THE GREEK WARS

The Greek Wars

The Failure of Persia

GEORGE CAWKWELL

OXFORD
UNIVERSITY PRESS

This book has been printed digitally and produced in a standard specification
in order to ensure its continuing availability

OXFORD
UNIVERSITY PRESS

Great Clarendon Street, Oxford OX2 6DP
United Kingdom

Oxford University Press is a department of the University of Oxford.
It furthers the University's objective of excellence in research, scholarship,
and education by publishing worldwide. Oxford is a registered trade mark of
Oxford University Press in the UK and in certain other countries

First published in 2005
First published in paperback 2006
Reprinted 2012

British Library Cataloguing in Publication Data
Data available

Library of Congress Cataloging in Publication Data
Data available

ISBN 978-0-19-929983-6

PREFACE

THE viewpoint of this book is no longer novel, and the concerns of scholars are different from what they were over four decades ago when I began to lecture on Xenophon and on the Persian Wars. One must salute above all Pierre Briant, but also Amélie Kuhrt and the late Heleen Sancisi-Weerdenburg, to whom all students are much beholden not only for their own wide-ranging and learned writings but also for their stimulation of the study of the Achaemenids and their world. They have certainly encouraged us all to rid ourselves of a Hellenocentric view of the Persian world. This viewpoint I would modestly claim to have shared, and this book is the fruit of many years of reflection on the Greek accounts of Persia and Persian policy towards the Greeks.

The book presumes in the reader a fairly ample knowledge of the period under review. It seeks to discuss, not to narrate. It is not meant to be what people call 'a good read', though matters more complicated or more peripheral have been consigned to Appendices. The list of works referred to in the notes is not, of course, a full bibliography, which would be vast. There has seemed no point in listing in print all the books and articles in my (old-fashioned) card index.

I am very grateful to various members of the Classics Office who uncomplainingly turned my manuscript into the legibility of the word-processor and, above all, to Rachel Chapman, to whom I owe especial thanks and for whom I, like all who deal with her, have the highest regard. I acknowledge too my debt to my wife, who has kept me from 'bestial oblivion'.

G.L.C.

25 October 2003

CONTENTS

ABBREVIATIONS

ANET[3]	*Ancient Near Eastern Texts*, 3rd edn., ed. J. B. Pritchard
ATL	*The Athenian Tribute Lists*, vol. ii (1949), ed. B. D. Meritt, H. T. Wade-Gery, and M. F. McGregor
CAH	*Cambridge Ancient History*
CHI	*Cambridge History of Iran*, vol. ii (1985)
CQ	*Classical Quarterly*
FGH	*Die Fragmente der griechischen Historiker*, ed. F. Jacoby
FHG	*Fragmenta Historicorum Graecorum*, ed. C. Müller
GHI	*Greek Historical Inscriptions*, vol. ii (1948), Oxford
Hell. Oxy. Chambers	*Hellenica Oxyrhynchia*, ed. M. Chambers (1993) Stuttgart and Leipzig: Teubner
JHS	*Journal of Hellenic Studies*
Kent	R. G. Kent, *Old Persian Grammar* (1953)
ML	*Greek Historical Inscriptions*, ed. R. Meiggs and D. M. Lewis (1969), Oxford
OGIS	*Orientis Graecae Inscriptiones Selectae*
PW	*Paulys Realencyclopädie der classischen Altertumswissenschaft*
SIG[3]	*Sylloge Inscriptionum Graecarum*, 3rd edn.

1

Introduction

To the Great King, seated on his throne at Susa or Persepolis, Greece and the Greeks were a very long way away, those of the mainland 2,000 miles or more as the crow flies. Nor can they have figured very largely in his mind. To the east, 1,200 miles or so, lay the satrapy of Bactriana and Sogdiana, the empire's north-east frontier where the pressures of nomadic migration were especially to be felt and where, as Alexander was to discover, men were fierce fighters.[1] Neither they nor those they kept in check could ever be neglected. Then there was Egypt, difficult to reach across its protective desert and difficult to hold in subjection. The mistake of incorporating it in the empire once made, imperial pride could not permit the sensible course of letting it go. That satrapy was out of control for about one third of the period between its conquest by Cambyses and the conquest of Alexander, and great efforts were constantly being made to recover it.[2] So there was much on the extremities of empire to engage the King's thoughts and, of course, he had constantly to be on the alert for troubles within.[3] Against all this the Greeks were a minor distraction and the Greeks of Greece itself a luxury, not a necessity. It must have been very far from the truth that the King had them constantly in mind. Herodotus' pretty story (5. 105. 2) of Darius appointing a servant to remind him of the Athenians each day before dinner was perhaps truer than Herodotus knew. The King had more important matters to think about.

It was quite different for the Greeks themselves. Of the coming of Cyrus, the prophet Isaiah cried (41: 5), 'coasts and islands saw it and were afraid, the world trembled from end to end' and though the brave message delivered to him by a Spartan embassy (Hdt. 1. 152. 3) hardly suggested fear and trembling, the fact and the proximity of Persian power mightily affected Greek political life for two centuries. The Persian invasion of 480 BC caused the Greeks to unite in the Hellenic League; the Persians' withdrawal and abandonment of thoughts of return led to the great division between Sparta and Athens which engrossed the rest of the century. From 449 BC onwards Persia secured her hold on western Anatolia by treaty, the Peace of Callias, and for two decades abstained from interfering in Greek affairs, but with the outbreak of the Peloponnesian War the chief land-power of Greece, Sparta, looked to Persia for help, and, after Athenian naval power had been gravely diminished by the Sicilian disaster, found in alliance with Persia the support she needed. For a decade and a half after the defeat of Athens, Sparta unwisely sought to take the Greek cities of Asia under her wing. Persia reacted strongly and in the King's Peace of 387/386 the Greek cities were recognized as belonging without qualification to the Persian Empire. That point established, the King took pains to see that it was not again called in question. His various interventions aroused the ire of Isocrates and all the Panhellenist tribe and made the ambitions of Philip of Macedon the more easily realized. Not until Darius III had been utterly defeated on the battlefield of Gaugamela was Greece free of thoughts and fears of Persian might.

These two centuries are the period of 'the Greek Wars', a term which covers not only the hostilities of the first half of the fifth century but also all the contacts between Greece and Persia, both diplomatic and military, ending with the Anabasis of Alexander the Great. The title is convenient not just because it avoids the narrow implications of the customary 'Persian Wars', but also because it encourages the effort to see Persian relations with Greece with other than Greek eyes.

That effort, by no means novel,[4] has become less demanding as the riches of the Oriental evidence are revealed and exploited. The evidence is ample and various, but one thing is lacking. Apart from the Behistun Inscription which gives an account of the opening of the reign of Darius I, there are no literary accounts of Achaemenid history other than those written by Greeks.[5]

Foremost amongst Greek writers is, of course, Herodotus. He survives in full, and furnishes a great deal of information about Persia, and so inevitably dominates any discussion about Greek knowledge and understanding of that great power. No matter how widely he did or did not travel, he would, living in Halicarnassus, have been well placed to hear a good deal about Persia. The city was very much a meeting-place of Greek and non-Greek, as Halicarnassian nomenclature shows,[6] and if he travelled in the Persian Empire no further than the cities along the Ionian coast he certainly would have gleaned a great deal. Much no doubt would have been anecdotal like stories of the now celebrated gold-digging ants of India, but there is also a certain amount of exact-seeming information, like the list he furnished his readers of the composition of the Persian army in 480 BC, which suggests careful research. So one's initial reaction is respectful.[7]

Serious doubts arise, however, when one asks how well he understood the Persian world. For instance in book 3 (ch. 117) he recounts Persian measures to control the use of the waters of the river Aces,[8] a matter the importance of which the modern world well understands, and it does not necessarily argue greed if there were charges for the service (§6), but Herodotus' account betrays an astounding misapprehension concerning space and time within the Empire. He speaks of a plain 'on the borders of the Chorasmians, the Hyrcanians, the Parthians, the Sarangians and the Thamanaeans', and of 'a mighty river, the Aces'. As far as we can determine, these peoples lived hundreds of miles apart and such a plain is hardly to be found. So, strictly, Herodotus did not know what he was talking about, but it is what he goes on to tell that is most tell-tale. For he envisages each of these peoples, women included, going to 'the Persians' and making a hullabaloo at the King's gates, and the ones who made the loudest noise being rewarded with the sluice-gates being opened to them first; and so on with the others in turn. The picture is delightful and absurd. For the Hyrcanians, for instance, to travel to Persepolis, they would have had to spend most of the year getting there and back! Herodotus can write like this only because he has no real idea of how vast the upper satrapies of the Empire are. There may be something behind it all, a garbled version perhaps of annual migration,[9] but the whole story suggests that Herodotus had no real understanding of the Persian Empire.

Nor is this case isolated. In book 3 he has the conspirators who have succeeded in killing off the Pseudo-Smerdis debate the form of constitution they will set up. This enables Herodotus to give us (80–82) our earliest discussion of political theory, but in reality there could have been in this vast feudal kingdom of the King of Kings no question of kingship being replaced by either democracy or oligarchy. How could Herodotus talk of things as if Persia was a Greek city-state? Only a wild misconception of the nature of the kingdom could have prompted such a discussion. Interestingly, he himself at a later point in his narrative (6. 43. 3) lets on that there were Greeks who did not accept his story, and Herodotus amazingly seems to think that because Mardonius in 493 BC put down the tyrants in Ionia it was credible enough that the conspirators of 522 BC seriously considered replacing kingship with democracy.

According to Darius himself, he acceded to the throne because he was of the blood royal, a direct descendant of Achaemenes, founder of the dynasty. He was thus no less royal than Cyrus the Great or his son Cambyses, members of the other line of the family.[10] According to Herodotus, he was chosen by means of a bit of horseplay (3. 84. 3–87), of which no doubt he enjoyed telling, but it does not read as if he supposed no one would take him seriously, and it suggests that he had little idea of the true nature of Persian kingship. The story was presumably an imaginative embroidery on the fact that Darius set up an equestrian statue with an inscription. 'Darius the son of Hystaspes, supported by the valour of this horse—which was named—and of his groom Oebares, gained the kingship of the Persians' (3. 88. 3). What was actually behind these words, was presumably what was behind one part of the list of treasures looted by Sargon in 714 BC which says that Sargon seized 'a statue of Ursa, with his two racers and his charioteer, with the body of the chariot, all in founded bronze, on which one saw his pride expressed thus: "With my pair of horses and my single charioteer, my hands have conquered the kingdom of Urartu."' Perhaps Herodotus had been given a garbled version of the Ursa story, or perhaps such inscriptions were conventional with Oriental monarchies.[11] But that Herodotus could pass on whatever he had heard made of this sort of story shows that he little understood the world where the essential for succession was royal blood.

Anyone who criticizes Herodotus is always in danger of being hoist with his own petard. We are greatly beholden to him for what he tells us of Achaemenid Persia; he provides the framework to which the diverse bits of Oriental evidence can be attached and without him we would be impoverished indeed. No matter how or whence he derived his information, that information is both central and very considerable. Whence then cometh misunderstanding?

The precise extent of his travels remains obscure. His account of Egypt is sprinkled with remarks which indicate autopsy and on-the-spot information. Some of these indications have been again challenged[12] but whatever the truth there, it is notable how little of what he says about the Persian Empire elsewhere bears such marks. He certainly had been to Sardis and to Gaza (cf. 3. 5. 2). How much further inland is very arguable. Certainly behind Herodotus' account of Babylon lies the eye-witness of someone, be that Herodotus or another on whose report Herodotus drew. Although there certainly do seem to be serious errors, there is no proving that Herodotus could not possibly have made them.[13] On the whole it seems best to accept that he did go to

Babylon, especially considering what he says of the height to which millet and sesame grow in that land—'though I know full well, I will not mention it, since I am well aware that with those who have not been to Babylonia what has been said about crops has been treated with great incredulity' (1. 193. 4). It seems very unlikely that anyone would speak like that if he had not himself been there.

One would very much like to know something of Herodotus' journey to Babylon. It is unlikely that any individual going there would do other than go by ship to Cilicia, cross to the Euphrates, most probably at Thapsacus, and go down the river by boat, i.e. the route followed by Conon in 397/396. [14] Perhaps Herodotus' journey is reflected in his account of the sort of boats used on the river (1. 194), but not a word betrays how he returned. It is therefore a serious warning against arguing that if he had gone further than to Babylon, he would have left some traces of his journey. He has so little to say about his journey to and from Babylon that he may well have gone further, and in any case he may have been reserving material for his 'Assyrian narrative' (1. 184, cf. 1. 106. 2).

It would, however, be a bold man who asserted that Herodotus did travel widely beyond Babylon. His account of Ecbatana, the Median capital (1. 98), might suggest autopsy, were it not that that of Polybius (10. 27. 3–13) surely reflects the report of someone who did know what he was talking about. It is unlikely that Herodotus got near the other great Royal palaces. When Greek ambassadors are recorded as being at Susa (7. 151), there is no hint that Herodotus himself had seen that remarkable building. (Indeed one might presume that he would have had to be an ambassador to get there at all.) Likewise with Persepolis. He rightly took for granted that there was a palace in Persia (cf. 3. 117. 5), but there is no sign that he had seen it. Indeed there is something of an indication that he had not penetrated into Asia beyond Babylon. In the return march of the Ten Thousand in 401 BC the Greek army encountered pontoon-bridging (Xen. *Anab.* 2. 4. 13, 24f.), by that date perhaps widespread in the Persian Empire (cf. ibid. 1. 2. 5), but in view of the manner in which Herodotus describes the bridging of the Bosporus (4. 87–9) one cannot help suspecting that he had not encountered such bridging on his own travels. If he had one would have expected some comment on whether the bridge of Mandrocles had been copied elsewhere; and when he described the bridging of the Hellespont by Xerxes (7. 33–6) there is no suggestion that such bridging could be seen in other parts of the Empire. [15]

There is then no reason to suppose that Herodotus travelled widely in Asia, and his failure properly to apprehend the nature of the Persian Empire is to some extent excusable. However, he had travelled far enough, one would have thought, to have done better and one wonders why he did not. After all, he gave an account of the Royal Road[16] from Sardis to Susa which took three months to traverse (5. 52–4), and must have had a good idea of the immensity of the Empire, good enough at any rate to have cautioned him against writing his chapter on Persian control of waters (3. 117).

Part of the explanation may be found in an addiction to the doctrines of Panhellenism. These reached their finished form in the writings of Isocrates, particularly in the *Panegyricus* of 380 BC, where he appeals to Sparta to join Athens in leading the Greeks against Persia; in this way Greece would rid itself of internal wars and share in the profits of the great crusade. Obviously such ideas would have been more favourably received after the Anabasis of Cyrus in 401 BC. Within seven years Agesilaus was talking grandly of setting out on a similar campaign himself.[17] Also one might be tempted to suppose that ideas of union against Persia were the product of the divisions in Greece effected by Persian policy in the later decades of the fifth century and it is to be noted that the celebrated Panhellenist utterance of Callicratidas (Xen. *Hell.* 1. 6. 7) as well as the explicit call for united action against the Barbarian made by Aristophanes' Lysistrata (*Lysis.* 1128–34) belong to the closing years of the War, also that that powerful advocate of the Panhellenist case, Gorgias, is not known to have been advocating it any earlier.[18] So one should approach the question of Panhellenism before the Peloponnesian War with caution.

Notions of common Greekness were widespread of course and the Persian invasion of 480 BC gave Greeks a common purpose expressed in the Hellenic League, but how far this represented more than a common resolve to be free might be questioned.[19] There are, however, pointers. When in 465 the great earthquake struck Sparta and a Spartan embassy came to Athens appealing for help in accordance with the terms of the Hellenic League, Cimon in urging Athens to help uttered his famous dictum, recorded by Ion of Chios. He called on the Athenians 'not to stand by and see Greece lamed and the city deprived of its yoke-fellow' (Plut. *Cim.* 16. 10). At first glance, this was curious. Athens had been getting along perfectly well without Spartan help since 478 BC, when Sparta 'desiring to be quit of the war against the Mede and thinking the Athenians were well up to the leadership' (Thuc. 1. 95) made a decision not to seek to recover the leadership on sea (Diod. 11. 50). The Delian League had been formed 'to take revenge on the King by ravaging his territory' (Thuc. 1. 96) and the Athenians had been doing so, without feeling any need for Spartan help. What, then, can Cimon have had in mind? Of course, if the Persians invaded Greece again, the grand alliance of 481 would have to be reactivated, but by 465, after the crushing defeat sustained by Persia at the Eurymedon, such an invasion was not seriously to be considered. It seems at least possible that Cimon was thinking of a joint attack on Persia, not mere ravaging, which had been happening effectively enough, with the forces of the Delian League, but a grand assault by all the Hellenes.

This may seem a far-fetched interpretation but that such ideas were current in Herodotus' time is strongly suggested by the justification for attacking Greece which he puts in the mouth of Xerxes (7. 11. 2): 'If *we* keep peace, they won't. Assuredly they will campaign against our land . . . it is not possible for either of us to draw back . . . the issue before us is whether to afflict or to be afflicted . . . either everything in our land is to come under Greeks or everything in theirs under Persians . . .'. Until the Great Invasion of 480 BC had failed, there could have been no thought of the Greeks conquering Asia and Xerxes would not and could not have uttered such sentiments. Such words seem much more likely to reflect Panhellenist dreaming, as indeed do other passages in Herodotus. When Aristagoras went to Sparta seeking support for the Ionian Revolt, he is made (5. 49. 8–50. 3) to urge Cleomenes to forget about petty, unprofitable wars against Messenians, Arcadians, and Argives which will produce no gold or silver, when it is open to him to 'rule the whole of Asia with no difficulty', and when Cleomenes asks how long a march it is from the sea to the King, Aristagoras is made to reply that it would be three months, when the truth should have been concealed by a man 'wanting to lead Spartiates forth against Asia'. Whatever Aristagoras was actually proposing (and presumably it was an attack on Sardis which was three days' march from the sea), he surely cannot have been proposing at that date, before Persian power had shown its limitations, a three-month march into the heart of the Persian Empire. This again is likely to be fifth-century Panhellenism. Similarly with the joint expedition proposed to the Spartans by the Scyths (6. 84), fantasy for the 490s but conceivable in the world of Cimon who 'tried to subject all Asia' (Plut. *Comp. Cimon and Lucullus* 2. 5).

Any man who, in the time that Herodotus was writing, could talk

of a Greek army marching up the Royal Road to do battle against
the Royal army must either have had colossal ignorance of the conditions such an army would encounter or have been talking without
really meaning it. Since Herodotus can hardly be considered colossally
ignorant, one wonders whether for his own artistic purposes he was
attributing to Aristagoras, Cleomenes, and Xerxes ideas which he himself thought absurd and which he meant his readers to take as signs of
the ill-judgement of each of these characters. Theoretically, that might
be so, but in the case of Xerxes at least (7. 11–18) it would seem otherwise. Xerxes had declared that there was no middle course between
total subjection of Greece and total subjection of Persia and the spirit
that appeared in sleep to both Xerxes and to his substitute, Artabanus,
threatened that if Xerxes called off the expedition he would suffer what
he must suffer if he disobeyed (7. 17. 2). The reference would appear to
be to the stark alternative of Persia being under the rule of Greeks (ch.
11. 3), and Xerxes' estimate of the situation seems to be shared by the
spirit in the dream. Xerxes could be wrong but in the world of Herodotus such a visitation cannot mislead. So the alternatives seem to be
those of the mind of the man who wrote up the debate, Herodotus. It
was the language of Panhellenism.

Such folly perhaps did in general little harm as long as there was
so little chance of a Greek army setting out on a march 'up-country',
but it was no help to the historian of the Persian Empire. Part of the
creed was the belittling of Persian military power and performance.
Isocrates did this at some length (4. 138–49), just as the envoy of the
Arcadian Ten Thousand reported back in the early 360s 'that the King
has bakers and cooks and wine-waiters and doormen galore but as to
real men who could fight against Greeks, though I looked hard for
them, I couldn't see any' (Xen. *Hell.* 7. 1. 38), words which Xenophon
echoed in his postscript to *The Education of Cyrus* (v.i. p. 18); as part
of the general moral decline of Persia, Xenophon dwelt at length on
military decline (§§19–26). Time would show that there was much to
be said against this, most notably that 'damned nice thing—the nearest thing you ever saw in your life', the battle of Gaugamela,[20] but
earlier in the fourth century Panhellenists believed it. Was it so in the
fifth? *The Histories* of Herodotus no doubt in some degree amused. For
instance, there was the delightful alternative version of Xerxes' return
from Greece, how he embarked with his entourage on a Phoenician
ship and when a storm arose and the steersman said there was no hope
of the King surviving unless they could get rid of this large entourage,

Xerxes called on the Persians to show how they cared for their King, and they 'kowtowed' and jumped overboard (7. 118). Kowtowing (προσκύνησις) always shocked and amused the Greeks and this picture of abject servility no doubt gave pleasure.[21] Herodotus professed disbelief (7. 119), for surely the Persians on deck would have gone below and sent the oarsmen overboard! Also, it was difficult to keep one's head when the King was displeased; witness the luckless builders of the first bridge over the Hellespont, which was destroyed by a storm (7. 35. 3), or the Phoenicians who went during the battle of Salamis to complain about the Ionians (8. 90). It was important not to let the King find out; careless talk cost heads (8. 65. 5), and the rich man who tried to keep his oldest son from the expedition kept him for burial (7. 39. 3).[22] All this, and much else, shocked and perhaps amused. But through it all ran a thread of contempt for the Persian army. Aristagoras was made to tell Cleomenes that with their big bows and short spears and pointed felt hats they would be easily conquered (5. 49. 3–4). They had to be whipped across the Hellespont (7. 56. 1), whipped into action at Thermopylae (7. 223. 3), the whip being considered necessary for good order and military discipline (7. 103. 4). Artabazus, who had argued for a different strategy for the Plataea campaign (9. 41), when he saw that the Persian division of the army had fared badly at the hands of the Spartans, led his command not just back to the security of the Persian camp or to Thebes but into Phocis, 'wanting to reach the Hellespont as quickly as possible' (9. 66), just as Xerxes' council had been much relieved when Xerxes had his first change of mind about invading Greece (7. 13. 3). There were 'many chaps, few real men' (7. 210).

But, it may be objected, such Panhellenist attitudes were merest frills and did not impair the underlying narrative. The Persians at Plataea, it is to be noted, 'were not inferior in fighting spirit or in strength but they lacked hoplite equipment, were untrained and no match in cunning for their adversaries' (9. 62), and at Thermopylae Persians fought and died in a manner beyond reproach (7. 211–12, 224. 2). That is true enough, but what one misses is any sense of the greatness of the Persian Army which had marched to and conquered the satrapies of Egypt and India, and had made a reconnaissance in force across the Danube. Such things are not accomplished by soft and effeminate men. Yet Herodotus would hardly have dissented from Isocrates when he said (4. 150) 'For how in such a way of life could there have been produced either a clever general or a good soldier? The largest part of them are undisciplined rabble with no experience of danger . . .?' There was no need to inquire into why the invasion failed. What could an army of Orientals, be it ever so large, do against Greek valour?

Herodotus may thus have been affected by sentimental and unrealistic Panhellenism. He was certainly subject to the wild lack of realism displayed by the ancient Greeks generally with regard to numbers.[23] Without a blush he calculated that Xerxes led into Greece a force of 5,283,220 (7. 186), combatants and non-combatants; more modestly he gives totals of 1,700,000 foot and 80,000 horse. This is fantasy with which one may compare the sort of totals furnished by Ctesias (*FGH* 688); e.g. the army of Semiramis (F1; Diod. 2. 54) had 1,700,000 foot, 210,000 horse, and 'almost 10,600 chariots'; this would have needed hundreds of miles to deploy! Not until we get down to Hieronymus of Cardia do Greek figures make good sense militarily. One suspects that Herodotus had no more exact idea of ten myriads than ordinary citizens today have of trillions. Fantastic totals were easy. One could count them by myriads (7. 60), a method one might wager that no commander of any army, no matter how large, has ever employed. One wonders indeed whether Herodotus himself had any experience of war.

Whatever the correct explanation is, the paradox remains that Herodotus, who had so much accurate information about the Persians and the Persian Empire, seems to have greatly misunderstood. With Thucydides there is a different paradox. Did he really know as little as he seems to know about Persia and the Persians? In asking such a question one does not think primarily of his celebrated omissions, the negotiations between Athens and Artaxerxes during the Pentekontaetia leading to the Peace of Callias, the renewal of peace with his successor, Darius II, the Athenian alliance with the rebel satrap Amorges which brought Persia into the War in support of Sparta. These omissions are baffling. Thucydides to some extent recognized the importance of the collaboration of Persia and Sparta and acknowledged the role of Cyrus the Younger (2. 65. 12), albeit perhaps inadequately.[24] For some dark reason, which cannot even be guessed, he omitted these matters although he cannot have failed to know something about them.

The question how much Thucydides actually knew about Persia and the Persians is raised above all by book 8. In earlier books he had seemed to know and not know. The digression on Pausanias the Regent (1. 128–34) shows familiarity with Royal phraseology[25] but does not shrink from recounting most improbable details in Pausanias' dealings with the King. The same can be said of the Themistocles story (1. 135–38).[26] In book 4 there is a difficulty raised by the account of the capture of a Persian emissary on his way to Sparta (4. 50). The solution may well be that Thucydides was in a muddle about the date of the death of Artaxerxes I.[27] In book 8, however, he gives very serious cause for unease. He provides the text of the treaty between Sparta and Persia (8. 58). It contains the full dating by the year of Darius' reign and the name of the Spartan Ephor as well as the place where it was made, in the plain of Maeander. He also states (8. 57) that Tissaphernes went to Caunus to make this treaty, and one is led to think that it was there in Caunus that he began to act on the clause concerning pay for the Peloponnesians and there too that the formal libations were made. This is surely a muddle, but much more serious is his conviction that the two earlier drafts of a treaty of alliance with Sparta were actual treaties (8. 18 and 37). One can only conjecture how he has obtained these texts. Neither has a prescript with a date and with neither is it said that the formalities of libations were observed. Yet Thucydides refers to each of these earlier texts as if they were treaties of alliance 'signed, sealed and delivered' as it were (cf. especially 8. 43. 3). The truth is in all probability that there was in 412/411 one treaty of alliance and one only, that the two earlier texts were merely drafts of treaties drawn up for submission to the two home governments, that the clear sign of this is that although the fully agreed version was drawn up in Caunus it was actually sworn to, as the text of the treaty asserts, 'in the plain of the Maeander', having been, in the time taken by Tissaphernes to move from Caunus, referred to Sparta and to Susa. Reference to Sparta is sure enough, although Thucydides did not mention it. A Spartan king might on occasion be expected to act on his own initiative (cf. Thuc. 8. 5. 3) but the normal position was that of Agesilaus in 395, when he declared to Tithraustes that he could not accept the terms Tithraustes was proposing 'without the approval of the home authorities' (Xen. *Hell.* 3. 4. 26) and he received his orders from Sparta shortly afterwards. An ordinary Spartiate would have been even more hamstrung. Reference to Susa is less sure. It would, of course, be quickly managed, but it is conceivable that Tissaphernes had his terms of reference and that if he kept within them, he did not need to secure Royal assent. However, earlier that same winter he had professed himself unable to take a decision about the rate of pay he would provide for the Spartan fleet (8. 29. 1); of course he may have been bluffing, but, later, Cyrus gave a similar response to Lysander (Xen. *Hell.* 1. 5. 5); reference to Susa was common (cf. Hdt. 5. 31. 4, Xen. *Hell.* 3. 2. 20, 3. 4. 5). In this case of the treaty of 412/411 BC it is almost probable. The first two efforts to define the area of the King's authority (8. 18 and 37) had spoken of 'territory and cities', and the status of the Greek cities of Asia is what is constantly at issue in the 390s and what is finally decided in the King's Peace (Xen. *Hell.* 3. 2. 20, 4. 5 and 25, 4. 8. 14, 5. 1. 31). Yet in the treaty of 412/411 the 'cities' are omitted (8. 58. 2) and it is hard to think that Tissaphernes would have taken it on himself to make such a change.[28]

It does seem therefore that Thucydides does not properly understand how the Persian machinery of government worked. Later Ephorus, as reflected in Diodorus (15. 41. 7), enunciated a general statement about the delay caused by generals having to refer everything to the King, but such insight was perhaps hardly to be expected in Thucydides' day. However, he displayed little curiosity about Royal policy and confined himself to speculating about the satrap Tissaphernes (cf. 8. 46. 5, 87. 2–4). Both his knowledge of Persia and his interest must be declared slighter than could be expected of the historian of a war on the end of which Persia had a very great influence.

With Xenophon one begins a new phase of Greek knowledge and understanding of Persia. In 401 BC he joined the army of Cyrus the Younger on its march 'up-country' passing through a good number of satrapies and seeing for himself the immensity and variety of the western half of the Empire. He did not see Babylon, but he saw for himself far more than Herodotus had seen, and one expects great illumination from his writings, not just from the *Anabasis*, which recounted the famous march of the Ten Thousand, but also from the *Education of Cyrus*, which professes very great knowledge both of the rise of Persia and of the Persian system of government, to which may be added the precious fourth chapter of the *Oeconomicus*. How and whence he obtained much of it is unclear. Certainly the part played by autopsy must be considered small. Even the *Anabasis*, which is commonly taken to be, as it were, a factual diary,[29] is not entirely that. For instance, when he records that the retreating army passed Larisa (agreed to be Calah at the junction of the Greater Zab and the Tigris, mod. Nimrud), he gives the dimensions of its wall, says that the circuit was two parasangs, and asserts that the city was once inhabited by Medes (3. 4. 7–9). Now although he might conceivably, during a halt, have quizzed, with the aid of an interpreter, some stray local who, perversely, had not joined 'the barbarians from the nearby villages' in getting away from

the oncoming army as far as possible, it is much more likely that Xenophon got this information from some written source, and he goes on to
give very much the same sort of information about Mespila, his name
for deserted Nineveh (ibid. §§10–12).[30] He was with an army trying to
get away from the vengeful Tissaphernes, not a band of curious tour-
ists measuring up and pacing out and quizzing whom they could, and
the dimensions he gives together with the 'historical' notes suggest that
he was drawing on a written source.[31] There is another indication of
this. Normally Xenophon recorded the progress of the army in stages
(σταθμοί) and parasangs, but when the march was through areas not
under Persian control, he spoke simply in days. Now, the 23rd book of
Ctesias' *Persica* furnished a record of the number of stages, days, and
parasangs 'from Ephesus to Bactra and India' (F33), and one cannot
help wondering whether this book like 'the Parthian stages' of Isidore
of Charax (*FGH* 781 F2),[32] recorded all the distances of the Empire,
a sample of the 'military and administrative itineraries' necessary to
a vast imperial power. Admittedly Isidore belonged to the age of
Augustus and the development of such itineraries doubtless owed
much to the so-called Bematists of Alexander's army (*FGH* 119–23),[33]
but Persian armies on the move had to be supplied and the Kings
had to know how much had to be provided and for how many days.
Itineraries would therefore have been necessary. Ctesias could either
have based his 23rd book on such or himself have provided for the
Greek world a full record of the distances of the Persian Empire, which
Xenophon was able to use. But if he did not use Ctesias, he seems
to have used some written source. So it is proper before estimating
the value of what Xenophon recounts of Persia and the Persians, to
consider those who preceded him in treating of the period of which
he treats. This comes down to Ctesias, whose *Persica* Xenophon was
aware of when he wrote the *Anabasis* (cf. 1. 8. 26, 27) though he by no
means followed him at all points.[34] The shadowy Sophaenetus (*FGH*
109) and the fragmentary Oxyrhynchus Historian do not allow us to
assess how much they knew of Persia, although one chapter of the
latter (22 Chambers) suggests that the full text would have been most
instructive. But we have to make do with Ctesias, of whose work in
epitome and fragments ample remains, too much in fact for the good
of his reputation.

One would expect that Ctesias had penetrated the *arcana imperii*.
He was no mere outsider, no remote observer. The Great Kings had
long esteemed Greek medicine more highly even than Egyptian and

had sought out Greek doctors in the Empire. The most celebrated, of course, was Democedes of Croton in the time of Darius I, whose queen, Atossa, he cured and by whom he was richly rewarded, as he was also by the Royal women. He 'dined with the King', as the phrase went.[35] Another celebrated doctor was the notorious Apollonides of Cos during the reign of Artaxerxes I. He behaved 'unprofessionally' with one of the Royal women and was buried alive for his sins (Ctesias F14 §44). How exactly Ctesias of Cnidus came to be at the court is unclear, but it is plain from his book that he knew full well what was going on. It is stuffed with court scandal and the revolts of eminent Persians. How long he practised his skill at court is uncertain. He certainly was in attendance on Artaxerxes II at the battle of Cunaxa (Xen. *Anab.* 1. 8. 26) and may have been at court for some years, amidst the intrigues of the fearsome Royal women, and thus admirably placed to gather material for his work.[36]

Ctesias claimed to have used the Royal hides on which the Persians kept, in accordance with a law, a record of ancient affairs (πράξεις)— that there were such archives is not incredible, considering that Darius had ordered that copies of the Behistun Inscription which had been written on clay and on parchment be sent to all parts of his kingdom, and the Persians were in general much given to keeping accounts, copies of documents, and the like.[37] Furthermore Ctesias professed (T8) either to have seen for himself the majority of events or, where autopsy was not possible, to have heard from Persians directly (παρ' αὐτῶν Περσῶν), and since the court spent winter at Susa, summer at Ecbatana, autumn at Persepolis, and the rest of the year at Babylon (Athenaeus 513b)[38] he had excellent opportunities to see for himself.

Unfortunately, his performance fell far short of his professions. His account of Xerxes' invasion of Greece is wild, putting Plataea before Salamis (F13 §§27–31).[39] His omissions astound; no mention of the Ionian Revolt which one would have supposed would have been of interest to a Cnidian, and no discussion of the relations of Greece and Persia during the fifth century. Whence he got his history of Assyria and Media is beyond conjecture. It is notable however that the man who berated Herodotus for his falsehoods placed Nineveh on the Euphrates (F1 b 3. 2). He must to some degree have gone around with his eyes and his ears shut. After all, he claimed to have seen a tiger sent to the King, but his description of it included a sting in the tail (F45 d β = Aelian, *NA* 4. 21). In one respect he was typically Greek, namely in the fantastic numbers he gave for Oriental armies; being at the heart of the Empire did not induce a more realistic view.[40] All in all, Ctesias remains a great disappointment.

Ctesias' work seems to have concluded with the early 390s. Xenophon's literary career came later and probably much later. Certainly the bulk of the *Hellenica* was written in the 350s,[41] and the *Anabasis* probably in the late 370s at the earliest.[42] The Socratic works may be his first literary efforts, possibly in the 380s after he settled at Scillus, near Olympia, and with them may be counted the *Oeconomicus* with the celebrated fourth chapter concerning the rule and administration of the Persian Empire. The curiously misnamed *Education of Cyrus*, which, as Cicero (*ad QF* I. I. 23) noted, was written to furnish 'a model of just rule and not a credible history', was composed, save for the added last chapter (8. 8), before, and probably well before, 362,[43] perhaps in the 370s. Had Xenophon been so minded, he could have drawn amply on Ctesias' *Persica*.

However, apart from the possible use in the *Anabasis* of the table of distances furnished in book 23 of the *Persica*, there is no sign of Xenophon's discussions of Persia being derived from Ctesias. Indeed much of the *Education of Cyrus* may be fiction, with the ample military descriptions being based on Xenophon's experience of soldiering and to a large extent on his imagination. A nucleus of what he recounts of Persia was no doubt based on his own experiences, both under Cyrus and under the Spartan commanders in Asia from 399 to 394 BC. For instance, the full account of what Cyrus the Great ordered by way of preparations for the twenty days' march (*Cyrop.* 6. 2. 25–41) probably enough was based on what Cyrus the Younger ordered for the march from the Euphrates crossing down to Babylon. But much of what might seem to be genuine information and merit serious consideration is nothing of the sort. Those wheeled towers which Cyrus was made to employ at the battle of Thymbrara (6. 1. 52–3), and many other details, give the game away; we have in the *Education of Cyrus* to a large extent a work of fiction.[44] One may be deceived, but there is no reason to suppose that Xenophon drew on some rich source of knowledge of the Orient.

The limitations of his knowledge are displayed in his two discussions of the Persian imperial system, briefly in the *Oeconomicus* (ch. 4) and at greater length in the *Education of Cyrus* (8. 6. 1–16). The first is somewhat puzzling. He concludes his discussion of the separation of civil and military authority by saying 'But wherever a satrap is appointed, he is in charge of both of these' (*Oec.* 4. 9–11). Since, as far as we know, there always was a satrap, even if he was a hereditary ruler rather than an

eminent Persian sent from Susa, Xenophon seems to be contradict-
ing his own claim that civil and military authority were separate. In
the other passage (*Cyrop.* 8. 6. 1–9) he asserts that garrisons and their
commanders were appointed directly by the King (§9) and that their
function was in part to provide a counterbalance to the satrap (§1),
and it is clear that Xenophon is dissenting from the claim made in the
Oeconomicus about 'wherever a satrap is appointed'.[45] Xenophon is, in
a word, muddled.

It would be pointless to speculate on the source of the muddle, but
it is to be remarked that Xenophon's own experience of the Persian
imperial system was limited. He had no direct knowledge of the world
far beyond the Tigris and it is hardly likely that he had time or opportunity to quiz people about the powers of satraps. The sort of discussions conducted with the aid of interpreters, which are reported in the
Anabasis,[46] seem far more practical and down to earth. So although he
had walked a long way, he probably learned little of the matters here
under discussion. He may have derived his (confused) account from
some written source or other, or else by oral report, but it seems much
more likely that his ideas were based almost entirely on his service
under Spartan command between 400 and 394 BC, particularly after
Agesilaus, with whom Xenophon quickly became intimate, came on
the scene.[47] The whole question of the powers of the satrap and his
relation to the King must have been raised by the making of the truces
with Tissaphernes; of that made by Dercyllidas (Xen. *Hell.* 3. 2. 20)
Xenophon may not have been precisely informed, but it may safely
be presumed that Agesilaus and he fully discussed the second truce
and Tissaphernes' conduct thereafter (ibid. 3. 4. 5 and 6). Likewise the
summary execution of Tissaphernes by Tithraustes (ibid. 3. 4. 25) must
have told Xenophon much,[48] as too the meeting with Pharnabazus
(ibid. 4. 1. 19–38). One cannot help suspecting that Xenophon based
himself in these matters on his own experience of the satraps of Lydia
and of Dascylium, and that is why he presents a picture of uniformity
when a great deal of variety may have prevailed.

No doubt there are many bits of genuine information about Persia
in the *Education of Cyrus*, but it would seem that in general Xenophon
represents no great advance in understanding.[49] For that one has to
wait for the opening up of the Iranian world consequent on the conquests of Alexander. An index of this is the realism that appears in
information given by Diodorus concerning the size of early Hellenistic armies.[50] Gone are the fantastic and comic totals of the world of

Herodotus and Ctesias. It is generally, and probably rightly, supposed that Diodorus' figures in books 18 to 20 derive from Hieronymus of Cardia, whose preoccupation with documents manifests his method, documents which revealed the business of the whole Iranian world.[51] Hieronymus really knew what he was talking about. Alexander had opened up Asia, as one can readily realize by a perusal of the fragments of the so-called Alexander historians, and men like Hieronymus could see for themselves.

Xenophon falls very far short of all this, and remains thoroughly Hellenocentric as far as numbers at any rate are concerned. One cannot be certain about the numbers engaged in the battle of Cunaxa but a probable enough case can be made to show that Xenophon's figures (*Anab.* 1. 8. 10–13) are wildly excessive. Beside them Ephorus' totals (Diod. 14. 22. 2) seem almost modest, lunatic though they too are. Like all the Greeks until the Hellenistic world was established, Xenophon dealt in fantasy.[52] No doubt in course of time he learned. The account of the mission of Pelopidas in 367 BC in the *Hellenica* (7. 1. 33–8) suggests that with every diplomatic exchange with the King Greeks in general, and Xenophon intent on writing his history in particular, were gaining knowledge and understanding of how the Persian system worked.

Nonetheless Xenophon's vision was seriously clouded. The Arcadian Antiochus, returning from the embassy sent to counter the efforts of Pelopidas, saw fit both to denigrate the famous golden plane-tree which he saw in Susa and to sneer at the Royal court generally (Xen. *Hell.* 7. 1. 38).[53] His *bon mot* was used by Xenophon himself in the last chapter of *The Education of Cyrus* when speaking of Persian military decline. 'In time past it was the custom for them not to be journeying on foot, for no other purpose than to become as skilled horsemen as possible, but now they have more coverings on the horses than on the beds, for they don't care about skill in riding so much as about having a soft seat. Indeed in matters pertaining to war, is it not to be expected that they should now be in every way worse than before? In days gone by it was the custom for those who held land to provide themselves from it with horsemen who would of course go on campaign if that was necessary, but for the defence forces of the territory to be hired men. Now the doormen and the bakers and the cooks and the butlers and the bath attendants, all serving them and clearing away and putting them to bed and getting them up, as well as the "beauticians" who make them up and rub them down and generally turn them out well—all this lot the men in power have turned into horsemen, for them to be their hirelings . . .' (8. 8. 19–20). This is Antiochus inflated. There is no reason to think that Xenophon had any new information to base himself on, and apart from a somewhat uncertain reference to the events of the Satraps' Revolt (§4) this is true generally of the whole chapter. For the most part he is putting a sour interpretation on what had previously not impeded his admiring Cyrus.[54] For instance, on the march back from Cunaxa, at least one Greek had accumulated a store of expensive carpets (Xen. *Anab*. 7. 3. 18 and 27), and Xenophon's sneer in this last chapter of *The Education of Cyrus* (§16) hardly shows that the Persians were going soft; at least one can hardly suppose that by the late 360s he knew anything more about such a matter than he had learned in 401 BC. Indeed the whole chapter is a feeble parade of trifling complaints, signifying nothing.

Why then did he add this weak final chapter? It will not do to say that the Persian treatment of the Greek generals in Cyrus' army had disillusioned him. On any view of Xenophon's literary activity, the whole of *The Education of Cyrus* was written long after Xenophon's military activity. The explanation would seem rather to lie in the decline after 371 BC in relations between Persia and the Sparta he so much admired. Xenophon and King Agesilaus had got on remarkably well personally, but there was more to it than that. Both, as it appears to me at any rate, had shared the fashionable, romantic attachment to Panhellenism. Through the 390s, the 380s, and the 370s this belief had hardly moved men to more than brave words. However when the Great King abandoned his policy of friendship with Sparta and supported Thebes in championing the independence of Messene, i.e. in the liberation of a large part of Sparta's servile population, the response of Xenophon and Agesilaus was furious. The aged king set about active opposition to Persia wherever he saw a chance, and the ageing writer dipped his pen in venom and added the contemptuous denunciation of the last chapter of *The Education*.[55]

A man with such prejudices is hardly one to whom one may look for a dispassionate appraisal of the power and importance of Persia. His omissions amaze, but should never be treated as other than manifestations of prejudice. All in all, from a writer from whom one might have hoped to gain great insight one gets disappointingly little.

It is matter for conjecture how much better off we would have been if the two Greeks who wrote about Persia in the three decades before Alexander's invasion had survived in full and not just in fragments, namely, Heraclides of Cyme (*FGH* 689) and Dinon of Colophon (*FGH*

690).[56] Both were subjects of the Great King and well placed to learn about the Persian system. Most of the fragments concern the customs of the court and no doubt Persian luxury was a fascinating topic. Nor were such matters trivialities. A full account of what went on at court would, if we had it, be revealing. It was, of course, the sort of discussion that particularly interested Athenaeus, the source of a large number of our fragments, and that helps to explain why there is so much about food and ceremony. But their scope was probably much wider. One fragment of Heraclides (F4) found in Athenaeus discusses the administration of justice by 'the King in the incense-bearing land',[57] and it is clear from the use that Plutarch made of Dinon in his *Life of Artaxerxes* that Cunaxa (cf. F17) and the diplomacy of Antalcidas (F19) were treated of. One would guess that he furnished a general political history of Persia. In Nepos' *Life of Datames* there is a detailed account of the Satraps' Revolt and since elsewhere Nepos asserted that his principal authority in the affairs of Persia was Dinon (*Conon* 5. 4) it would seem likely that it was on Dinon that he drew for his account of that Revolt. If Dinon had been preserved in full, we would surely have had a great deal of information about the workings of Empire and the relations of satraps and the King, and the general impression one gets that before the conquest of Alexander Greece had only moderate understanding of Persia might well have been falsified.

Nonetheless, there is an index of Greek understanding in the writings of Plato and Aristotle. In the *Laws* (694a–698a) Plato finds the secret of the success or the failure of a particular King in the sort of education he has received. His account of Cyrus seems to depend to some extent on the picture presented by Xenophon in *The Education of Cyrus*, and there is no case for regarding it as history; Cambyses turned out badly because he had been badly brought up, a cause, one suspects, deduced from the events of the reign; Darius turned out well because he had not had the lax education of a Royal prince, when in point of fact Darius had been of the blood royal, in a collateral line. And so on, theorizing without any real knowledge. His conclusion (698a) that Persia is now ill run because of the excessively servile condition of the subjects, and the excessively domineering conduct of the rulers seems to be a piece of pure Greek moralizing. One searches Plato in vain[58] for illumination of Persia and its empire. Nor would it appear that Aristotle was in this matter much different. He does seem to have treated of the Magi, as had Dinon in the fifth book of his *Histories*,[59] and to have interested himself in the ideas of Zoroastrianism (Diog. Laert. 1. 8), and in the

Politics he claimed that the measures taken by Periander of Corinth to safeguard his tyranny were similar to those practised in the Persian system of rule (1313ᵃ34–1313ᵇ12). But there may not have been much to this other than thoughts of the Eyes and Ears of the King, beloved of Greeks talking of Persia,[60] just as his assertion in the *Nicomachean Ethics* that Persians treat their sons as slaves (1160ᵇ27) may have nothing more to it than the common Greek reaction to the term which was misleadingly translated as 'slave'.[61] Perhaps this does the learned philosopher less than justice. What is clear, however, is that Persia figures very little in his works. Carthage and the Carthaginian constitution are discussed in some detail (*Pol.* 1272ᵇ24–1273ᵇ26), but of Persian monarchy and the relation of the Great King to his subject kings there is virtually nothing specific. Of course, it might be that the topic did not happen to occur to him when he was seeking instances, and in his general discussion of types of monarchy (1284ᵇ35–1288ᵃ32) he does include 'another type of monarchy such as are Kingships among some of the barbarians' which 'by reason of the more servile character of the barbarians compared to Greeks and of those in Asia compared to those in Europe' they put up with uncomplainingly (1285ᵃ16–22). So he seems to have had oriental monarchies in mind, but not the Persians and the Persian Empire specifically. He may have been well informed about it all, but he certainly does not show that he was.

It would be pointless to call on Isocrates to provide an index of Greek knowledge and understanding of Persia. All he can offer is a spectacle of Panhellenist folly. His purpose was to talk the Greeks into attacking the King, an attack that, he asserted, would be both easy and profitable. He was not interested in the truth of the matter.[62] However, when one considers how much material concerning Persia there is in Ephorus (as reflected in Diodorus) and in Plutarch's *Life of Artaxerxes*, it is clear that by one means or another Greeks had in the course of the fourth century come to learn quite a lot about Persia. This material is not just events which involved Greeks and could easily have been known about within Greece but also events which occurred well within the confines of the Empire such as the Cadusian War described in Plutarch's *Life of Artaxerxes* and the Satraps' Revolt; to write about them must have required deliberate inquiry and the existence of these narratives is proof that the Empire was being 'opened up' in the fourth century. All in all, it may be quite wrong to denigrate the work of fourth-century writers.[63] Not enough of their work has survived to justify such a judgement.

However, no matter how much or how little post-Xenophontic

writers would have helped if they had survived in full, we are reduced to making the best of what we have. Since what we have is so limited, and since there is so little Oriental evidence bearing directly on the relations of Greece and Persia, the 'best' will on occasion involve conjecture. But, as Sir Ronald Syme declared in the preface to his *Tacitus*, 'conjecture cannot be avoided, otherwise the history is not worth writing'.

NOTES

1. For Alexander's problems in suppressing the insurrection of the great Bactrian satrapy, cf. Bosworth 1988: 110–13, 116. For Cyrus the Great and the Massagetae, Hdt. 1. 201, 204, 214. It was on the north-east frontier of Iran that settled people had to confront great nomadic hordes. Cf. Tarn 1951: 79–81, 117. Alexandria in Margiane (Merv) was overrun by nomads (Pliny, *NH* 6. 47) and, when it was refounded by Antiochus I, he surrounded it with a wall nine miles long (Pliny, *NH* 6. 47; Strabo 11. 10. 2 516C is clearly a confusion of Pliny's source). Cyrus had tried to check the invaders with strong points like Cyropolis (Arr. *Anab.* 4. 2. 2, 3. 1). Alexander founded cities as 'defence against the incursions of the barbarians dwelling on the far side of the river' (Arr. *Anab.* 4. 1. 3), larger than previous foundations (cf. the size of Alexandria sub Caucaso, CR 7. 3. 23, and of Chodjend, CR 7. 6. 25), sometimes consolidating a number of previously founded cities in one large one (Justin 12. 5. 12). But, as the fate of Merv showed, the pressure of nomadic invasion continued. Cf. Will: 1979: 268–70 for the 3rd cent. BC, and Will 1982: 401–2 for the Chinese incursions of the 2nd.

2. For the revolt of 486–484 BC (Hdt. 7. 1. 3) and that of 464(?)–454 (Thuc. 1. 104. 1, 110. 1, and 112. 3) cf. *CAH* iv² 141–5. For the revolt of 404–343, cf. *CAH* vi² 345–9. Not only was the approach march across desert a difficult logistical problem (cf. Hdt. 3. 5–7) but the annual inundation of the Nile valley required a strict timetable. Any delay en route made for a washout. See Ch. 10, n. 22.

3. The frequently disputed succession is an index of what the King had to beware of, as Photius' Epitome of Ctesias shows (*FGH* 688 FF13–15). There was constant danger of rebellious satraps, e.g. Pissouthnes, later his son Amorges, Megabyzus in Syria, Artabazus, and of course the great Satraps' Revolt, and occasionally the King had to take the field, e.g. the war against Bactria (F14) or the war against the Cadusians (Plut. *Art.* 24, 25). Uneasy lay the head that wore the crown. The deal made with the mountain Uxii is suggestive (Arr. *Anab.* 3. 17. 1, Strabo 15. 3. 4 728 C). To a

degree the mountainous places were beyond pacification. The King, who travelled with a not inconsiderable military retinue, had to pay a toll on journeys between Susa and Persepolis. Small parties must have been, and felt themselves, very insecure and it is no wonder that we hear of embassies at Susa but never at Persepolis.

4. Cf. Hornblower in *CAH* VI² 45.

5. Dandamaev–Lukonin 1989: 368–87 usefully surveys the written sources. Hallock in *CHI* II 588–609 discusses the tablets found at Persepolis. The text and a translation of the Behistun Inscription is provided in Kent 116–34, and another translation by Frye 1983: 363–8. For Babylonian chronicles, esp. the Nabonidus Chronicle and the Cyrus Cylinder, see *ANET³* 305–7, and 315–16. Lewis 1977: 13–15 proposes that Greek secretaries played a part in the transmission of Oriental information.

6. S. Hornblower 1982: 346–51 discusses the admixture of Greek and Carian names in Halicarnassus. In ML 32, in addition to Carian names, a Persian name appears borne by a magistrate, evidence of Persian influence rather than of Persian presence; cf. Hornblower 140 for other Persian names in Greek cities of Asia Minor. The Mausoleum too was a mixture of the Greek and the non-Greek; Hornblower 251 speaks of its 'unhellenic eclecticism'.

7. The gold-digging ants of Hdt. 3. 10. 2 have excited derision and been regarded as a typically 'fringe of empire' tale, almost beyond the fringe (cf. Asheri 1990 ad loc.); Peissel 1984: 144–9 and 176 discovered that there are gold-digging marmots in the Dansar Plain near the Indus and suggests that Herodotus was not so much misinformed as misunderstanding the name in Old Persian of the *Arctomys Himalayanas*. As to the so-called Army list of 7. 61–80, whatever it is and wherever it comes from, it cannot be the list of contingents in the army that invaded Greece in 480 (cf. Briant 1996: 207–9 and Appendix 3). Lewis 1977: 13–15 showed that there were Greek secretaries in the Persian administration, and one could readily accept that they may have been to some extent the source of such information; the ethnographical and geographical notes seem characteristic of Hecataeus and Herodotus may have drawn on him, but the list is hardly to be dismissed as worthless. However, as Armayor 1978*b* makes clear, much of the detail is at variance with the Oriental evidence. Lewis 1985 showed that many of the names are respectable but accepted that much of Armayor's case is irrefutable.

8. The Aces is perhaps the Atrak which flows into the Caspian (cf. Asheri ad loc.).

9. For transhumance and nomadism in modern Persia, see PERSIA, Geographical Handbook, Naval Intelligence Division 1945, chs. VII and VIII. ('As in all stock-breeding countries where rainfall and vegetation are limited, pastoral nomadism or seasonal migration is the rule', p. 336.)

10. Behistun Inscription I §§1–4. For Darius' relation to Cyrus, see the genealogical table of the Achaemenids in Kent 1953: 158–9, or Asheri 1997 (on Hdt. 1. 107) 335.

11. For the item of the treasures, looted by Sargon in 714 BC, cf. Herzfeld 1968: 289 and Volkmann 1954: 49–50.

12. Cf. the list in Lloyd 1975a: 72–3. The attack of Fehling 1989 revives the approach of Sayce (cf. Lloyd ad 2. 29. 1), and is sceptical about Herodotus' assertions of autopsy. Some of these assertions are hard to swallow (e.g. 2. 75. 1, 2. 104. 2, 3. 12), but they do not necessarily discredit assertions of autopsy in other parts of the *Histories*.

13. A balance sheet of the acceptable and the unacceptable in Herodotus' account is presented by MacGinnis 1986: 81–2. The latest major discussion is that of Rollinger 1993, who argues that Herodotus was not speaking from autopsy. As Kuhrt 1997, in her review of Rollinger, pointed out, there has been a tendency to presume that Herodotus was accurately recounting what he had seen and to interpret the archaeological evidence to suit him. Only those who suppose him incapable of error would argue that such details as the wall three hundred feet high (1. 178. 3) show that Herodotus had not seen the wall for himself.

14. For Conon's journey to Babylon, Diod. 14. 81. 4. The Royal Road from Sardis to Susa was the route for land armies. Herodotus plainly had not travelled by it and did not know what he was talking about in 5. 52 (cf. Calder 1925). The army of Cyrus the Younger crossed the Euphrates at Thapsacus (Xen. *Anab.* 1. 4. 11); the river was exceptionally low and his troops waded across easily, though normally there were boats, presumably a bridge of boats (ibid. §§17, 18). (Thapsacus is Semitic *tiphsah*, 'crossing place'.) Alexander also crossed the river at Thapsacus using a double bridge of boats (Arr. *Anab.* 3. 7. 1). One would dearly like to know what was the reality behind Damastes' account of the journey of Diotimus to Susa (Strabo 1. 3. 1 47C), which began in Cilicia. Diotimus may have been a contemporary of Herodotus (cf. Davies 1971: 161).

15. For bridging in the Persian Empire, cf. Briant 1996: 174–6.

16. Herodotus (5. 53) speaks of 'the royal road'. There were other royal roads (cf. Diod. 19. 19. 2 and Welles 1966: no. 20), though what earned a road the title 'royal' we do not know. Cf. Briant 1996: 369–74.

17. Cf. Cawkwell 1976a: 67–71.

18. The date at which Gorgias delivered his *Olympic Oration* is unclear but it cannot be shown to belong before 411 BC, the date of Aristophanes' *Lysistrata*, the only evidence being the account Philostratus gives of the gist of the speech in the *Lives of the Sophists* (1. 9. 4). What he says of the *Funeral Oration* (in §5) seems to suit the period of the Corinthian War when Athens could well be said to be 'yearning for empire'; earlier she had held it.

19. The term 'Panhellenism' is modern and is a convenient title for the

doctrine espoused by Isocrates but a common feeling of being Greek had gradually developed and was expressed by the term *Panhellēnes* (cf. Strabo 8. 6. 6 370C, and M. L. West ad Hesiod *Works and Days* 528), which meant little more than *Hellēnes* (cf. e.g. Euripides, *Trojan Women* 764 and 412). When the comic poet, Cratinus, spoke of Cimon as 'in every way best mortal of the *Panhellēnes*' (Plut. *Cim.* 10. 4), he was lauding Cimon's character, not his politics.

20. V.i. pp. 211–12.

21. For *proskynēsis*, the crucial passage is Hdt. 1. 134. 1 (cf. Asheri 1997 ad loc.). Herodotus makes plain that various forms of salutation were appropriate to the varying social rank of the man saluted and that full self-abasement (προσκύνησις) occurred when there was the greatest social disparity. Despite what Greeks chose to make of it, it had nothing to do with religion (cf. Bickerman 1963, who discusses the archaeological evidence). For Greeks such self-abasement was reserved for religion, and there were stories of rigid refusal to submit (Nepos, *Conon* 3. 3–4, Hdt. 7. 136) though the tricky Themistocles judged submission a price worth paying (Plut. *Them.* 27. 2–7) as doubtless did a great many others. It was not just at the Great King's court that Greeks were compelled to kowtow and in Agesilaus' campaign of 395 BC satisfaction was obtained by the Greeks in making Persians do unto others as they had compelled others to do unto them (Xen. *Ages.* 1. 34) even though this sort of thing belonged to holy religion (Xen. *Anab.* 3. 2. 9). For the whole topic, cf. Briant 1996: 234–6.

Similarly the Greeks made play with the 'subjection' of the King's subjects. The term *bandaka*, common in the Behistun Inscription, used to describe the condition of subordination to the King, was translated into Greek by the word *doulos*, which besides being regularly used for those politically subject (cf. Hdt. 1. 89. 1, 5. 49. 2, 6. 44. 1, 7. 8β 3 etc., and in Thucydides *douleia* is the opposite of 'empire' in e.g. 5. 69. 1) yet kept something of the flavour of 'slave'. So Euripides, *Helen* 276, says "τὰ βαρβάρων γὰρ δοῦλα πάντα πλὴν ἑνός", which is matched by Socrates asking in Xenophon's *Memorabilia* (4. 2. 33) 'how many others do you think have, for their wisdom, been taken up before the King and are there slaves?' For *bandaka*, see Briant 1996: 336.

22. Cf. Gibbon, *Decline and Fall*, ch. 3, 'there is a saying recorded of a young nobleman that he never departed from the sultan's presence without satisfying himself whether his head was still on his shoulders'. Persian punishments were, of course, appallingly brutal, burial alive (Xen. *Anab.* 1. 6. 6–11) of which 'dusting' was a devilish refinement (Val. Max. 9. 2. 6, Ctesias F15 §§50 and 52; cf. Hdt. 2, 100), mutilations of robbers (Xen. *Anab.* 1. 9. 13), abominable stoning of prisoners (Plut. *Art.* 19. 9). The penalty of death was common enough; perhaps the manner of execution was left to the whim of the judge or of the executioners (cf. 'boating' Plut. *Art.* 16).

The Royal women were horrifyingly cruel (ibid. 17, 14. 10, Hdt. 9. 110–12). But one need not believe all of Herodotus' stories. Senseless executions do not serve an army well.

23. See Appendix 3.

24. The Persian alliance with Sparta was all important, not so much for the amount of money the King provided, allegedly 5,000 talents (Andoc. 3. 29, Isoc. 8. 97) about which considerable doubts have been entertained (cf. Lewis 1977: 131 n. 138), but rather because Sparta was given confidence to persist. After the defeat of Arginusae the Spartans might well have despaired of ultimate victory had not Cyrus kept them at it (Xen. *Hell.* 2. 1. 11 and 14). Thucydides might at 2. 65. 12 have laid more emphasis on the part of Persia in the defeat of Athens.

25. One presumes that the letter which Pausanias allegedly sent to Xerxes (Thuc. 1. 128. 7) was a free composition, deploying the known usages. Likewise in the case of 1. 137. 4, the letter allegedly sent by Themistocles. It is vastly more likely that Thucydides wrote up what he considered suitable than that Pausanias and Themistocles kept copies of their treasonable communications. Xerxes' reply to Pausanias (1. 129. 3) must also be a free composition; if there had been an original in those terms it would have been far too incriminating for Pausanias to keep. See S. Hornblower 1991 ad 1. 128. 6, 129. 3, 137. 4.

26. It seems wholly improbable that Pausanias would have written to the Great King saying he wanted to marry his daughter, in the bald manner of 1. 128. 7. Likewise the story of Themistocles' letter to Xerxes (137. 4) is very improbable. It claimed that Themistocles could do the King great services but asked the King to wait for a year until these were revealed to him, as if the King did not have secretaries and interpreters to render unnecessary Themistocles having to learn the Persian language (which would have been a serious obstacle to communication); all this too when Themistocles was 'up-country' (ἄνω §3), in a position to 'send in' his message!

27. For discussion of the difficulties arising from Thucydides' narrative in 4. 50, see S. Hornblower 1996 ad loc., both the introductory note to the chapter and the note on §3 concerning the date of the death of Artaxerxes I. Thucydides appears to set the death in winter 425/424 and before the eclipse of the sun of 21 Mar. 424 (4. 52. 1), whereas Oriental evidence shows that Artaxerxes died considerably later. It is fashionable to save Thucydides' credit by supposing that the return of the Persian envoy Artaphernes to Persia was a good year after his capture and that it was only then that the King died. This may be right, but it leaves unexplained not only why the Athenians took so long to send Artaphernes and their own embassy with him but also why the King made no protest about his being detained. Thucydides *may*, however, have simply got it all badly wrong.

28. Andrewes's commentary on 8. 58 sets out the complications which the three 'treaties' present. For the time which reference to the King demanded, see Lewis 1977: 57 and n. 51; if the King replied promptly, the whole exchange could have been carried through within two to three weeks, in the course of which Tissaphernes could have moved his army to the valley of the Maeander. Presumably §1 of ch. 58 was added when the consent of the King arrived in Magnesia (cf. Hdt. 3. 125. 2), though the formal libations would have been made outside the city, at a place agreed on in Caunus, perhaps at the mouth of the river.

29. Cf. Breitenbach 1967, who discusses (cols. 1649–55) Xenophon's method of composition and, typically, supposes that he must have kept and used a diary of some sort; how could one small head carry all he recounts? There must have been some supplement (v.i.) but when human memories can vary so greatly and when the physical difficulties of writing, alluded to but not explored by Breitenbach, are considered, to suppose that Xenophon *must* have kept a diary is unjustified. There is, furthermore, no reason to suppose that Xenophon had any notions of writing an account of the march up-country when he set out with his friend Proxenus. He does not appear to have begun on his *Anabasis* before he was settled at Scillus *c.*392 BC and at least ch. 3 of book 5 was not written before his sons were grown up sufficiently to go hunting wild boar (5. 3. 10). I believe, though it can hardly be argued within a note, that Xenophon began with his Socratic discourses, passed perhaps to the *Education of Cyrus* (to which he was in the late 360s to add the sour footnote of the last chapter), then to the *Anabasis* conceivably after he settled in Corinth but not so old as to have forgotten. He had a good memory on which he was led, and misled, to rely. Cf. Cawkwell 2004 for the dating of Xenophon's *Anabasis* and v.i. n. 43. For the whole question whether Xenophon kept a diary, Cawkwell op. cit.

30. For Larisa and Mespila, see Lendle 1995: 172–7.

31. Mallowan 1966: 79–81 remarked that Xenophon (*Anab*. 3. 4. 7) was correct about the height of the walls (100 ft.) 'which is exactly in accord with a calculation made by Tiglath-Pileser III' and his *estimate* for the width (25 ft.) 'obviously refers to that of the quay', and went on to speak of him 'jotting down for posterity notes, substantially accurate'. It would be indeed remarkable if Xenophon had time on the march to 'estimate' and 'jot down'. A written source seems to me far more likely.

32. Rostovtzeff 1941: 1038.

33. Cf. Tarn 1951: 55 n. 1.

34. Dürrbach 1893: 363 n. 1 proposed to remove the references to Ctesias at *Anab*. 1. 8. 26 and 27, to which drastic surgery others have not assented. Ctesias would seem to have written his *Persica* in the 390s (cf. Jacoby 1922: col. 2036) and it is all too likely that Xenophon would have read it. Plainly, however, he did not entirely agree with it. Ctesias' numbers (F22) are quite

different from Xenophon's (1. 7. 11–15) and the two accounts of the battle represent two separate viewpoints (compare 1. 8. 26 and 27 with Ctesias FF 20 and 21). Indeed at one point Xenophon (2. 1. 7 and 8) is suspected to be giving the lie to Ctesias' claim to have been on the party sent to demand surrender (F23). Ctesias was interested in the fate of Clearchus and his account of Clearchus' response to the summons of Tissaphernes (F27 §68) differs from Xenophon's (2. 5. 28–30).

35. Cf. Hdt. 3. 1. 1, 129–30, 132. 1.
36. Cf. Syme 1988: 139.
37. For the Royal hides, Ctesias F5 (Diod. 2. 32. 4). Drews 1973: 111 and 198 n. 67 gives expression to the scepticism widely felt about such archives, but much undeserved. Cf. Dandamaev–Lukonin 1989: 113–15. Whether Ctesias actually used them is a quite different matter.
38. Cf. Briant 1996: 199–200.
39. Cf. Bigwood 1978.
40. Cf. Appendix 3.
41. As was argued in Cawkwell 1979: 18–21. Part of that argument raised, but did not fully treat of, the relation of the *Agesilaus* and the *Hellenica*. The encomium was written after the death of Agesilaus in 359 BC, and since the two works deal with the lifetime of Agesilaus and for the period 396–394 BC often in very similar language but after that with no such linguistic 'overlaps', the question which version was written first inevitably occurs. *Pace* Tuplin 1993: 29–31, I adhere to my view, but this is hardly the place for a full statement.
42. I cannot accept the argument of Delebecque 1957: 83 and 199 that the *Anabasis* was composed in two portions. The date of the work is fixed by 5. 3. 4–13 where he talks of his life at Scillus seemingly in the past, and if his sons went out on wild boar hunts (§10) a longish time must have elapsed since he established himself there.
43. The dating of Xenophon's writings is a very subjective matter. Delebecque 1957 places the composition of the *Education of Cyrus* between 364 and 358 (pp. 344, 384–410 esp. 405) with unjustifiable precision. The central consideration is that the whole book idealizes Cyrus and the Persian way of life until the last chapter of book 8, a bitter postscript in which Xenophon castigates everything Persian. What caused him to change his attitude? One can only guess that it was the change in Persian policy towards Sparta and Thebes first manifested at the Conference of Susa in 367 BC (Xen. *Hell.* 7. 1. 33–8), after which Xenophon as well as his hero Agesilaus became μισοπέρσης (Xen. *Ages.* 7. 7). So the *Education of Cyrus* may well belong to the 370s or earlier, in the 'sandwich' period between the Socratic works and the historical, of which the first was the *Anabasis* of, say, 370–368 BC. But there is ample room for different views. Cf. Gera: 1993 23–5, who accepts the idea of Anderson 1970: 211 that Xenophon's

account of the battle of Thymbrara in book 7 reflected what had happened in 371 at Leuctra; with which one doubts that many will concur.

44. Cf. Anderson 1970: 139. The wheeled towers which came on the scene at
6. 1. 52 and 53 and which must have had a merry time bumping along on
the march presumably did not have their one hundred and twenty men
each aboard until the approach to battle began at 7. 1. 3. They seem not to
have much part in the battle, though Cyrus used one of them as a look-out
point (7. 1. 39), but they were a nice idea foreshadowing the Hellenistic
helepolis—or the modern tank.

45. Dandamaev–Lukonin 1989: 100–3 do not address the question of the
apparent discrepancy between the *Oeconomicus* and the *Education of Cyrus*.
Cook in *CHI* II 267–8 discusses the inconsistency: 'the picture [Xenophon]
presents is on his own showing fictitious'. Pomeroy 1994 ad *Oec.* 4. 9–12
concludes that 'Xenophon is telling the truth for the most part . . . the vastness of the Empire, the variety of the territories and peoples ruled, and the
fact that not all parts of the Empire had been conquered at the same time
resulted in a system of administration that was not uniform throughout
. . . Xenophon has probably exaggerated the division of power for didactic
and literary purposes' (pp. 246–7). Alternatively, he did not know as much
as he is generally supposed to have known.

46. Cf. *Anab.* 1. 2. 17, 8. 12; 2. 3. 17; 4. 2. 18, 4. 4, 5. 34.

47. Cf. Tuplin 1987*b*: 232–4.

48. The story (in Polyaenus 7. 16. 1) must have fascinated the Greeks.

49. The apologia of Hirsch 1985: 61–97 seems to me wholly wrong-headed.

50. Cf. Launey 1987: i. 7–14, where the evidence for the size of armies is listed,
all on a quite different scale from the sort of figures Greek authors of the
pre-Hellenistic period furnish.

51. Cf. J. Hornblower 1981: 132–3.

52. Cf. Appendix 3. It is to be noted, however, that the Macedonians who
recorded the campaigns of Alexander did no better than record the fantastic figures provided by hearsay. Cf. Arrian, *Anab* 3. 8. 6 and 3. 15. 6 on
the battle of Gaugamela, on both of which passages see Bosworth 1980.

53. Other Greeks were more impressed (Briant 1996: 248).

54. His admiration of Cyrus and the Persians had not at an earlier stage been
diminished by the treatment of the Greek generals in 401 BC, which a careful reading of the *Anabasis* shows not necessarily to have been a matter of
Persian perfidy rather than of Greek treachery (cf. Cawkwell 1972: 24–5).

55. Cawkwell 1976*a*: 63–71.

56. See Drews 1973: 116–18, 121 and 202 n. 127.

57. i.e. not the Great King.

58. In *Alcibiades* I 121–4 there is a discussion of Persia which includes reference
to teaching the King's son 'the *mageia* of Zoroaster the son of Oromazos'
(122a) and also to the vastness of the Royal estates (123b). However, it is

generally accepted that the dialogue is spurious. Cf. Taylor 1948: 522, though Ledger 1989: 79–80 and 118 treats it as genuine.

59. *FGH*690 F5.
60. Hirsch 1985: 101–31 argued that there was in fact no official called the King's Eye or another called the King's Ear and that Xenophon's discussion of the matter in *Cyrop.* 8. 2. 10–12 is proof of his accuracy concerning Persia, a circular argument. But no matter here. Aristotle may like other Greeks have believed there was some sort of secret service which resembled what he believed existed in Corinth under the tyrants. (Since it is likely enough that Plutarch's reference to the King's Eye, Artasyras, at the battle of Cunaxa (*Art.* 12. 1) derives from Ctesias, it is wholly credible that such officials did exist, and that Xenophon was in error.)
61. The term *bandaka* occurs ten times in the Behistun Inscription (see Kent 1953: 199), where it is used, for instance, of Hydarnes (col. II §25), and of the commander of an army (col. II §33). When Euripides wrote in the *Helen* (276) τὰ βαρβάρων γὰρ δοῦλα πάντα πλὴν ἑνός, he was saying no more of all the King's subjects than was said of the satrap Gadatas in the document translated into Greek and familiar to us as the Letter of Darius (ML 12). Cf. Briant 1996: 335–7.
62. Cf. Stevenson 1985: 70–4.
63. As does Momigliano 1975: 132–5. S. Hornblower (*CAH* VI² 11) rightly typifies as 'facile' the 'view that all fourth-century Greek writing about Persia was trivial gossip'.

2

The Subjection of the Greeks of Asia

IN the first book of his *History*, Herodotus described the subjection of the Greeks of Asia first by the Mermnad dynasty of Lydia, then by Cyrus of Persia, and he concluded his account of the suppression of resistance by the Ionians with the remark, 'In this way Ionia had been subjected for the second time.'[1] A question automatically arises. What difference did subjection to Persia make?

Herodotus' account is curious. The Ionians were, it would seem, part of the army that Croesus led outside his kingdom and across the river Halys; Cyrus had sent heralds to the Ionians and tried to get them to abstain, but to no effect. After that battle Croesus dismissed them, and they had no part in the battle fought in the valley of the Hermus, not far from Sardis itself, nor in the unsuccessful defence of the city which ensued.[2] Once Cyrus was established there and clearly master of the Lydian kingdom, the Ionians sent messages to him asking to be accorded the same terms of subjection as they had had under Croesus. Cyrus angrily refused; they had had their chance to secure lenient treatment but they had not taken it. As far as Herodotus' account goes, there was no discussion of what the Ionians could expect, but when the cities got report of how Cyrus had reacted, they each began putting up walls around their cities and continued to assemble at the Panionium and to plan concerted action including appeal to Sparta (Hdt. 1. 141). The only exception was Miletus. That city had successfully defended itself against Lydia in an eleven-year war early in the century and secured special terms of friendship and alliance, and presumably had had no part in Croesus' attack across the Halys, for Cyrus accorded them precisely the status they had had vis-à-vis Lydia, the status of 'friend and ally'.[3] For the rest, the wrath of Cyrus was to be expected. Curiously, while Cyrus was in Sardis, it did not come.

How long Cyrus stayed in Sardis is not known. It was certainly long enough for the Ionians to make their unsuccessful appeal to him and then to summon Spartan aid, and for the Spartans to send an embassy to Cyrus. It may have been no more than the winter months,[4] but clearly nothing was done for the while to molest the Greeks. No army began operating until after Cyrus' departure. He had appointed a Persian, Tabalos, to be in charge of Sardis and a Lydian, Pactyes, to collect 'the gold of Cyrus and the other Lydians' (Hdt. 1. 153. 3) which makes one think of the arrangements made at Sardis by Alexander the Great in 334—someone to be responsible for the defence of Sardis and someone to assess and collect the tribute.[5] Yet although Alexander also appointed someone to replace the Persian satrap, Herodotus does not record the appointment of anyone to be in charge of more than Sardis itself, and Tabalos stayed shut up in the acropolis. There was certainly no army operating outside Sardis. When, shortly afterwards, Pactyes revolted and summoned the 'seaboard people' to join him, there was no army to prevent him besieging Tabalos (Hdt. 1. 154). A general with an army was dispatched by Cyrus, according to Herodotus (1. 156), only when Cyrus received news of the revolt. This general, Mazares, came with instructions to disarm the Lydians, to enslave 'all the others who joined in the attack on Sardis, and to bring Pactyes to him alive'. Only thereafter did the task of reducing the Greek cities begin, somewhat delayed by the death of Mazares but carried through by his replacement, Harpagus.

One can only guess Cyrus' reasons for this delay in taking over the whole of Croesus' kingdom. Perhaps he was unwilling to reduce his own conquering army, which needed a rest after what must have been a severe campaign, and which he intended to take with him undiminished when he returned to deal with Babylon and much else (Hdt. 1. 153. 4). Perhaps Mazares with a suitable army had already been summoned, and was already on his way when Cyrus marched east from Sardis. Whatever the reason, it is clear that nothing had been done to the Greeks before Mazares and Harpagus began on the task of reducing them by siege.

Yet from the outset the Greeks were greatly afraid of what Persian rule would mean. They had been prepared to resist both by putting walls around their cities and, to judge by the appeal for Spartan help, by conflict in battle. The Phocaeans, the first Ionians to be attacked by Harpagus, were so 'aggrieved by the subjection' that they took ship and sailed west. Indeed the Greeks even went so far as to join Pactyes in his foolhardy revolt.[6]

The condition of the Greeks under Lydia had certainly been subjection. With the exception of Miletus all 'the Greeks in Asia had been subjected to paying tribute',[7] and to judge by the fact that Miletus,

privileged as it was, obliged itself to military alliance, all the cities were
liable to military service.[8] That was probably not very severe, but what
it meant to be within the reach of Croesus' power is well shown by
the story Herodotus tells of how Croesus cowed the Lampsacenes into
releasing Miltiades, who had attacked Lampsacus and got himself
taken prisoner (6. 37). Lampsacus as part of Croesus' kingdom might
have expected not to be threatened with destruction when an outsider,
albeit friendly with the king, made war against it. The Ionian cities
were indeed vulnerable. When Cyrus refused to guarantee them the
same condition as they had been in under Croesus, they put up walls
around their cities. That is very remarkable indeed. Why had they
been without them before that? At what stage archaic Greek cities put
walls around the urban settlement as distinct from the secure acropolis
may be debated. The sixth-century wall of Athens would be, if it was
not for the firm statement of Thucydides (1. 93. 2), mere hypothesis.[9]
But it is not to be conceived that the Ionian cities which had been
attacked by the Mermnad kings from Gyges onwards would not have
taken the elementary precaution of putting up walls. In any case Miletus had walls, which it seems to have maintained (Hdt. 1. 17. 1), and
Ephesus had had walls until Croesus reduced the city (Hdt. 1. 26. 2),[10]
and Smyrna had walls, until the city was captured by Alyattes and its
walls were destroyed.[11] Why should other cities not have provided for
their defence in the same way?[12] The conclusion must be that when
the cities were captured they were required to demolish their walls.
Threats from Sardis would not be empty threats. There was to be no
barrier to the formidable Lydian army.[13] So what did the Greek cities
have to fear from Persia which they did not already suffer at the hands
of the Lydian?

The question is not necessarily rightly answered by describing how
the Persians actually treated them. By supporting the revolt of Pactyes,
the Greeks had alienated themselves still further from Cyrus, and if it
were to prove that the cities were much worse off under Persia, that
might be thought to be in large measure punishment. However, to
judge by the scant account of Herodotus, the punishment was confined
to the capture and enslavement of those who had actually participated
in the attack on Sardis, and to pillage. Mazares in carrying out his
orders 'enslaved' the Prienians, overran and pillaged their territory,
and proceeded to treat Magnesia on the Maeander likewise (Hdt. 1.
156. 2, 161). But the population of Priene had sufficiently recovered
by 494 BC to be able to furnish twelve triremes; it was not complete

depopulation and presumably the effects of the pillaging were not overwhelming. Of Magnesia sufficient remained to provide the satrap in Sardis with some sort of administrative centre (and later to be the 'bread' of Themistocles' sustenance).[14] So punishment for their part in the revolt of Pactyes may have been short, sharp, and shocking, but not of lasting effect. The difficulty is indeed all the other way. It is hard to see in what way the Greeks in Asia were worse off for the coming of Cyrus than they had been under Croesus. Cyrus had threatened worse but as far as one can tell from Herodotus subjection to Lydia was fairly complete. So did the Greeks of Asia in fact fare worse under their new masters?

The customary answer has been that the Persians imposed tyrants on the Greek cities.[15] There is no direct evidence that Cyrus did any such thing, but since Herodotus (4. 137. 2) represents Histiaeus the tyrant of Miletus as saying to his fellow tyrants at the bridge over the Danube that 'it is thanks to Darius that each of us is tyrant of his city, for each city would prefer to be under democracy than under tyranny', it is presumed that it was Persian practice to establish tyrants, or to use existing tyrants to maintain firm control of the Greek cities.[16] Certainly there were tyrants before Cyrus came down to Sardis but there is no evidence that any of them were replaced or any sustained to secure their city's subservience. In general, tyranny in the East Greek world was longer lived than in mainland Greece, as the history of Samos shows. There, tyranny, hardly affected by the Lydian power which never took to the sea, flourished in the 530s and 520s and the fair name of *Isonomia* was not heard until the Persians intervened in the early 510s (Hdt. 1. 27, 3. 142. 3). So the mere existence of tyrants in mainland cities under Darius by no means proves that the Persians made tyranny the mainstay of their power. Indeed Miletus with its tyrant Histiaeus with his deputy Aristagoras shows quite a different state of affairs. It was able to continue in the special relationship to the power of the hinterland which it had achieved for itself vis-à-vis Lydia, and the existence of tyranny there would seem to be in no way due to Persia. It had risen and fallen and risen again entirely, it would seem, for internal reasons (Hdt. 1. 20–2, 5. 92). Histiaeus was certainly not imposed by the Persians, and if he said that he and the other tyrants owed their position to Darius he must have meant that they had secured themselves by reliance on Persia against the surge of notions of *Isonomia* (cf. Hdt. 5. 37. 2), not that they had been imposed by Persian power on reluctant cities. Certainly we do hear of impositions. At Samos Theomestor, who had

distinguished himself at the battle of Salamis, was installed as tyrant by
Xerxes, just as Aeaces had been re-established there after the Ionian
Revolt, and as his father, Syloson, having won the favour of Darius,
was installed when the Persians took over the island in the first place
(Hdt. 8. 85. 2, 6. 23. 1, 3. 144). Samos, whose tyrant Polycrates 'had
nourished large ambitions' (Hdt. 3. 122. 3), may have been untypical.
Although Coes of Mytilene, who was 'general' of the Mytileneans on
Darius' Scythian Expedition, was not at that time tyrant but had by
499 BC been 'given Mytilene' by Darius, he was one of the few tyrants
to suffer the vengeance of his countrymen when he was deposed.[17] The
lenient treatment accorded to the rest suggests that they had not been
imposed; they might, but for the Persians, have been earlier deposed
and, when it came to revolt, they could not be trusted not to serve the
Persian cause, but, unlike Coes, they had been home products; they
had come to suit the Persians; they had not been established to do
so. Indeed, presuming that Herodotus' list of tyrants on the Scythian
Expedition was meant to be complete, it is remarkable how few they
were.[18] Either there were a good many he did not know about or the
Persians had not made it their practice to install tyrants.[19] The evidence is thin, but on the whole it looks as if it was not by the imposition
of tyrannies that the Greeks of Asia were more harshly treated under
Cyrus than they had been under Croesus.

Were there then garrisons installed in the Greek cities, or, at any rate,
in the more important of them? There certainly was a Persian guard
installed by Cyrus' general, Harpagus, when the Phocaeans evacuated
the city, but that was an exceptional state of affairs; the Persians were
guarding an empty city surrounded still by exceptionally strong walls
(Hdt. 1. 164. 3). Clearly at the outbreak of the Ionian Revolt there were
no garrisons for the rebels to have to deal with; if there had been, the
deposition of tyrants would have been much more complicated and
Herodotus records no case in which plans went awry. That was almost
half a century after the coming of Cyrus, in the course of which there
may have been important changes, but on the whole it seems unlikely
that there ever were garrisons in those early decades. Garrisons were
costly in men and money and hardly necessary if the cities were without walls. Harpagus had reduced them all by siege, and, regardless
whether Lydia had required cities to be without walls, the Persians
would hardly have allowed them to continue to have a means of causing them trouble.[20] Phocaea was perhaps the exception that proved the
rule. Harpagus, not wishing to be detained by the siege of the first city

he attacked, offered curious terms. To get the Phocaeans to submit, he declared he would be content 'if a single bastion were razed and a single building dedicated' (Hdt. 1. 164. 1), a partial demolition and a symbolic surrender. It was not so much that Phocaea was exceptionally well provided with walls. Harpagus took the cities that did not submit by building mounds by which he could make the assault, and there is no reason to think that such a method would not have worked for Phocaea. What was special about that siege was that it was the first city of Ionia to be attacked; a quick decision would have a suitably dispiriting effect on the other Ionian cities, and a delayed decision a correspondingly inspiring. The Phocaeans realized that their subjection could only be a matter of time and withdrew leaving the Persians an empty city.[21] No other Ionian city save Teos was quite so resolute, but Teos and the rest of the rebellious Ionians were taken by assault.[22] Common prudence would have suggested that the walls must be, and stay, pulled down. In that way, the Lydian way, garrisons were needless.

As to tribute, it is to be presumed that Cyrus did not discontinue what Croesus had established. When he provided for the administration of the new satrapy, he assigned to Pactyes the collection of 'the gold of Croesus and that of other Lydians', which hardly sounds like an abiding task, but which may have been somewhat misrepresented by Herodotus.[23] In his third book (3. 89. 3) he would have it thought that tribute (the so-called *dasmos*) was not formalized before the reign of Darius, that under Cyrus the subject peoples 'brought gifts', but his own narrative is not consistent with this statement (cf. 3. 13. 3, 3. 67. 3, 4. 165. 2),[24] and in his seventh book he makes Artabanus assert that 'Cyrus made all Ionia tribute-paying' (7. 51. 1). It would seem that Cyrus continued the system of Croesus.

What difference then did the coming of the Persians make? Did they take over the seaboard towns and plains which the Lydians had left alone? In the fifth century ample enough evidence appears for Persians owning large estates in western Anatolia and for the King giving cities to favoured Greeks.[25] These latter gifts may, however, be left out of consideration here. It would appear that what the gift of a city amounted to was not necessarily more than the grant of the tribute due to the King. Themistocles was 'given' 'Magnesia on the Maeander for bread, Lampsacus for wine, and Myous for meat' (Thuc. 1. 139. 5) but both the latter cities paid tribute to Athens in the 450s and there is no reason to suppose things were any different in the previous decade.

If the descendants of the Eretrian, Gongylus, and of Demaratus, the deposed Spartan king who chose to serve the King of Persia, were in active control of cities late in the fifth century after the collapse of the Athenian Empire,[26] that is no proof that the families had been in control all through the century. In short, such gifts may not have always amounted to very much. The real point is raised by Persian estates and land settlements of various sorts. When Xenophon in winter 400/399 BC was leading the remains of the Ten Thousand southward to join up with the Spartans, he raided an estate in the valley of the river Caïcus where a Persian, as his name Asidates proclaims, lived in a strongly fortified tower with an ample number of defenders. Calls for help both with fire-signals and by shouting brought another Persian, Itamenes,[27] 'with his own force' and from the nearby strongpoint of Comania there came 'Assyrian hoplites, Hyrcanian cavalry, about eighty, King's mercenaries, eight hundred peltasts, others from Parthenium, others from Apollonia and the nearby places including cavalry' (*Anab.* 7. 8. 17). These places were at no great distance from Pergamum or from the sea, but clearly Xenophon had stirred up a very hornets' nest of Orientals. It is to be noted, however, that Pergamum was a Greek city. From it, Gongylus led out 'his own force' to assist Xenophon's force and save it from disaster (ibid.). Although we do hear of two cities near Cyme, which were settled by Egyptian soldiers, Larisa and Cyllene, it would seem from the history of the Spartan campaign between 399 and 387 BC in the war with Persia that no city presented the Spartans with difficulties caused by divided loyalties. So it may safely be affirmed that in the Caïcus valley at any rate there was a strong Persian presence but the Greek cities were left alone.

How typical, then, was the situation in the Caïcus valley? The rest of the evidence for western Anatolia is not as vivid or as unequivocal as the story of Asidates, but there is enough to indicate that the sort of colonization to be found in the Caïcus valley was widespread. Strabo (13. 4. 13 629C) speaks of 'the Hyrcanian Plain, the Persians having conferred the name and brought settlers there just as the Persians gave its name to the Plain of Cyrus', and the assemblage of forces to save Sardis at the start of the Ionian Revolt in 499 BC must have been drawing on these settled areas (Hdt. 5. 102. 1). It is all, it would seem, in accord with the arrangements for controlling the Empire which Xenophon, in the *Education of Cyrus* (8. 6. 4 and 5), has Cyrus the Great spell out. His idea was that those sent out to the provinces ($\tau\grave{\alpha}$ $\check{\epsilon}\theta\nu\eta$) should have estates and houses there so that the tribute should come to them at court and that if they went out there, they should have their own places to reside in, also that they should establish a cavalry force of the Persians in their retinue and of the allies as well as charioteers (8. 6. 10).[28]

Xenophon was here no doubt describing the situation that pertained in his own day. How much of all this had been begun when Cyrus took over the Lydian Empire? The only measure specifically attributed to Cyrus is the grant of seven cities to Pytharchus of Cyzicus (*FGH* 472 F6), and it might be thought that if Cyrus had time for such a minor matter he might well have given thought to the major problem of how to maintain control over these new lands and have given orders to that effect, which perhaps Pactyes the Lydian by revolting sought to prevent. The Plain of Cyrus, to which Strabo referred, may at that early date have been designated for occupation. Certainly enough Cyrus did settle Egyptian troops from Croesus' army in Larisa and Cyllene near the coast in the area of Cyme as well as in 'cities up-country' (*Education of Cyrus* 7. 1. 45).[29] So plans for settlement may well have been made as soon as Croesus and Sardis had been dealt with. The manner in which the Persians punished the Milesians in 494 BC for their part in the Ionian Revolt is suggestive (Hdt. 6. 20). The people were led away into captivity and settled beside the Red Sea. The Persians did not, however, occupy the city, which is later found paying tribute to Athens,[30] but they took possession of the area around the city and of the plain. Miletus had enjoyed a special relationship with Lydia which Cyrus had continued (Hdt. 1. 141. 4) and so would have been saved from any settlements in the 540s. Elsewhere in 494 men were rounded up and cities burnt (Hdt. 6. 31–2), but Herodotus says nothing about the Persians in settling the Revolt occupying the best land. It is at least possible that that had happened to the rest fifty years before, or had begun to happen. One cannot be sure. Persian colonization may not have begun immediately after the conquest of Lydia, but when the Ionians and the Aeolians appealed to Cyrus to be allowed the same condition of subjection as they had had under Croesus, Cyrus refused (Hdt. 1. 141. 1–3). They had paid tribute to Croesus. They no more had under Cyrus garrisons imposed than under Croesus. Indeed the cities themselves seem to have been left to get on with their business as before. So what did Cyrus have in mind to do to them and why did the Greeks in fear prepare to resist and to stand siege, to plan what must have seemed a fairly hopeless revolt even with Spartan help (Hdt. 1. 141. 4)? At least the theory of Persian colonization provides an answer.

Of course, Cyrus and Persia came into the Greek world as an

alien power, where Croesus and Lydia had been congenial enough. Croesus' mother was Carian, his stepbrothers Ionian (Hdt. 1. 92. 3). When Croesus laid siege to Ephesus, that city had as tyrant a grandson on his mother's side of Alyattes, and thus a nephew of Croesus, namely Pindar son of Melas (Aelian, *VH* 3. 26). Perhaps such marriages were common enough. Certainly Croesus before he became king had readily enough turned to Ephesus for help; on one occasion, if we may trust Dionysius of Halicarnassus (*FGH* 90 F65), when Alyattes required his son to bring mercenaries to Sardis, Croesus in need of money and rebuffed by the richest of the Lydians (a merchant with the royal name of Sadyattes) visited Ephesus, prayed to Artemis, and got what he needed from a rich Ephesian. Many a Greek had, in turn, been to Sardis. The Alcmaeonid family of Athens were said to have owed their wealth to a successful visit by Alcmaeon, who had by luck or prudence taken pains to help Croesus' envoys to Delphi (Hdt. 6. 125). Miltiades the Elder was known to, and was saved by, the King (Hdt. 6. 37), and before ever he sought the Spartan alliance, he had earned the gratitude of the Spartans when they went to Sardis to buy gold and had received it as a gift (Hdt. 1. 69. 4). Trade between the Greek world and Lydia had, in fact, a very long history.[31] The gift of three hundred boys by Periander of Corinth to Alyattes probably reflects more than mere friendship (Hdt. 3. 48. 2). Solon's visit to Croesus was alleged to be motivated by curiosity and perhaps 'all the other Sophists from Greece', who, according to Herodotus, visited Sardis, were similarly inspired.[32] But clearly there was a lot to be got from Croesus. His wealth was advertised to the Greek world by generous gifts to many shrines in Greece, not just to Delphi.[33] This was not an innovation. Not only his father but Gyges himself, founder of the dynasty, had similarly given (Hdt. 1. 25. 2 and 14. 1). Consultation of oracles may not have been as important to the Lydian kings as Herodotus would lead us to believe, but they certainly indulged in it freely, not just Croesus but his father too (Hdt. 1. 19); the gifts represent appeals and their continuance considerable confidence in the oracles concerned.[34] In this way the Lydian kings were much imbued with Greek religious notions, and the compatibility of Greece and Lydia is equally well shown by Lydian religious exports. The cult of Dionysus originated in Lydia as the opening of Euripides' *Bacchae* declares (esp. ll. 72–82), Baki being the Lydian name for the god. Just as Artemis, 'the greatest divinity of Sardis in the Lydian period',[35] made a bond with Ephesus, so the cult of Baki made a bond with Teos, where Dionysus was honoured especially.[36] This integration of Lydian and Greek was to be felt in all spheres. Lydia can be considered 'as a marginal province of Greek art' and 'with the rise of the dynasty of the Mermnadae, we see in architecture and sculpture the emergence of a stylistic grouping which I should like to define as "Lydo-Ionian" '.[37] Lydian empire over the Greeks of Asia was domination, but not foreign domination.[38]

By contrast the Persians were wholly alien. The Colophonians for instance could be said to have picked up the luxurious ways of the Lydians (Xenophanes F3 West). The Persians had no such charm. Phocaeans and Teans preferred to abscond rather than endure, and before the effects of Persian rule were felt, the cities put up their walls in fear against the alien intruders. Their attitude was shared in mainland Greece. The Spartans would have gone to the help of Croesus, according to Herodotus, if the speed of Croesus' advance had not prevented them, and the subsequent message to Cyrus showed that he was viewed as a menace to Greek liberty in a way the Lydian kings had not been (Hdt. 1. 82 and 152).

'Coasts and islands saw it and were afraid, the world trembled from end to end,' according to the author of Isaiah 40–55 as he prophesied the coming of Cyrus, and the relation of the islands close by the mainland of Asia to the new power of the hinterland is a matter of some importance.[39] According to Herodotus (1. 27. 1), Croesus had been minded to build a fleet and attempt to subject the islanders but was dissuaded, making instead a treaty of friendship (ξεινίη).[40] Similarly when Harpagus had completed the subjection of the mainland Ionians, those occupying the islands, the Chians and the Samians, in fear 'gave themselves to Cyrus' in the phrase of Herodotus (1. 169. 2). This seems to denote more than mere friendship, and when Cambyses was assembling his forces to attack Egypt, he called on Polycrates of Samos to contribute a naval contingent (Hdt. 3. 44). Herodotus would have it that Polycrates invited Cambyses so to call on him, but the Samians were not the only islanders who served in Egypt. We happen to hear of a Mytilenean trireme in the course of the operations, and it seems likely that all the major islands close to the Asiatic shore were in some sense subject to the Great King.[41] Of course, until the Persians had conquered Phoenicia and taken the Phoenician fleet into service, the islands had no immediate fear of invasion, but since the major islands had dependencies on the mainland, it was in their interests to conform.[42]

The regular method of conforming to Persia while remaining outside the Empire itself was to satisfy the Persian demand for earth and water. There are enough mentions in Herodotus of such demands to make clear that they constituted, as it were, diplomatic overtures; when and only when the demand had been complied with, 'alliance' could be formed.[43] It is to be presumed then that Harpagus called on the larger offshore islands to give earth and water and that they complied. Polycrates knew the limits of his independence. Early in his rule he harboured large ambitions. According to Herodotus he had taken 'both numerous islands and many cities on the mainland', and he had won a naval victory over the Lesbians and made them prisoners of war. In the story of his death, his large ambitions play a part.[44] Yet he not only sent the forty ships to Egypt, but he also obeyed the summons of the satrap at Sardis and appeared before him at Magnesia on the Maeander (Hdt. 3. 44. 2, 124–5). His daughter was said to have tried to dissuade him from answering the fatal summons, but he knew his place just as he knew that after the Persians had gained the Phoenician navy he could not act independently. That was the position in the reign of Cambyses. Darius, his accession troubles over, moved to incorporate the island in the Empire. Herodotus would have it thought that Darius acted to satisfy a request for restoration by Syloson, the exiled brother of Polycrates (3. 139, 140). That is, one guesses, the reverse of the truth, namely, that Darius resolved to incorporate Samos in the Empire and Syloson was a fit instrument.

The precise status of other islands is uncertain. Presumably it was not the Ionian islanders alone, who, on Harpagus' urging, 'gave themselves' to Cyrus. The Aeolians had joined the Ionians in the revolt against Cyrus (Hdt. 1. 151) and so deserved the same treatment. Thus it is no surprise that, like the Samians, the Mytileneans served in the invasion of Egypt (Hdt. 3. 13. 1). Whether Mytilene was taken over as Samos was, is uncertain, but it is likely. The presence of naval contingents from island states on the Scythian Expedition of Darius argues no more than does their presence in Egypt under Cambyses, but since at the end of the Scythian Expedition Darius installed a Mytilenean as tyrant on Mytilene, he either then or earlier took Lesbos into the Empire (Hdt. 4. 138, 97. 1; 5. 11). How widely this happened is unsure. We hear of the islands giving earth and water when required before the Marathon campaign but that may have been the limit of their subjection (Hdt. 6. 49). As to the more southerly offshore islands, nothing is heard. Herodotus records the subjection of Caria very briefly and makes no mention of Cos or Rhodes in that connection.[45]

Despite the paucity of information it would seem that the demand for earth and water was the warning shadow of what was to come. No doubt what was happening in Ionia was reported in mainland Greece by traders, and in any case the annual meeting of Ionians on Delos, revived by Polycrates, gave ample opportunity for leading Athenians to hear from their fellow Ionians themselves (Thuc. 3. 104. 3). The reaction of the Greeks generally seems lukewarm, but quite apart from the fact that there was little that could be done it was also the case that once Persian rule had been established in the East Aegean there was little to distinguish it from the rule of Lydia with which the Greeks had lived comfortably enough.

NOTES

1. 1. 169. 2 At the end of the Ionian Revolt of 499–494 he declared (6. 32) οὕτω δὴ τὸ τρίτον Ἴωνες κατεδουλώθησαν, πρῶτον μὲν ὑπὸ Λυδῶν, δὶς δὲ ἐπεξῆς τότε ὑπὸ Περσέων. Cf. 1. 6. 2, 27. 1 and 4.

2. When Croesus had crossed the Halys, Cyrus sent a message to the Ionians in the army trying to get them to revolt (Hdt. 1. 76. 3). Croesus' army was said to be ξεινικός (Htd. 1. 77. 4). According to Xenophon (*Cyrop.* 6. 2. 10), 'both Ionians and Aeolians and pretty well all the Greeks settled in Asia had been compelled to follow Croesus'.

3. Hdt. 1. 22. 4, 141. 4. According to Diogenes Laertius (1. 25), when Croesus summoned the Milesians as allies, Thales dissuaded them from going and this saved them from Cyrus' wrath. According to Herodotus (1. 75), Thales was with Croesus and got his army across the Halys, an unlikely story.

4. The statement in the Nabonidus Chronicle (cf. J. B. Pritchard, *ANET*[3] 306) concerning the movements of Cyrus in 547 is no longer to be taken as an allusion to the campaign against Croesus (cf. M. Mallowan, *CHI* II 404 n. 5, who rejects both 547 and 546 as possible dates for the fall of Sardis, and concludes that 'the city could have fallen at any time between 545 and the attack on Babylon in 540'; also cf. Cargill 1977, and Briant 1996: 44). If it is right to date the beginning of Pisistratus' third tyranny in 546 (cf. Rhodes 1981: 191–9), the narrative of Herodotus would have it both that Croesus did not seek alliance in Greece before that date (1. 59. 1, 69. 1) and that Cyrus did not attack him for some time; for Miltiades the Elder had been in the Chersonese long enough to build a wall across it before he engaged in war against the Lampsacenes, got himself captured, and was

released after dire threats by Croesus (6. 37). For the appeal of the Ionians and Aeolians to Sparta and the Spartan embassy to Cyrus, Hdt. 1. 152. Cyrus must have been some months in Sardis, but he had pressing business elsewhere (Hdt. 1. 153. 4) and a long stay seems wholly unlikely.

5. Arr. *Anab.* 1. 17. 7. According to Herodotus 1. 153. 3, Pactyes was instructed to κομίζειν 'the gold of Croesus and the rest of the Lydians'. If he had been intended to convey it to Cyrus, he would have needed a substantial military escort and one would hardly expect such a task to be entrusted to a Lydian, and so there is much to be said for the view that κομίζειν here means 'manage' (cf. Boffo 1983: 24 n. 94).

6. Hdt. 1. 163, 164. 2. Athens built a new wall in 479/8 in a very short time, a matter of perhaps not much more than a month, to judge by Thucydides' narrative (1. 90–2), and the haste was plainly to be seen in the masonry (93. 2). Similarly the walls of unwalled East Greek cities could have been quickly erected after Cyrus reached Sardis; since they were demolished (v.i.), there are no remains to proclaim the haste of construction. Phocaea, however, is a serious difficulty; a wall of 'not a few stades' and 'entirely of large stones well fitted together' (Hdt.1. 163) was not built in a day, and in any case, although there does seem to have been quite an interval between Cyrus' capture of Sardis and Harpagus' campaign against the Ionian cities, the Phocaeans were not to know that they would have so long to prepare their defences. Besides, they appealed to the king of Tartessus and he gave generously, having learned from them 'that the power of the Mede was increasing' (πυθόμενος τὸν Μῆδον παρ' αὐτῶν ὡς αὔξοιτο), a phrase hardly suitable for the period after the capture of Sardis. One is forced to conclude, despite the silence of Herodotus, that Phocaea had secured permission to rebuild her walls some time before Cyrus descended on Sardis. Perhaps that is why Phocaea seems to have had a leading part in the revolt (Hdt. 1. 152), and why Harpagus attacked it first (163. 1). For the problem of the walls of Phocaea, cf. Boffo 1983: 17 n. 60, and Özyiğit 1994, who argued for a date of 590–580 BC for the construction of the 'Archaic' walls, which seems too early for the Phocaeans to be alarmed at the rise of the Mede.

7. Hdt. 1. 6. 2, 27. 1. Despite these general statements, one presumes that Miletus' position in this regard was exceptional (cf. 1. 22. 4, 141. 4).

8. Xen. *Cyrop.* 6. 2. 10 speaks of 'the Ionians, the Aeolians and pretty well all the Greeks settled in Asia' being compelled to serve in Croesus' army. Herodotus described the army of Croesus that crossed the Halys as ξεινικός (1. 77. 4), but that term was used to distinguish τῶν Λυδῶν ἡ δύναμις from the Lydians themselves (cf. 1. 79). Pactyes raised mercenaries (1. 154), just as Croesus, during the reign of his father Alyattes, is alleged by Nicholas of Damascus to have done (*FGH* 90 F65), but was able to secure the Greeks on the seaboard for his army. So evidently they were ready for war. In any

case it is hardly to be conceived that Lydia, having reduced the cities, did not make use of their armies.

9. Cf. S. Hornblower 1991: 135.

10. Cf. Polyaenus 6. 50; Aelian, *VH* 3. 26.

11. There is some obscurity about Smyrna. Hdt 1. 16 records its capture by Alyattes, and Strabo 14. 1. 37 646C says that 'after the Lydians had razed Smyrna, it continued for about four hundred years dwelling in villages' (Λυδῶν δὲ κατασπασάντων τὴν Σμύρνην, περὶ τετρακόσια ἔτη διετέλεσεν οἰκουμένη κωμηδόν). The excavations of the 1950s had therefore no hesitation in ascribing to Alyattes the siege-rams which they unearthed (cf. Nicholls 1958–9: 128). However, it is clear that after an interval life at the temple of Athena continued as busily as ever, and the real break came in the middle of the century. This break is inevitably connected with the campaign of Harpagus by Akurgal 1983, esp. 72–5, and he supposes that the hastily erected barrier across the main entrance to the temple was a desperate attempt to keep the Persians out. Cf. Cook and Nicholls 1998: 170.

12. Priene did, to judge by *Suda* s.v. Ἀλυάττης.

13. Cf. Tozzi 1978: 151 n. 86 and Boffo 1983: 18–19. Cf. Strabo 13. 1. 42 601C (where Croesus having captured a city put a curse on the rebuilding of its walls).

14. For Priene Hdt. 6. 8, Paus 7. 2. 10 (who speaks of them being 'extremely harshly treated' by a Persian, but the context is uncertain). Under the Athenian Empire Priene paid in the years before 431 a single talent in tribute, while Erythrae, which had provided only two-thirds as many ships in the Ionian Revolt (Hdt. 6. 8), paid nine talents. Herodotus mentions (1. 61) only the enslavement of the Prienians and the ravaging of Magnesian territory; perhaps after the death of Mazares the programme was dropped. For Magnesia, Hdt. 3. 122. 1, 125. 2, Thuc. 1. 138. 5.

15. Cf. Huxley 1966: 144, Hammond 1959: 178, Berve 1967: 85 and 91. For an attack on the conventional view, see Graf 1985. The scattered and disparate evidence is assembled by Tozzi 1978: 118–21. Cf. Boffo 1983: 60–1. For the view of Austin 1990, that Darius began a policy of establishing tyrannies, v.i. pp. 71–2.

16. Boffo 1983: 60–1, remarking on the scarcity of evidence relating to the arrangements made by Cyrus, claims that it was only under Darius that the tendency to 'una progressiva generalizzazione del sistema tirannico' asserted itself. The two cases cited for Cyrus are hardly impressive. At Cyme in Aeolis, according to Heraclides Ponticus (*FHG* II 217), Cyrus καταλύσας τὴν πολιτείαν, μοναρχεῖσθαι αὐτοὺς ἐποίησεν. Since Cyme was one of the places that let its tyrant go free and unharmed at the start of the Ionian Revolt in 499 (Hdt. 5. 38) and was minded to shelter the rebel Pactyes after Cyrus had gone away (1. 157–9), it is hard to see how a

Persian-nominated and supported ruler fits in. The other case is positively harmful to the thesis that Cyrus installed tyrants. According to a Hellenistic historian, Agathocles, in a work on the history of Cyzicus, 'Cyrus bestowed on his friend Pytharchus of Cyzicus seven cities', a well-scattered lot, 'but he proceeded to try to make himself tyrant of Cyzicus' (*FGH* 472 F6 = Athenaeus 30a). Such gifts meant no more than that the recipient received the tribute which otherwise would have gone to the King. Cf. Briant 1985. Pytharchus profited from but did not rule the cities. But the important point is that Cyrus did not make him tyrant of Cyzicus and the Cyzicenes did not fear to resist his attempt.

17. Hdt. 4. 97. 2, 138 (where he is not listed), 5. 37. 1, 38. 1.
18. Hdt. 4. 138. 2 lists ten, of whom only four were Ionians.
19. It is possible, but unlikely, that the only Ionian states involved in the Scythian Expedition were those whose tyrants Herodotus named.
20. Hdt. 1. 162. 2 for the building of ramps, costly in time and effort.
21. Phocaea was the most northerly of the Ionian cities, but Harpagus attacked it first possibly because of the city's geographical position near the mouth of the Hermus and the route to Sardis, more probably because of its leading part in the Revolt (v.s. n. 6).
22. Hdt. 1. 168, where 'all' the Teans are said to have departed. Seeing that the city contributed seventeen ships to the Ionian Revolt (Hdt. 6. 8. 1), Strabo's statement about some of the Teans later returning from Abdera (14. 1. 30 644C) must be correct.
23. V.s. n. 5.
24. For Persian taxation see the discussion in Dandamaev–Lukonin 1989: 177–93. Also Boffo 1983: 62–3.
25. Cf. Briant 1985: 53–70 esp. 58–9 and Cook 1983: 176–80, and 258 nn. 27–32.
26. Xen. *Hell.* 3. 1. 6, *Anab.* 2. 1. 3, 7. 8. 8.
27. A name familiar from Thuc. 3. 34. 1, where it is spelt Itamanes. Possibly the two are one and the same man, for on each occasion there are troops involved and twenty-seven years is perhaps not too long for the one man to be in command. Itamenes may have been another 'settler' like Asidates. Cf. Briant 1996: 662.
28. Cf. Briant 1996: 812–15 for the composition of satrapal armed forces.
29. Larisa, invested and besieged in 399 by Thibron, stoutly defended itself (Xen. *Hell.* 3. 1. 7).
30. Similarly the Prienians were said by Herodotus to have been enslaved in the 540s, but they played their part in the battle of Lade (1. 161 and 6. 8. 1).
31. Cf. Hanfmann 1983: 89.
32. Hdt. 1. 29. 1 and *FGH* 70 F181.
33. Hdt. 1. 50, 51, 92. 1, 5. 36. 3.
34. Cf. H. Flower 1991: 47–8.

35. Hanfmann 1983: 91–3.
36. Cf. Ruge, *PW* v a 560.
37. Hanfmann 1983: 28.
38. Cf. Mazzarino 1947: 21 and 107.
39. The quotation comes from the New English Bible, Isaiah 41: 5. 'The "isles" here and throughout these chapters are the coastlands and islands of the eastern Mediterranean' (Smith 1944: 50).
40. When Alyattes concluded hostilities against Miletus, the settlement was of 'friendship and alliance' (Hdt. 1. 22. 4), but there is no mention of alliance in Croesus' settlement with the islands (1. 27. 5).
41. Hdt. 3. 13. 1, and 14. 4, 5. (The numbers involved show that Herodotus thought the Mytilenean ship was a trireme.)
42. Hdt. 1. 143. 1. For Mytilenean interests on the mainland, Hdt. 5. 94. 1, Strabo 13. 1. 38 599C, and cf. Ruge, *PW* xix. 1 583–5. For the Samian *Peraea*, Plut. *Mor.* 296 a, and Welles 1966: no. 7, and cf. S. Hornblower 1991 ad Thuc 3. 19. 2. Chian interest in the mainland is shown by Hdt. 1. 160. 4.
43. Cf. Kuhrt 1988.
44. Hdt. 3. 39. 4, 122; Thuc. 1. 13, 3. 104. 2. His treaty of friendship with the Pharaoh Amasis (Hdt. 3. 39. 2, 43. 2) may have been made to protect Samos' interest in Naucratis (Hdt. 2. 178). For the relations of Polycrates and Persia, Shipley 1987: 94–7.
45. Hdt. 1. 171, 174. 1. The story of the Coan woman at Plataea (Hdt. 9. 76) might suggest that the Persians had taken her over with the island. Nothing sure is to be inferred about the condition of Rhodes in 490 BC from the entry in the Lindian Temple Chronicle (cf. *CAH* iv^2 503).

3

'The lands beyond the sea'

By the late sixth century Persia was firmly established in Europe. In the inscription which Darius caused to be set on the upper edge of the south wall of the terrace at Persepolis there is included in the list of subject peoples, at the end of the western section, 'countries which are across the sea', and in the list given in the first Naqš-i-Rustam inscription after Ionia come 'Scythians who are across the sea, Skudra, petasos-wearing (*takabara*) Ionians'. Both inscriptions thus refer to the European conquests of Darius.[1]

They are to be kept sharply distinct from the Scythians of the eastern part of the Empire whom Darius included in his list of the countries at the time of his accession, 'the countries which came to me'. These were the Scythians, later, in the first Naqš-i-Rustam inscription, distinguished as *Saka haumavarga* (hauma-drinking Scythians, Amyrgian Scythians) and *Saka tigrakauda* (Scythians with pointed caps). Against this latter division of the eastern Scythians Darius proceeded early enough in his reign for the attack culminating in the capture of their chief, Skunkha, to be recorded in the postscript to the Behistun Inscription, that is, in the third year of his reign, 519 BC.[2] The precise date of Darius' advance into Europe is uncertain, but since one of the Greek tyrants with the fleet was Aeaces of Samos (Hdt. 3. 149 and 4. 138. 2), who succeeded the tyrant Syloson some time after the accession of King Cleomenes of Sparta in 519, it is clear that the expedition that led to the capture of Skunkha is not to be confused with the so-called Scythian Expedition of Darius, the date of which is now generally accepted as *c*.513 BC.[3]

Herodotus' account of this latter event must be largely fantasy. He has Darius, having passed by a bridge of boats across the Bosporus, send the fleet to await him on the Danube, and himself proceed to meet them by a route which is unspecified save for the mention of two Thracian rivers; then having crossed the Danube by another bridge of boats and having charged the Greeks who formed and guarded it not to abandon it until a full sixty days had passed, Darius is made to cross the mighty rivers of South Russia without the aid of his fleet and commence the building of eight forts on, as it would appear, the Volga;[4] despite the suasions of the Scythians, the Greeks reject the idea of breaking up after the sixty days had passed, and Darius was able to cross to safety. There is no point in castigating this account, nor is it relevant to the relations of Greece and Persia to seek to determine what precisely happened across the Danube. He certainly did cross the Danube on a bridge of boats. In this Herodotus is confirmed by Ctesias, who has Darius' journey last a mere fifteen days (F13 §21). He certainly cannot have crossed the Dniester, for he would have needed another bridge of boats to do so, and whatever the value of Strabo's source of information (7. 3. 14 305C) he must be right in asserting that Darius operated between that river and the Danube.[5] The solid result of Darius' so-called Scythian Expedition was the incorporation of Thrace within the Empire, Skudra as it is named on the lists, and the operations across the Danube were in all likelihood a demonstration rather than an attempt at conquest, aimed at deterring Scythian incursions into Persian territory, comparable to Caesar's operations across the Rhine in 55 BC.[6] That is all that need be here said about the matter.

Herodotus' story about the Scythians and the bridge over the Danube is more worth consideration. We are in no position to deny that they did call on the Greeks of the fleet to break up the bridge and leave Darius and his army to their fate, though it is notable that in Ctesias it was the bridge over the Bosporus the destruction of which was considered, and by the people of Chalcedon. That is indeed likely to have been the case, for the Chalcedonians and the Byzantines, according to Herodotus, had to be dealt with after the conquest of Thrace had been completed; Darius had recrossed to Asia by ship from Sestos presumably because he had had word of treasonable talk at the Bosporus, and, according to Ctesias, Darius had Chalcedonian houses and temples burned.[7] So it is not inconceivable that the whole story of the Scythians and the Danube bridge was a fanciful adornment of events less remote. However, that is perhaps to take scepticism about Herodotus' account too far. What is very questionable is his account of the debate amongst the Greek commanders, in which the proposal of Miltiades, tyrant of the Chersonese, that the bridge should indeed be broken up, was successfully opposed by the tyrant of Miletus, Histiaeus (Hdt. 4. 137–8). If Miltiades had proposed this, it is very unlikely that word of his doing so would not have reached Darius and punishment not have been promptly administered. Instead Miltiades returned to the Chersonese, was not molested by the Persians, and was only forced to withdraw

when confronted by an incursion of Scyths (Hdt. 6. 40), very probably
in 496. [8] As was long ago suggested, the story of the debate at the bridge
is much more likely to have formed part of the *apologia* of Miltiades at
his trial in Athens in 493; he was then in the difficult position of having
been not only a tyrant, with which he was formally charged, but also a
tyrant sustained by Persian favour, and the story of his conduct at the
Danube would have been most apt, asserting at once his hostility to
Persia and the shameful subservience of Histiaeus, of whom no doubt
much was being said after the Ionian Revolt.[9] Of course, to doubt that
the debate at the bridge actually occurred does not deprive the story
of its real historical interest. Regardless of whether it occurred or was
only said to have occurred, it marvellously illuminates Greek views
of the relationship between the East Greek tyrants and the imperial
power.

There is one feature of the story which is especially provoking.
Darius relied on the bridge of boats for the recrossing of the Danube,
and it is frankly impossible that he would have told the Greek captains
to await his return for no more than sixty days (Hdt. 4. 98). He had
no other means of return. Herodotus could cheerfully think of Darius
over-leaping the rivers of South Russia and contemplating a return
through the Caucasus. Darius was a soldier who knew about times and
distances, and about supply. Whence then this fantastic story of the
sixty days? It is to be noted that it was not a necessary part of the story
of the debate about breaking up the bridge. The sixty days are said to
have passed when the debate took place (4. 136. 3). It could have been
supposed to have taken place at any time after Darius crossed the river.
So there was no need for Miltiades at his trial to say anything about
a period of sixty days.

It may be proposed therefore that Darius did indeed tell the fleet to
wait sixty days not for his return from the other side of the Danube but
for his arrival at the Danube from Thrace. When he began his Thracian campaign, he could have had no idea how much real resistance
he would encounter, nor how long his advance to the Danube would
take. His route is unclear. Herodotus mentions only two points, the
headwaters of the river Tearos (which cannot be certainly identified)
and the crossing of the river Artescus, but only because at each point
Darius did something memorable. If the Artescus is indeed the Arda
which flows into the Maritsa from Rhodope, he must have crossed the
latter near Edirne and his march will have taken him over the Balkan
range by the Kotel Pass, a journey to the Danube of over 700 kilo-

metres.[10] Even if he did make for the coast from Babaeski east of Edirne (which seems less likely, since he had severed contact with his fleet until he reached the Danube), the journey will have been not much shorter. So at an average rate of 15 kilometres a day,[11] he would have needed forty-seven days simply for the march. As it turned out, the only opposition of which we hear was from the Getae living between the Balkan range and the Danube (Hdt. 4. 93). So he could have reached the fleet within sixty days comfortably enough. Nor would such a period have been improbably long for the fleet to reach the mouth of the Danube, sail two days' journey upstream, and construct the bridge. (Once constructed, the bridgehead would have been guarded against attack by what Herodotus—4. 97. 1—terms 'the army from the ships'.) So if there is any truth in the tradition of a sixty-day wait, it is likely to represent the time Darius allowed for the march to the Danube.[12]

Such considerations do at any rate help to put the crossing of the Danube in perspective. Herodotus seriously distorts the whole campaign, by representing it as essentially directed against the Scythians, and he makes Darius' motive the desire to revenge the Scythians for their incursion into Asia in the first half of the seventh century (4. 1. 1). That is interesting about Herodotus but it is not history. The real motive of Darius in extending his power into Europe, one divines, was simply to extend his power. The 'King in the great earth far and wide'[13] was simply claiming his own, with suitable pomp. Armies in future years were to cross and recross the sea dividing Europe and Asia without the aid of a bridge. Mardonius' army returning from Plataea was not stranded in Europe in 479, although the bridges had been broken up, just as he was able to ship his land army across the Hellespont in 492. [14] But Darius, in a supreme gesture of *folie de grandeur*, had to have a bridge, just as his successor had to.[15] He would do nothing common or mean. The advance into Europe would be led by the Great King in person, just as the Emperor Claudius would do when Roman power formally established itself in Britain. Glory (and prudence) dictated that as far as possible the Great King himself would acquire new lands, just as Cambyses had done with the conquest of Egypt and probably Darius himself with the subjection of 'India' (Hdt. 4. 44. 3). Others could mop up pockets of resistance after the initial glory had been gained. As Xerxes in 480 (and Claudius in AD 43), so too Darius in the invasion of Europe. The extension of Persian power to include Thrace was his real aim, the crossing of the Danube a sideshow.

More mundane considerations have been alleged. It was long ago suggested that the gold of Transylvania was the lure, a suggestion too absurd to deserve discussion.[16] But it has also been claimed that[17] the Asiatic Greeks gladly joined in the expedition in the hope that Persian dominion in Thrace would relieve the Greek cities on the Black Sea of the debilitating attacks of Scythians and so foster trade; witness the fact that the tyrants named by Herodotus as taking part in the debate on the Danube (4. 138) are all from 'the great commercial and colonising centres of Ionia' save for Aristagoras of Cyme 'of which we do not have knowledge of any specific colonial or commercial activity that would set it in relations with the Black Sea, but that is probably merely the defect of our information'! It is to be noted, however, that Herodotus was listing the names of such tyrants as he knew to be present. He was not listing all the Greek cities contributing to the fleet; elsewhere (4. 97. 2) he mentions the Mytileneans whose commander was not a tyrant; 'the only Aeolian of note who was present' is named, which does not exclude that there were others. Further Darius, according to Herodotus, issued orders to those whom he wanted to provide ships. He is unlikely to have considered their wishes. Service was not voluntary.[18]

Greeks were pleased to regard the campaign as a fiasco. Both Herodotus (4. 134–5) and Ctesias (F13 §21) treated Darius' return to the south bank of the Danube as virtual flight, with large numbers of the sick and 'those whose destruction mattered least' left to be massacred, which may be doubted; that is hardly the way those who depend on their armies conduct themselves.[19] In a broad sense the operations across the Danube might be thought to have failed of their purpose, if that purpose was to check future nomadic incursions into the European part of the Empire; Miltiades was forced to retire from the Chersonese by such an incursion (Hdt. 6. 40. 1). That, however, was probably during the unsettled times of the Ionian Revolt, and Darius may well have deterred the Scyths from attacking the Persian-controlled territories in more settled years. For the rest, the European campaign was strikingly successful. No opposition was encountered south of the Balkan range. The Getae of the Dobrudja, the 'most courageous of the Thracians', according to Herodotus (4. 93, 96. 2), were foolish enough to resist and were made subject, allegedly joining the Persian army. Meanwhile a bastion of empire, the fort at Doriscus on the lower Hebrus (Hdt. 7. 59. 1), was established. Darius could return to Asia well satisfied with his achievement.[20] How much of the great Thracian plain between Rhodope and the Balkan range was secured in that year must remain uncertain, but the work of 'taming every city and every people' in Thrace (Hdt. 5. 2. 2) could be left to Megabazus who carried out the task without great difficulty.[21] Whether there was ever a formally established satrapy of Skudra or by what stages the formal establishment was made is here indifferent. The important fact is that Darius' European expedition led to Persian control of Thrace from the Strymon to the Black Sea[22] and must be pronounced a great and glorious success, let Greeks concentrate their vision on its trans-danubian aspect and find there what satisfaction they could.

The preparations for Darius' great advance are not described by Herodotus, but must have been considerable and thorough. His later casual mention of the establishment of the bastion at Doriscus in the course of his campaign (7. 59. 1) gives no hint of how it was done; some part of his force must have been dispatched for the purpose and materials and food brought in by sea. No word escapes him about how the main army was supplied. Nor do we get any picture of how the necessary intelligence was gathered, but it is inconceivable that a large army would have been taken into alien country without it. Talk of the use of spies is common enough in accounts of Persian campaigns.[23] Major preliminary reconnaissance must have been conducted, of the sort suggested by the story of Democedes and the fifteen Persian grandees (Hdt. 3, 134 and 13. 8. 4), and intelligence gathered from traitorous or unsuspecting Thracians, as is suggested by the story of the two Paeonians in Sardis, who sought to ingratiate themselves there with Darius.[24] Perhaps it is in this context that we should understand the expedition of Ariaramnes recorded in Ctesias (F13 §20). He was instructed by Darius to cross by sea 'against the Scythians and take prisoner both men and women'. In the event the brother of a Scythian chieftain was treacherously delivered to him. No wonder that Darius had the confidence to take forces across the Danube, and in general a good deal of information must have been gathered about the interior of Thrace. All this is obvious enough, even if it can only be presumed.

More importantly, one must note that since Darius had the bridge across the Bosporus constructed in advance he must have known that the Byzantines could be counted on not to destroy it. The tyrant of Byzantium was one of those named by Herodotus as sharing in the debate at the Danube, and he must have been won over with promises and threats. After the expedition Megabazus began the task of consolidating Persian power by subjecting those of the Hellespontines 'who had not gone over to Persia' (τοὺς μὴ μηδίζοντας), most notably

Perinthus. It is clear that diplomacy had gained Darius the necessary bridgehead.[25]

This is characteristic of Persian imperial expansion. The most striking instance is Samos. After Harpagus had completed the subjection of Ionia, 'the Ionians occupying the islands' according to Herodotus 'in fear gave themselves over to Cyrus'. This will have included the Samians, but their submission must have been no more than the formality of giving earth and water, for they continued to act very independently in the time of Polycrates, not only for a period allying with Amasis of Egypt but also taking 'many cities even on the mainland'. So while they could be required by Cambyses to send a contingent for the invasion of Egypt, Polycrates continued to act in an offensively high-handed and ambitious manner. This led to his downfall, but it was not until some years later that Darius ordered Otanes to take over the island.[26] The demand for earth and water seems to have regularly been the first step, taken when there was no immediate prospect of Persian authority being exercised.[27] Presumably that happened in the case of Byzantium. Before Persian power was established in Europe, the city could be counted on.

The case of Macedon is similar. The final stage was reached during Mardonius' campaign of 492. His army operated within Macedonia, and had some hard fighting against the Brygi. That was consolidation of full Persian control, for now the Persians had 'acquired the Macedonians as subjects to be added to those already subjected'.[28] The early stage is reflected in Herodotus' story of the seven Persian ambassadors sent by Megabazus to demand earth and water. Herodotus would have it believed that the whole party was murdered, a story no one accepts. In any case Herodotus asserts that King Amyntas did give earth and water, and not long after there was a marriage between his daughter and Megabazus' son, Bubares. So Macedon came within the Persian sphere.[29] The two stages are distinct, and it was not until Mardonius had completed his work that Macedon became 'tribute-paying' (δασμοφόρος). But by 500 the kingdom was firmly enough within the Persian sphere, and they appear in the first Naqš-i-Rustam inscription as the 'Ionians wearing the petasos' (*Yauna takabara*).[30]

The shadow of Darius was spreading over the Greek world. Of the major Greek cities brought under Persian control, Perinthus, Aenos, Maroneia, and Abdera all had east Greek metropoleis and the shock of their subjection would have been less severe. In the cases of Byzantium and the cities of Chalcidice, Stagirus, Acanthus, Mende, Torone, and

Potidaea, their changed condition must have been keenly felt within Greece itself, in Corinth particularly, which annually sent out a magistrate to Potidaea (Thuc. 1. 56. 2) and which had an unusually strict idea of the connection of colony and metropolis. Above all, Athens itself was well aware. Not only must the changed condition of the Chersonese have been noted but also, when the tyrant Hippias took refuge with Persia, the Persian threat was fully appreciated (Hdt. 5. 73). Why Sparta had expelled him from Athens is unclear. It may have been because he had shown some sympathy for Persian support in seeking a marriage connection with the tyrant of Lampsacus whom, according to Thucydides (6. 59. 3), he 'realized to be of great influence with King Darius', just as the Spartans had sought to oust Polycrates from Samos because he had medized. But in the aftermath of the Samian rebuff, the Spartans may have had enough for the while of opposing medism and their motive in expelling Hippias may have been rather different. In any case it is clear that Athens herself did not feel revulsion for the idea of Persian support, for Clisthenes sent an embassy to seek alliance. It was only when Artaphernes made clear that alliance meant for the Persians formal submission that the position was fully appreciated. He demanded and received 'earth and water', and the Athenian people showed that they fully appreciated what this meant; when the Athenian ambassadors returned, they were greatly blamed for what they had done; the demand for earth and water was seen as a clear advertisement of Persian ambitions (Hdt. 5. 73). In general, Greece must have been well aware by the late sixth century of the menace from the east and indeed from the north. The seemingly feeble response of the Greeks to the opportunity of the Ionian Revolt is indeed remarkable.

NOTES

1. D Pe 14–18 (Kent 136), D Na 15–30 (Kent 137). Cf. Cameron 1943: 307–13.
2. D B 1 16 and 17 (Kent 119), D Na 25 and 26 (Kent 137), D B v 20–30 (Kent 133). (Herzfeld 1968: 291 identified the Skunkha campaign with the European campaign of Darius on the grounds that the inscription speaks of crossing the sea, not a river, and supposes that the reference must be to the crossing of the Bosporus. But the crossing of whatever sea was involved was after the Scythians had withdrawn and refused battle. Balcer 1972:

99–132 concurred, but retracted in 1984: 474 n. 69. Harmatta 1976: 15–24 argued that the sea crossed was the Aral.)

3. The date furnished by the Tabula Capitolina (*IG* xiv 1297 ii 24) may be right but is unreliable (cf. Balcer 1972: 103). However, *c*.513 BC is widely accepted (cf. Briant 1996: 154 and 931—'la bibliographie est inflationniste, mais toujours contradictoire, sauf sans doute sur la date . , .').

4. For the identification of Herodotus' Oarus (4. 124. 1), see A. Hermann, *PW* xvii. 2 1680. The eight uncompleted forts are a mystery. One might suppose they are a confused memory of what Darius did against the eastern Scyths, if it were not that Herodotus said the ruins were still there up to his own time. It is very doubtful whether Herodotus had been to South Russia (cf. Armayor 1978*a*: 45–62), for if he had been he could hardly have had Darius moving a large army two thousand miles as the crow flies and o'erleaping those mighty South Russian rivers in just over two months. (Hammond in *CAH* iv² 240–3 displays remarkable credulity.) Perhaps the report of the forts derived from Hecataeus, Herodotus attributing their construction to Darius but not explaining why he did not complete the work! Μῦθοι indeed.

5. Cf. Beloch 1927: 5–6.

6. Cf. Momigliano 1933: 350–9. For 'Skudra', Kent 210; speculations about the origin of the name (as in Herzfeld 1968: 348) are pointless. It is curious that quite large bodies of Skudrians are found in the Persepolis Fortification Tablets (cf. Hallock 1969: nos. 852, 1006, 1010, etc. and cf. Balcer 1984: 474 n. 75). See also Cook 1983: 58–9.

7. Hdt. 4. 98, 128, 136. 4–139; Ctesias F13 §§21 and 25; Hdt. 5. 26, 4. 143. 1. (Strabo 13. 1. 22 591C speaks of Darius having cities on the Propontis burnt.)

8. That is, rejecting the solution of Powell 1935: 162, followed by Wade Gery 1958: 162 and Berve 1967: 2. 567, and preferring Stein's insertion of πρό in Hdt. 6. 40. 1 to Powell's excision of πρότερον and τῶν κατεχόντων πρηγμάτων. Stein preferred the inferior reading καταλαβόντων, but that is not necessary. By τῶν κατεχόντων πρηγμάτων Herodotus meant the situation in which Miltiades found himself with the approach of the Phoenician fleet. The repetition of πρότερον τῶν τότε μιν κατεχόντων is characteristic of Herodotus' method of marking off digressions. Herodotus' motivation for the Scythian raid is no more to be regarded than his similar motivation of Darius' Scythian Expedition (4. 1. 1), historically speaking an absurdity; Ctesias (F13 §21) with talk of 'bridges' would have Darius chased out of Europe by the Scyths, but since they lacked the means of immediately crossing the Danube he cannot be correct.

The matter is of some importance here since it affects judgement of the effectiveness of Darius' whole European campaign. On the one hand, there is the picture of a grandiose military venture ending in a shambles.

On the other, which I hold to be the truth, we have a picture of an orderly extension of empire with an expedition to impress the trans-Danubians (cf. Caesar, *BG* 4. 16) who, future centuries would show, would not be cowed.

9. Hdt. 6. 104. 2 for the charge. Cf. Wade-Gery 1958: 165 for the thesis that the story of the bridge over the Danube derived from Miltiades' trial. It goes back to Thirlwall 1846: ii. 486–8.

10. This is the route proposed by Hammond 1980: 53–5, which depends on the identification of Herodotus' Artescus (4. 92) with the river Arda, which joins the Maritsa just above Edirne.

The central consideration concerning Darius' route is that, to judge by Herodotus' account, he completely lost contact with the fleet until he arrived at the Danube, which renders unlikely the common opinion that he crossed the Istranca range and followed the coast up to Apollonia (modern Sozopol), for if he had done so he would undoubtedly have kept contact with his fleet and so been supplied, in the customary Persian fashion. Unger 1915: 3–17 was perhaps right in placing the springs of the Tearos near Pinarhisar, though the inscription with letters 'like nails' reported to Col. Jochmus (*Journal of the Royal Geographical Society*, 24 (1854), 43–4) which led Unger to that area may well not be the inscription set up by Darius; the Persians were in Thrace long enough to have left epigraphic remains of their presence (cf. the inscription found at Gherla in Transylvania, for which see Harmatta 1953), and one must note that the inscription reported by Herodotus was not said to be in Ἀσσύρια γράμματα nor to be bilingual as it must have been if Herodotus' report is essentially correct. (For a review of his handling of non-Greek inscriptions, cf. West 1985, which hardly gives one confidence.) Herodotus' remark that the sources of the Tearos were equidistant from Heraeum Polis (near Perinthus) and Apollonia (Sozopol), being each a two-day journey, is disquieting; on any method of calculation the latter must have been much further away, and both journeys would surely have taken more than two days. But even if the Tearos was where Unger placed it, that by no means proves that Darius was moving towards the Black Sea coast at that moment. He may have gone by the route of the south-western side of the Istranca range to impress the Thracians there and cow them into submission, and then have passed from Kirklareli into the valley of the Maritsa.

The real problem is the location of Herodotus' Artescus (4. 92). Those who, like Danov 1976, are persuaded that Darius followed along the Black Sea coast to the Danube, easily enough fix on a river; Danov pronounced that the 'Buük Dere if not completely secure is yet probable'. V. Velkov is reported by Danov 1976: 265 n. 118 to have argued in an article 'über den antiken Namen des Flusses Arda' (in Bulgarian) that the Artescus is to be identified with the Arda. Danov rejected this principally on the ground that Herodotus said that his Artescus 'flows through the Odrysians' and in the late 6th cent. the Odrysians could not be said to have lived in the area of the lower Arda. They may, however, have done so by the time Herodotus was writing. If Hammond is right to follow Velkov, one might expect Herodotus to have remarked the crossing of the Maritsa, which would have required boats, but Herodotus' whole account is sketchy in the extreme. His comment about the Thracians who occupy Salmydessus and live above Apollonia and Mesambria (4. 93) surrendering without a battle is no sure indication of route; Darius himself can have gone nowhere near Salmydessus (for the location of which, cf. *PW* IA 2 1991). Further, if Darius was concerned to subdue the whole of Thrace from the middle Maritsa to the east, his army may well have been divided.

So Darius' route must remain uncertain. With the identification of the Artescus with the Arda goes the wider view of the whole expedition. Darius' intention was to incorporate Thrace in the Empire. The core of it was the valley of the Maritsa, and Doriscus, the 'royal fort' built in connection with the campaign (Hdt. 7. 59) was to serve as *arx aeternae dominationis*, to adapt Tacitus' phrase describing the temple of the Divine Claudius at Colchester (*Ann.* 14. 31).

11. Herodotus calculated a day's journey at 200 stades, i.e. about 40 kilometres (4. 101. 3). That is inconceivable for a large army. Cf. Engels 1978: 153–6, who states that 'the maximum recorded rate for the *entire* army (sc. of Alexander) is 19. 5 miles per day'. As his table shows it was often much less. When one considers that Darius was moving through potentially hostile country, 15 kilometres a day does not seem too little.

12. To suspect Herodotus of such confusion is not all that shocking when one considers the skimpiness of the account of Darius' march to the Danube and the fantasy of what he did beyond the river.

13. The phrase of D Na §2 (Kent 138).

14. Hdt. 9. 89. 4, 114. 1 for the breaking up of the bridge which meant that the remnants of Mardonius' army in 479 BC had to cross on merchant ships from Byzantium. At 8. 117. 1 he remarked that when the troops that had escorted Xerxes on his return journey in 480 reached the Hellespont they crossed to Abydos on 'the ships', the bridges having been broken up by bad weather. This destruction was presumably after Themistocles had counselled the Greeks to break up the bridges (8. 108. 2) but it is curious that in 479 after the battle of Mycale Herodotus says the Greeks who went north to the Hellespont expected to find the bridges still in place (9. 114. 1). In 492 Mardonius' army crossed by means of 'the ships' (6. 43. 4).

15. It is perhaps not utterly contemptible to question whether the bridging of the sea between Asia and Europe did not have religious significance. Xerxes was accompanied by Magi (Hdt. 7. 43. 2, 113. 2; Pliny, *NH* 30. 8). Doubtless Darius also. (For the role of the Magi cf. Boyce 1982 *passim*.)

The story of Tiridates' journey to Rome in AD 66 is suggestive. He at first professed himself unable to travel to Rome, detained *sacerdotii religione* (Tac. *Ann.* 15. 24). According to Pliny, *NH* 30. 16 and 17, he was himself a *Magus*, and 'had refused to go by sea, since they do not think it right to spit into the sea or violate its nature with other human necessities'. So he went by land. Of course he must have crossed the Hellespont by ship, and he returned by sea from Brundisium to Dyrrhachium (Cassius Dio 66. 7. 1). But perhaps the bitter sea could be tamed and enslaved with lashes and fetters (Hdt. 7. 35). (Cf. Boyce 1982: 166, 'However unworthy this act, it was performed to the letter of evolved Zoroastrian doctrine, which is that salt water is sweet water tainted by the assault of the Hostile Spirit.') Once tamed it could be crossed with honour (Hdt. 7. 35, 54). Perhaps that is why Darius crossed on a bridge but returned by boat, though there is no mention of his having the sea flogged for the misbehaviour of a storm!

Tiridates' religious scruple, which required that he go the long way by land rather than cross from Dyrrhachium by sea, did not stop him returning by sea (a point not discussed in Cumont 1933). Perhaps his scruple had been more diplomatic than real. As to Darius and Xerxes, the bridges may just have been *folie de grandeur*. They could perhaps perfectly well have got their armies to Europe as Alexander the Great would get his across to Asia and as they got theirs back again.

16. Cf. Bury 1897, who would have Darius' expedition taken into Transylvania for the sake of Dacian gold, a failure marked by the eight uncompleted forts! Balcer 1984: 184 claimed that it was 'to obtain tribute of the famed Scythian gold (Hdt. 4. 104)', a lot to build on the statement that the Agathyrsi were 'gold-wearing' ($\chi\rho\upsilon\sigma\sigma\phi\acute{o}\rho\sigma\iota$).

17. Momigliano 1933: 355–8.

18. 5. 11. 2, 4. 138. 2, 4. 83. 1.

19. For modern estimates, see Castritius 1972: 1 n. 3. Cook 1983: 63 thought the enterprise 'an imprudent one that showed up Persian limitations'. Cf. *CAH* IV² 235–46.

20. Two matters complicate judgement. First, the account of Herodotus of Darius' operations south of the Danube is most inadequate. If the river Artescus (4. 92) is indeed the Arda (v.s. n. 10), he must have crossed the Maritsa, operations which could have been assisted by the foundation of Doriscus (7. 59. 1), which was part of the campaign. But whatever route Darius followed to the Danube, Herodotus leaves us guessing. Secondly, the absence of Persian material remains hardly encourages one to believe that Darius established Persian power in the central Thracian plain. However, Persian power was not long exercised in Thrace if, as seems likely (cf. Hdt. 5. 98. 4), Persian hold had to be relaxed during the Ionian Revolt, and there are no material remains at Doriscus where the Persians certainly were for possibly as long as sixty years. We know there was 'a

Persian city, Boryza' on the Black Sea coast (*FGH* 1 F166) but that area has produced no material remains. Finally, it must be kept in mind that Darius and his army fleeing for the safety of Asia may be a purely Greek picture. If Darius intended to open the campaign but to leave its completion to Megabazus and a substantial army, a very different picture presents itself.

21. When at 5. 10 Herodotus speaks of Megabazus subjecting τὰ παρα- θαλάσσια, he does not mean to exclude the territory of western inland Thrace. In 5. 9 and 10 he is contrasting the sphere of Megabazus' operations with the uninhabited places across the Danube, *pace* Castritius 1972: 2. As Hammond 1980: 56 points out, Megabazus approached the Paeonians by the inland route (Hdt. 5. 15. 2).

22. Opinion has been much divided on whether there was a satrap and a satrapy of Thrace as well as hyparchs of the cities which it was the special concern of Darius to keep firmly under control (Hdt. 7. 105 and 106. 1 'in Thrace and everywhere in the Hellespont'). The chief proponent of there being a satrap is Hammond 1980. Borza 1990: 293 summarizes the case against. Cf. Lenk, *PW* VI A 1 420 and Danov 1976: 268–9, who pointed to the absence of Thrace from Herodotus' Satrapy List (3. 89–94) and from his list of combatants in 480 (7. 62–83). But if Herzfeld 1968: 288 and 295–6 is right in regarding the former as derived from Hecataeus, it may have been drawn up by Hecataeus before Darius expanded into Europe, and while the source of the list of combatants is quite uncertain, it too may derive from a document deriving from a time when Skudra was not part of the Empire. It is true no satrap can be named nor do we know of a satrapal capital, though it may have been Doriscus, described at 7. 59. 1 as τεῖχος βασιλήιον (cf. 3. 74. 2) from which the hyparch could never be dislodged (7. 106. 2). Despite our lack of evidence a satrapal capital is not inconceivable and may be the source of the inscription found at Gherla in Transylvania, a site far beyond the range of Darius' trans-Danubian operations (it was pronounced by Harmatta 1953 to be possibly 'a Persian inscription erected in the North Balkans and carried off to Transylvania after the collapse of Persian rule in Thrace'; it runs 'Darius, the Great King, the King of Kings, the King of countries, son of Hystaspes, the Achaemenian (is the one) who had this palace built.'). The lack of evidence from the central Thracian plain proves nothing. The Royal Road through Thrace (Livy 39. 27. 10 and 42. 51. 5) led through Paroreia on the upper Strymon and had nothing to do with the military road which Xerxes used when he cut inland after crossing the Strymon (Hdt. 7. 115); it may have been made long before 480. Some sort of road system is suggested by Herodotus' remark (5. 21. 1) that the Persian embassy to King Amyntas had 'carriages' (ὀχήματα). A tribute collection system is implied by Herodotus' statement (3. 96. 1) that 'tribute came in both from islands and those living in Europe

as far as Thessaly', τῶν ἐν τῇ Εὐρώπῃ μέχρι Θεσσαλίης οἰκημένων, a curious phrase covering presumably more than just the cities (cf. 5. 2. 2). The hyparchs of Hdt. 7. 106. 1 may have collected the tribute, but why should there not have been the regular satrapal organization? Megabazus' purpose had been 'to subjugate to the King every city and every tribe of those living in this area', the order from Darius having been 'to conquer Thrace' (5. 2. 2). Was this likely to have been realized by no more than a set of hyparchs here and there? Castritius 1972: 10–11 claimed that the subjection effected by Megabazus was in the highest degree 'nominell', that the real subjection followed on Mardonius' campaign of 492 BC. That, however, is by no means the impression created by Herodotus' remark (6. 44. 1) when he recorded the subjection of the Macedonians that 'all the peoples (ἔθνεα) as far as the Macedonians had been made subject to them previously'.

On the whole therefore I incline to accept Hammond's view.

23. Cf. Hdt. 3. 19. 1 and 21. 2, 23 and 25. 1; 7. 208. 1, Xen. *Cyrop.* 6. 1. 31, 2. 2 and 9. Hdt. 4. 44 makes Scylax's voyage of discovery precede the conquest of India, an ordering of events frequently rejected (cf. Frye 1984: 104 and Cook 1983: 62).

24. Hdt. 5. 12–14, which would make Darius' decision to transplant the Paeonians the consequence of this encounter in Sardis after returning from Europe. That may be doubted, but the story is suggestive of how intelligence was, in part, gathered.

25. 4. 138. 1, 144. 2; 5. 1. 1, 2. 1. Herodotus would attribute the subjection of the Perinthians to Persian numerical superiority, but it is more probable that their reluctance to submit reflects their confidence in the city's natural defensibility, which made siege difficult for Philip of Macedon in 340. Persian siegecraft seems to have been much in advance of Greek. They captured Sardis in 14 days, though perhaps the Lydians were much to blame (Hdt. 1. 81, 84), also Olynthus though they apparently failed at Potidaea (8. 126–9). Although some of their sieges took a long time (Babylon 19 months, 3. 152; and Barca 9, 4. 200; Memphis 'in time' 3. 13. 3; Naxos 4 months to no avail, 5. 34. 2), they reduced Ionia in 546 easily enough, the Phocaeans retiring before the inevitable (1. 164) and the Chians not daring to run the risk of a siege (1. 160). We hear of the use of mines at Barca (4. 200), and also at Miletus in 494, where they also used 'all kinds of siege engines' (6. 18), just as at Babylon they tried 'every cunning device and every siege engine' (3. 152). Neither the Samian nor the Athenian acropolis could hold out (3. 147. 1, 8. 52–3). The Thasians had strengthened their defences (and in the 460s the city took the Athenians over two years to reduce—Thuc. 1. 101. 3), but they dared not test them against Mardonius in 492 (6. 46–8).

26. Hdt. 1. 169. 2; 3. 39. 2 and 44. 1, 121. Paus. 7. 5. 4 attributed the burning of

the Samian Heraeum to the Persians and so Balcer 1984: 104 postulated Persian intervention in 546. The burning of the first Heraeum probably preceded the rise of Polycrates (cf. Mitchell 1975: 83–4), but Persian naval activity in 546 is very improbable and the notice of Pausanias should be rejected.

27. Cf. Kuhrt 1988.

28. Hdt. 6. 44. 1 (by τὰ ἐντὸς Μακεδόνων ἔθνεα, he means the peoples to the east of Macedonia), 45. 1. Hammond and Griffith 1979: 61 placed the Brygi 'between lake Doiran and the Strumitsa valley on the slopes of Mt. Orbelus' (cf. his map 2, p. 66) i.e. on the modern Greek border with Yugoslavia and Bulgaria, a good index of the Persian penetration.

29. Hdt. 5. 18–21, and for Bubares' patronymic 7. 22. 1. In *Philip of Macedon* (1978: 24) I briefly suggested that the truth behind Herodotus' story of the murder of the Persian envoys may be that the political subjection of Macedon was sealed by multiple marriage akin to the Susa marriages of 324. Certainly if envoys had been murdered there would have been reprisals and Herodotus' account of how the alleged murder was hushed up is absurd. The fullest account of the Susa marriages was furnished by the Court Chamberlain, Chares of Mytilene (*FGH* 125 F4), who was well placed to know what happened; he recounted the great feast with couches adorned with wedding raiment. All this was done, according to Arrian (*Anab.* 7. 4. 7), 'in the Persian mode'. It seems likely enough that a similar set of marriages was celebrated in Macedon in the late 6th cent. to mark the subordination of Macedon to Persia. Cf. Hdt. 5. 18. 2, where the Persians are made to say 'Since you give earth and water to King Darius, follow our custom.'

30. Hdt. 7. 108. 1, D Na 29 (Kent 137), D Sm 10 (Kent 145). For the identification of the *Yauna takabara*, Herzfeld 1968: 349. The term is found also in A? P (Kent 156), the inscription on the south tomb at Persepolis, normally assigned to Artaxerxes II (404–359); which is curious, for the same inscription also contains Skudra, India, and Egypt.

4

The Ionian Revolt

'I am Darius the Great King, King of Kings, King of countries containing all kinds of men, King in this great earth far and wide . . .' Thus Darius' boast of power in the inscription at the tombs of Naqš-i-Rustam.[1] Certainly by 500 BC Persian power was well advanced in the West. Early in his reign Darius had incorporated Samos in his empire, and by the date of the Scythian Expedition Chios and Lesbos were on a par with the Greek cities of the Asiatic mainland.[2] As the abiding consequence of that expedition, Persian power was established in Thrace, and the islands of Lemnos and Imbros had been occupied (Hdt. 4. 97, 138, 5. 26). Reconnaisance for further expansion had been made on at least one occasion, as the story of the fifteen grandees guided on a grand tour of Greece suggests (Hdt. 3. 134. 6).[3] The next alluring plum was Naxos, 'outstanding amongst the islands for its prosperity', 'possessed of great wealth and many slaves', a suitable stepping-stone to Euboea (Hdt. 5. 28, 31. 1 and 3). In 499 the Persians attacked, but failed to take the city despite a siege of four months. When the fleet returned to Asia, the Ionians, that is those states that together formed the Panionium,[4] revolted and shortly the King was confronted with revolt all along the Aegean seaboard and in Cyprus also. It was a serious set-back for Darius' plans, delaying expansion for seven years.

Unfortunately, for knowledge of the course and for understanding of the Ionian Revolt, we have to rely almost entirely on Herodotus of whose account the most varied interpretations have been made ranging from the most radical scepticism to despairing credulity. No one can hope to win general approval. The view adopted in this book amounts to substantial rejection of Herodotus, and I can do no more than state what I *believe* to have been the truth.[5]

There are, however, three major criticisms to be made of Herodotus' account which have been widely accepted. The first is that it is indeed far too personal. Even if Herodotus is right in attributing to Aristagoras final responsibility for setting Ionia in revolt, some account was due of how Aristagoras persuaded a large number of his fellow Greeks to act out his plans, be they ever so self-serving. Perhaps it is right to see in 'the members of the faction' (στασιῶται) no more than his own supporters in Miletus and they may have been ready blindly to follow his lead.[6] But there must have been a great deal more to it all than this. When Aristagoras sent Iatragoras to arrest by trick the Greek captains of the fleet harboured at Myus (near the mouth of the Maeander, not far north of Miletus), he could not have done it single-handed nor without justifying his action to the crews. How they were persuaded to join in an affair that could have such serious consequences, Herodotus does not explain. Again, not all the tyrants deposed were with the fleet (Hdt. 5. 37. 2). Their deposition must have required some co-ordination and synchronization, for if any were forewarned they might have tried to keep control of their cities until Persian help arrived rather than 'flee to the Medes' (Hdt. 6. 9. 2). There must, in short, have been a conspiracy and Herodotus gives no account of its genesis or what moved the conspirators other than Aristagoras. Similarly with the military narrative. The events of the period of Aristagoras are reasonably clear as are those of the period of Histiaeus, but Herodotus does not make clear exactly when the latter came to Ionia and he provides no picture of any sort of the development of the Persian grand offensive which culminated in the sack of Miletus in 494.[7] It is particularly troubling that he gives no account of the Persian navy, of its strength in 499 or of the role of Greek naval contingents. Much is left to speculation.[8] His account is indeed far too personal. Of course, historiographically speaking, it is illuminating that the Father of History should so write in the third quarter of the fifth century but for historical understanding he leaves us sadly in the dark.

The second criticism to be made of Herodotus' account is that he dismissed the Revolt as from the outset a hopeless endeavour and so was the more inclined to attribute the responsibility to the self-seeking of Aristagoras and Histiaeus. When he recounted that Aristagoras, having failed at Sparta, persuaded the Athenians to send help, he commented that it would seem that it was easier to mislead thirty thousand Athenians than the Spartan king (5. 97. 2). Not for a moment does he speculate on what might have happened if mainland Greece had supported the rebels; from the outset the Revolt brought nothing but evils for the Ionians, and when the Ionian tyrants appealed from the Persian camp shortly before the decisive naval battle of Lade, the Ionians were pronounced blind to their interests, refusing to betray the cause; but the cause was in Herodotus' eyes hopeless.[9] Aristagoras had begun it, he asserted, simply to get himself out of a difficult situation, and Histiaeus had counselled revolt simply in the hope of getting back to Miletus (5. 35).

Herodotus' attitude is a matter of some complexity. It is commonly thought that the failure of the Revolt was due to lack of unity and to treachery.[10] Especial emphasis is placed on the treacherous withdrawal of the Samians (Hdt. 6. 13–15), who had played the leading part in what Herodotus presents as the defeat of the Phoenician naval force off Cyprus in 498 (5. 112. 1); if they had stayed at Lade and fought with as much valour as the Chians, the Persian navy could have been defeated and the liberation of Ionia assured. If this view were correct, Herodotus' dismissal of the chances of the Revolt succeeding would have to be regarded as a monstrous defamation. But it is not necessarily, *tout simple*, correct.

Paradoxical as it seems, the truth is that the defence of the liberty of the Asiatic Greeks was essentially naval. No doubt if Persia had sent and maintained a large army in the western satrapies, the Greek cities could have been reduced one by one and treated with the severity accorded to Miletus in 494 (Hdt. 6. 18), but the demands of empire were such that large Royal forces might be needed elsewhere and in practice the King had to leave the satraps to manage their own defence with their own satrapal forces. As long as the Greeks maintained control of the sea, even the reduction of cities could be rendered difficult. In the sixth century the Milesians had successfully resisted the Lydians, being able by their control of the sea to maintain their food supplies (Hdt. 1. 17. 3), and in the first three decades after 479 Athens secured the freedom of the Greek cities by her naval power. But in the early years of the fifth century naval superiority belonged to the Phoenicians. Much has been made of the defeat of the Phoenician fleet off Cyprus in 498, but it is remarkable that Herodotus makes little of it and it seems possible that most of the defeated naval force were troop-carriers which had transported the large Persian army to the island, a very minor triumph.[11] The real test came with the battle of Lade, where the true state of affairs is reflected in the efforts of Dionysius of Phocaea to prepare the Greeks for the coming struggle, whereby he sought to train the Greeks for a sort of naval warfare to which they were quite unused. Perhaps Dionysius, commander of only three ships, was chosen to train the Greek fleet because he had had the chance to observe Phoenician naval tactics during the Persian invasion of Egypt.[12] He certainly knew that their standard manoeuvre was to sail in column through the

opposing line of ships, turn quickly and by superior oarsmanship over-
take the enemy ships, tie up side by side and with a substantial force of
marines board and capture the enemy vessel. This was the so-called
diekplous, or, rather, the early version of *diekplous* practised by the Phoenicians at the time of the Persian invasion of Greece which involved
boarding (the later version involving ramming).[13] For this the rowers
had to be skilled in quickly turning the ship once it had sailed through
the enemy's line of battle and in quickly getting alongside an enemy
ship. But in this period the Phoenicians, although having the heavier
ships, were able to row their ships faster than the Greeks rowed their
triremes, as the events of 480 were to make clear (Hdt. 8. 10. 1; cf. 7.
179–82). Such skill, as Pericles was later to remark (Thuc. 1. 142. 6), was
not quickly acquired, and it is unlikely that in the brief period of training Dionysius succeeded in making the Eastern Greeks the equals of
the Phoenicians. He tried, but the Ionians, 'in as much as they had not
experienced such hard work and were exhausted by the constant effort
and the heat', jibbed and refused to continue (Hdt. 6. 12. 2). Dionysius
had intended to use the marines as hoplites[14] and in hopes of winning
a form of sea-battle which Thucydides was later to term 'more like a
land than a sea battle' he had put forty picked soldiers on each ship as
marines, foreshadowing Cimon at the battle of the Eurymedon but
for the rest unheard of in Greek naval warfare. When it came to the
actual battle of Lade, Dionysius' preparations bore some fruit, if we
may trust Herodotus' statement (6. 15. 2) that the Chians 'took many of
the enemy ships' though they 'lost the majority of their own', though
there is no knowing whether in their roughly central position in the line
of battle they encountered the Phoenician division of the Persian naval
force.[15] By contrast, the Samians who Herodotus says distinguished
themselves against the Phoenicians off Cyprus in 498, at Lade (6. 13.
1) abandoned the struggle. Part of their apologia was that 'the power
of the King seemed to them insuperable' (6. 13. 1). The Lesbians and
others followed suit (6. 14. 3). It may be that treachery was the real
cause, and that if the whole right flank of the Greek line had seen the
battle through, the result would have been different. It may also be
that the cause was recognized as hopeless, that the Phoenician navy
at that date was invincible. The might-have-beens of history remain
mere speculations. But the very severity of Dionysius' training suggests
that in his view the Greeks had a lot of skill to acquire before they could
face the Phoenicians. If treachery had been the real cause of the deser-
tions, they might have been expected before, not during, the battle.

As it was the Greeks accused each other of cowardice and Herodotus could not say 'which of the Ionians had shown themselves cowardly or brave in this sea-battle' (6. 14. 1), and this is consistent with the view that the Greeks were simply outclassed.

So Herodotus' dismissal of the Revolt as hopeless from the outset is not to be treated as plainly bad history. However, he does not seem to have appreciated the true position with regard to the development of naval warfare in the fifth century, as his scrappy account of the battle of Salamis shows. That battle involved the tactic of the future, viz. ramming, but its employment there was due to the exceptional circumstances of fighting in confined waters where the Phoenicians could not exploit their superior seamanship and it did not become general until the Peloponnesian War. Herodotus passed over the matter in silence. For him the Persian defeat in 480 BC was due to cowardice. No other explanation is advanced.[16]

Given, then, that for Herodotus it was courage (and divine favour) that won the day at Salamis, and given that for thirty years thereafter the Persians were kept from recovering the Greek cities of Asia by the Athenian fleet, he might have been expected to affirm that if only the Greeks had stood together and fought with courage and resolution in the 490s, the Ionian Revolt could have succeeded. Why then did he dismiss it as hopeless from the outset?

Various explanations have been proffered. It is notable that his native city, Dorian Halicarnassus, had no part in the Revolt. Herodotus' attitude may well have been conditioned by his father and his fellow citizens who had a strong interest in justifying their abstention. Again, he may well have been impressed by the judgement of Hecataeus (5. 36) who counselled Aristagoras against revolt, who regarded operations on land as hopeless, and who, if we may trust Diodorus (10. 25), was sufficiently acceptable to Artaphernes to be sent, on the conclusion of the Revolt, to plead for clemency for the Ionians. Not, of course, that Herodotus is likely to have known Hecataeus personally,[17] nor that Hecataeus' views on the Revolt were available in written form,[18] but Herodotus may well have been impressed by what he heard about his great literary forebear. Again, he must have heard a lot about the Revolt from various Ionian sources. He records that they blamed each other for what happened at Lade (6. 14. 1) and no doubt these informants were not silent about the Revolt as a whole. In particular, it would seem that his contacts with Samians were a fruitful source.[19] To justify their conduct in the battle, Samians could well have treated the Revolt as a hopeless venture and have blackened the character of Aristagoras. All in all, Herodotus' attitude may have been variously conditioned.

There is one element, however, that must not be neglected, the influence of Athenian isolationists. There was probably considerable division at Athens about support for the Revolt. After joining in the raid on Sardis and suffering in the defeat at Ephesus, the Athenians refused many appeals for further help (Hdt. 5. 103), and those responsible for this change of policy had strong reason to denounce the Revolt as hopeless and Aristagoras as a self-seeking blackguard. Now when Herodotus recorded the decision to send twenty ships, he made a very curious comment. 'These ships proved a cause (or 'a beginning') of evils for Greeks and barbarians' (5. 97. 3). For the Ionians 'evils' had begun when Cyrus incorporated them in the Persian Empire, and though there could be said to have been 'a cessation of evils' after the operations in the Hellespontine region at the end of the Scythian Expedition, 'evils' for the Ionians began a second time with the Naxian appeal to Miletus (5. 28). So in making his comment Herodotus was thinking of the Greeks of mainland Greece and of the disasters sustained at the hands of 'the barbarians' in the invasions of Greece, and was giving a mainland Greek view of the cause of the Persian invasion of Greece. There were, however, two views which find expression in Herodotus. One, which it has already been argued on the basis of the Old Persian inscriptions is the true explanation of Persian westward expansion,[20] was that in this great contest of East and West, the beginning of which was to be found centuries before, the Persians were moved by desire for universal conquest (cf. 1. 1–5). Thus the reconnaissance of 'the coastal areas of Greece' led by Democedes early in the reign of Darius was for the purpose of 'turning against' the Greeks, for Darius had his dreams of world conquest and the Greeks of Europe, Mardonius was made to counsel him, must be added to the list of conquered peoples and not be left to scorn the Persians.[21] But here the other view obtrudes. The Greeks have 'begun wrongdoing' and must suffer vengeance. Indeed the King must each day be reminded at dinner 'to remember the Athenians' (5. 105). When the Spartans appealed to Athens in 480/479 not to treat with the Persians, they are represented as saying to the Athenians (8. 142. 2) 'You stirred up this war when we would have none of it'—the reference is to the Spartan refusal of aid to the Ionians in 499—'and originally the contest was for your land'—that is, the Marathon campaign. Both views appear in

Herodotus' introduction to that campaign (6. 94. 1). The servant constantly reminded Darius 'to remember the Athenians' and 'at the same time Darius wished, seizing on this pretext, to subject those in Greece who refused to give him earth and water', the tokens of submission demanded generally of the Greeks by Darius before 490. [22] But how did Herodotus come to the idea that the Persians invaded Greece to revenge the burning of Sardis? It cannot be proved but it seems more likely that he was influenced by mainland Greeks who had opposed help for Aristagoras, pre-eminently the Athenian isolationists whose concern it would have been to justify their failure, principally perhaps the Alcmaeonids whose policy earned them the charge of medism and who seem to have been an important source of information for Herodotus.[23] Those who opposed help for the Revolt were only too likely to belittle its chances of success and to denigrate Aristagoras. It is here proposed that their apologia infected Herodotus' view and account of the Ionian Revolt. One hesitates therefore to accept the judgement of Herodotus, grounded as it is, at least in part, on such partial evidence. His bias is plain and calls for compensation.

The third criticism that must be made of Herodotus' account of the Revolt is that he displays remarkable misunderstanding of the nature and operation of the Persian Empire. This matter has already been discussed in a general way.[24] Here the particular case of the Naxian expedition (5. 30–5) must be called in question in two respects. First, there is the status of Aristagoras. As tyrant of Miletus, he was a Persian vassal and in no position to undertake an expedition on his own initiative. The Naxian exiles may have been under the illusion that Aristagoras could do so and their appeal to him is credible enough. But that Aristagoras should for a moment have thought that if the exiles were successfully restored he would have rule over Naxos is wholly incredible; the only possible result would be that the Persian King would include the island in his empire as he had already included the Aegean islands. But there is worse to follow. When the Persian commander, Megabates, cousin of Artaphernes and of the King himself, disciplined the captain of a ship from Myndus in Caria, Aristagoras is made to protest as if Megabates had exceeded his authority (5. 32). Now it is hardly likely that the Myndian was the subordinate of the Milesian, though it is not inconceivable that Aristagoras had some position of command over more than his own Milesian ships, but it is quite inconceivable that he should have said to the Persian grandee in command of the whole expedition (5. 33. 4) 'What has this got to do with you?

Didn't Artaphernes commission you to obey me and sail wherever I order? Why don't you mind your own business?' Herodotus has somehow got things upside down in his mind and he has done so because he so little understands how the Persian Empire works. The second point concerns the response of Megabates. Far from dealing with this insubordination in the way that the commander of any military force, let alone a Persian force, would, he is made by Herodotus to get his own back on Aristagoras by forewarning the Naxians, thus making it possible for them successfully to frustrate the King's purposes. This is frankly incredible. If Megabates had done what Herodotus has him do, he would have rendered himself liable for the most severe punishment for damaging the King's interests. The Naxians were no doubt forewarned, though probably long before the Persians landed on the island, for a city is not likely to have supplied itself for a four-month siege in a mere day or two,[25] but it cannot have been Megabates who did the forewarning. Herodotus' whole account exemplifies his serious misunderstanding of how the Persian Empire worked.

These three criticisms of Herodotus principally affect judgement of Aristagoras and the outbreak of the Revolt, but some discussion of the value of his account of Histiaeus cannot be avoided. What Herodotus affects to know of what happened on the Persian side is difficult to evaluate. He may well have had reliable information about what happened to Histiaeus after his capture. The news of his execution at Sardis could well have reached Greek cities on the coast, and it is perfectly conceivable that Herodotus' account of Darius' honorific treatment of the severed head was based on reports brought to Greece by such a person as Zopyrus, the high-born Persian who deserted to Athens in the 440s.[26] But it is most unlikely that the exchange between Darius and Histiaeus, which resulted in his being sent down to Sardis (5. 106–7), was recounted by any such Persian source. Indeed the chronological vagueness of Herodotus' account of Histiaeus' movements suggests that he did not know anything very reliable about him before he reached the coast. The interview with Darius is pictured as taking place promptly after the burning of Sardis in 498, but Histiaeus would seem in Herodotus' account (6. 1. 1) not to have arrived at the court of Artaphernes until after the death of Aristagoras, which was in 497/496 (Thuc. 4. 102), nor is it clear how long Herodotus supposed that Histiaeus was in Sardis before he fled to Chios, though he certainly envisaged a period of time long enough for treasonable discussions with 'Persians' there (6. 4). One suspects therefore that what Herodotus tells us of Histiaeus before he arrived in Chios is principally based on what he said to the Chians by way of self-defence (6. 2. 2), hardly reliable in the case of so tricky a customer. But there is an even more disquieting possibility. When Miltiades, who had been a Persian-supported tyrant, returned to Athens in 493, he was put on trial for 'tyranny in the Chersonese' (6. 104). From his defence at that trial much of Herodotus' account of the family may well ultimately derive; in particular, the story of the Bridge over the Danube may have been produced there to counter accusations of his having been hand in glove with the Persians (v.s. p. 48), and the whitening of Miltiades required the blackening of Histiaeus, whose conduct in the Ionian Revolt must have been very much in Athenian minds at that moment. His interference with merchant shipping passing through the Bosporus[27] may have affected Athens, even been directed against Athens as a state that had let the Ionians down, and he would have been a suitable person for Miltiades to abuse as the real medizer. Nothing much therefore should be made of Herodotus' account of his capture. There was unlikely to be solid evidence that 'when he was running away and was caught up by a Persian and was about to be struck down, he declared himself in Persian speech to be Histiaeus the Milesian' (6. 29. 2). Greek witnesses who understood that language were probably not present. As to the statement that 'Histiaeus expected that he would not be put to death by the King for his present mistake' (6. 29. 1), even if it was true, it is most unlikely that Histiaeus, who alone knew what he expected, ever said as much; leading men into battle, he would hardly have indicated that whatever happened to them, he would be all right. It looks much more like slander, the slander of Attic legal oratory where statements could be made without a shred of evidence. Whatever is to be said about Histiaeus, must be tempered by the recognition that the account of Herodotus may stem more from what was said to malign him than from what he actually intended and did.

One question raised by Herodotus' account of Histiaeus is of special importance. Did Histiaeus send a message to Aristagoras telling him to revolt? and, if he did, what prompted him to do so?[28] Herodotus would have us believe that at the very moment that Aristagoras, in fear of the consequences for himself of the failure of the Naxian expedition, was planning revolt, a message arrived from Histiaeus urging exactly that course (5. 35). The story of 'the slave with the tattooed head' is picturesque but hardly acceptable. If the slave was reliable enough to carry the message on his head, he was reliable enough to carry it

in his head; the device hardly made the secret more secure, for, if the
slave was suspected, he could easily respond to torture by telling his
torturers to shave him and read for themselves, and while the hair was
growing again after the tattooing, the chances of discovery were considerable; nor does one imagine slaves with messages passing up and
down the Royal Road, as if it were the road from Athens to Megara.
The detail must be dismissed, but is it a colourful adornment of the fact
that Histiaeus did indeed send a message to Aristagoras? Artaphernes
may have suspected the complicity of Histiaeus (6. 1. 2) (though he
could not have been certain of it, for in that case he would have acted
decisively to punish or restrain him), but it is equally possible that
Histiaeus invented the whole scene with Artaphernes to ingratiate
himself with the Ionians.[29] However, after Histiaeus had been released
by the Chians, he was, according to Herodotus, 'asked by the Ionians
why he had so eagerly sent a message to Aristagoras to revolt from the
King'. Of course, Herodotus may simply have invented the question
to maintain consistency with his earlier story, but that would seem to
be carrying incredulity too far. Reports of what Histiaeus said by way
of self-justification must have been widely spread amongst the Asiatic
Greeks, and the reply that Histiaeus is said to have given is very striking—'Darius planned to remove the Phoenicians and settle them in
Ionia and the Ionians in Phoenicia'. On the face of it this is so improbable that one finds it hard to believe that anyone would have invented
it. Transplantation was a Persian practice, but not transplantation of
such a pointless kind. If the Ionians were a danger in Ionia, they would
be a danger in Phoenicia and all the more so for such treatment, and
the uprooting of the Phoenicians would have a most unsettling effect
on their loyalty. One wonders therefore whether the transplantation
of the Ionians which Histiaeus said Darius planned did not concern
'the Ionians' in the sense that the Persians used the word, a general
term for the Greeks,[30] whether in reporting to the Ionians what he
had heard, Histiaeus was not misreported or misunderstood. He knew
Old Persian[31] and no doubt understood perfectly well what the term
'Ionians' meant to Darius, but if his statement of what the King said
was partly rendered in a literal translation, he could be misunderstood
and misreported. Indeed the Phoenicia that Darius could have had
in mind, could have been the Sidon, Tyre, and Aradus of the Persian Gulf whence Herodotus and Strabo believed that the Phoenicians
derived; such an area would have been much more conceivable for
the settlement of deported Greeks.[32] However, whatever explanation

one gives of Histiaeus' reply to the Ionian question, it suggests that he had indeed heard of some revolutionary development of policy related to Darius' plans for westward expansion, and had tried to warn Aristagoras to act before it was too late. Herodotus' account of why Histiaeus sent the message (5. 35. 4) is in any case very improbable. Histiaeus could hardly have expected that if Ionia revolted, he would be allowed to return to the sea. It looks suspiciously like the slanderous motivation produced in an Athenian court, not sober history. It cannot be excluded therefore that Histiaeus did indeed send a message and that he did so because he became apprised of a development of policy seriously affecting Greeks and Greece.

All in all, Herodotus has presented historians with a sorry choice. We must either blindly accept or pick and choose on no criterion other than that of probability, a dangerous and subjective procedure. But in view of the criticisms here made of his account, blind acceptance is unacceptable. One can only say what one considers to be probable, with little hope of general agreement.

Let us begin with the question why the Ionians revolted. Three answers have been given: that the tyrants supported by Persia had become by 499 intolerable, that the Greeks of Asia were suffering economically under Persian rule, and that the revolt was a revolt against Persian domination in general, an assertion of the Greek passion for liberty. It is here to be argued that the third is the correct explanation.

The debate in Herodotus about the breaking up of the Danube Bridge (4. 137), no matter whether it actually was held or, as has been argued, was said by Miltiades at his trial to have been held,[33] makes clear the position of the tyrants of the Asiatic Greek cities. Histiaeus is said to have opposed Miltiades' proposal to break up the bridge and to set Ionia free, by arguing thus: 'As things are now each of us is tyrant of his city because of Darius, but if the power of Darius is destroyed neither will I be able to rule the Milesians nor will any of you be able to rule anyone else. For each of the cities will wish to be under a democracy rather than a tyranny.'[34] Secondly, the opening of the Revolt was marked by Aristagoras' deposition of the tyranny of Miletus and the arrest and expulsion of the tyrants generally (5. 37). Finally, part of the Persian settlement of affairs after the Revolt was the abolition of the tyrannies,[35] which must have been re-established as the Revolt was crushed, and the institution of democracies (6. 43). On the basis of these three facts it has been argued that what the Ionians really wanted was to be free not of Persian rule in itself but of the system the Persians adopted to maintain their rule; as time passed, the attractions of democracy as witnessed elsewhere, particularly in the Ionian metropolis, Athens, must have become ever greater[36] and by 499 tyranny within a city could no longer be endured.

It would be foolish to suggest that there were no Greeks for whom such considerations were compelling. Wherever a number of men take a decision, their reasons for supporting it can be very diverse. However, the case for fixing on hatred of the system of tyranny as the real cause of the Ionian Revolt is weak. What the Persians did after the Revolt may have been no more than palliative, an attempt to remove unnecessary causes of resentment. When, according to Diodorus (10. 25), Hecataeus was sent by the Ionians to Artaphernes after their total defeat, he pleaded for generous treatment as the right method of avoiding bitter hatred incurred by their sufferings in the suppression of the Revolt, and Artaphernes in consequence 'gave back to the cities their laws', that is, the right to have whatever constitution they wished. It is to be noted that Hecataeus is not represented as saying that the tyrannies had been the cause of the Revolt. There is no necessary inference from what was done after the Revolt to why the Ionians revolted. The cause may have been irremovable, Persian domination, the changes merely means of reconciling the Ionians to that fact. It is also remarkable that both the Carians and most of the Cyprians joined in the Revolt, but there is absolutely no reason to suppose that either of these peoples was at all agitated about tyranny or whatever form of rule the Persians chose to maintain.[37] The motive in these cases was, presumably, uncomplicated desire to be rid of Persian domination. But, it may be countered, what moved these lesser breeds proves nothing about the motives of the pure Greeks north of Caria. However, one may fairly presume that the Hellespontine Greeks shared Ionian attitudes. They too had their Persian-supported tyrants (Hdt. 4. 138. 2). But there is no mention of their expulsion, when the Ionian fleet appeared and got the cities to join the Revolt (5. 103). They may have been expelled, but Herodotus thought it not worth mention. One may note also that when Herodotus recounted the appeal of Aristagoras to King Cleomenes of Sparta (5. 49), there is no reference to Sparta's opposition to tyranny in which, whether rightly or wrongly, Herodotus certainly believed (5. 92α 1). Aristagoras is made to appeal to Sparta 'to rescue the Ionians from slavery',[38] and the foe is quite simply Persia. There is no hint here that the real aim of the Ionians was to be free of their own local tyrants rather than of foreign domination. All in all, the case for supposing that the basic desire of the Ionians was to be rid of tyranny as a political system is weak. The tyrants were deposed not because they were tyrants, but because they were the instruments of Persian power.

Similarly the case for supposing that the Revolt was essentially against the economic ill effects of Persian rule is to be rejected. What was done after the Revolt proves nothing about the root cause. Herodotus recorded two measures taken by Artaphernes in 493. The first was the establishment of a system of arbitration of disputes between Ionian cities (6. 42), the working of which is illustrated by an inscription of a hundred years later (Tod, *GHI* 113). The purpose of this measure was declared to be that the Ionians should not settle their disputes by harrying and pillaging each other. The relevance of all this at that moment is obscure, but it may be that in the past harrying and pillaging had provoked Persian police action which had been resented.[39] It certainly has no bearing on the question of whether Persian rule disadvantaged the Ionians economically. The other measure, however, is more in question. Artaphernes established an equitable system of tribute. Before Darius, there was tribute but it seems to have been unregulated, and Darius earned himself the reputation of a money-grubber by his regulation of it. The dating of this administrative reform is uncertain. If in Ionia it was carried out before the Revolt, it may have been felt to be inequitably arranged. If on the other hand it was first implemented in 493, the previous lack of regulation may have been felt to be burdensome and unjust.[40] So it might be supposed that this measure of 493 argues that the cause of the Ionian Revolt was in some degree economic. Again, however, the Diodoran version of Hecataeus' embassy to Artaphernes (10. 25) suggests otherwise; 'the imposition of tribute fixed according to ability to pay' was, like the establishment of democracies, a measure of leniency aimed at obliterating the bitter memory of what the Ionians had suffered in defeat. Furthermore, the Ionians were well used to tribute as a necessary part of political subjection. The Persians merely continued the practice of the Lydian kings. Whatever happened under Darius, it was not so sharp a change as Herodotus would lead us to think, and it is unlikely that the Revolt was inspired by Persian taxation, rather than by Persian domination as a whole of which the collection of tribute was only one aspect.

It is common in rejecting theories of economic decline as the mainspring of the Ionian Revolt to point to Herodotus' remark (5. 28) that in 499 Miletus was 'at its peak and was indeed the show-place ($\pi\rho\acute{o}\sigma\chi\eta\mu\alpha$)

of Ionia', and that is probably correct. If Ionia went into decline in the fifth century and began to recover in the fourth,[41] that may well have been the consequence of punishments meted out after the Revolt. But it may be that Persian grants of land to individuals and Persian settlements[42] had taken away much of the best land of the Greek cities, that therein was the real impoverishment and a cause of bitter resentment.

Since Herodotus did not trouble himself to explain why so many followed Aristagoras into revolt, it cannot be excluded that Persian empire was felt burdensome in this way, and in view of the paucity of the evidence any argument from silence would be particularly unsatisfactory. But it must be noted that Persian occupation of Milesian territory was part of the punishment of Miletus, and in his report Herodotus gives no hint that such a thing had been happening to cities earlier.[43] *Non liquet*. At present there is no reason to suppose that the Revolt was due to economic discontent.

The remaining hypothesis is that the Ionians revolted, not because they resented particular aspects or effects of Persian rule, but because they resented Persian rule *tout simple* and aimed at recovering their liberty which they had lost first to the Lydian kings, then to Cyrus (Hdt. 6. 32). This at any rate is the impression one derives from what Herodotus makes Histiaeus and Aristagoras imply in pursuit of their allegedly selfish purposes. When Darius confronted Histiaeus with the news of the Revolt, part of Histiaeus' deceptive reply was to assert that the rebels were doing 'what they had of old longed for' (5. 106. 5). Aristagoras made his appeal at Sparta in terms of liberty. 'By the gods of the Greeks, save the Ionians from Slavery', just as Dionysius of Phocaea put the issue in terms of liberty (5. 49. 2, 3; 6. 11. 2). So it would seem that in Herodotus' mind the aim of the Ionians, though not of their leaders, was the recovery of long-lost liberty, the result was renewed subjection. That, unfortunately, is all that can be said, and the hypothesis is weakly grounded, more properly to be called a presumption, but such a presumption is not surprising, given the Greek hatred of foreign rule. 'Remember freedom first of all' was the proclamation of the Spartan king to the Ionians in 479 (9. 98. 3), but they had never forgotten it and in 499 they had seized their chance.

499 presented a unique opportunity. When Megabates was frustrated in his attack on Naxos, he did not disband his fleet but kept it together at Myus. This would have been pointless if he had intended to renew his attack in the spring. It suggests rather that his purpose was very

shortly to return to Naxos, more suitably prepared this time with the necessary instruments of siege warfare. But it was an advertisement of intention and it also provided an opportunity for action. It has been argued above that whatever the private intentions of Aristagoras, some preliminary organization was necessary if the plan to eliminate unsympathetic captains in the fleet and tyrants in the cities was not to go awry. Even in Herodotus' account, by 498 'the Ionians' would seem to be formally involved. Early that year 'the Ionians', 'the league of the Ionians' (τὸ κοινὸν τῶν Ἰώνων) deliberated on help for Cyprus (5. 108. 2, 109. 3). Indeed immediately after the raid on Sardis and the Athenian withdrawal, 'the Ionians' were 'none the less preparing for the war against the King' (5. 103. 1). So at some point the Revolt passed from the mind of Aristagoras to the supervision of the league, and in view of the need for concerted action one may guess that it happened in the very early days.[44] Too little is known of the meetings of the Panionium to be precise; the Apaturia, which was the common festival of all the Ionian people and which fell at Athens in Pyanopsion (i.e. autumn), would have been a convenient assembly, but no doubt there were frequent meetings for religious purposes which would have afforded opportunity for planning revolt.[45] It is not clear from Herodotus' narrative whether the man sent to secure the arrest of unreliable captains in the fleet at Myus, Iatragoras, went from Miletus or from the temple at Mycale. The latter is possible, perhaps even preferable; for Aristagoras' deposition of the tyranny followed in Herodotus' narrative the action in the fleet (5. 37). If the Panionium was the focus, it was readily possible for Aristagoras to convert a conspiracy into a formally sanctioned movement. He was 'sent as an envoy' to Greece (5. 38. 2). One may guess that he was the envoy of the league.

The concentration of the fleet made concerted action more easily effected. But was there something which made the action at that moment peculiarly attractive? One may suggest there was. When the expedition to Naxos was mounted, it must have been plain to many a Greek that success at Naxos would be followed by an attack on Euboea. Herodotus pictured Aristagoras enticing Artaphernes with the prospect of gaining for the King not only Naxos itself 'but also the islands dependent on it, Paros, Andros and the rest of the Cyclades, and from this base you will easily attack Euboea' (5. 31. 2). It needed no great acumen for Greeks to see what was in store. Under Cyrus the Asiatic Greeks had been absorbed. Cambyses had taken Phoenicia and so gained a fleet, and gone on to incorporate Egypt.

Darius had engrossed the offshore islands and occupied Thrace to the Strymon. The Persians must have seemed by 500 well on the way to making the Aegean *mare nostrum*. The prophet of Deutero-Isaiah (40: 15) had cried of the coming of Cyrus 'Why, to the Lord nations are but drops from a bucket . . . coasts and islands weigh as light as specks of dust . . .'. 'Coasts and islands saw it and were afraid, the world trembled from end to end.' He was talking at that time of 'the coastlands and islands of the eastern Mediterrranean'[46] but by 500 they had all been absorbed, and the trembling must have extended, or would have been thought by Aristagoras to have extended, to Greece itself. While Megabates was gathering forces shortly to renew the onslaught on Naxos Aristagoras and his ilk had an unprecedented opportunity. He could appeal to the main powers of mainland Greece in terms such as these: 'We are in revolt. Come and help. It is plain that you will fight in defence of your liberty, either with us in Ionia or without us in Greece itself. You cannot avoid the fight.' He failed at Sparta. Athens (and perhaps Eretria),[47] nearer the danger, complied. Whether a message from Histiaeus alerted him to the menace and to the possibilities must remain somewhat uncertain, but even without it Aristagoras could read the writing on the wall.

The truth can no longer be avoided. I believe that de Sanctis[48] was right when he pronounced Aristagoras one of the heroes of Greek liberty. Herodotus' account of him is so plainly unsatisfactory that one inevitably suspects that his denigration of Aristagoras was the result of prejudice, apologia, and misunderstanding. He makes Aristagoras a coward ($\psi\upsilon\chi\dot{\eta}\nu$ $o\dot{\upsilon}\kappa$ $\ddot{\alpha}\kappa\rho os$), choosing escape to Thrace when his ill-conceived, self-seeking plans miscarried. I see him as a man of political vision, who when the mainland Greeks failed him took the sensible decision to move the Ionians to a colony on the Strymon.[49] Since this involves rejecting Herodotus, it will be derided by some, the fate of believers. But whatever the truth of that, we are dealing with more than the one man, Aristagoras. Whatever his motives, the others had to be persuaded. The situation, as I have pictured it, was indeed persuasive.

The real business of this chapter is to consider the Persian response, but before turning to that, one must discuss the rebels' strategy. Hecataeus was right. Control of the sea was crucial (Hdt. 5. 36). But something had to be done on land. If the territory on which the cities depended was not to be so ravaged as to deny them food, there had to be an army operating, as Agesilaus was to operate in 396 and 395. Herodotus would have it thought that Aristagoras planned a march up-country, an *anabasis*, and has him show Cleomenes a bowl with a map of the world (5. 49). That is fantastic invention. Such thoughts are anachronistic and the fruit of Panhellenist dreaming after the repulse of the Persian invasion of Greece.[50] One might, however, guess that Aristagoras had in mind, and indeed proposed to Cleomenes, more limited and more practicable operations of which the attack on Sardis was the first and, because it ended in a serious reverse at Ephesus, the last. Perhaps his land strategy was to attack, like Agesilaus in 395, 'the strongest points of the area' (τὰ κράτιστα τῆς χώρας—Xen. *Hell* 3. 4. 20),that is, the seats of satrapal authority, Sardis, Dascylium, perhaps Colossae and Celaenae.[51] Unseated, the satraps would have found the reduction of the Greeks much more laborious, but for the success of such a strategy Aristagoras needed the help of the leading military power in Greece, Sparta. When Sparta failed him, he was left to the forlorn flourish of a raid on Sardis, and after that he could expect nothing other than what happened, the reduction of the rebel cities one by one.[52] Once the Revolt had failed in Cyprus, with clear strategic vision Aristagoras saw that the Ionians must get out or endure the sufferings brought by the inevitable restoration of Persian power.

One might wonder whether Aristagoras went further and envisaged the longer term condition of Sardis. It has been plausibly suggested[53] that he hoped for an uprising of the Lydians. Half a century of pacification by excluding them from military service, as Herodotus would have it that Croesus suggested to Cyrus (1. 155), had not perhaps extinguished memories of independence. They had earlier revolted under Pactyes (1. 154). Aristagoras may have hoped for another revolt. If he did so hope, he was disappointed; a descendant of King Gyges, Myrsus son of Gyges, actually died in Caria fighting for the Persians (5. 121). But the hope was not absurd. Perhaps Histiaeus' conversations in Sardis with 'Persians', as Herodotus terms them, were with eminent Lydians.[54] All in all, Aristagoras may not have lacked strategic vision.

It is time to turn to the Persian response to the crisis. The Revolt took over five years to suppress and that might be thought curiously long, suggestive perhaps of incompetence. But that would be wrong. Not until Mardonius came down in 492 when the Revolt was already ended, did the King send a large land army into the western satrapies, to resume the westward expansion of the Empire (Hdt. 6. 43. 1). For the Revolt itself the satrapal forces of the area west of the Halys were deemed sufficient, and indeed they dealt with resistance piecemeal

effectively enough. By the time of the battle of Lade in 494, the list of
rebel states, to judge by the list of combatants (Hdt. 6. 8), was very small.
The Carians had been dealt with. They disappear from Herodotus'
narrative on a victorious note, but their reduction must have followed
(5. 121). Byzantium and many of the Hellespontine and Propontic cities
had been recaptured. Nearer the heart of the Revolt Cyme in Aeolis
and Clazomenae had fallen (Hdt. 5. 117, 122, 123). Ephesus is not heard
of again after the defeat of the force that raided Sardis; presumably it
too had been occupied. The Persian land forces were both adequate
and successful. For Miletus, however, naval forces were necessary. The
city had, early in the sixth century, held the Lydians at bay for eleven
years, 'for the Milesians controlled the sea so that there was no use the
army laying siege', as Herodotus put it (1. 17. 3), and the attack on the
mainland centre of the Revolt had now to await the assembly of a large
naval force, always a matter of two or three years. Once the Persian
navy had fought the battle of Lade, the city was promptly taken by
assault.[55] What delayed the preparation of the fleet was the revolt of
Cyprus which took a year to subdue (Hdt. 5. 116). So not until later
497 was Darius free to proceed with the final settlement of Ionia. The
Persian response was not dilatory.

Incompetence might be suspected in the opening phases of the
Revolt. How was it that Sardis could be raided? Artaphernes appears
to have been taken by surprise. At the very time of the raid, the satraps
of the area west of the Halys were assembling, presumably at Castolus,
and learning what had happened they went to the rescue of Artaphernes. Too late, they pursued the Ionians and their allies and caught
them in Ephesus.[56] So military preparations were afoot. But how had
the Greeks been able to take the offensive?

The answer depends on the exact dating of these events; which
Herodotus denies us. However once the banner of revolt had been
raised, it was so much in the Ionians' interest for Aristagoras to seek
help from Greece as speedily as possible that one is justified in supposing that he was sent on his mission within a few days of the deposition
of the tyrants. The appeals to Sparta, to Athens, and perhaps to Eretria
and his return to Miletus could have been effected within, say, three
weeks of the beginning of the Revolt, and the Athenians and Eretrians could have been in Ionia shortly afterwards. In short, the raid on
Sardis could have taken place not much more than a month after the
outbreak.[57] If that was in fact the chronology of events, the Persians
were prompt enough in assembling their forces. Hymaies, who was

probably satrap of Dascylium,[58] had after summoning his own forces and arranging for supplies to make a journey of over a hundred miles as the crow flies, and other satraps must have been similarly placed. So it may well be that there was neither delay nor incompetence.[59]

Of course, if Aristagoras had been successful in his appeal to Sparta and the Persian generals had had to deal with an army like that of Agesilaus in 396 and 395, more substantial forces would have been necessary, and the army that the King sent down with Mardonius in 492 (Hdt. 6. 43. 1) might have been required four years earlier. But in this period Persia was fully equal to dealing with Greek resistance. Indeed it is striking that Darius felt able to resume the offensive in the West so soon after the settlement of the Revolt. He must have had ample confidence in the effectiveness of the measures taken after the fall of Miletus, and in the event his confidence was on the whole justified. The Ionians who fought at Salamis were accused of not doing their utmost, and Xerxes may have taken some action by way of punishment, but in general they seem to have served the King well enough. None of the Ionian ships deserted, and it was not until the Greeks moved to Asia Minor that the Ionians again moved to revolt.[60]

The settlement was a mixture of severity and leniency. Herodotus speaks of the Persian forces conducting man-hunts, of castration of boys, of good-looking girls being carried off to Susa, of the burning of cities and shrines (5. 102, 6. 19. 3). The Persians could be frightful, and no doubt were in dealing with the rebels. It was not, however, as complete as Herodotus would have us think. He concluded his account of the punishment of Miletus by saying 'Miletus was emptied of Milesians', but this is plainly an exaggeration. There were Milesians in the Persian forces at the battle of Mycale in 479. Not all of them can have been deported to a settlement on the Tigris. Hecataeus continued to exercise influence, and to judge by the list of Aesymnetae families prominent in the three decades before 494 continued to flourish in the succeeding years; the most striking case is that of the office-holder for 492/491, if it is correct that there was no break in the list, namely a son of Molpagoras which was the name of Aristagoras' father. The real penalty for Miletus must have been the loss of territory, which for all we know was permanent.[61] Although the record of Milesian payments of tribute in the Athenian Empire is difficult to interpret, being complicated perhaps by revolts and factional strife, it is to be noted that the highest amount of tribute recorded was ten talents, substantial enough but for a state that could provide eighty ships at Lade surprisingly less than what one would expect. So the Milesians suffered and were spared.[62] If the treatment of the state which led the Revolt was so mixed, no doubt other places suffered less severely, and the decision of Darius, implemented in 492 by Mardonius, no longer to sustain tyrannies (Hdt. 6. 42. 3) was a remarkable piece of leniency and prudence. Nor, would it seem, was the Panionium dissolved, as might have been expected. It had provided a ready forum for political opposition both at the coming of Cyrus and during the Revolt. Indeed the league was in origin political rather than religious, and must have been regarded by the Persians with suspicion. Yet the festival of the Ionians continued. Its site was moved to near Ephesus by the time of Thucydides, and its name became the Ephesia, but the Ionians continued to assemble and there is absolutely no reason to suppose that formal assemblies ceased after 494, as has been often thought.[63] Herodotus recorded the institution of a system of arbitration (which an inscription shows to have flourished still in the late 390s). If at the same time the league itself had been dissolved, he would presumably have said so; instead he introduced his notice by saying 'During this year nothing further than this was done by the Persians tending to strife with the Ionians', which is hardly consistent with the dissolution of the league.[64] Darius seems therefore to have done what Cyrus did, when he left untouched the league that had organized resistance to Persian power.[65] All in all, the Persian settlement was in large measure lenient.

The real long-term result of the Ionian Revolt was that Darius, one of the greatest of the Kings, was prevented for seven years from westward expansion. If the Marathon campaign had come in 497, the mainland Greeks would have been less psychologically prepared to resist. If it had at the earlier date failed as it did in 490, it would have been Darius not Xerxes who launched the land invasion of Greece. Under his effective leadership it might well have succeeded.[66] The Ionian Greeks did not suffer wholly in vain.

NOTES

1. D Na 8–15 (Kent 138).
2. Hdt. 3. 139–44, 4. 138. 2. For the progress of Persian power in the West, cf. V. Martin 1965: 38–48 and Briant 1996: 152.

3. Herodotus evidently believed that the reconnaissance happened early in the reign (cf. 3. 138. 4).

4. For the varying senses of the term 'Ionians' in Herodotus, cf. Tozzi 1978: 227–30.

5. As will emerge, I side with de Sanctis 1932: 63–91. There is a full bibliography on the Ionian Revolt in Tozzi 1978: 231–6, to which is to be added Wallinga 1984 and Murray 1988.

6. Hdt. 5. 36. At 5. 124. 2 the word is συστασιῶται. At 5. 104. 2 Onesilos of Salamis takes counsel with his στασιῶται. Cf. Tozzi 1978: 138.

7. Cf. Murray 1988: 472–3. The Histiaeus narrative is ill connected with the rest. At 6. 1. 1 Herodotus makes him arrive in Sardis after the death of Aristagoras in 497/496 (as it would seem from Thuc. 4. 102) but he places Histiaeus' conversation with Darius which prompted his dispatch (5. 105–7) shortly after the raid on Sardis of 499. Histiaeus' death is set after the fall of Miletus in 494 (6. 26. 1).

8. Cf. Wallinga 1984.

9. 5. 28, 30. 1, 6. 3, 19. 2. At 5. 105. 1 Darius declares that the rebels 'would not get off scot-free'. Note ἀγνωμοσύνη at 6. 10.

10. e.g. Waters 1970: 506 ('The whole account of the war shows that Herodotus realized, and meant us to realize, that the principal reasons for the failure of the revolt were lack of unity and treachery'). Representative opinions cited in Tozzi 1978: 204 n. 119, and 222 n. 51.

11. Hdt. 5. 112. The battle was against the ships which had transported the 'large army' from Cilicia (5. 108), and the Phoenicians were sailing perhaps, in the phrase of Thuc. 2. 83, οὐκ ὡς ἐπὶ ναυμαχίᾳ ἀλλὰ στρατιωτικώτερον παρεσκευασμένοι (cf. 2. 87. 2). The naval victory off Cyprus before the raid on Sardis, fetched by Plutarch (*Mor.* 861 A-D) from the otherwise unknown Lysanias of Mallos, must be pure invention. Cf. Tozzi 1978: 167–8.

12. For Greeks in Cambyses' Egyptian expedition, Hdt. 2. 1. 2, 3. 1. 1, and for a Greek ship 3. 13. 1.

13. For a discussion of the tactic called *diekplous*, see Appendix 1.

14. Such I take to be the meaning of the phrase, τοὺς ἐπιβάτας ὁπλίσειε (Hdt. 6. 12. 1). Cf. 7. 100. 3. Marines would always have been armed. So ὁπλίζειν must mean 'to furnish them with hoplite arms'.

15. Hdt. 6. 8 gives the Greek order of battle but omits to do more than notice the mixed Persian array (6. 6). Lateiner 1976: 283 takes as literal truth Herodotus' statement at 6. 9. 1 that the Persian generals were afraid that they would not defeat the Ionians in 494. Whence would such information have come? Generals keep their fears to themselves.

16. Cf. Appendix 1 on development of naval warfare and p. 109 on the battle of Salamis.

17. Cf. *PW* VII. 2 2668–71 for the little that is to be told of Hecataeus' life, and some of that is dubitable (cf. West 1991).

18. Cf. Tozzi 1978: 32–3.
19. Cf. Mitchell 1975: 88–90.
20. V.s. p. 49.
21. 3. 134. 6, 136. 1, 7. 19. 1 and 9. 1.
22. 6. 48. 2, 7. 133. 1.
23. *Pace* Fornara 1971: 53–6. Hdt. 6. 115, 121–4 for the charge of medism; Herodotus' apologia culminates in 6. 131 with the birth of the lion-hearted patriot, Pericles, whose mother was Alcmaeonid. Cf. 5. 96. 2, where those who had given earth and water, i.e. Clisthenes and supporters, became ἐκ τοῦ φανεροῦ enemies of Persia, having been earlier, it is left us to infer, secretly so. Cf. Cawkwell 1970: 45.
24. V.s. pp. 3–4.
25. Herodotus is not specific about the interval between Megabates' message and the invasion, but it seems to be short.
26. Hdt. 3. 160, Ctes. F14 §45.
27. 6. 5. 3, 26. 1 (in which passage, however, Herodotus speaks of 'the merchant ships of the Ionians'). It is doubtful whether Athens imported Pontic corn directly in this period. If it came, it came presumably by way of Aegina (Hdt. 7. 147. 2). Cf. Garnsey 1988: 107–13.
28. Tozzi 1978: 135–7.
29. If it is correct that Herodotus is most unlikely to have received information from a Persian source about the conversation of Darius and Histiaeus, it may stem from what Histiaeus said he said, and his colourful remark about 'not changing the shirt I wear down to Ionia until I make the very great island of Sardinia tributary to you' (5. 106. 6) may have been part of his account of how he tricked Darius into letting him go, an absurd promise that showed how the boundlessly ambitious monarch could be gulled. Likewise the remark of Artaphernes 'You stitched the shoe, Aristagoras put it on' (6. 1. 2) may be another colourful invention of Histiaeus.
30. For the extension of this title over the centuries, cf. Mazzarino 1947: 107–68, esp. 165–8 for Achaemenid usage.
31. Hdt. 6. 29. 2. It was claimed that he had heard all of Darius' councils (5. 106. 3).
32. For the belief that the Phoenicians came from the Red Sea, see Hdt. 1. 1, 7. 89. 2, Strabo 16. 3. 4 766C, and 16. 4. 27 784C. 'Tyre' was presumably Arrian's Τύλος (*Anab.* 7. 20. 6), modern Bahrain. The islands in the Red Sea where deportees were settled (Hdt. 7. 80, 3. 93. 2) may have been those of which Strabo spoke.
33. See p. 48.
34. Cf. Artaphernes' demand that the Athenians take back Hippias (Hdt. 5. 96).
35. Hdt. 6. 43. The expelled tyrants 'fled to the Medes' (6. 9. 2).

36. Cf. Murray 1988: 474–5.
37. One of the captains in the fleet who was arrested at Myus was Oliatus, son of Ibanollis of Mylasa (Hdt. 5. 37. 1), but his brother presumably, Heraclides son of Ibanollis, was in command of the Carians who ambushed a Persian force (5. 121). He was probably the man of whom Scylax of Caryanda wrote in his Τὰ κατὰ Ἡρακλείδην τὸν Μυλασσῶν βασιλέα (*Suda* s.v. 'Scylax'). The brothers may have differed in their attitude to Persian rule, but it is equally possible that once the Carians had decided to join the Revolt the ruling house of Mylasa proved loyal to the cause. In Cyprus the leading rebel Onesilos of Salamis was 'king' (5. 108. 1, 111. 3).
38. In Herodotus δουλοσύνη is always subjection to a foreign power (save at 1. 129. 1 and 9. 76. 2 where it means literally 'the condition of servitude').
39. One may note the severity of Cyrus the Younger's policing (Xen. *Anab.* 1. 9. 13).
40. As Leuze 1935: 13–16 made clear, Herodotus is not literally correct in stating (3. 89) that before Darius there was no regular tribute. The date of Darius' regularization is obscure. Cf. Cook 1983: 242 n. 2, and *CHI* II 271. If Darius' real contribution to the Imperial system was to establish an equitable method of assessment, that could well have taken time and not have been carried out in the western satrapies before the Ionian Revolt began.
41. Cf. Cook 1961: 9–18.
42. Cook 1983: 174–82.
43. Hdt. 6. 20. His story of the return of the Paeonians to their homeland whence Darius had settled them in Phrygia (5. 98) does not suggest that Asia Minor was at that date bristling with Persian barons and their retainers.

It is unfortunate that the one piece of evidence pertaining to the period of Cyrus the Great, *FGH* 472 F6, is so dubitable. It runs 'Cyrus the Great bestowed on his friend Pytharchus of Cyzicus seven cities, according to Agathocles of Babylon, to wit Pedasos, Olympion, ⟨A⟩kamantion, Skeptra, Artypson, Tortyre. "But he" to quote Agathocles "resorted to such violence and folly that he made an attempt to become tyrant of his native land after assembling an army. And the people of Cyzicus set out against him in haste, bearing down rank on rank on the danger."' The seventh name is irrecoverable (*pace* Ruge, *PW* VIA 657). Pedasos may well have been the town of that name in the Troad (*Iliad.* 20. 92 and cf. Ruge, *PW* XIX. 1 29). Akamantion is described by Steph. Byz. as 'a city of Phrygia'. There is no reason to think that the seven places were clustered together or particularly near Cyzicus. A reasonable guess would be that they were part of the 'royal lands' of Croesus, whose dominion had embraced all of Asia Minor west of the Halys (Hdt. 1. 28, 6. 37, Strabo 13. 1. 42 601C) and who may be presumed to have appropriated land for himself just as later rulers did (cf. Rostovtzeff 1910: 245–8 and Magie 1950: ii. 1013–16). Lydian royal lands are unattested, though it is to be noted that Atramyttium, in which Pharnaces settled the Delians (Thuc. 5. 1), was said by Strabo (13. 1. 65 613C) to have once been 'under the Lydians' and to have had in his time a 'Lydian Gate, since the Lydians allegedly founded the city'. If the seven cities granted by Cyrus to Pytharchus had previously belonged to Croesus, this fragment of Agathocles furnishes no evidence of Persian colonial settlement on Greek territory.

44. Cf. Tozzi 1978: 151–4 for the varying views on this question, with a resolution here rejected.

45. Hdt. 1. 147 (and Deubner 1956: 232–4 for the date). Thuc. 3. 104 sets the celebration of the *Delia* in winter 426/5 and remarks that 'there was at one stage in time past (πάλαι) a great concourse of the Ionians and surrounding islanders on Delos', a celebration 'like the Ephesia at the present day'. So the winter was a time for such assemblages, and the fleet may well have been at Myus in 499 at the moment when one took place.

46. Smith 1944: 50.

47. Tozzi 1978: 162 and n. 136 ('It is of course not necessarily the case that Aristagoras visited Eretria.').

48. V.s. n. 5.

49. Hdt. 5. 124–6. That Thucydides (4. 102. 2) said that Aristagoras tried to found a city on the Strymon φεύγων βασιλέα Δαρεῖον does not necessarily mean that he accepted Herodotus' interpretation of Aristagoras.

50. See pp. 6–8, and cf. de Sanctis 1932: 84.

51. For Colossae, Polyaenus 7. 16. 1. For Celaenae, Xen. *Anab.* 1. 2. 7–9 (but Xenophon ascribes its fortification to Xerxes; Livy 38. 13. 5 says 'caput quondam Phrygiae').

52. It is notable that after the battle outside Ephesus (Hdt. 5. 102. 2) that city is not mentioned again in the history of the Revolt, that the temple of Artemis was not burned (Strabo 14. 1. 5 634C), and that the Ephesians attacked the Chians making their way home after the battle of Lade (Hdt. 6. 16. 2). Probably they had come to terms early (cf. Bürchner, *PW* v. 2 2789).

53. Tozzi 1978: 168.

54. V.i. pp. 233–4.

55. For Oriental siegecraft, cf. Winter 1971: 110 n. 20 and 292–300, and Lawrence 1979: 39–41.

56. Hdt. 5. 102. For the plain of Castolus, Xen. *Anab.* 1. 1. 2, 9. 7, *Hell.* 1. 4. 3. Presumably Thymbrara (*Cyrop.* 6. 2. 11) was a village on this plain, for the site of which see Dittenberger, *OGIS* ii 488. Cf. Cook 1983: 84 and 243 n. 17.

57. It is conventional to place the raid on Sardis in spring or early summer 498 (cf. Tozzi 1978: 111–12) but there is absolutely no reason for doing so.

It is unlikely that Megabates would have been keeping the fleet together at Myus all winter, when he could have avoided feeding and paying the sailors of Ionian ships by dismissing them with orders to reassemble in the spring. Presumably the fleet was being kept together to return promptly to Naxos and a later summer date for the revolt is credible enough. Aristagoras would only have been summoning the mainland Greeks to help during the season of navigability.

58. After his death, Oebares became satrap (Hdt. 5. 122. 2, 6. 33. 3).

59. No doubt the Revolt came as a great surprise to the Persians and there may have been initial confusion. As soon as Aristagoras returned from Athens and before the Athenians arrived if we may trust the sequence of events in Hdt. 5. 98, he sent a message to the Paeonians who had been transplanted to a village in Phrygia. Some escaped, although they were nearly caught up with by a large body of Persian cavalry. There is no knowing where they had been settled, nor by what route they reached the sea; presumably they did not come down the valley of the Hermus past Sardis. But in the early days of the Revolt a stray body of men, women, and children was of little importance when the full military power of the satrapies had to be concentrated for action against the rebel cities. However, it is to be noted that there are some dubitable elements in the story (cf. Macan 1895 ad loc.).

What became of Megabates and 'the really large collection of Persians and the other allies' which he took against Naxos (Hdt. 5. 32)? Megabates is not heard of again, though his son was an admiral in 480 (Hdt. 7. 97). Once the Revolt had broken out, there was no further use for the admiral, and he may have been recalled.

60. Hdt. 8. 10 (no Asiatic Greek ship deserted at Artemisium). Themistocles after that battle incited them to desert (8. 22), which none did, or at least to fight half-heartedly, which Herodotus claims that the Phoenicians accused them of at Salamis (8. 90), but that few did (8. 85). Paus. 8. 46. 3 speaks of Xerxes punishing the Milesians for their half-hearted performance at Salamis, but removing a statue of Apollo hardly seems an apt punishment, and before the battle of Mycale the Milesians were treated with no more than suspicion (Hdt. 9. 99).

61. For the 'emptying' of Miletus, 6. 22, but cf. 9. 99. 3, 104 and a similar 'emptying' of Samos early in Darius' reign 3. 149; presumably Syloson did not take over a city literally 'empty of men'. Doubtless when men had been rounded up (6. 31), only some were deported. Pliny 6. 28. 159, Hdt. 6. 20 for the settlement on the Tigris. For Hecataeus, Diod. 10. 25, and for the list of Aesymnetae in this period, most conveniently Tozzi 1978: 98; cf. Mazzarino 1947: 230. For Aristagoras' father, Hdt. 5. 30. 2, and for confiscation of land, 6. 20.

62. For the rebuilding of Miletus, see Kleiner 1968: 25–7, 29, 50.

63. Hdt. 1. 141. 4, 170 for the league's political aspect. For the Ephesia, Thuc.
    3. 104 (on which cf. S. Hornblower, 1991: 522 and 527). Von Wilamowitz-
    Moellendorf 1937: 141 presumed that the Persians dissolved the league.
64. 6. 4. 2, *GHI* 113 (the first fragment is not such as to allow a clear picture
    of the circumstances in which the King and his satrap became involved;
    perhaps the intransigence of Myus was all through the affair the obstacle
    to normal procedure; but the mention of 'the dicasts of the Ionians' in
    line 42 strongly supports the view that the Ionians continued as a political
    entity: cf. S. Hornblower 1982: 57).
65. For the Carian league, equally blameworthy in Persian eyes, cf. Tozzi
    1978: 176 n. 193, and S. Hornblower 1982: 58.
66. The happy discovery of the rich vein of silver at Laurium (Ar. *Ath. Pol.*
    22. 7) would have come too late, and Greek naval resistance would have
    been negligible.

5

The Conquest of Greece

THERE is no real evidence for why the Persians invaded Greece in 480. The pretty debate furnished by Herodotus at the start of book 7 of his *History* is almost certainly the product of his imagination; it is highly unlikely that he had any evidence about the parts played by Mardonius and Artabanus in the innermost councils of the King. But there is no need to ask why empires expand. Extension of power is the natural consequence of power. No less than Rome, Persia aspired to *imperium sine fine* and from the moment that the expedition was mounted against Naxos in 499 it was plain that Greece would face invasion.[1]

Herodotus did not entirely concur, and the view that the Persian invasion was inspired by Athenian help for the Ionian Revolt is freely expressed in his book. Mardonius is made to argue that not only would Greece be a desirable acquisition but also the King must punish Athens and dissuade anyone else from attacking his land; Xerxes responds in similar terms (7. 5. 2, 3 and 8β 1). Likewise, the Spartans in winter 480/479 are made to assert that the invasion was caused by Athens (8. 142. 2). All this reflects perhaps no more than Greek wrangling, and is of no great consequence. But it is a serious question whether the invasion of 490, for which Herodotus provides in part the same motivation (6. 94. 1), was indeed of limited scope and directed at the punishment of Athens and Eretria for their part in the raid on Sardis. If the expedition of Datis and Artaphernes, which ended ingloriously at Marathon, had succeeded in its aim, would no more have ensued than that the Athenians would have shared the fate of the Eretrians, deportation to a remote place in Asia, or would Athens have been made the base for the Persian conquest of Greece and the capital of a new satrapy?

The answer would seem to be provided by Herodotus' report of Darius sending messengers to Greek cities to demand 'earth and water', the tokens of submission. Darius is presented as wishing to subject those Greeks who refused (6. 94. 1). They included, it later emerges, not just Athens but also Sparta (7. 133. 1). No other mainland states are named, though the Aeginetans and 'the other islanders' submitted (6. 49. 1, 99.

1). If all this is true, the scope of the Marathon expedition must have been much wider than merely to punish Athens and Eretria. Although Herodotus' report of these embassies has been doubted and the thesis posed that embassies sent by Xerxes have been attributed to Darius,[2] there is no good reason for such scepticism. The Persian aim in 490, as in 480, was not just to punish. It was rather to begin the incorporation of mainland Greece within the Empire.

The Persians had in 490 two courses. One was to invade Greece by the route followed by Xerxes in 480. The other was to continue the 'island-hopping' strategy begun in 499. The advantage of the former was that a larger army could be employed, the serious disadvantage that the penetration of Thermopylae presented a most difficult strategic problem of which the King was doubtless well aware.[3] So the expedition by sea seemed much to be preferred, though the general intention of 490 was no different from that of 480.

But were the forces Persia deployed in 490 suitable for more than a punitive raid? There is no way of determining the numbers of troops on the Persian side. Herodotus' figure of six hundred triremes (6. 95. 2) is hardly to be trusted; he gave the same figures for the Scythian Expedition (4. 87. 1) when the fleet had neither to transport troops nor to expect naval opposition and one suspects that the figure is conventional, and worthless. Nor is the figure he furnishes for the approximate number of Persian casualties ('about six thousand and four hundred') of any real use for calculating the size of the whole. The most that can be said is that Datis and Artaphernes could not know that they would have to face only the Athenian army and the best one can do is to presume that they took a force of up to thirty thousand foot with a quite indeterminable number of cavalry. That would have been adequate to deal with such Greeks as were likely to resort to arms.[4]

Why then did the expedition fail? Judgement of what happened at the battle of Marathon turns on how one explains Herodotus' omission of any notice of the part played by the Persian cavalry. He had made clear that cavalry came on specially constructed ships (6. 48. 2), and that the Persian commanders chose to land at Marathon because of its suitability for cavalry operation (6. 102) (and local tradition about horses whinnying in the night (Paus.1. 32. 4) confirms that there was Persian cavalry), but, though he remarks the Athenian lack of cavalry (6. 112. 2), the Persian cavalry made no appearance in his account of the battle.[5] However, on the south frieze of the temple of Athena Nike which was erected in the 420s, there is represented a battle of Greeks and Persians, which has often been regarded as the battle of Marathon.[6] It contains four horsemen. This has been taken as proof that the Persian cavalry was indeed involved in the battle, and Marathon has been regarded as a glorious victory of Athenian hoplites over the full Persian army of Datis and Artaphernes. This may be right. But there are strong reasons for doubting it. The re-embarcation of cavalry must have taken no little time. Although we have no precise evidence about the construction of horse transports, getting the horses aboard was hardly to be hurried.[7] Yet although Herodotus reports the flight of the Persians to the ships with the Athenians in hot pursuit, only seven ships were captured and there is no mention of cavalry left stranded (6. 114 and 115). This strongly suggests that the withdrawal had begun before the battle started, indeed that Miltiades only attacked when the Persians were no longer able to use all their army. Similarly, the small number of Athenian casualties suggests that the cavalry was not engaged. The Persian centre broke through the Athenians and pursued them fleeing inland (6. 113. 1). If the cavalry had been in the pursuit, surely more than one hundred and ninety-two Athenians (6. 117. 1) would have been killed.[8] One inclines therefore to the view that the full Persian cavalry was not involved in the battle, which was thus not the great affair that the Athenians represented it to have been.[9] It is consistent with this that, after withdrawing, the Persians sailed round to Phalerum. If they had sustained defeat in a full-scale engagement, they could hardly have hoped for disloyal Athenians still to be interested in them.

The Persians had been much deceived. No doubt it was the aged Hippias who was responsible. He had memories of Pisistratus his father's return in 546, when the Athenian opposition to the advance on the city had been of no avail (Hdt. 1. 62), and he had thought he could count on treachery to receive him back. Instead the whole Athenian army went out to Marathon, took up a defensive position and waited. So the Persians had to withdraw and in doing so enabled the Athenians to strike. The battle of Marathon proved only that if Greece was to be invaded it would have to be by land and Darius began preparations immediately. The revolt of Egypt and the death of Darius, however, delayed the invasion (7. 1–4) and gave Greece time to make ready.

Yet there was little that the Greeks could do. The first to hear that Xerxes was leaving Susa to lead the campaign were, according to Herodotus (7. 239), the Spartans. They informed the rest of the Greeks and there was, it would seem, general recourse to the oracle at Delphi

(7. 220. 3, 140. 1, 148. 2). This must have been in the middle of summer 481 (or a bit later) and led to a meeting of the Greek states who were minded to resist (7. 145. 2). They decided to settle the enmities and actual wars between Greek states, most notably the war between Athens and Aegina, and what Thucydides (1. 102. 4) was to term 'the alliance against the Mede' came into being; appeal was made to Argos, Syracuse, Crete, and Corcyra to join in, and spies were sent to secure information about the Persian force (7. 145. 2). So, as soon as Greeks knew that Greece was to be invaded, they took effective action to unite, and they were successful in discouraging any states south of Boeotia from giving a favourable reception to the envoys of the Great King as they went around Greece in autumn and winter 481 demanding the tokens of submission, earth and water (7. 132).

By way of military preparations there was little possible. They had had good reason to suppose that the invasion would, unlike that of 490, be by land. The canal dug through the neck of the peninsula of Acte took three years to complete (7. 22. 1) and must have made men wonder as to its purpose, but surely not for long. The trafficking of the Aleuadae, the powerful family of Larisa in Thessaly (7. 6. 2, 130. 3), was doubtless no secret,[10] and must have reinforced the expectation of invasion by land. When Athens in 483/2 had the good fortune to strike a rich seam of silver at Laurium and Themistocles turned it to good effect with the proposal to build two hundred triremes (*Ath. Pol.* 22. 7, Hdt. 7. 114), he did so, according to Thucydides (1. 14. 3), at a time when 'the Barbarian was expected'. But there was nothing much the Greeks could do. There was only one strategy possible, viz. to try and keep the Persians out of the Gates, Thermopylae, but that, it would have seemed, depended entirely on the Greeks being able to stop the Persians outflanking the defences by use of their navy, and that was not a very happy prospect. Delphi clearly expected the Greeks to be largely overrun, and issued 'dire oracles' (Hdt. 7. 139. 6). Phoenician seapower was famously formidable and though Athens had the luck to be able greatly to increase her fleet, other states had not. In any case, the larger the Greek fleet the greater the difficulty of manning it.

Indeed it is miraculous that Athens was able to find anything like the thirty thousand necessary fully to man the fleet at Artemisium.[11] But the problem for the Greeks was not merely assembling an adequate number of properly manned ships. Even if cities like Corinth and Megara had been rich enough to double their number of triremes and populous enough to man them,[12] the real difficulty remained. Nautical skill was, as Thucydides made Pericles remark (1. 142. 6), not quickly acquired. When it came to battle, the Phoenicians were able to move through the water faster (Hdt. 8. 10, 7. 179). It was all very well for the Plataeans to contribute 'valour and enthusiasm' (8. 1. 1). They had no experience of things nautical and must have been more of a hindrance than a help. When the Greeks first formed up at Artemisium to face the Persian fleet, they lacked experience of its manner of warfare and in particular of the manoeuvre of 'sailing through', the so-called *diekplous*, for which Dionysius of Phocaea had sought to train the Ionians fourteen years earlier. The Chians had at that time some success but it had required forty marines on each ship and, presumably, ships fully decked, and finding another ten thousand hoplites for this aspect of the war was probably beyond Greece's resources in 480. Greece did what she could in merely getting the fleet for Artemisium manned and moderately competent. Phoenician finesse was not so quickly attained, and the chances of success seemed slender indeed. Once the strategic nut of Thermopylae was cracked, there could be little to be hoped for in conflict with the Persian land army. Unless the gods took a hand or the Persian command misused its opportunities, Greek liberty was lost.

The Persians failed, and failed ignominiously. Why they did, it is the purpose of this chapter to inquire. For Herodotus and his latter-day admirers, there is no problem. For them the Greek victory was a moral victory, the triumph of free men over slaves; the Persians came, in locust-like numbers, over five million in all, but as events at Thermopylae quickly proved there were 'many human beings, few real men'; they had to be driven into action with whips, and they died in their myriads; of the allegedly three hundred thousand at Plataea, forty thousand got away with Artabazus when he fled, but of the rest barely three thousand escaped being slaughtered; numbers were of no account before the valour of free men.[13] Such is the Herodotean view, and very satisfying it is to moralists. Of course even the most moralizing cannot trust everything that Herodotus says but the general impression lingers on that the Persians failed because they lacked the valour of their free opponents. This impression is false. One must try to stand apart from Herodotus.

Herodotus on the Great Invasion

It is remarkable how little of books 7, 8, and 9 can with any confidence be presented as furnishing a reliable account of what actually happened in 480 and 479. It goes, or should go, without saying that Herodotus is most unlikely, as already remarked, to have had any account of what was said in the inner councils of the Great King. It is not to be excluded that some account of strategic discussions during the campaign derived from Artemisia, the ruler of Herodotus' native city, who may have had, or may have claimed to have had, a favoured place among the King's councillors, or similarly from Demaratus, the exiled King of Sparta who may have been similarly placed, but accounts of discussions between Xerxes and Mardonius or Xerxes and Artabanus are almost certainly entirely fictitious and must be rigorously excluded from the mind when one considers Persian aims and strategy. Even the discussions in which Demaratus or Artemisia have a part inspire little confidence; the former's proposal to split the fleet (7. 234–7) seems to presuppose a size of fleet which Xerxes probably did not have, and although it is credible enough that Artemisia counselled Xerxes against fighting the battle of Salamis (8. 68), the debate (8. 100–3) in which she is made to argue after the defeat at Salamis that Mardonius and a Persian army should stay in Greece is absurd; they had not fought their way in only to abandon it so lightly or to discuss abandoning it. All this is obvious enough. So too without scruple one rejects what Herodotus has to say about the size of the forces at Xerxes' disposal. Scholars debate how far the numbers are to be reduced but the 'countless, voiceless, hopeless' hordes of Herodotus must go, and so too, for almost all, must the 'vast fleet' the Persians are credited with.[14] With all this goes too the comic apparatus of an army numbered by myriads stuffed into a walled counting house (7. 60)—such a method would take far too long. Likewise the stories of the army drinking rivers dry (7. 43, 58, 108); armies move in separate units which do not all arrive at a river bank at the same moment. Likewise, the story of Xerxes' trying to build a mole from Attica to Salamis immediately after the naval battle (8. 97) is too absurd to excite criticism; one has only to think of the time and trouble it took Alexander to build a mole half a mile long, in very shallow water for the most part, at Tyre in 332 BC.[15] All this is transparently absurd and no sensible person will waste ink on it, but it does raise serious doubts about a historian who could write such things.

Even geography has fared badly. The scouts posted on the high points of Euboea would have had to be able to see round corners to do what Herodotus reports them to have done (7. 183, 192). He seems ignorant, or at least confused, about the route the Persians followed into Thessaly (7. 128. 1, 173); if they passed 'through the Perrhaebians' they did not, however, go by Gonnus.[16]

The reading of Herodotus constantly delights and frequently disquiets. For instance, Herodotus reads as if Aristides returned from ostracism the night before the battle of Salamis, but he is also presented as commanding the Athenians who landed on the island of Psyttaleia the following day. The two points are unlikely both to be correct, quite apart from the fact that the Aristotelian *Constitution of Athens* declares (22. 8) that the ostracized had been recalled the previous year. This is perhaps a minor matter. The famous circumnavigation of Euboea is not. According to Herodotus (8. 7), Xerxes dispatched two hundred ships to sail round Euboea and cut the escape route of the Greek fleet, intending to delay his attack until he received 'the signal from those making the circumnavigation that they were coming'. No such signal could possibly have been received until the squadron had reached a point in the strait which it could have reached from the Persian base at the beginning of a battle, and the prudent considerations long ago advanced by Beloch[17] remain compelling; for Xerxes to send such a force on a voyage of two hundred and fifty nautical miles, the duration of which would be quite unpredictable, to do a task that could more simply be done otherwise, the task of denying the Greek fleet an escape route, is wholly improbable.

Indeed the whole account of the Greeks' behaviour at Thermopylae and Artemisium is suspect. Both the Greek army and the Greek navy are represented as singularly timid in the face of Persian might. Were most of the Greeks very poltroons? In the case of the navy not only does Herodotus have them plan to withdraw after the battle of Artemisium in which the Greeks had been 'roughly handled, not least the Athenians half of whose ships had been disabled' (8. 18), a plan to which it would seem there was no alternative, but he does not speak merely of withdrawal. He speaks of their planning 'to run away into Greece', the identical phrase he had used to describe their reaction earlier at the sight of 'many ships drawn up on the beach at Aphetae and army everywhere' (8. 4. 1). His navy is a very runaway lot. Still earlier, learning that ten enemy ships had pursued and proved too fast for three Greek ships on guard off Sciathus the Greeks took fright and retired to Chalcis to guard the Euripus channel (7. 179–83), thus leaving their army at Thermopylae fatally vulnerable to the landing of troops in the rear. They were in this way lucky enough to be safe at Chalcis when the Persian fleet was being lashed by the storm on the Sepiad strand and able to return when it was over (7. 189. 2, 192. 2). One cannot help suspecting that Herodotus is here quite unreliable. There is a simple explanation, namely that the Greek commanders, knowing well what storms in the Aegean were like, at the first sign withdrew to safe shelter somewhere, and returned when the storm had blown itself out.[18] Herodotus even adds that the Greeks expected that they would find few enemy ships to oppose them and implies that that was why they hastened back to Artemisium, a timid lot. One cannot help but sympathize with Plutarch's charge of malice in these matters (*Mor.* 867 B–F).

Similarly with the Greeks of the land army. When the Persian army came near, 'out of fear the Greeks in Thermopylae were considering going away, but while the Peloponnesians were in favour of going to the Peloponnese and guarding the Isthmus, the Phocians and the Locrians were greatly incensed with this decision and Leonidas' vote was for sending messengers to the cities bidding them help, since they were themselves too few to ward off the army of the Mede' (7. 207). They were in fact four thousand strong and in position to prevent the enemy penetrating a strip of land in places no wider than a cart-track (7. 207), with mountains on one side and sea on the other.[19] There is no proving that Herodotus is not right. The Peloponnesians other than the Spartans may indeed have wanted to let the Persians into Greece without a struggle. When later they all knew that the Persians would shortly shut off their route for withdrawal, Herodotus records a debate as to whether they should stay and die or live to fight elsewhere; the honour of Sparta required Leonidas not to abandon the position to which he had been sent; the others with good sense saw there was no longer any purpose to be served by remaining and chose to withdraw. This debate is indeed credible, though it was no doubt short. Herodotus, however, describes those who withdrew as 'lacking enthusiasm and unwilling to share the danger' (7. 220. 2) and so has Leonidas dismiss them. Men who avoided needless and useless deaths were not spared the censure of Herodotus. His Greeks other than Athenians and Spartans were a cowardly lot. So they may have been. But one is less inclined to believe it than to attribute it to the malice of Herodotus.

It may, however, be thought that if Herodotean malice has coloured the motives of some of the Greeks, none the less he can be fully trusted in his account of the main matters of Greek strategy and the Greek implementation of it; at least in these central matters he must, one would think, have inquired fully and recorded faithfully. Unhappily one cannot trust even here. He is not clear about Greek strategy as far as excluding the Persians from Greece is concerned. Quite apart from the highly dubitable claim (7. 172–4) that the ten thousand hoplites sent to Thessaly before Xerxes had crossed the Hellespont had been intended to keep the Persians out of Thessaly,[20] there is an unresolved ambiguity concerning the defence of Thermopylae. Did the Greek command deem that the force under Leonidas was adequate provided the Greek navy was not defeated, or did it not? Having listed the Greeks who assembled at Thermopylae, Herodotus added that the Opuntian Locrians and the thousand Phocians were summoned with a message that declared that those already at Thermopylae came as 'forerunners of the rest', but where the rest were to take their stand is obscure. On the one hand, one finds expressed the notion that the full force of the Greeks was to be assembled in Boeotia. When the fleet got back to Salamis from Artemisium, the Athenians are at that point declared 'to have been deceived of their expectation, for thinking that they would find the Peloponnesians in full force in Boeotia in a position to resist the barbarian, they found no such thing' (8. 40. 2). On the other hand, elsewhere Herodotus speaks as if those who went to Thermopylae were to be reinforced there. Leonidas, he says (7. 207), proposed to summon help to Thermopylae itself, on the grounds that his forces were too few to ward off the army of the Mede. This uncertainty on Herodotus' part is troubling. It is hardly likely that the Greek high command was itself unclear. Geography showed and history would prove that no great force was needed to hold Thermopylae provided it was not outflanked,[21] but the Greeks in 480 may just conceivably have been mistaken about this and planned to reinforce Leonidas. Whatever the truth, however, one would expect Herodotus to have discovered it and been in no doubt. Indeed with regard to the defence of Greece which depended on the navy keeping the enemy from getting behind the army at Thermopylae, he says something quite astounding. Noting the synchronism of the land and sea battles, he added 'And the whole struggle for those on the sea was *for the Euripus* just as for those with Leonidas it was to guard the pass' (8. 15. 2). The man who wrote this did not properly understand the Greek strategy.[22] One is bound to wonder how thoroughly he had tried to do so.

Herodotus constantly depicts the Greeks of the Peloponnese inclin-
ing towards the strategy of abandoning all of Greece north of the
Isthmus and establishing a defensive position there supported by the
Greek navy offshore. In the highly suspect debate of the land-force
at Thermopylae when the Persian army was approaching (7. 207), he
represents the Peloponnesians other than the Spartans as preferring
'to go to the Peloponnese and guard the Isthmus', that is, preferring to
guard a strip of land six kilometres wide at its narrowest point to holding one no more than twenty to thirty metres at its widest. This one can
readily dismiss, but when Herodotus represents the Peloponnesians on
Salamis preferring to abandon the position in the bay of Salamis and
to fight a sea-battle off the Isthmus in defence of the Peloponnese (8.
49, 56), he has been generally regarded as giving a truthful statement
of the strategy preferred by a majority. Some of the Greeks were said to
have taken to their ships and begun to raise their sails 'intending to run
away', while those who were remaining 'ratified the proposal to fight a
sea-battle before the Isthmus', from which they were only checked by
the decision of Eurybiades, the Spartan admiral, to fight off Salamis
(8. 56, 63). Themistocles is made by Herodotus to give the compelling argument against such a strategy (8. 60a): 'if you engage near the
Isthmus, you will fight a naval battle on open sea, which is least to our
advantage since our ships are slower and fewer in number'. But surely
it did not need Themistocles to put this point to the Greek captains. In
the battle of Artemisium the Greek navy had been 'roughly handled'
(8. 18) and the only hope of not suffering similarly again was to fight
within the confined waters of the strait between Salamis and Attica
where superior Phoenician seamanship would not have the space to
assert itself. If they feared that they would be stranded on the island
of Salamis and powerless to help in the defence of their own cities,
that was an argument for abandoning the struggle altogether, not for
facing it in a hopeless position. Eurybiades chose rightly, according to
Herodotus, because Themistocles threatened to sail off to Italy if there
was to be no battle off Salamis. He may not have realized that Themistocles' whole argument was sound. The other captains too may have
been muddled in their thoughts of where best to fight. But one cannot
avoid suspecting that Herodotus' whole account of the debate about
strategy is fictitious and misleading.

It will be contemptuously said in reply that the wall across the
Isthmus which the Spartans and the other Peloponnesians constructed
and behind which they proposed to shelter when the Persian army

began its onslaught on the Peloponnese shows how deeply all the Peloponnesians were drawn to what one may term the Isthmus strategy.
But that wall is a very curious thing. Admittedly it is recorded by Diodorus,[23] who was almost certainly following Ephorus and since the
terminal points are named as they are not by Herodotus one might
suppose that Ephorus had independent information about a wall built
in 480. That, however, is highly dubitable, and what Herodotus tells
us about the matter hardly inspires confidence. The Peloponnesians
were, he says, already engaged in building the wall when the fleet got
back from Artemisium (8. 40. 2), the work having been begun under
the command of Leonidas' brother, Cleombrotus: 'in as much as they
were many myriads and every man was engaged, the work was getting
on, for stones, bricks, timber, and bags full of sand were being brought
in and those who had come to assist were ceaselessly at work, night
and day' (8. 71. 2). An eclipse of the sun, to be assigned to 2 October
480,[24] moved Cleombrotus to lead the army away from the Isthmus,
the army which 'built' the wall (9. 10). Thus one would suppose that,
in Herodotus' mind, the wall was completed in 480. Nevertheless the
Spartans were still, he says (9. 7. 1), building the wall in summer 479 at
the time of the festival of the Hyacinthia,[25] and were already putting
parapets on it. At the moment of the Athenian appeal to Sparta the
wall was said to be in its final stages, and while the Spartans delayed
their response, 'all the Peloponnesians were walling the Isthmus, and
it was near completion' (9. 8). Herodotus goes on to opine that the
reason why the Spartans had disregarded the Athenian appeal at first,
although in winter 480/479 they had pleaded with Athens not to abandon the Greek cause (8. 140–4), was that in mid-479 they thought that
once the Isthmus had been walled off they had no longer need of the
Athenians. Having thus opined, he goes on to depict them hasten-
ing out to Boeotia (9. 19) as if the wall was of no importance. So his
wall was a very long time in not being completed; it was all-important
to the Peloponnesians before it was done and quite neglected once
it was. No explanation is offered for all of this. The Peloponnesians
knew that Mardonius was still in Greece (Herodotus speaks of him
wintering in Thessaly (9. 1, cf. 8. 113. 1), but he must have continued
to occupy Thermopylae at least, for the Persians had not fought their
way past it only to give the Greeks a second chance to deny access),
and the Greeks could not be safe as long as Mardonius had not gone
away. The Themistoclean ring of walls round Athens, roughly comparable in length to the distance from sea to sea at the Isthmus itself was

constructed in, it would seem, about a month; Herodotus' wall was not completed by the tenth month. He was convinced that it was made (cf. 7. 139. 3). No doubt it will cause outrage amongst his faithful admirers, but one must beg leave to doubt.

It is true that some sort of ineffective barrier was put across from Lechaeum to Cenchreae, consisting of ditches and palisades (Diod. 15. 68), in an attempt to keep Epaminondas out of the Peloponnese in 369 BC, but that was not at all the sort of wall Herodotus (8. 7. 1) was talking about with his stones and bricks and bags full of sand. In any case, before the Long Walls from Corinth to Lechaeum were built in the middle of the fifth century,[26] a wall from Lechaeum to the eastern side would have been pointlessly long. Indeed if there were a wall built in 480, it would surely have had to be to the north of the Diolkos, the slipway from sea to sea not infrequently used for ships of war,[27] for it would greatly have complicated the defence of the Peloponnese if part of the Persian fleet had been free to operate in the Gulf of Corinth.[28] Yet no traces remain of such a wall north of the Diolkos either on the ground (where perhaps it would not be reasonable to expect them) or in the history of the wars between Corinth and Athens in the fifth century. The suspicion arises, though it can be no more than a suspicion, that Herodotus' wall did not in fact exist.[29] One should be cautious therefore about developing an account of Greek strategy based on it. There may not have been an 'Isthmus strategy'.

When it comes to battles, Herodotus does not, generally speaking, so much arouse our suspicions as leave us largely in the dark. Yet although in the case of the defence of Thermopylae where there was no manoeuvre there is nothing seriously to trouble us,[30] the naval operations off Artemisium are perplexing. According to Herodotus, there was a string of Greek successes, beginning with the capture of fifteen ships that mistook the Greek ships for their own, followed by the capture of thirty ships in the course of the first formal engagement, then a day's lull with no more than the capture of 'Cilician ships', and finally the battle in which although 'many ships of the Greeks were being destroyed, far more ships and men of the barbarians were lost' (7. 194; 8. 11, 14, 16). Of all these captured ships no more is heard, nor indeed of any prisoners of war, and although the Greeks had acquitted themselves, it would seem, so well, Themistocles was sure that they could only succeed at Salamis if they gave the Persian no chance to exploit the nautical skills of his navy. Herodotus, as already remarked, seems to have been concerned to glorify the Athenians by discrediting the other members of the fleet and his claim that the Greeks planned to run away (8. 18) may be quite unfair; once it was known that Thermopylae had fallen (8. 21. 2), withdrawal was the only sensible course and so in no way argues that the Greeks generally understood the lesson of Artemisium. But they probably did understand it, as their unwillingness to stay and fight at Salamis shows, and those preliminary successes recounted by Herodotus are hard to credit.[31] Xerxes may have had no reason whatsoever to feel less than complete confidence in the capacity of his fleet to defeat the Greeks.

Herodotus' report of the battle of Salamis is in essence a rag-bag of stories and a proper account cannot be given. Part of our difficulty is not his fault; vastly divergent pictures of where and how the battle developed are given depending on where one locates the island of Psyttaleia,[32] about which no Athenian would have been in any doubt. It is his fault that it is unclear whether the opposing fleets faced each other in a roughly east–west direction or whether the Persian fleet attacked in a southerly direction, also that it is unclear whether Xerxes sent a squadron to cut off the Greek escape route,[33] that there is no notice of how many ships on each side were destroyed, disabled, or captured.[34] If one seeks to explain why the Persians lost that battle, Herodotus is of remarkably little help.

It is the same with the battle of Plataea. Again there is uncertainty about the topography, for the so-called 'island' on the battlefield (9. 51), mysterious to us, would perhaps have been readily identified by a fifth-century Greek. But no proper account of the battle can be given. The Persians relied very much on their cavalry and in the preliminary engagements it had operated to devastating effect, but although Herodotus says the cavalry was posted separately (9. 32. 2), he omits to say where and how it operated in the battle. So again it is not easy to explain the Persian defeat.

The final battle of Herodotus' *History*, the battle of Mycale, is quite obscure. Herodotus asserted that the Greek fleet numbered one hundred and ten ships in winter 480/479, and gave no hint of it being reinforced when it moved to the East Aegean in the course of the following summer (8. 131. 1). Nothing is said to make us think that the Greek force was other than purely naval.[35] So the number of marines cannot have amounted to much more than two or three thousand. As to the Persian forces, he had declared that in late 480 there were three hundred ships wintering in Cyme (8. 130. 2). By the late summer of 479 the Phoenician ships had been sent home (9. 96. 1) and rather than fight a sea battle against the Greek fleet the rest of the ships were at the time of the battle of Mycale beached and protected by a stockade (9. 98. 2). The Persian land forces Herodotus set at sixty thousand (9. 96. 2), declaring that they were in Mycale and that the Persian fleet moved there from Samos for protection. One suspects that the numbers are wildly inflated and that the engagement was a very minor affair.[36] Herodotus' whole account of the battle can hardly raise his credit.

One arrives at an awkward position. We have Herodotus and cannot do without him, but one cannot have great confidence in what he says. One would not wish to impugn the glory of the Father of History. One just cannot believe a great deal of what he says and one is suspicious about a great deal more. Whence then cometh understanding of why the great invasion failed? Not, at any rate, by the method of following Herodotus sentence by sentence accepting whatever one has no compelling reason to reject. The truth may well be in Herodotus but one needs some criterion for discerning truth from fancy and fiction.

Thucydides on the Great Invasion

One turns to Thucydides. His *History* does not say much about the Persian Wars, but what it does say should give one furiously to think. The principal passages are these, in the order in which they occur in the printed text.

1. In the first Corinthian speech to the Spartans in book 1 Spartan inertia in the face of both the Persian invasion of 480 BC and the present Athenian menace in 432 BC is remarked; the Spartans are told 'both that the barbarian for the most part failed because of his own mistakes, and that confronted by the Athenians we have already survived in many ways more by their mistakes than by your taking reprisals against them' (1. 69). What Thucydides makes the Corinthians refer to in the second part of this sentence is obscure.[37] Perhaps this first part is what really furnished support for what had been said about Spartan inertia.

2. In the Athenian reply to the Corinthians (1. 73. 4–74. 4), the role of Athens in the Persian Wars is discussed at length. '. . . For we declare that at Marathon on our own we faced the peril from the barbarian on behalf of Greece, and that, when he came the second time, not being able to defend ourselves by land we boarded the ships in full force and

played our part in the sea-battle at Salamis which checked him from sailing against the Peloponnese and ravaging it city by city since the Peloponnesians would have been unable to help each other confronted by many ships. The barbarian himself furnished most ample testimony to this. After he had been defeated by the navy, he promptly withdrew with the major part of his army on the grounds that he no longer possessed adequate force. Such was the outcome of that affair and the demonstration was clear that the fortunes of the Greeks lay in the ships. It was we who provided the three things most useful to that end, a very great number of ships, a commander of the highest intelligence, and thirdly resolution of the most unflinching kind, namely, a little less than two-thirds of the [three hundred][38] ships, as commander Themistocles, who was most responsible for having the sea fight in the confined waters (the thing that most plainly saved the day, and for this you paid him the greatest honour you have paid to an outsider visiting you), and as for our resolution, we displayed it to the most daring degree. When no one was coming to our aid on land and the rest of the Greeks as far south as us were already subjected, we thought fit to abandon the city and destroy our own property and even so not to quit the alliance of the remaining allies nor by scattering to become of no use to them, but we thought fit to board our ships, to face the peril and not to be enraged because you had not come to our aid in time to prevent all this . . . .'.

3. In the speech of Hermocrates to the Syracusans in 415 BC (6. 33. 5–6), he is made to say 'Few great expeditions of either Greeks or barbarians having set out a great distance from their own land have been successful. For they do not come in greater numbers than the local inhabitants and their neighbours (since out of fear there is a general banding together), and if they come to disaster in a foreign land through shortage of supplies, they leave those they plotted against a glorious reputation, even if for the most part they owe their failure to themselves. Indeed in just such a way these very Athenians, when unexpectedly many disasters befell the Mede, were magnified on the ground that he was going against Athens.'

These are challenging statements indeed, reflecting on the reasons for failure of the Great Invasion. But do they reflect Thucydides' own views? All three passages come from what others are alleged to have said and the question naturally arises whether it is right to assume that Thucydides was making his speakers express his own opinions. It would, of course, still be interesting that others should have had such thoughts, but it is much more striking if we are dealing with what the great Thucydides thought himself.

No one can be sure that Thucydides did not have detailed reports of what the Corinthians and the Athenians said at Sparta or Hermocrates at Syracuse, but he did not claim that he had such reports nor does it seem at all likely. The only real question, at any rate for most of us, is whether he fleshed out 'the general drift of what was actually said' (1. 22. 1) with his own knowledge and views of the Persian Wars, or with the sort of things that he supposed the various speakers thought. It is here argued that the comments are indeed Thucydides' own.

The claim made in Hermocrates' speech that the Persian invasion force did not outnumber the force the Greeks assembled to face them stands alone in Greek historical writing. For the rest, the fantastic picture of Herodotus prevails or, at any rate, similar totals, wild if not as wild. It is one of Thucydides' main strengths that he is, or seems, remarkably hard-headed about the numbers engaged in conflict[39] and eschews the abandoned totals one finds in Xenophon, and in the Alexander historians, as well as in Herodotus. Of course, Hermocrates may have been similarly hard-headed and similarly independent-minded but it seems more likely that this unparalleled view of 480 BC is Thucydides' own. It is not after all what one would expect to come to mind with a Syracusan; the massive but unsuccessful Carthaginian expedition of 480 would have been much more relevant.[40]

The second sign that we are dealing with Thucydides' own views is the repeated claim that the Persian failure was largely the Persians' own fault. That is absolutely without parallel, or echo.[41] Herodotus set the tone and the orators in panegyric and funeral oration, not surprisingly, do not deviate. One looks in vain in Plutarch's *Themistocles* or his *Aristides*, which in Plutarch's manner draw on a variety of sources, for any trace of such a view. It is unique to Thucydides' text. It is, one dares to assume, unique to Thucydides himself.

Thucydides' judgements are always considerable. Where he so remarkably differs from everyone else, one should pay special heed. But there is one point in which he seems to follow Herodotus that should put us on our guard against slavish acceptance.[42] He makes the Athenian speaker at Sparta argue that the greatest proof of the vital importance of the Athenian share at Salamis was provided by Xerxes himself, for 'after he had been defeated by the navy, he promptly withdrew with the major part of his army, on the grounds that he no longer possessed adequate force' (1. 73. 3). It is, however, dubitable that

Xerxes took the bulk of his army home with him directly after Salamis, though in speaking of Mardonius selecting the troops he wanted to keep (8. 113), Herodotus has fostered that impression. Xerxes was escorted by a force under Artabazus which promptly returned to the army of Mardonius (8. 126), and if Xerxes had indeed taken the bulk of his army with him as Thucydides' speaker is made to assert, there would have been no need of this escort.[43] Furthermore, a view of Persian strategy is implied in this passage that, as will be argued shortly, is unsound. As far as the Persian occupation and control of Greece was concerned, the Greek victory at Salamis was of very little importance. It was at Plataea, not at Salamis, that the new satrapy was lost and if Thucydides thought that it was Salamis that was of decisive effect, that effectively reminds us he is not infallible.

Thucydides' view of Persian numbers is, however, both startling and consonant with the other considerations which lead me to postulate low totals for the invading army and navy in 480/479. [44] If he is correct in this, one is encouraged to investigate those other striking assertions, namely, that the failure of the invasion was largely due to the Persians' own mistakes and that shortage of supplies played an important part.

The Failure of the Great Invasion

Xerxes' purpose, we may assume, was to incorporate mainland Greece within the Persian Empire and there must have seemed but one serious obstacle in his way. He had an army that had conquered India and taken Egypt, not the motley array that Herodotus' so-called Army List (7. 61–88) has led scholars into imagining, not the 'countless, voiceless, hopeless' throng of the Herodotean totals (7. 184), but a well-trained force accustomed to marching great distances and defeating the King's foes. The serious obstacle was the pass of Thermopylae, the only route into Greece for a large army with transport.[45] Once he was through that, central Greece was open and on the plain of Boeotia or on the plain of Eleusis the Greek army could be broken and he had no reason to doubt that it would. Greeks had not stood together and faced the Persian army, either in the conquest of Ionia or in the Ionian Revolt. The Marathon campaign had failed, but only because the Athenians would not risk conflict until the Persian force was withdrawing, its cavalry already, literally, *hors de combat*.[46] The Greeks of mainland Greece would be no match for his Grand Army.

Xerxes must have been well aware of the problem of Thermopylae. The basis of all successful military endeavour is reconnaissance, and Persian reconnaissance can be presumed; the voyage of the Persians accompanied by Democedes (Hdt. 3. 134. 6), spying out 'the seaward parts of Greece' was not, one may presume, untypical (cf. 3. 17. 2); in any case, Xerxes had a ready source of intelligence in the Aleuad family of Larisa, and Thessalian experience of Thermopylae had been too painful for Thessalians not to explain and emphasize the difficulty of passing through the Gates.[47] He was not to know, until he got there, of the path which the Immortals took to attack the Greeks from the rear, though he would of course have known of the route over the mountains into Phocis which Leonidas set the Phocians to guard (Hdt. 7. 212). Such a guard was only to be expected, and so in prospect he had to concentrate on assaulting and penetrating Thermopylae.

Whatever one makes of Herodotus' account of two days' fruitless assault and heavy casualties (Hdt. 7. 210–11, 8. 25), Xerxes must have realized that something else would be needed, and he therefore must have decided to use his navy to outflank the Greek defence. In the event he was successful on both land and sea and the Great Invasion began with a brilliant success. The losses suffered in the storm on the Magnesian coast are, doubtless, wildly exaggerated by Herodotus (7. 190), but they may have done sufficient damage to make it more uncertain that the Persian fleet would prevail over the Greek and render the defensive position at Thermopylae untenable. The discovery that there was a way round the Greeks by land was a piece of luck, effectively exploited, but the victory on sea was what had been planned. When it was all over, Xerxes had every reason to congratulate himself.

It may be questioned whether Artemisium really was a Persian victory. According to Herodotus (8. 16–18), the loss of ships and men on the Persian side was far heavier, and since the Greeks were 'roughly handled, not least the Athenians half whose ships had been damaged' we are left to suppose that the Persian fleet must have been very badly mauled indeed.[48] Although Herodotus asserted that the Greeks after the battle were 'planning to run away' (8. 18), his imputations of cowardice are not necessarily, as has already been remarked, to be taken seriously. Once Thermopylae had fallen, there was no point in the Greek fleet remaining, and Herodotus himself indicated (8. 21) that the withdrawal did not begin until the news of the fall of Thermopylae had arrived. So was the battle of Artemisium really a Persian victory?

The answer is provided by the conduct of Themistocles at Salamis.

He was willing to fight a sea-battle only if it was within the confined waters of the strait. Whether or not the scepticism already expressed about the Isthmus strategy (v.s. pp. 96–8) is just or excessive, Themistocles was, according to an Athenian speaker in Thucydides (1. 74. 1), 'the man most responsible for fighting the sea-battle in the strait—which most clearly saved the day'. This remark comes as no surprise, when one considers that the Phoenicians could at that stage outrow the Greeks[49] and that in the final engagement at Artemisium the Greeks adopted a defensive position, having earlier had an experience similar to that of the Corinthians in 429 when Phormio circled round them and caused them to back-water and crowd together.[50] What the Greeks had to fear was the Phoenician 'sailing through', the *diekplous*, which was followed by boarding by the large number of marines on each ship, and Themistocles was resolved to have no more of it.[51] Herodotus would have it believed that the attempt by the Persians to bring on a battle outside the strait came to nothing because it was too late in the day (8. 70). That seems unlikely. If the Persians had wanted a battle, they would have allowed time for it to be fought. It is much more likely that the Greeks would not oblige. They had learnt the lesson of Artemisium, which was that if they faced a sea-battle in the open water they would suffer most dreadfully. That battle had indeed been a Persian victory.

Once Thermopylae was cleared, Greece lay open and Xerxes must have thought that the new satrapy was virtually secured. Presumably what he most wished was a grand and decisive battle in the open space of Boeotia. At least, he must have half expected it. Would the Greeks abandon Attica? The Athenians returning to Salamis from Artemisium expected to find all the so far unengaged forces of Greece 'in full force in Boeotia in a position to resist the barbarian' (Hdt. 8. 40). The Athenians did not, according to the Athenian speaker in Thucydides (1. 74. 3), give in to fury because the Spartans did not go to the help of Athens before it was occupied by the Persians, and he is clearly referring to the plan to confront the barbarian in Boeotia, the very plan the Athenians got the Spartans in winter 480/479 to undertake to fulfil (Hdt. 8. 144. 5, 9. 6. 1 and 7β1). Since all of Boeotia save Plataea and Thespiae had signified submission to Persia and the Greeks would be in honour bound to try to save them, Xerxes could expect the defence of Attica, if defence was attempted, to be made in south and south-west Boeotia. This consideration helps to explain why, having cleared the way through Thermopylae, he seemingly turned back to begin to deal with the Greeks behind Mount Kallidromos, principally Phocis, which had not as yet medized; Xerxes doubtless meant to have no unfinished business to his rear, whence trouble could come for his army engaged in finishing off the Greek army.[52]

If Xerxes did expect battle in Boeotia, he could not have instructed the navy to sail directly to Athens without knowing what was happening in Boeotia. According to Herodotus, Xerxes did indeed arrive in Attica before the fleet sailed in to Phalerum, but that that should have happened a mere six days after the fleet and the King went their separate ways is wholly improbable (8. 51, 66). That part of the army that went through Doris and Phocis had to cover something like one hundred and fifteen kilometres to reach Thebes, through terrain at first difficult and then requiring caution as it advanced through hostile people. After Thebes lay another seventy-odd kilometres march to Athens. So even if Xerxes had expected no opposition, six days is far too short for the army to reach Athens, and something must be wrong with Herodotus' timetable,[53] but whatever the correct timetable was, the fleet's arrival must have been planned not to precede that of the army. Since Xerxes must have expected that the Greeks would not let him pass into Attica unopposed, he must have had some system of communicating with the fleet to keep it apprised of where he was. This in itself is of no great consequence, but it does raise the major question of what Xerxes wanted the fleet for, once the strong point of Thermopylae had been cracked.

One important use of the fleet was to convoy supply ships. As long as the army was in Persian-controlled territory, carefully prepared supply dumps provided for the army, and although Herodotus does not say as much, by winter 480 Thessaly must have been suitably supplied to feed as much of the army as wintered there. In summer 480, however, south of Macedonia supplies must either have been carried on the person and transported by wagon or beast of burden, or have been provided by the supply ships.[54] Herodotus puts the number of such ships at three thousand, too low for his invading millions, probably considerably higher than the truth, but they certainly must have played a vital part. So regardless of the use of the fleet for battle, it was essential for convoying. But this was the case only for the summer of 480. Once these supply ships had discharged their cargoes finally in Athens, there was nothing further for them to do and presumably they returned whence they had come. Many of them had probably departed after Thermopylae, the rest by the time that Salamis had been fought and lost. The use of the battle fleet for the protection of lines of supply was finished once the last supply ships had reached Athens.[55]

After Salamis the Persian occupation of Greece continued, unaffected by the lack of a naval force. In 479, after the fleet had departed, Mardonius is alleged to have advanced into the territory of Megara (Hdt. 9. 14). The fact that there were Greek ships possibly at no great distance seems not to have deterred him. In the long history of armies passing and re-passing to and from the Peloponnese, to and from Attica, naval power never asserts itself, and after Salamis Greek naval power and Persian lack of naval power was utterly irrelevant to whether the new Persian satrapy could be maintained.

The question therefore arises what use his naval power was to Xerxes after Thermopylae apart from the work of convoy. Did he have to fight the battle of Salamis at all or indeed any naval battle anywhere? It is constantly asserted that until the Greek navy had been defeated at Salamis or induced to move elsewhere the Persian army could not advance towards the Isthmus. If, later, Sparta was never to be deterred from advancing into Attica, one finds it hard to believe that Persia was deterred in 480. Herodotus at any rate does not seem so to have believed, rather the reverse. He reports (8. 71. 1) that the night before the battle the Persian infantry began to march towards Peloponnese, a barely credible story, for no more is heard of the matter and it was far too late to be seeking to influence the Greek naval commanders by such a move, but Herodotus believed it, unmoved by the thought that until the Greek navy had been defeated, no advance of the land army would alarm anyone. Indeed, if Xerxes had dismissed his fleet after the battle of Artemisium, what could the Greek fleet have done to impede his progress? His army had marched from Thermopylae to Athens carrying its own supplies. It could have done likewise in marching from Athens to the Isthmus. Is it to be thought that the marines on the Greek ships might be landed to the rear of the Persian advance? But one never hears of Greek naval forces adopting such strategies. In any case the Persian High Command could have taken precautions. There was, in short, no need to have a sea battle before the land army advanced.

Was there any need to have a sea battle at all? Of course, if the Greek navy was ready to come out and fight in open water, Xerxes could be confident of the result. But if the Greeks persisted in staying within the strait, what harm to his cause would ensue if he let them continue there? The answer will be made that if Xerxes could advance to the Isthmus without his navy, to get past the famous Isthmus Wall he needed the navy to outflank it. But if there ever was such a wall in 480 and 479, if, that is, one's doubts about Herodotus' account of it must be swallowed, is it really to be thought that such a wall, six kilometres long, would have been impenetrable by the Royal Army? Whatever there was there, it can hardly have been a veritable Great Wall of China, built to keep out hordes of barbarians for centuries. The troops that escorted Xerxes back to Thrace were not long delayed by the wall of Olynthus (Hdt. 8. 127). The Plataeans and the Thespiaeans did not think it worth their while to stay trusting their walls (Hdt. 8. 50). The Greeks knew what had happened to Sardis in 546 and to the cities of Ionia in the Ionian Revolt. Are we then to suppose that the Persians needed the navy to outflank this wall? It frankly seems absurd. If the Persians had wanted to get on with the assault on the Peloponnese, they could happily have set out to do so without naval assistance.

Why then did Xerxes want a naval battle that was not strictly necessary? His campaign had been brilliantly successful. He had achieved the most difficult military feat in breaking in to Greece, victorious on land and sea, and the Greeks would neither come out to face his army nor sail out to face his fleet. How long was he to stay? The Emperor Claudius spent a mere sixteen days in Britain at the head of his army— *satis diu vel naturae vel gloriae*. One cannot know but one suspects that just as Darius' so-called Scythian Expedition involved him personally in only one season's campaign and he returned home leaving Megabazus to mop up and round off the conquest; so too Xerxes never intended to spend more time in Greece than the time he actually did spend; Mardonius could be left to finish it off. The fleet had done what he had needed it for, and it could be sent home. But the total destruction of the Greek fleet must have been appealing to the grandeur of the King of Kings. If the Greeks would not fight in open sea, they could not be expected to put up much resistance anywhere.

Herodotus would have it thought that Xerxes was moved to order battle by a message sent the night before the engagement by Themistocles saying that the Greeks were planning to run away and their morale was so bad that they would turn on each other rather than put up a fight against the Persian fleet. There should be no doubt that a message of some sort was sent; the slave who carried it was rewarded after the invasion, and the ruse was alluded to in 472 by Aeschylus in the *Persae*.[56] There should equally be no doubt that the message had no part in persuading Xerxes to fight. The fleet set out at midnight and in Herodotus' account the message was sent by night, too late therefore to influence the Persian High Command, for preparations would have had to be begun long before that. But if Aeschylus' version is the correct one and the message was sent the day before, even so it would hardly have stirred the Persians to go in and fight within the strait, if they had not already decided to do so. Of course, if they had so decided, news of low morale and the likelihood of some Greeks medizing would have been encouraging. But if the Persians were still hoping for the Greeks to come out, the news that they were about to run away would have been good news indeed;[57] either they would fight in open water or they would scatter, never to reassemble. It would certainly not prompt the Persians into entering the strait. The message went but it did not influence the course of events.

Xerxes himself in his grandeur for the sake of his own grandeur took the fatal decision to fight the needless fight—*folie de grandeur* indeed—and whatever other Persian errors Thucydides had in mind, this was the error *in excelsis*. By entering the strait the fleet was deprived of room to manoeuvre. The Phoenicians could outrow the Greeks but they needed space for that and for their favourite manoeuvre that depended on it, the *diekplous*. Instead of 'sailing through', turning, overtaking and boarding enemy ships, they were rammed, a new experience. Where previously they had always 'captured' enemy ships, they were now finding themselves disabled (cf. Appendix 1). Xerxes' whole plan had gone sadly awry. He had not destroyed the Greek fleet and he had to set out whence he came without this crowning glory.

But how serious was the defeat? Many Greek ships were 'taken' according to Herodotus, but he gives no casualty figures. Diodorus says that forty Greek ships were destroyed, 'over two hundred Persian quite apart from those which were captured with all hands'. Ctesias (F13 §30) says that in the battle seven hundred Greek ships confronted 'over a thousand' Persian, of which five hundred were destroyed. Justin (2. 12. 27) says that 'many were captured, many sunk'. From Aeschylus (*Persae* 272–330), one gets the impression of enormous carnage. One suspects that all this is more colourful than truthful. Certainly the Corinthians, who the Greeks in general attested played a leading part in the battle (Hdt. 8. 94), had some casualties, and 'the sailors of Diodorus', one of the Corinthian trierarchs, made a dedication of Persian arms, 'memorials of the sea-fight'.[58] It is also to be remarked that in late 480 the Greek fleet that came to Aegina was one hundred and ten ships strong (Hdt. 8. 131), that is, just over one third of the figure of Aeschylus for the battle (*Persae* 339–40). No doubt a good number were kept at home and in the case of Athens she would shortly need a good number of those who had fought in the sea-battle to fight on land. Even so, one wonders whether the Greek naval losses had been heavier than Herodotus and Aeschylus let on. What is more striking is that, according to Herodotus (8. 96. 1, 108. 1), after the battle the Greeks expected that the Persians would renew the conflict and even as they followed after the departed fleet they still so expected. Perhaps the truth was that the glorious battle of Salamis was above all the demonstration to the Persians that they were not all powerful; if the Greeks continued to stay within the strait, they were invincible. Prudently the Persians sent the fleet home rather than try again to win the battle they had not needed to fight.

It has been argued above that once the Persian army had broken the Greek hold on Thermopylae and the supply ships had reached Attica, the fleet was no longer necessary for the securing of the new satrapy. But how was the army to proceed? Mardonius' strategy in 479 seems clear enough. He was looking for a major engagement on suitable terrain, which in effect meant Boeotia, where his cavalry could manoeuvre more freely than it could on the plain of Eleusis (Hdt. 9. 13. 3) and where he could base himself on a friendly Thebes. According to Herodotus (9. 3. 2), and it is one detail about his dates for events in the Great Invasion that seems secure, Mardonius reoccupied Athens nine months after Xerxes had captured the Acropolis. The delay is a clear sign that Mardonius was hoping, as indeed the Athenians were expecting, that the Greeks would come out and fight in Boeotia, and that if he could induce them to do so he would not approach the Isthmus. He did, before leaving Attica, make a move towards Megara, and his cavalry did overrun the territory of Megara (Hdt. 9. 14), and his purpose is unclear, for he shortly withdrew. Herodotus would have it thought that he withdrew because he was informed that the Greeks were assembled at the Isthmus, thus implying that his purpose in moving towards Megara was to move to the unguarded Peloponnese. If, however, he had intended to go to the Isthmus, he was remarkably slow doing so. It seems more likely that he thought that by ravaging the Megarid he would provide one more inducement for the Spartans and the Peloponnesians to come out and fight for those in the Greek alliance and not leave them to suffer; when he heard that the Peloponnesians were assembled at the Isthmus, he withdrew hoping the Greeks would follow.

It may be countered that a story in Herodotus (9. 12) about the Argives argues the opposite, that Mardonius did not want the Spartans, or presumably the Peloponnesians generally, to come out of the Peloponnese. The Argives are said to have sent a runner to Mardonius to inform him that they had been unable to prevent the Spartans marching out, although, according to Herodotus, they had previously promised Mardonius that they would do so. So, if this story is literally correct, Mardonius must have wanted the Spartans and their following to be confined to the Peloponnese. The story is, however, very unsatisfactory. As Macan, with his customary irony, commented, 'how this *hēmerodromos* (runner) got past the Isthmus wall, which was no doubt guarded from sea to sea, Herodotus does not say'. If, as has above (see pp. 97–8) been wickedly opined, there was no wall, Herodotus' runner does not need to have been a hurdler into the bargain, but what did the Argives pretend to Mardonius that they could do to stop the Spartans marching out of Sparta? Perhaps they could have deterred the Spartans by fear of the troubles that might be caused in their absence but the Argive promise that they would check the Spartans from marching out implies something more active. Nor was their alleged undertaking held against them, it would seem, after the Persian defeat and withdrawal. Perhaps it was only a story, expressing the same hostility as the story (7. 152) that it was the Argives who actually summoned the Persians to attack Greece. The truth is probably told elsewhere in Herodotus (8. 73), viz. that 'by sitting on the fence they favoured the Persian cause'. No more than that, and this fabled message should not be allowed to make one suppose that Mardonius was not wanting a great and decisive battle in Boeotia.

479 is clear. Was it different in 480? Did Xerxes intend to march to and through the Isthmus? Not a word is said by Herodotus to suggest that Xerxes was wanting to draw the Peloponnesians out to ground of his choosing. When Demaratus is made to give his opinion on strategy (7. 234–5), he counsels naval attack on Laconia, which is the alternative to having to confront the confederate Peloponnesians in the 'narrow Isthmus'; the presumption seems to be that Xerxes will, one way or another, be penetrating the Peloponnese. Artemisia (8. 68) counsels him not to fight a sea-battle at Salamis, but to keep his fleet at Phalerum or even, leaving it there, to advance against the Peloponnese;[59] again, Xerxes' sole objective would seem to be the Peloponnese. As already remarked, Demaratus' speech seems to presuppose a numerical naval superiority which existed in Herodotus' mind rather than in fact, and one can easily disregard it. Artemisia's is more credible, in that it is not to be excluded that Herodotus heard in his native city report of what

Artemisia said she had said to the Great King, but it seems more likely that all Herodotus heard was that she had opposed the plan of bringing on a sea-battle within the strait and that the rest is his own. One must add that the night before the battle he has the Persian land army 'marching against the Peloponnese' (8. 71. 1). Nothing more is heard of this movement. Herodotus gives it neither purpose nor consequence. It sounds like nothing so much as the sort of groundless rumours that sweep through all armies. It certainly should not be taken as evidence that Xerxes intended to push on to the Isthmus. There is in fact no good evidence for what he planned to do with his army in October 480.[60] The battle of Salamis may have been an appalling upset to his plans. Alternatively, he may have decided before this battle that unless the Peloponnesians came out very shortly there was no chance of a decisive engagement while he was himself in Greece and he would have to leave the work of pacification to Mardonius and the next summer. Certainly a decisive battle would have been much preferable to a series of sieges within the Peloponnese which would have caused problems of supply, not only severe but probably insuperable.

The Persian decision to retire from Attica was, it would seem, a serious error. A winter on Salamis for the Athenians without adequate provisions and no sure prospect of return would have been unendurable, and they would either have had to submit or do what Themistocles is said to have threatened in the debate before the battle of Salamis, migrate westwards (8. 62). The explanation of the Persian withdrawal is presumably that the army could not be properly supplied if the bulk of it did not winter in Thessaly, where provision had been made. That may have been partly what Thucydides (6. 33. 5) had in mind when he made Hermocrates speak of 'shortage of supplies'.

Nonetheless, Mardonius must have returned to the task in 479 confidently enough. On the plain of Boeotia, if only he could get the Greeks there, his cavalry would assert its power and the Greeks would not be able to withstand it.

He waited in Boeotia. They did not come. He moved to Attica, reoccupied Athens, and invited the Athenians to join him. The Peloponnesians had not yet assembled at the Isthmus, this allegedly impenetrable place, and he could have invaded had he chosen. Why were the Spartans and the Peloponnesians so slow to come to the defence of their allies, Athens and Megara? Certainly to claim that religious festivals detained the Spartans will not suffice. Although, at the moment the Athenians issued their threatening appeal, the Spartans were scrupulously observing the festival of Hyacinthia (Hdt. 9. 7–11), there was plenty of time earlier for them to take the field. Religion did not impede Sparta and her allies from invading Attica before the Hyacinthia in the Archidamian War. So as an explanation for their delay in 479 religion will not do. It is commonly believed that it was fear of a Helot Revolt that deterred the Spartans.[61] In 490 they sent only two thousand to Marathon (Hdt. 6. 120), and too late at that, and the assertion of Plato (*Laws* 698e) that they were prevented by 'the war at that time against Messene' provides an explanation probably correct. So they certainly had good reason to fear in 479. Yet they did finally march out taking, Herodotus alleges (9. 29. 2), seven Helots a Spartiate. Why did they not do so earlier? The Spartans at any rate did not lack courage and the best explanation one can give is that the Peloponnesians, generally speaking, did or that they were all so pessimistic about the chances of victory that they preferred to stay at home and avoid the inevitable defeat.[62] Herodotus, however, represents the dilatoriness as entirely Spartan, and the Spartan failure to act before Athens threatened to submit to Persia and so put their navy at the disposal of Mardonius remains somewhat mysterious.

Mysterious too is the Greek strategy once the assembled Greek army advanced into Boeotia. Refusal to do battle on terrain not advantageous to one's own army is of course sound strategy provided other advantages are not being lost thereby, but Pausanias' inactivity was very far from masterly. During the ten days the Greeks delayed, they were sorely afflicted by the Persian army. The supply column which was bringing food from the Peloponnese was cut off (Hdt. 9. 39). Mardonius' cavalry kept attacking and inflicting casualties (9. 40); in Herodotus' words, 'when the cavalry rode against them, they did damage to the whole Greek army with their javelins and arrows, since they were mounted archers and difficult to engage' (9. 49. 2). Mardonius then had the Gargaphian spring fouled up, thus depriving the Greeks of their water supply, and the Greeks were forced to plan their move to the celebrated (and, to us, mysterious) 'island' (9. 50). Mardonius, not Pausanias, was master. Why did not Pausanias act? He could hardly withdraw from Boeotia for that would have been, in effect, to acknowledge that the Greeks could not win and that it was time for individual states to secure for themselves what terms they could. If he moved the army along the northern slopes of Cithaeron, it would not cease to be exposed to the attacks of mounted archers which were proving so costly. The only thing he could do if he was not to be at the mercy of the Persians was to advance across the Asopus river to the plain and fight a battle. There can be only one explanation why he did not. He and the other generals felt there was no hope of victory. Indeed a mood of something akin to despair came on the Greek army generally, if Herodotus (9. 52) is to be believed. Once the plan to move to the island during the following night had been taken 'all that day the cavalry kept attacking and the Greeks had unabating toil, and when the day was drawing to a close and the cavalry had desisted, night was coming on and it was the time at which it had been agreed that they should move off, then the majority once they had risen and begun to move, not having it in mind to move to the place which had been agreed, gladly fled from the cavalry to the city of Plataea . . .'. The Persian cavalry had been too much for them.

The Greek inactivity is inexplicable. The Persian decision to attack likewise needs explanation. The strategy of cavalry attack was proving so successful that, as long as the Greeks were not willing to cross the Asopus and fight, it was the best way of attack. If the Greeks moved westwards to secure themselves a different line of supply,[63] what the cavalry had done once could no doubt be done again and that route too could be cut off. So Mardonius' decision to attack is somewhat surprising. The day of the general engagement began, if we may trust Herodotus (9. 57. 3), with an attack of the whole Persian cavalry. Earlier attacks had been by divisions (9. 20, 22), and that was no doubt how they were kept up all day long. The full-scale cavalry attack argues that Mardonius intended a full-scale battle even before he knew of the Greeks changing their position, if, that is, Herodotus is to be trusted when he says that the cavalry expected to find them where they had previously been. Consistently with this, he represents Alexander of Macedon as saying that Mardonius was intent on a full engagement (9. 45. 2), at least two days before the battle took place. So it can hardly be argued that Mardonius rashly attacked when he thought the Greeks were on the run. Why then did he decide to attack?

In Herodotus' account of the night visit of Alexander of Macedon to the Athenian generals he is made to assert that Mardonius' food supplies would last only a few days (9. 52. 2), which accords with what Artabazus is said to have said to Mardonius in advising withdrawal to Thebes (9. 41. 2). One would hesitate to make much of such remarks, if it were not that Thucydides ascribed Persian failure in Greece to 'shortage of supplies' (6. 33. 5), a remark to which considerable importance should be ascribed. It may therefore be proposed that the real reason why Mardonius attacked was that he was going to have to with-draw shortly and he could not leave the Greeks in possession of the field, seemingly victorious.

In a broad sense the battle of Plataea made plain what had not been plain before, namely the superiority of the Greek hoplite to Oriental infantry. The minor engagements of the Ionian Revolt and earlier had involved only small numbers of hoplites probably well outnumbered. Marathon was no real contest, if it is correct that the Persians were withdrawing when the Athenians attacked. Plataea was a 'fierce battle that went on for a long time' (9. 62. 2). 'The Persians were not inferior in courage or strength' Herodotus continues, 'but not being hoplites and in addition not being trained, they were no match for the skill of their opponents . . . it was a contest of men without the protection of hoplite armour against hoplites'. As Aeschylus noted (*Persae* 85–6, 147–9, 239–40), it was a match between spear and bow, and ever after the Persians would seek to have in their armies hoplites when hoplites were to be faced, even in remote zones as the story of Xenophon's *Anabasis* shows. So the battle was lost.

Yet it was a needless battle. If Mardonius had been able to continue his cavalry's harassing attacks, the Greeks would in all likelihood have begun to melt away, leaving all Greece north of the Isthmus secure-ly in the new satrapy and the Athenians and the Megarians to save themselves either by migration or by submission; in either case their not inconsiderable forces would not be available for the Peloponnese. Sooner or later, starting with the populous cities of the north, Mar-donius would have had his way. A needless battle indeed, save for the failure of the commissariat. For Persia a tragic mistake due merely to shortage of supplies. As to the Greeks, for their victory at Plataea, as at Salamis, they had only themselves largely not to thank. That, at least, is the view of the speakers in Thucydides.

Plataea was decisive. No matter what condition the Persian army was in after the battle (Herodotus' account barely allows us to know),[64] the shortage of supplies which had forced them to fight forced them to depart quickly, and so they went from Greece, 'bag and baggage' from the satrapy they had 'desolated and profaned',[65] and though loyal commanders clung on at the crossing of the Strymon and at Doriscus dominating the lower Hebrus (Hdt. 7. 106–7), with the siege of Sestos ended in the winter the Asiatic power in Europe was virtually beyond recovery, and though the Kings might dream of and scheme for return, they never would. Indeed, shortly the Greek cities of the Aegean seaboard were in revolt. For much of this the Persians were themselves to blame. The dismissal in Asia of the main part of the fleet before the battle of Mycale (Hdt. 9. 96. 1) was indeed a serious error. The Greek naval offensive of 479 seems to have come as a complete surprise (Hdt. 9. 116. 3). The Persians never had a true naval strategy; if there was no army for a fleet to move along the coast beside, they saw no point in having a fleet. Just as the un-nautical Spartans in 479 thought that the Greeks of Asia could not be defended from the power of the hinterland (Hdt. 9. 106), so too the even more landlubberly Persians could see no use in keeping the fleet in readiness in 479, though it must be admitted that if Mardonius had not failed, the Greeks of Asia would probably have continued to submit. It was left to the highly nautical Athenians to perceive that the defence of Ionia was naval, paradox indeed. The battle of Mycale was a minor matter. Its consequences were major.

NOTES

1. The prophet Isaiah (41: 5) shows how 'coasts and islands' viewed the coming of the Persian. For Darius' strategic plan, Briant: 1996 171.
2. Cf. Beloch 1916: 86. He is followed by Hignett 1963: 87, but not by Lazenby 1993: 45–6.
3. V.s. p. 51.
4. At Chaeronea in 338 BC Philip of Macedon with an army of 'over 30,000 foot and no less than 2,000 horse' (Diod. 16. 85. 5) faced the united Greeks, and whatever one makes of Herodotus' tally of Greek hoplites at Plataea in 479 (9. 28 and 29), concerning which differing views have been held (cf. Hignett 1963: 435–8), Mardonius in 490 could have had as many as he considered adequate to deal with the Greeks, as many perhaps as he had at Plataea in 479 (cf. pp. 249–50).
5. The notice in the *Suda* s.v. Χωρὶς ἱππεῖς has been variously employed. Cf. Shrimpton 1980.
6. Cf. Harrison 1972. M. Robertson 1975: i. 348 more circumspectly speaks of 'scenes from the Persian wars', and there seems no reason to identify this scene with one incident of the Persian wars rather than another. (Similarly, Vanderpool 1966: 105 declared that the scene on the Brescia Sarcophagus concerned Marathon.) The temple of Athena Nike belongs to the 440s at the earliest (cf. *CAH* v² 125 n. 21 and 219). It is absurd to treat the sculpture as a precise record of events forty or fifty years past, and it is a refinement of fancy to suppose that the artist of the temple of Athena Nike was reproducing what he saw in the painting in the Painted Porch.

7. Cf. Morrison, Coates, and Rankov 2000: 227–30. According to Thuc. 2. 56. 2, triremes were converted for horse transport for the first time in 430 BC, which is consistent with Herodotus speaking of ἱππαγωγὰ πλοῖα (6. 48. 2, 7. 21. 2). Whatever these were like, one could hardly suppose that getting horses aboard them was as quickly accomplished as getting tanks onto tank landing-craft.

8. Shrimpton 1980: 29 argued, however, that the Sacae in the Persian centre (6. 113. 1) were cavalry.

9. Cf. Loraux 1986: 157–69.

10. The early issues of Larisan coinage were on the Persian standard (Kraay 1976: 115). Cf. T. Martin 1985: 34.

11. According to Herodotus, Athens had 180 ships both at Artemisium and at Salamis (8. 1. 1 and 14. 1 and 8. 44. 1). The figure for Salamis is highly suspect, for he seems to have taken no account of the losses at Artemisium where 'half the Athenian ships had been damaged' (8. 18), 'many Greek ships having been destroyed' (8. 16. 3), and that the Plataean help in manning the Athenian ships at Artemisium was not available for Salamis (8. 1. 1 and 44. 1). But even if the Athenian numbers were reduced to, say, 120, that would still have required over 21,000 oarsmen fully to man them.

Wallinga 1993: 171–8 presented a picture of habitually undermanned ships. Obviously on occasion generals had to make do with less than a full complement. Quite apart from disease, an ever present possibility for large forces, desertion by non-citizen oarsmen was common (cf. Xen. *Hell* 1. 5. 4 and Thuc. 1. 143. 1, 7. 13. 2, 8. 45. 2, etc.), but since a fully manned ship must have been more effective than a partly manned, it would have been madness regularly to send out ships that would be at a disadvantage against a fully manned enemy. (For Wallinga's theory, see p. 229.) There was no point in the Athenians building in the late 480s ships they could not put to the best possible use against the Phoenicians. They must have relied then, as later, on mercenary labour. Wallinga points triumphantly to the figure of 100 Athenians per ship in the Themistocles Decree (l. 32) as confirmation that in 480 the Athenian navy was considerably undermanned. For reasons advanced elsewhere (Appendix 6) I side with those who hold that that decree is not authentic, but it may still be asked whence the 4th-cent. forger fetched this figure of 100 per ship, if it was not regular practice in the navy of his day to have in an emergency two-thirds of the oarsmen citizens and metics and to complete the manning as best could be done. The navy at all times needed mercenary oarsmen. In 480 even the Plataeans, who were quite inexperienced in such matters, had to be used to complete the manning of the ships (Hdt. 8. 1. 1) and one possible explanation of the late arrival of 53 Athenian ships at Artemisium (Hdt. 8. 14. 1) is that there had been delays in completing the manning of ships.

       Herodotus did not mention this mercenary element perhaps because it was so normal by his time that it could be taken for granted.

12. Corinth provided 40 triremes and Megara 20 (Hdt. 8. 1. 1, 43, 44. 2). If Aegina which provided 30 ships could hold some in reserve (8. 46. 1), presumably Corinth and Megara could have done better than they did.

13. 7. 210. 2, 223. 3, 9. 70. 5, 7. 101–4.

14. Cf. Appendix 4. Hammond in *CAH* IV² 532 pronounces Herodotus' totals for the land army 'absurd exaggeration' but clings to his total for the navy.

15. Arr. *Anab.* 2. 18 and 19, Diod. 17. 40–2, Curtius Rufus 4. 2 and 3 describe the building of the mole at Tyre by Alexander. Clearly the Persians would have had great difficulty in completing and landing from a mole over to Salamis. Ctesias F13 §26 has Xerxes begin to build the mole *before* the battle of Salamis, but if the Persians had won the sea-battle, the mole would have been unnecessary and, if they lost it, militarily useless. Hammond, *CAH* IV² 569 credits the account of Ctesias but does not discuss the time the mole would have taken to complete or its military use, merely describing it as a 'serious undertaking begun before the battle and continued after it'. Burn 1984: 467 appears of a like mind: 'Xerxes resumed (Herodotus says, began) preparations for bridging the strait.' Such comments make one blush.

16. On the various possible routes, see Hammond in *CAH* IV² 546, a discussion that causes amazement if it were true that Xerxes chose to cut a road where Herodotus says (7. 131) rather than use the available routes. On any view of Xerxes' route, however, Gonnus, which certainly was Perrhaebian (Strabo 9. 5. 19 440C), must be a mistake.

17. Beloch 1916: 87–90.

18. Cf. Hignett 1963: 162–7.

19. For the strategic importance of Thermopylae, see Appendix 5. Four thousand in Thermopylae itself (cf. Hignett 1963: 116) was a force quite adequate for its defence (cf. Evans 1969: 393–5). The position was secured in 352 against Philip by five thousand Athenians and though a further three thousand Lacedaemonians and Aetolians were expected, the Athenian force alone was sufficient to deter Philip from trying (Diod. 16. 37. 3, Dem. 19. 318–19). Likewise in 346 a force of fifty triremes which could hardly transport more than a moderately sized force of land troops was, it would seem, deemed sufficient to prevent Philip getting through the Gates (Aesch. 2. 37).

20. The principal difficulty in Herodotus' account is that the ten thousand hoplites which he says were sent out while Xerxes was still engaged in crossing the Hellespont, would have had to be in position for about two months before confronting the Persian army, a quite unprecedented situation which would have required elaborate provisioning of a sort undreamt

of by the Greeks of the early 5th cent. (N. Robertson 1976 argued that Damastes, *FGH* 5 F4, which he took to mean that the Greeks encamped not in Tempe but at Heracleum between Olympus and the coast, made more strategic sense than Herodotus' version. On this one may beg to differ, but the problem of how such a large force was to be supplied for so long remains.) Hignett's notion of a 'demonstration in force' 'intended to encourage the anti-Persian elements in Thessaly to come out into the open' (Hignett 1963: 103) is probably the best that can be made of it. When this large force withdrew from Thessaly, it returned, according to Herodotus (7. 173. 4), to the Isthmus, and it was not until the Persians were in Pieria (7. 177) that a force was sent out to defend Thermopylae. That must have been quite a time after the Thessalian venture, and suggests that it had not been intended that the force should take up and hold a position denying Xerxes access to Thessaly.

21. V.s. n. 19.

22. There is another troubling matter. According to Herodotus (7. 175. 2), the Greeks did not know that there was a route by which their defensive position at Thermopylae could be attacked from the rear. This is curious, since the Phocians were not of those who gave earth and water to the King's heralds (7. 132. 1) and presumably shared in the deliberations at the Isthmus (7. 145. 1). Why did they not put the rest of the loyal Greeks right when the decision was made to hold Thermopylae (7. 175. 1)? Leonidas did not know about this route, Herodotus asserts, until they reached Thermopylae. Yet the thousand Phocian hoplites had, he further asserts (7. 212. 2), been posted on the mountain to guard the path. When, one wonders, did they receive these orders? They are said to have volunteered to guard the path across the mountain (7. 217. 2). Yet when Hydarnes' troops came on the scene, after a preliminary skirmish the Phocians withdrew to the top of the mountain (7. 218. 3), expecting destruction, only to be disregarded by Hydarnes, who descended to the destruction below. So, when and how did the Phocians receive the orders which they largely disobeyed?

It may therefore be postulated that the thousand Phocians placed themselves to 'defend their own land' (Herodotus' phrase at 7. 217. 2), and the further role of guarding the path Anopaea was added by Herodotus himself who did not fully understand what he purported to recount.

23. Diod. 11. 16. 3, which makes the fortification of the Isthmus the result of a decree of the Hellenic League passed when some of the Greeks were restive at the prospect of fighting the naval battle off Salamis. (So in 11. 15. 3 the genitive absolute clause must have a conditional sense.) It is to be noted that Diodorus said that the extent of this wall was of forty stades, from Lechaeum to Cenchreae, precisely those terminal points he named for the defences of 369 BC (15. 68. 3) to which they seem more apposite. His two notices are remarkably similar.

24. Cf. Busolt 1895: 715 n. l.
25. For the date of the Hyacinthia, cf. *PW* ix.i 1. It appears to have taken place during the Attic month of Thargelion, roughly May/June. Hdt. 9. 3. 2 says that Mardonius reoccupied Athens in the tenth month after its capture by Xerxes.
26. Cf. Salmon 1984: 180.
27. Salmon 1984: 136–8.
28. This consideration rules out the suggestion that a stretch of wall on the crest of high ground further south was part of a wall constructed in 480; it has been pronounced by Wiseman 1978: 60–2 to have 'a fifth century appearance', but the dating of walls is notoriously uncertain.
29. Macan's comment (1908) on the Argive courier (9. 12. 1) is to be savoured. 'How this ἡμεροδρόμος got past the Isthmus wall, which was no doubt guarded from sea to sea, Herodotus does not say.' There was either no wall or no courier, or possibly neither.
30. For the theory of Szemler, Cherf, and Kraft 1996, see Appendix 5.
31. Herodotus (8. 11. 2) gives the name of a prominent Cyprian captured in the penultimate engagement and declares that Lycomedes on that occasion was the first Athenian to capture a barbarian ship and so won the prize of valour, details which seem to give his narrative credibility. Plutarch (*Them.* 15. 3) assigns Lycomedes' exploit to Salamis, but, as Lazenby 1993: 195 remarks, at Salamis ramming largely prevailed and the capture of a ship by Lycomedes seems more likely to have occurred at Artemisium. So that episode cannot be used to discredit Herodotus' account of the capture of these thirty ships. One can only suspect his account because it seems to have been all too easy. Did the Greeks suffer no losses in this first engagement, so differently from the main battle (8. 16. 3 and 18)? And what of the action of the next day when striking at the same late hour of the day the Greeks destroyed 'Cilician ships' (8. 14. 2)? Was the Persian High Command caught off their guard a second time? Some scepticism is inevitable.
32. Hammond (cf. *CAH* iv² 579) adheres to his view that the island of St George is Psyttaleia, but most scholars agree in identifying it with Lipsokoutali (cf. Lazenby 1993: 179 n. 44, and Ernst Meyer, *PW* Suppl. xiv 566–71).
33. Diodorus 11. 17. 2 says as much explicitly; Aeschylus, *Persae* 368 seems to assert it. Hdt. 8. 79. 4 can be taken to suggest it and the part played by the Corinthians, in flight on the Athenian story, was in the eyes of the rest of Greece of major importance (8. 94), but he stops short of explaining what the Corinthians actually accomplished, even though their epitaph (ML 24) claimed that they had 'captured Phoenician ships and Persians and Medes'. What Herodotus did do was create great uncertainty (contrast Hignett 1963: 220–2 and Burn 1984: 453). He cannot be blamed for not

explaining what did not happen but he is much at fault for not explaining what the Corinthians were about.

34. Diodorus 11. 19. 3 gives losses of forty Greek ships and over two hundred of the Persians' apart from those captured with all those on board. Whatever the truth was, some statement was due.

35. Herodotus' mention (9. 98. 2) of gangways (ἀποβάθραι) is curious, in that all ships must have had one (cf. Morrison, Coates, and Rankov 2000: 162). How otherwise would the crew have got on or off? Herodotus must have mentioned them here because the Greeks would have needed them for boarding ships which were taller (Plut. *Them.* 14. 3), no doubt at least two per trireme. (Cf. Masaracchia 1998: 203, and Flower and Marincola 2002: 273.)

36. The figure of 60,000 at 9. 96. 2 is 'obviously excessive' (Masaracchia 1998: 202) and the concentration of such a force on Mycale would be baffling if it were not wholly improbable. The Tigranes said to be in command is a shadowy figure. If he was the Tigranes named at 7. 62 (as accepted by Flower and Marincola 2002: 271), that can only reinforce arguments against taking seriously the list given by Herodotus (7. 61–99) to record the army of 480 BC (cf. pp. 239–43). (If the name Tigranes given in most manuscripts at 8. 26 and retained by Stein and Macan was what Herodotus wrote, he cannot be the same man, present at Artemisium and left behind in Ionia.) Whoever the Tigranes of 9. 96 was, he had presumably no great force of troops to judge by their feeble performance against what must have been a small number of hoplites. Perhaps the Persian naval force that moved from Samos to Mycale was too weak in numbers to take on the fleet of Leotychidas, and made the move because Tigranes' force happened to be in that area. It is hard to accept Herodotus' statement (9. 96. 1) that the Persian commanders dismissed the Phoenician ships at the very moment when they might be useful. All in all, the battle of Mycale was in itself a very minor one, though of course its outcome had the major consequence of the revolt of Ionia (9. 104).

37. Gomme 1945 ad loc. thought that the speaker was referring to Athenian rashness before the battle of Coronea and in going on the Egyptian expedition, but if that is all there is to the remark it does not seem much.

38. *Pace* Gomme 1945 and also S. Hornblower 1991 ad 1. 74. 1, it seems best to follow Poppo and Stahl in their preference for the reading τριακοσίας found in one manuscript.

39. Thucydides did not furnish numbers indiscriminately. Cf. Rubincam 1979 for analysis of his method. At 2. 98. 3, in giving the number of that innumerable throng of Thracians that swarmed down on Macedonia, like locusts (Ar. *Ach.* 150), Thucydides carefully added, 'it is said'. For the rest, his numbers are cautious and credible. 'Over 40,000' on the last march from Syracuse has been questioned but, since there is no knowing

how many camp-followers there were, questioned vainly. He was well aware of the range of numbers involved in the battle of Mantinea in 418 BC and the total number cannot have been very large. When Thucydides pronounced it 'the greatest battle between Greek armies for a very long time' (5. 74. 1), he showed his sober approach to numbers generally. His statements of naval strengths are careful. He is emphatic that precisely 147 Phoenician ships came as far as Aspendus in 411 (8. 87. 3); he qualified with μάλιστα the seemingly unrounded number of 73 ships, which Demosthenes took to Sicily in 413, although 'the several constituents of this fleet enumerated by Thucydides add up to exactly 73' (Rubincam 1979: 82). The impression one gets is of great scrupulousness in regard to numbers. For omitting at 1. 23. 1 to lambast Herodotus for his absurd totals, he has been labelled 'innumerate' (cf. S. Hornblower 1985: 108–9), but in that passage he was contrasting the brevity of the Persian invasion, which involved only two sea-battles and land-battles, with the long-drawn-out Peloponnesian War, the numbers engaged being hardly relevant.

40. Hdt. 7. 165, Diod. 11. 20 and 21.

41. Cf. Starr 1962, esp. p. 329.

42. It is worth noting one point in which Thucydides may not have followed Herodotus. In the letter of Themistocles to Artaxerxes (1. 137. 4), which was in all likelihood of Thucydides' own composition, he does allude to the message sent to Xerxes on the eve of Salamis, but the Greek failure to break up the bridges at the Hellespont is not, as it is in Herodotus, made the substance of a second message. One may add that when he declared (1. 74. 1) that Themistocles was the man 'chiefly responsible for the sea-fight being in the strait', the alternative strategy may in Thucydides' mind have been to confront the Persians to the east of the island where the Persians had hoped for battle (Hdt. 8. 70. 1); there is no reason to think that Thucydides must have had in mind 'the Isthmus strategy'.

43. Cf. Busolt 1895: 712 n. 4.

44. See Appendix 4.

45. See Appendix 5 for discussion of the theories of Szemler, Cherf, and Kraft 1996.

46. V.s. pp. 88–9.

47. Hdt. 7. 6. 2 and 130. 3 for the Aleuads; 7. 176 for the topography; 8. 27–8 for the Thessalian experience.

48. Hignett 1963: 192 opined that 'if the Greek army had held out a few days longer at Thermopylae, the Greek fleet might have fought again with greater success'. According to Hammond (*CAH* iv[2] 558), the Greeks 'had more than held their own against greatly superior numbers'. Burn 1984: 402 is more tempered: 'the Greeks were indeed no longer in a condition to renew the fight'.

49. Hdt. 8. 10. 1, 7. 179–82. For discussion of 8. 60α, where Themistocles is

made to assert that the Greeks had heavier ships (βαρυτέρας), see p. 231, where the possibility is raised that Stein's conjecture was correct. Cf. Plut. *Them.* 14. 3.

50. Hdt. 8. 16, 10. 1; Thuc. 2. 83–4.

51. V.s. p. 98 for the alleged preliminary operations at Artemisium, seemingly so successful for the Greeks. The thirty ships allegedly 'captured' at 8. 11. 2 would have produced about 6000 prisoners of war; neither they nor their ships are ever heard of afterwards. It is true that the only prisoners taken by the Persians that we hear of are the 500 who had been found lingering in Attica and who were ransomed in Samos (Hdt. 9. 99. 2). Herodotus may simply not have known what happened at the hands of the Persians to the main body of captive Greeks, but he would have been able to ascertain what happened to the ships and crews allegedly captured by the Greeks. One is inevitably sceptical.

52. For the theory that there was no road through the Gates, see Appendix 5. If there was such a road, it is unclear how suitable it was for wheeled traffic. Even Greek armies had wheeled transport (cf. Thuc. 5. 72. 3 and Xen. *Resp. Lac.* 11. 2 for the Spartan army). In the Iranian world there is frequent mention (cf. Xen. *Anab.* 1. 7. 20 and 10. 18, *Cyrop.* 6. 2. 36 etc.) as with Alexander's army (cf. Engels 1978: 15 n. 13 and 17 n. 19), but they could be limiting to movement (cf. Xen. *Anab.* 3. 2. 27, where Xenophon advocated burning the waggons 'so as not to be under the command of our transport', and Curtius Rufus 6. 6. 15, where Alexander burned his waggons before he moved north-east against Bessus). The Persians had waggons in 480 BC (Hdt. 9. 80. 2 and 7. 83. 2, also 7. 41. 1, 7. 176. 2, 9. 76. 1). Perhaps the route used by Xerxes (Hdt. 8. 31; cf. Pritchett 1982: 211–33) was, once the threat of Phocian resistance was cleared, better suited for wheeled transport. (It must be remembered that ancient four-wheeled transport did not have the blessing of a swivelling front axle (cf. Landels 1980: 180) and roads with sharp turns were to be avoided.)

53. For doubts about Herodotus' timetable, cf. Hignett 1963: 195.

54. Hdt. 7. 25 for supply dumps as far as Macedonia. For supply ships, 7. 184. 3, 186. 1, and 191. 1.

55. If Xerxes had indeed planned to advance into the Peloponnese in 480, wheeled transport and beasts of burden (Hdt. 7. 83. 2) would have sufficed as they did ever afterwards for Greek armies passing to and fro.

56. Hdt. 8. 75, Aesch. *Persae* 355–63. Hignett 1963: 403–8 dismissed the whole Sicinnus story as a fiction (as had Beloch 1916: 119), principally because the versions of Herodotus and Aeschylus seriously differ, although happily for history he was not induced by the differing versions of when the Persian fleet set forth to deny that it did so! Sicinnus must have done something big to be given citizenship at Thespiae and to be enriched by Themistocles. Hignett rightly argued that a message would not have been

acted on so recklessly by the Persians but wrongly supposed that therefore no message was sent. The message, sent the night before the battle
actually took place, may have arrived too late to influence the decision
already taken and already being put into effect but may have been sent
in complete ignorance of which day battle would be sought. Pelling 1997:
2–5 argues that the differing accounts of when precisely Sicinnus was sent
or when the battle began are hardly seriously to be pressed, since they may
derive from differing views of the artistically appropriate time; 'any inferences about historicity would be most precarious'. So one may remark
that if the Persian navy was not to be caught by day streaming in columns
into the Bay of Salamis, it would have had to set out at night sufficiently
early for the rearmost ships to be at battle stations by daybreak, and since
the distance from Phalerum was at least ten kilometres, the first ships must
have set out no later, one would guess, than midnight. By then orders
would have had to be given, and the crews prepared, fed, and rested. So if
the message of Sicinnus arrived in the early evening, that would have been
too late to initiate a move that night, let Greeks with their inadequate feel
for logistics say of it what they would.

57. Cf. Beloch 1916: 119.
58. ML 24, Plut. *Mor.* 870 E, F. According to Vitruvius 5. 9. 1, timber from
    Persian ships was used to roof the Odeum.
59. It is to be noted that Artemisia is represented as presuming that naval
    victory is not the indispensable preliminary to advancing on the Peloponnese, that such advance can be made without the fleet, and that the Wall
    will not be an insuperable obstacle.
60. Mardonius is made after the battle of Salamis to suggest that if Xerxes so
    chooses, the Peloponnese could be attacked forthwith (8. 100. 3). (Again,
    it is to be noted that naval defeat had not rendered such strategy inconceivable.)
61. Cf. e.g. Burn 1984: 504.
62. Burn 1984: 504 ('their most deep-seated motive was an intelligible one: the
    desire not, if it could be avoided, to commit their limited man-power to
    a severe and bloody campaign'!).
63. For the topography, Pritchett 1985: 92–137.
64. Herodotus' figures for Greek casualties (9. 70. 5) can, in view of 9. 85 and
    69. 2, Plutarch, *Aristides* 19. 5–7, and Pausanias 9. 2. 5, be argued about;
    his statement about Persian casualties (9. 70. 5—out of 300,000 not even
    3,000 survived) is absurd. When the Greeks had captured the Persian
    camp, there was nothing the disordered remnants of Mardonius' army
    could do but make for the security (and the food-supplies) of Thessaly.
    Artabazus' flight before the battle in Herodotus' version (9. 66 and 89) is
    mysterious, in that earlier (8. 126. 1) Herodotus had declared that his reputation was much increased as a result of the Plataean campaign. Perhaps

Mardonius was blamed for not following the strategy recommended by Artabazus (9. 41), but his abrupt departure before the batttle on Herodotus' account could hardly have improved his reputation.

65. The phrases of Mr Gladstone in 1876 about the Turks.

6

The War in the East Aegean

IN the *Persae* of Aeschylus the chorus of Persian elders, having heard the news of the failure of the invasion of Greece, are made to sing

> Throughout the land of Asia
> No longer do men heed Persian law,
> No longer do they pay tribute
> Under compulsion of their masters,
> Nor do they fall to the ground
> In reverence. For the King's might
> Is utterly destroyed.
> No longer is men's speech
> Kept in check. For the people is set free
> To walk in freedom
> Now that the yoke of force is broken.　　(ll. 584–94)

The truth was less dramatic. The power of Persia was confined to Asia, and a handful of Greek cities on the Asiatic seaboard of the Aegean were in revolt. Herodotus (9. 104) concluded his account of the battle of Mycale with the statement that 'thus for the second time Ionia revolted from the Persians', and Hellespontine cities did the same (Thuc. 1. 89. 2, 95. 1). Doubtless walls were rebuilt just as they had been in 499 (cf. Hdt. 1. 141), and the help of mainland Greeks was to be expected. Xerxes would not easily restore his authority over the Greeks of Asia even though the rest of his realm was, despite his defeat, untroubled, but the task can hardly have seemed impossible.

The Persian efforts seem feeble. No major Persian forces are heard of operating in Ionia as had happened in the 490s. The initiative seems to lie entirely with Greeks. In 478 Pausanias, the victor of Plataea, set out with a mere twenty ships from the Peloponnese together with thirty from Athens and an unstated number from the other allies, but probably not many, and sailed first for Cyprus where he 'subjected the major part of the island' (Thuc. 1. 94). No Persian naval force seems to have challenged his progress. This is perhaps not surprising in view of Persian naval losses at Mycale the year before, but the Phoenician contingent had not been affected by that battle and some sort of naval resistance was to be expected in 478 (Hdt. 9. 96. 1 and 106). None is recorded. Nor do we hear of any until the Eurymedon campaign of 469, when a large Athenian naval force under Cimon won on a single day a double victory, first destroying a Persian navy at sea and then in a master stroke of daring and surprise inflicting a humiliating and decisive defeat on the land army (Thuc. 1. 100). The Persian response seems all too feeble indeed. The Eurymedon river was the nearest a major army came to Ionia for decades. Was 'the King's might utterly destroyed' as far as the Greeks were concerned?

One must first remark the paucity of the evidence. The Delian League was formed late in 478 'to exact vengeance for Greek sufferings by ravaging the King's land' (Thuc. 1. 96. 1), but we hear remarkably little of Greek ravaging. Comparatively small forces of fifty ships under Pericles and of a mere thirty under Ephialtes were mentioned by Callisthenes in his belittling of the importance of an Athenian peace-treaty with Persia (Plut. *Cim.* 13. 4); one is left to guess what their mission was, but presumably forces of that size were engaged on some sort of raiding, possibly on merchant shipping (cf. Diod. 15. 3) but more probably on land. The famous casualty list of the Erechtheid tribe (ML 33) gave the names of members who had died in the same year 'in Cyprus, in Egypt, in Phoenicia, in Halieis, in Aegina, at Megara'. The last three are plainly shown by Thucydides' narrative to refer to operations on land; likewise with Egypt. He does not refer to operations either off or in Cyprus, but all the Cyprian campaigns of which we are apprised involve fighting on land and it is reasonable to suppose that those casualties of the Erechtheid tribe were on land. So too, then, in the case of Phoenicia one may suppose a raid on the mainland. But apart from that we have no information about what was done to fulfil the purpose of the Delian League. Yet it must have been done, especially in Asia Minor itself, where ample opportunities of the sort suggested by Xenophon's account of a raid on the estate of a Persian in Mysia in 400/399 (*Anab.* 7. 8. 8–19) doubtless existed; indeed Xenophon in his *Education of Cyrus* (8. 6. 4–5) asserted that Cyrus the Great formally provided for the settlement of eminent Persians on estates throughout the Empire, and that these estates continued to be held by their descendants in his own day. In their defence the satraps would not sit idly by. Each satrapy had its own satrapal army, responsible for the defence of the King's subjects (Xen. *Oec.* 4. 9). The system of command delineated by Xenophon may not have pertained precisely throughout the Empire, but it is probably accurate for the western satrapies with which he was familiar, and he flatly asserted that 'if the defence force commander does not adequately defend the land', he is denounced by the satrap (ibid. 4. 10). So we should suppose that in the three decades after 479 satrapal forces, like those of Tissaphernes and Pharnabazus in the 390s, were constantly engaged. The Delian League had undertaken to ravage the King's land. Where more profitable than in the fat lands of Asia Minor? The Persians defended, even though our sources do not describe such petty warfare.[1]

Indeed, the King plainly showed that he was of no mind to retire gracefully from any part of his heritage. Despite the loss of Sestos in winter 479/8 and of Byzantium in early 478, the Persian commanders in those two 'bastions of empire', Eion on the river Strymon which then commanded the only point of crossing on its lower reaches, and Doriscus on the river Hebrus, where Xerxes had established one of his main supply dumps and had reviewed his army, remained firmly held. Boges in Eion, despite the seeming hopelessness of his position, preferred to die rather than to abandon the place. Presumably his orders were to hold on. Doriscus is even more remarkable. The stubborn resistance of Boges was made in 476, when the prospects of Persian recovery of Thrace were not yet clearly dim, but Mascames in Doriscus 'no one could ever capture, despite many attempts' and he seems to have lived on when Herodotus was writing, in enjoyment of annual gifts from 'whoever was king'. So the Persian flag, as it were, was kept flying in the satrapy of Skudra, a continuing assertion of the King's intention to return.[2] The Greeks recognized that intention in all probability. Much has been made of Thucydides' remark (1. 100. 2) that the Thasians revolted 'over a dispute about the trading posts on the mainland opposite the island and the mining area which they were exploiting', as if Athens was embarking on a measure of naked greed. It must be noted that the revolt coincided with a decision to send a colony of ten thousand 'Athenians and the allies' to found a city on the future site of Amphipolis, a city of vital strategic importance as Thucydides later noted (4. 108) and as the history of Philip of Macedon would in the fourth century underline, and one suspects that the League was induced, or beguiled, by strategic considerations. The Thasians could contest the danger of Persian return after the Athenian triumph in the battles of the Eurymedon; Athens in the name of the League could respond by pointing to the immovable Mascames in Doriscus, and the League accepted the implication, whatever Athenian statesmen privately thought. Yet even they feared, to judge by Thucydides' explanation of Themistocles' attachment to the idea of naval power (1. 93. 7)—namely, that it was easier for the King to attack by sea than by land. So attack by land was not out of the question, and it was to be presumed that Persia would come again.

Indeed, the whole story of the alleged medism of Pausanias implies considerable nervousness that he might soon have the opportunity to exercise his disloyalty to bad effect. He had been alleged to have 'medized' in dress and way of life in 478 and escaped unscathed, but he was held guilty of the most damaging communications with the King years after his second return to Sparta when he was in no position to serve him unless the King came against Greece again. The charges were credited because the King was expected. Similarly with Themistocles. He too was credited with medizing at a time when he was discredited at Athens and in no position to serve the King, unless the Persians came again.[3] The Greeks must have feared. Plato (*Menex.* 241d) declared that messages were received in Greece that the King intended another attempt—in a passage concerning the period before the Eurymedon campaign. But even later, fears of a Persian resurgence prevailed. Thucydides (1. 138. 2 and 4) believed that Themistocles had promised to secure the subjection of Greece, though he expressed no opinion on whether Themistocles had any such intention, merely remarking that 'some assert' that Themistocles committed suicide when he realized he could not, when required, deliver what he had promised. According to Plutarch (*Cim.* 18. 6), Themistocles thereby acknowledged that Cimon was too good for him. Thus the slander of Themistocles persisted, but the presumption of it all was that the King would try again if he could, and when the disaster in Egypt befell the Athenians, the Samians proposed (Plut. *Arist.* 25. 3) that the Treasury of the Delian League be moved to Athens. Such was 'the fear of the barbarian', in the phrase used by Pericles' opponent, Thucydides son of Melesias, to explain the transfer (Plut. *Per.* 12. 1). Nor do we have to seek explanation of why Athens, having suffered so severely in Egypt in 454, was ready to return there with sixty ships within four years and sustain 'the rebel king in the marshes'. The commonplace of fourth-century rhetoric, according to Aristotle (*Rhet.* 1393[a]34)—'we must prepare against the King and not allow him to get hold of Egypt'—was no doubt to be heard in 450. The Persians would come if and when they could.

Why then did the Royal army not go into the satrapies on the Aegean seaboard and do what the satrapal armies were proving unequal to?

Was it that the mighty Persian Empire was kept on the defensive, as the barbarians box, in Demosthenes' famous simile (4. 40), constantly covering the part of the body where a blow has just been received? It is not to be denied that Cimon, who might have been spoken of as Lucretius (3. 1043) spoke of Scipio ('thunderbolt of war, terror of Carthage'), secured for himself the reputation of having tried 'to subject the whole of Asia' (Plut. *Comp. Cimon and Lucullus* 2. 5), and he tried to maintain concord with Sparta, the more effectively to fight the war against Persia. His famous dictum (Plut. *Cim.* 16. 10) uttered when he urged the Athenians to go to the rescue of Sparta at the time of the Great Earthquake and the Helot Revolt of 465 is suggestive; he called on them 'not to stand by and watch Greece lamed or the city deprived of its yoke-fellow'. The theory of the dual hegemony of the Greeks first emerged in the debate in Sparta in late 478 when it was decided not to contend with Athens for the hegemony on sea; implicitly Sparta would continue to lead on land. But what was the relevance to Cimon in 465 of Spartan land hegemony? He may have been thinking that if ever the Persians came again to Greece, Spartan leadership on land would be needed, but it is unlikely that he so thought. His whole effort was directed to ensure that the Persians never could return. What use then could he see in Spartan leadership on land? One suspects that he and others like him had begun to dream the Panhellenist dream, so obsessive in the fourth century, of a great Anabasis, a march up-country into the heart of the Persian Empire to unseat the King from his very throne. As will emerge, the doctrine gathered strength later in the fifth century, but that it had already cast its spell may be suspected from the *History* of Herodotus, which was composed for the most part before the outbreak of the Peloponnesian War in 431. [4] He thus provides evidence for what some Greeks were thinking in the period under discussion in this chapter, and, if they were, it would seem likely that the satraps of the western satrapies would have known and reported to the King. So one wonders whether he remained on the defensive out of fear of a great Greek offensive?

It was a long way from Ephesus to Susa and a long time before a Greek army under Alexander would successfully make the Anabasis. Whatever Greeks in the fifth century might say, in reality only on the Mediterranean seaboard could attacks be made, and there were no solid gains east of Phaselis, which lay on the eastern coast of Lycia. As a base for attacks on the Levant, Cyprus proved wholly unreliable. In 478 Pausanias' naval force 'subjected the greater part of the island'

according to Thucydides (1. 94. 2), avoiding any suggestion of liberation, and although in *The Persians* of 472 Aeschylus could include
three of its cities in his list of places the King had lost, Paphos, Soli,
and Salamis (ll. 892–3), that was by no means 'the greater part of the
island'. Evidently much of what Pausanias had gained had been lost.
What the position was in 460 is obscure. The expedition 'to Cyprus',
merely mentioned by Thucydides and not reliably attested elsewhere,[5]
may have been intended to recover what Pausanias thought he had
secured. Certainly Athenians died 'in Cyprus' in 459 (ML 33), but in
what sort of action there is no telling. By 450, when Cimon went on his
last expedition (Thuc. 1. 112), not only Citium, the centre of Phoenician influence, but also Salamis had to be laid siege to (Diod. 12. 3 and
4), and thereafter the break with Cyprus was complete until late in the
century. The explanation is obvious. As the *Cyprian Orations* of Isocrates
make plain, Phoenician influence was too strong. 'Before Evagoras
took power, they [sc. the Cyprians] . . . thought those rulers best who
happened to be the most savagely disposed towards the Greeks' (Isoc.
9. 49). No wonder that Cyprus was in the time of Cimon not available
as a base for attacks on Persia,[6] and that, apart from two major efforts
to establish there the power of the Delian League, one of which was
distracted by the revolt of Egypt, and from fitful marauding squadrons,
the King's real military problem was to recover the Greek cities on the
seaboard of Asia from the mouth of the Pontus to Lycia. There were
no major Greek assaults planned, let starry-eyed Greeks talk as they
would, and no reason why the King should not assume the offensive
and recover what he had lost.

So why did he not? Part of the explanation plainly is that so vast an
empire constantly presented the King with more pressing problems
than dealing with a handful of Greek cities.[7] In the Epitome of Ctesias'
Persica, provided for us by Photius, two major challenges had to be
faced by Artaxerxes I, the revolt of Bactria, which was the real danger
spot of the Persian Empire, and the long-drawn revolt of Egypt. These,
added to the insecure period at his accession, would in themselves
suffice to explain why the recovery of power in the West was delayed.[8]
There were too in all probability serious, if minor, troubles of which
the Epitome does not inform us. There is no mention of the troublesome Cadusians,[9] described by Xenophon (*Cyrop.* 5. 2. 25) as 'a populous and warlike tribe'. They are found engaging the military attention
of Artaxerxes II in the 380s, a campaign fully enough described in
Plutarch's *Life* of that king (ch. 11), and also of Darius II shortly before

his death, of which we would not be informed but for a stray allusion in Xenophon's *Hellenica* (2. 1. 13). Such troubles were endemic and it is not to be presumed that their absence from the Epitome's record of the last days of Xerxes and of the reign of Artaxerxes I argues that the King had nothing to divert his full energies from Greece and the Greeks.

More importantly, it is to be remembered that the Persians did not keep a standing army and navy.[10] When a major force was needed, major efforts were necessary to assemble it. The most striking instance of this is found in the history of the revolt of Cyrus the Younger in 401. Artaxerxes had, one would have thought, ample enough notice of his coming, but it was not until the decisive battle of Cunaxa had been fought in the heart of the Empire not far from Babylon, and the Ten Thousand were on their way north beside the Tigris that they encountered the King's bastard brother on his way south with a large army from Susa and Ecbatana to help the King (Xen. *Anab.* 2. 4. 25). Of course, in a sense there was a standing navy. Ships prepared for an earlier expedition would still be available. But in ancient navies the main brunt of the fighting was done by new ships, and to assemble a navy for a major expedition a substantial amount of ship-building was necessary, which was not quickly accomplished.

Major expeditions therefore required major efforts. Given the known distractions of revolts in Bactria and Egypt, and other minor troubles which may be presumed, and the unsettled conditions after the death of Xerxes, the Persian response was not feeble. There was a major expedition in 469, checked at the battle of the Eurymedon within a decade of defeat in Greece, and another major expedition in the late 450s immediately after the settlement of revolt in Egypt. The only period where Persia seems to be inert is in the mid-470s, but after the shock of 479 prudence may have counselled caution. Egypt subdued in the 480s (Hdt. 7. 1, 5 and 7) remained unreliable. Disaffected nobles could well look to Bactria as a base and a spring-board for reprisals. Indeed one, Masistes, had sought some time after 479 to make it so and had moved the King to military action (Hdt. 9. 113). The seeming quietude of the mid-470s is not necessarily the sign of a failure of nerve on Xerxes' part.

Assembling a Royal army and navy took time and if ships were being built, the Levant could not contain the news. Just as in the 390s it was the news of Persian preparations which moved the Spartans to send Agesilaus to Asia (Xen. *Hell.* 3. 4. 1), so too the preparations for the major efforts of the 460s and the 450s would have been known in

Greece well in advance. Indeed it seems likely that it was the rumour of Persian preparations which excited the major naval expeditions of Cimon. Thucydides did not explain the circumstances in which a large Persian navy and army happened to be in Pamphylia at Aspendus in 469 (1. 100. 1), but we may be sure that the preparations took quite a long time, perhaps two full years, and the Athenians will have known about it. Plutarch's narrative of the campaign (*Cim.* 12) suggests that Cimon only went south and east from Caria when he heard that 'the King's generals were lying in wait with a large army and many ships in Pamphylia', as if Cimon had gone out with a large fleet not to confront the Persians but to carry on the business of liberating Greek cities from which he was distracted by news of the Persian expedition. This may be quite misleading. He did not need a large fleet to liberate cities and he probably knew of the Persian preparations. What surprised him was perhaps the news that the Persians had got as far as Pamphylia, or alternatively that the land army was not on the Royal Road to Ionia, but had come down into Pamphylia and was preparing to restore Persian power by coming along the coastal road (used by Alexander in 333 in the opposite direction); for such must have been the point of the army being in Aspendus. Thus, whereas Cimon had expected, as Pericles was to expect in 440 (Thuc. 1. 116), that the Persian navy would have to be stopped 'off Caunus and Caria', he suddenly learned that the whole double force would be moving along the coast. So he secured Phaselis to block the land army, and hastened to deal with the Persian navy. There is nothing in the story, which we derive entirely from Hellenocentric sources, to argue against the idea that Cimon went out with so large a navy because of the news of Persian preparations to resume their control of the Asiatic Greeks.

Similarly in the late 450s. The revolt of Egypt was crushed by 454. No doubt the Persian army and navy under Megabyzus and the mysterious Oriscus[11] were detained for some time thereafter in the settlement of the satrapy but by the late 450s Megabyzus was free to move his army into Cilicia, where he is found in command when Cimon sailed for Cyprus on his last campaign (Diod. 12. 3. 2). Just as in 342 BC the reconquest of Egypt was followed by the dispatch of the victorious general to take command along the seaboard of Asia Minor (Diod. 16. 52. 2), so too it would appear that Megabyzus, the victor of 454, was given some commission which involved a substantial army in Cilicia. But the King did not keep such an army there for no purpose and the Athenians would have known it. The response, it may be guessed, was

that the Athenians made a five-year truce with the Spartans, having
recalled Cimon from ostracism, and dispatched him with a large fleet
to Cyprus, to counter a renewed Persian offensive. The King was not
lacking in resolve and effort.

But, it may be riposted, these expeditions were not just unsuccessful; they were disasters. We have it on the authority of Thucydides
(1. 100) that at the Eurymedon the Athenians 'captured triremes of the
Phoenicians and destroyed them all to the number of two hundred',
and although he refrains from giving a figure for Persian losses in 450,
Diodorus recorded that 'Kimon sank many of the ships and captured
one hundred with all hands'. In each campaign the disasters on sea
were accompanied by defeats on land. One double defeat on sea and
land might be regarded by the King as a misfortune; a second, it may
be thought, must have convinced him that further effort was bound
to fail.

This may indeed have been the case, but one must point out how
unsatisfactory the evidence is. Diodorus' account of the Eurymedon
(11. 60 and 61) is famously unsatisfactory. That of Plutarch in his *Life of
Cimon* (ch. 13) introduces a subsidiary action involving a force of eighty
Phoenician triremes which were on their way to join the main Persian
force and which the Athenians attacked and destroyed, but the truth
is unattainable.[12] It seems best to stick to Thucydides. If two hundred
ships were 'destroyed', the destruction was probably to a large extent
on land. It is hard to believe that Phoenician seamanship had so far
declined within a decade that such a large number of ships was sunk;
the destruction is more likely to have been achieved, as at Mycale in 479
(Hdt. 9. 106. 1), on land and by fire. The whole disaster is to be attributed to inept leadership. For the defeat of 450 the loss of 100 ships with
all hands is firmly enough attested by the epigram, wrongly linked by
Diodorus with the epigram on the Eurymedon, for it speaks of Cyprus
which could not have been the scene of any part of the fighting at the
Eurymedon, and of the capture of 'one hundred ships of the Phoenicians at sea'. That was an amazing feat for a fleet of one hundred and
forty ships, sixty having been dispatched to Egypt at the beginning
of the campaign. Again one wonders whether there had been such a
decline in Phoenician skill. More remarkably, despite control of the
sea, the Athenians gave up the siege of Salamis and abandoned their
partial hold on Cyprus (Diod. 12. 4, Thuc. 1. 112. 4). An explanation
presents itself. The one hundred captured ships were perhaps troop-
carriers and the Athenian success was against a naval force taking

reinforcements to Cyprus, a serious set-back for the Persian resistance on the island but not the final proof of the invincibility of Athenian naval power. The Persian garrison in Salamis, however, proved equal to their task and the Athenians had to withdraw unsuccessful, not just from Salamis but from Cyprus, concealing Cimon's death (Plut. *Cim.* 19. 2). The campaign was a draw, not a victory.

The Eurymedon campaign had illustrated the real strategic problem for the Persians. As already remarked, Persia was a land power which used its naval forces in close conjunction with its armies, not free ranging in enemy waters. In any case secure bases were necessary. In the Ionian Revolt with land forces already operating in Ionia and elsewhere along the Aegean seaboard, it was easy for a Royal army and navy to deal with the revolt (cf. Hdt. 6. 6), but in view of the general revolt of the Greek cities in 479 and the subsequent successes of Greek navies the only way for Persia must have seemed to be to move along the coast restoring order in city after city, with fleet and army moving together. The battles of the Eurymedon checked such a strategy in 469. In 451 the force assembling in Cilicia had the extra difficulty of renewed trouble in Egypt (Thuc. 1. 112. 3) and to the King control of Egypt was always more important than resumption of empire over the Greeks. With the Athenians again operating in Cyprus it was clear that for the moment no further attempt could be made in the West.

It was time therefore for the King to see whether he could secure by diplomacy something of what he had not been able to secure by force. Already in the 460s, the precise date being much disputed but most probably in 462/461 when Athens gave up her alliance with Sparta against Persia, the so-called Hellenic League of 481, and allied with the King's chief ally in Greece, Argos (Thuc. 1. 102), Callias had gone to Susa to discuss terms of peace (Hdt. 7. 151); Herodotus darkly says 'on other business', but in the context of his whole discussion of Argos' refusal to share in the defence of Greece in 480 discussion of peace seems likely.[13] No agreement followed and, shortly after, Athens was going out to Cyprus on campaign, but what had been broken off could be resumed.

Athens for her part was ready. Cimon's death had removed the great proponent of unrelenting conflict. The Egyptian disaster had had ill consequences with her allies.[14] If ever the Greek fleet sustained a severe defeat, there could be widespread revolt, and constant naval activity was costly. No more had been accomplished than that Persia's former Greek subjects remained free, and if this could be established by agreement, there was no point in fighting on. So when ambassadors came from the Persian generals on the instructions of the King, Athens responded by sending an embassy fully empowered to come to terms (Diod. 12. 4). It included Callias, whose name has been attached to the Peace then made.

NOTES

1. Cf. Rhodes, *CAH* v² 46.
2. For the loss of Sestos and Byzantium, Thuc. 1. 89. 2 and 94. 2. For Persian supply dumps at Doriscus and at Eion, Hdt. 7. 25. Eion was captured by the Greeks in 476 (Thuc. 1. 98. 1, for which cf. S. Hornblower's note ad loc., and Schol. ad Aeschines 2. 31). For the repeated attempts to capture Doriscus, Hdt. 7. 105; presumably the governor, Mascames, had to with-draw after the Peace of Callias though he continued to receive annual gifts from the King. Herodotus (5. 98) described Doriscus as a 'Royal fort' and Livy (31. 16. 4) referred to it as a fort in recounting the doings of Philip V in 200 BC. Pliny, *NH* 4. 43 asserted that it could accommodate 10,000 men, but at no point did it become a proper city until it was superseded by Tra-ianopolis; Demosthenes kept listing its seizure among Philip II's villainies (8. 64, 9. 15, etc.) and arousing the scorn of Aeschines (3. 82). But after 449 BC there would have been no point in the King maintaining his hold nor would the Athenians have tolerated it.
3. Thuc. 1. 128–38 for the Pausanias and Themistocles stories which have been repeatedly discussed. See S. Hornblower 1991: 211–22.
4. See pp. 6–8.
5. Cf. Barns 1953: 170–2, but see S. Hornblower ad Thuc. 1. 104. 2. Whatever confusions there are in Diodorus' accounts of Eurymedon and of Cimon's last campaign in 450 BC, it seems best to take this Thucydides passage to mean that at the moment the revolt of Egypt began Cimon was already engaged in a campaign against Cyprus; for ἐς Κύπρον cf. Thuc. 2. 6. 4.
6. Cf. Maier in *CAH* vi² 308–9.
7. Cf. Theopompus (= *FGH* 115) F87 οὐ πάνυ τι τοῖς Ἑλληνικοῖς πράγμασι βασιλέως προσέχοντος ὑπ' ἀσχολιῶν περὶ τὰς ἄνω πράξεις.
8. *FGH* 688 F14 §§30–2.
9. For the Cadusians, see Stylianou 1998 ad Diod. 15. 8. 5.
10. V.i. Appendices 3 and 4.
11. Ctesias (= *FGH* 688) F14 §33. He is not heard of again. Artabazus shares command with Megabyzus in Cilicia.
12. The difficulty for the ancient historians was that battles on both sea and

land were easily confused, a confusion which Barns 1953 sought to disentangle. It is notorious that Plutarch (*Cim.* 12. 5), describing the Eurymedon campaign, remarked that Ephorus and Callisthenes furnished different names for the Persian commanders. Callisthenes, wherever he discussed the Eurymedon, to my mind quite as probably in the *Deeds of Alexander* as in his *Hellenica* and likely enough in the introduction (cf. Bosworth 1990: 5–10, esp. 8 n. 48), had no occasion formally to describe the Eurymedon campaign. Plutarch may have been mistaken in his understanding of what Callisthenes was talking about. His account of the naval operations must be held unreliable.

13. Three dates have been favoured for Callias' embassy to Susa: 449, under which date Diodorus (12. 4) sets the making of the Peace through an embassy led by Callias; 465 or very shortly after, when Artaxerxes acceded to the throne; and 462/461, when Athens ceased to belong to the Hellenic League against Persia and made an alliance with Argos (Thuc.1. 104. 2). Discussion has been bedevilled by two improper presumptions. First, it has been presumed that Callias was engaged in negotiations with Persia only once. There is no justification for this. His descendant, another Callias, son of Hipponicus, boasted that on three occasions he had been engaged in negotiating a peace treaty between Athens and Sparta (Xen. *Hell.* 6. 3. 4), and our Callias may have been sent twice, or more, to negotiate with the Persians. Antalcidas was involved in such negotiations on behalf of Sparta on several occasions (Xen. *Hell.* 4. 8. 12, 5. 1. 6 and 25, 6. 3. 12, Plut. *Artaxerxes* 22). One does not have to choose between one date and another. Callias may have been engaged on both occasions. Secondly, it is often presumed that when Callias made the Peace, he must have gone to the Persian court where he is to be seen in Hdt. 7. 151. According to Diodorus' account of the making of peace in 449 (12. 4–5), the negotiations were between the Athenian ambassadors and leaders of the Persian forces in the Levant acting in accordance with a Royal rescript, precisely the situation to be found when Tiribazus held peace talks in Sardis in 392 BC (Xen. *Hell.* 4. 8. 12), and when the talks miscarried, Tiribazus went up to the King to secure a change of policy. (It may be added that Pyrilampes, who received a gift of peacocks on one of his numerous embassies to the King or 'to some one else on the continent' (Plato, *Charmides* 158a), did not have to be at Susa to receive them; he may have been given such an oriental gift by an oriental grandee in the Levant.) For both these confusing presumptions, cf. Cawkwell 1997: 116 and n. 4.

For 449 BC as the date of the embassies of Argos and of Callias alluded to in Hdt. 7. 151, there have been many supporters (cf. Meister 1982: 23 n. 48), but it is wholly unsuitable as a date for Argos to be asking Artaxerxes if their friendship with Xerxes, fifteen years dead, still held. Cf. Meister 1982: 22–3. A date shortly after the death of Xerxes was argued for most notably by Meister loc. cit. and Badian 1993: 3–4; both suppose that the Argive embassy is to be understood in terms of 'the traditional and necessary mission of securing a new ruler's friendship after his accession'. The only possible parallel case is the renewal of the Peace which was effected not long after the accession of Darius II (cf. Badian 1993: 72), but since Athens had been sending an embassy just before Artaxerxes I died (Thuc. 4. 50. 3), the peace made with Darius may have been the consummation of that initiative rather than a routine renewal. As far as I am aware, there is no other evidence touching this question.

As I have already argued (Cawkwell 1997: 115–16), Badian's theory that Athens and Persia actually did make peace in the aftermath of Eurymedon can only be considered if Thucydides' order of events is regarded as sadly misleading. According to Thucydides (1. 100–2), Athens did not renounce her membership of the Hellenic League against Persia until after the end of the revolt of Thasos and the dismissal by the Spartans of the Athenian force at Ithome. Peace with Persia before that renunciation is, if we follow Thucydides, unthinkable, but even secret negotiations seem unlikely. Athens might have been going behind her allies' backs, but it was the dismissal from Ithome that caused the Athenians to rethink their whole position and make alliance 'with their enemies, the Argives' (Thuc. 1. 102. 4). A later date for Callias' embassy is therefore preferable.

Meiggs 1972: 92–3 argued for 461 BC and he was followed in this by Fornara and Samons 1991: 175. This seems to be right. Whether the two embassies coincided by accident or design, Argos having allied with the King's arch-enemy Athens had some explaining to do. As to the business of Callias' embassy, what else was there to discuss than the ending of hostilities? Of course Herodotus' dark phrase, 'on other business', is a clear enough sign that that particular embassy did not immediately lead to a Peace, but it must be understood in the whole context of chs. 148–52, where Herodotus was dealing with the charge against the Argives of medizing. Ch. 151 prepares for the climax of ch. 152; Athens was in a sense medizing in 461 and had no right to be calling Argos black.

14. Cf. Meiggs 1972: 109–24.

7

Peace with Athens, 449–412 BC

FOR nearly four decades following on the death of Cimon and the withdrawal of Athenian forces from Cyprus and Egypt (Thuc. 1. 112. 4) there was no fighting between Royal armies and navies and Athens. The only time, as far as we know, when there was thought to be danger of a Royal intervention in Greek affairs was in 440 BC during the revolt of Samos. The Samians appealed to the Phoenician navy for help; Pericles left the siege of Samos in haste on report that Phoenician ships were on their way to attack the Athenians; but they did not appear and nothing happened (Thuc. 1. 116. 3).

Much has been sometimes made of the two appearances in Thucydides' narrative of Pissouthnes, the satrap of Sardis, first in connection with the rebel government in Samos (1. 115) and later with the division between Colophon and its port, Notium (3. 34).[1] In each case mercenaries, of which there appear to have been an ample number in the western satrapies,[2] were made available by Pissouthnes to support the party he favoured, but clearly he was not prepared himself to act as was expected. In 427 BC Greeks who planned serious opposition to Athens thought that the satrap could be persuaded to join them in a war of liberation (Thuc. 3. 31), but he failed them just as he had failed to give real assistance to the Samians in 440. Persia remained at peace.

It may be argued that in the 440s and the 430s Persia remained on the defensive because she had had enough at the hands of the Greeks. But once the Peloponnesian War had begun, Persia declined to exploit Athens' preoccupation.[3] It emerged in 425 that Sparta had sent 'many embassies' to the King (Thuc. 4. 50. 2), doubtless seeking as they had intended in 431 to seek (ibid. 2. 7. 1) and as Archidamus before the war had counselled seeking (ibid. 1. 82. 1), whatever support, financial or military, the King could be persuaded to provide. Time would make plain that Persia aimed to control all of Asia unconditionally, and in 431 the Greek cities of Ionia and probably of the whole Aegean seaboard were without walls (Thuc. 3. 33. 2).[4] There was no obstacle. Why did not Artaxerxes seek to resume control of the dissident parts of his kingdom?

The answer that is generally given and generally accepted is that he was bound by a treaty of peace, the Peace of Callias.[5] He might, of course, when provoked have renounced it as the Spartans clearly sought to persuade him to do. Yet not until Athens gave military aid to the rebel Amorges did the King change his policy.[6] Even if we did not have Diodorus' explicit notice of a peace in 449 (12. 4. 5.), its occurrence would be strongly suspected.

The 'principal points' of the treaty of peace are, in Diodorus' account, these:

1. 'all the Greek cities in Asia are to be autonomous';
2. 'the satraps of the Persians are not to go down further than a three days' journey from the sea';
3. 'no warship is to sail within Phaselis and the Cyanean Islands';
4. 'and if the King and his generals fully abide by these clauses, the Athenians are not to campaign against the territory over which the King exercises sovereignty'.

These clauses at first sight seem to be more restrictive of the King than of the Athenians and they do raise questions and excite speculation.[7] Nothing in them seems to go against Plutarch's notion that the King had been humbled (*Cim.* 13. 4). But did he have no cause for satisfaction? According to Plutarch (*Cim.* 19. 2.), Cimon on his deathbed bade the Athenians to sail home immediately, and to conceal his death. This does not sound as if the Athenians had won a crashing victory, and Thucydides, despite his thunderous silence as to the reasons why, let the cat out of the bag when he said (1. 112. 4)[8] that the Athenians 'after their victory on both land and sea went away home and the ships from Egypt went with them'. Why was Amyrtaeus, 'the King in the swamps', left in the lurch? The answer is obvious, the Peace of Callias. The King had regained both undisputed control of Egypt and unchallenged rule over Cyprus at least. The whole deal, however, may have been even more satisfactory from the Persian point of view.

Autonomy was a nebulous concept. It seems clear enough that there was a clause in the Thirty Years Peace of 446 BC between Athens and Sparta guaranteeing the autonomy of the members of the Athenian Empire.[9] That clause did not, however, save Athens' allies from the tightening of her imperial grasp, and this was not so much because Athens happily disregarded the autonomy clause as because the clause was so vague. Autonomy certainly did not preclude the payment of tribute, as a clause of the Peace of Nicias in 421 would show (Thuc. 5. 18. 5) and as the demand made by Tithraustes in 395 (Xen. *Hell.* 3. 4. 25) would presume. Similarly in 449 the guarantee of autonomy for the Greek cities could have been thought consistent with a clause requiring the Greek cities of Asia to pull down their walls.

It would be otiose here to restate the case, first proposed over sixty years ago by Wade-Gery, for believing that the right explanation for the state of affairs revealed by Thucydides' comment in his account of 427 BC (3. 33. 2) about 'Ionia being without walls' is that demolition of walls had been required by the Peace of Callias.[10] That case is here accepted. If it is correct, it makes a vast difference to how the Peace was regarded in Susa. It meant that at any moment the King could resume unqualified control over all of Asia, if Athens did not keep her side of the bargain. In the fourth century the Peace would be extolled as a glorious triumph for Athens. Thus Plutarch in his *Life of Cimon* (chs. 12 and 13), drawing on fourth-century sources could speak of humbling the King and curbing his pride, just as Isocrates in his *Panegyricus* of 380 BC (§120) speaks of the peace made under the Athenian Empire 'limiting', 'fixing', and 'preventing'. In the fifth century it was perhaps not so. Callias on his return was fined heavily for taking bribes (Dem. 19. 273), just as Philocrates, the chief author and agent of the peace of 346 BC that bears his name, was prosecuted and, in absentia, condemned to death on a charge that included the element of bribery (Hyperides 4. 29–30). Accusations of bribery were indispensable but incidental. The real question at issue was how the recently made peace was judged. What fault had the Athenians to find in this glorious triumph of 449? It was perhaps this clause about walls that stuck in the Athenian gullet. After his death in 449 the 'divine' Cimon 'in every way best of all the Hellenes' was lauded by the comic poet Cratinus (Plut. *Cim.* 10. 4), at the very time that Callias was censured.[11] Nor is this surprising when one considers the general withdrawal after Cimon's death. All in all, there was no walkover victory. A bargain was struck by the King's generals on the basis of the status quo. The King had his pound of flesh as well.

The peace lasted for three and a half decades and hostilities only recommenced because Athens chose to give support to the rebel Amorges, the bastard son of Pissouthnes, who himself, by birth near to the King,[12] had revolted, had been defeated by a Royal army and captured, and was put to death by the King (Ctes. F15 §53). The only evidence for Athens deciding to support Amorges is provided by the orator Andocides in a speech made twenty or so years later (3. 29). Yet it is clear from Thucydides' account of 412/411 that Amorges was in league with the Athenian commanders in Ionia (8. 54. 3), and there is no reason to reject Andocides.[13] Athens, in short, chose to incur the King's hostility, an act of imperial arrogance and madness.

Of the years of peace the term Cold War has been used.[14] Such a view was based principally on very dubitable interpretations of entries on the Athenian Tribute lists; if states did not pay, there is no reason to presume that Persia was egging them on or that every time an Athenian general is found seeking to collect tribute or in some other way enforcing imperial discipline, a technical breach of the Peace of Callias was being committed. It is true that the satrap in Sardis, Pissouthnes, lent help in the shape of mercenaries to the Samians (Thuc. 1. 115) and to the Colophonians (ibid. 3. 34. 1), and indeed was thought to be open to persuasion to join an Ionian revolt (ibid. 3. 31. 1). But he never did fully commit himself or his satrapal army, and despite rumour, which may well have been wholly idle, Persia never presented military or naval opposition.

Of course, once the Peloponnesian War began, seeking Persian aid was an obvious way for the Spartans to counter Athenian naval and financial superiority. Thucydides represents King Archidamus of Sparta saying as much (1. 82. 1) when the decision for war was being taken, and during the last uneasy weeks before Attica was first invaded, the Spartans preparing for war intended to send to the King to seek his help (2. 7. 1). Whether Athens did the same is dubitable,[15] but they may have sought to encourage the King to maintain his neutrality. In Aristophanes' *Acharnians* of 425, the scene with the Persian ambassador (ll. 61–125) with its jibe about Royal tightfistedness (l. 104) did not necessarily reflect the rebuff of Athenian requests for financial aid; it may well have been based on Peloponnesian experience. The Peloponnesians certainly did need money to man large fleets and no doubt the embassies to Persia, both the one formally reported (2. 67. 1) and those merely alluded to in the Royal letter of 425/424 (4. 50. 2), primarily perhaps sought Persian gold. But the King gave nothing.

The Royal letter of 425/424 represented a major change. For the first time the King took the initiative. One can only guess why, but it is an easy guess. It would not have taken long for the King to hear of the Athenian success at Pylos whereby it must have seemed that the Spartans would have to concede that they could not liberate the Greeks from Athenian rule. The mood of Athens was promptly manifested in the great Reassessment of Tribute of 425, with swingeing increases all round and provocative assessments of places not in the Empire, such as Melos, portent of things to come, and including places within the Persian sphere, Aspendus, Celenderis, Perge, and a wholly new 'province' of the Empire, the Euxine district, an advertisement of plans of imperial expansion.[16] Such matters could have quickly reached the ears of the King. Though he may have 'laughed loud and long' at the news that a place in the Levant[17] had been, if indeed it had been, assessed for tribute, things could prove more serious if Sparta accepted failure, and Pericles' successors were free to realize his expansionist designs. 'There is no one who will stop us sailing the seas with our present naval armament, neither the Great King nor any other people that now exists' is what Thucydides (2. 62. 2) has Pericles declare. From the Persian point of view this was sinister indeed. Hence the King's change in 425. Athens had plainly enough contravened the Peace.

The King would have had his terms. The Spartans had entered the war with a proclamation that they were freeing Greece (Thuc. 2. 8. 4, 4. 85. 1). They meant freedom from Athenian rule, but the sort of considerations later put before Tissaphernes by Alcibiades, which Tissaphernes hardly needed (8. 46. 3–5), were perhaps in Artaxerxes' mind in 425 BC. He would have had no wish to replace Athenian empire with Spartan protectorate. Any deal with Sparta would have to make clear that, in Herodotus' words (9. 116), 'the Persians think that the whole of Asia belongs to themselves and to the King for the time being' and that Sparta had abandoned any claim to be liberating *all* the Greeks. In his letter to the Spartans in 425, Artaxerxes said that 'although many ambassadors had come, none said the same thing' (Thuc. 4. 50. 2). Clearly the Spartans had been havering and avoiding the central concession on which for the King all depended. How long negotiations with Sparta would have gone on before Persian gold or Persian ships were forthcoming there is no knowing. The envoy with the message was captured and sent to Athens. Athens' counter-embassy was turned back by news of Artaxerxes' death (Thuc. 4. 50. 3), and the crisis in Athenian–Persian relations subsided amidst the accession confusions of the new reign (Ctes. F15 §§47–9). The situation in Greece itself also changed with the emergence of Brasidas the liberator (cf. Thuc. 4. 86. 1). If he had his way, Sparta would not be abandoning the Greeks of Asia.

Persia was perhaps better informed about Greek affairs than the

Greeks were of Persian. The Athenians may well have misunderstood the reasons for Persian quiescence in the early days of Darius II, knowing nothing of Royal distractions and thinking it was Royal indifference. Thus they missed the lesson of 424 BC and let themselves be persuaded by the rebel Amorges. The result was Spartan–Persian alliance and, in time, the end of the Peloponnesian War and the end of the Athenian Empire. There must have been a debate in the Athenian Assembly when the alliance was made, and one would dearly wish to know what arguments were deployed. Did anyone plead for the maintenance of the Peace made with Darius in 424/3[18] and warn against provoking Persian hostility again? Unhappily, Thucydides cared for none of these things. Persia reappears in his narrative only when the King is reported to be requiring Tissaphernes to collect tribute despite the Athenians, and Tissaphernes turned to Sparta (8. 5. 4–5).

NOTES

1. See e.g. Eddy 1973: 250–1, but cf. Lewis 1977: 59–61 and Badian 1993: 33–5.
2. After, and partly as a consequence of, the Ten Thousand there were abundant mercenaries in Asia Minor, but even before then the western satraps had many in their pay, not only Pissouthnes (Thuc. 1. 115. 4, 3. 34. 2 and 3) but also the satrap of Syria, Abrocomas, whose mercenaries deserted to Cyrus (Xen. *Anab*. 1. 4. 3), and Artyphius who rebelled against Darius II in the first half of his reign and who relied largely on his Greeks (Ctes. F15 §52). When not long afterwards Pissouthnes revolted he had 'the Athenian, Lycon, and the Hellenes he commanded' (ibid. §53). When the remnants of the Ten Thousand made their night raid on Asidates, an ample force including 'eighty mercenaries of the King and about eight hundred peltasts' came to his aid from nearby cities and estates (Xen. *Anab*. 7. 8. 15), a situation not much different from that in 411 BC when a party on Lesbos hired about two hundred and fifty from the mainland (Thuc. 8. 100. 3).
3. Cf. Cawkwell 1997: 118.
4. Certainly, later on, Hellespontine cities were without walls (Thuc. 8. 62. 2 Lampsacus, 8. 107. 1 Cyzicus). In general, Thucydides seems to mean by 'Ionia' the area of the cities of the Panionium (cf. Hdt. 1. 142. 3), but at 8. 56. 4 when Alcibiades speaks of 'all Ionia', one presumes he refers to all the Greek cities of the Aegean seaboard of Asia (cf. Andrewes 1981 ad loc.) as perhaps at 3. 36. 2.

5. Lewis in *CAH* v² 121–7 provides a statement of the case. Extreme sceptics are becoming rare. Few would now insist that the silence of Thucydides is decisive, as did Stockton 1959. The glib presumption that the 4th cent. invented the Peace is ill-based; cf. Cawkwell 1997: 119–21. For the theory of Badian 1993 that there were two peaces, see Ch. 6, n. 13.

6. The aid given to Pissouthnes by 'Lycon the Athenian and the Hellenes' (Ctes. F15 §53) is clearly that of a band of mercenaries. The date of Pissuthnes' rebellion is quite unclear (cf. S. Hornblower 1982: 31 n. 198, and Lewis 1977: 80 n. 198), and the date of the appeal to Athens by his son, Amorges, is also uncertain, the only evidence being the record of a payment from the Treasury of Athena to a 'general in Ephesus' who is presumed to be there in support of Amorges (ML 77 l. 79, and comment p. 236). So the connection, if any, between the rebellions of father and son is only to be guessed.

7. See Appendix 7, 'The Peace of Callias'.

8. The other passage where Thucydides lets the truth emerge is 8. 56. 5, where Alcibiades is found demanding on behalf of Tissaphernes that the Athenians 'allow the King to make ships and sail along the coast of his own land'.

9. Cf. Badian 1993: 137–40.

10. Cf. Cawkwell 1997: 122–5.

11. Cawkwell 1997: 122 n. 20 suggests that Herodotus' account of the Argive response to the Hellenic appeal of 481 BC (7. 148–52) plays on Athenian bad conscience about having made the Peace. To whom was Herodotus referring when he said (7. 152. 2) that 'it was not by the Argives that basest things have been done'?

12. For the standing of Pissouthnes, see Lewis 1977: 55.

13. Westlake 1989: 103–12 ('Andocides . . . is almost certainly guilty of falsification', p. 110) has not been widely followed.

14. By Eddy 1973.

15. S. Hornblower ad 2. 7. 1 takes the word ἑκάτεροι to show that Athens as well as Sparta appealed to the King, but this may not be right. The Athenians, for their part, may have appealed 'elsewhere to the barbarians' (who are clearly different from the Persians), perhaps to the Thracians, whose king, Sitalces, was won over to alliance with Athens in 431 (Thuc. 2. 29. 1). At the start of the War Athens needed neither Persian gold nor Persian naval power.

16. The cities in Pamphylia occur only in the assessment of 425, never in the preserved tribute lists. The assessment of Aspendus was particularly provocative, in that, lying on the river Eurymedon, it had been and would continue to be a Persian naval base (Thuc. 8. 81. 3), as fully in the 5th cent. as in the 4th 'barbarian', as Alexander would discover (Arr. *Anab.* 1. 26 and 27).

17. Dōros in Phoenicia may have been included in the assessment of 454 BC (cf. *ATL* I 203–4). If it was assessed then, the empty gesture may have been repeated in 425.
18. For the peace with Darius II, see Wade-Gery 1958: 207–22 and cf. Lewis in *CAH* v² 422 n. 132.

8

The Recovery of the Greeks of Asia

'ARTAXERXES thinks it just that the cities in Asia be his.' Thus began the Royal Rescript of 387/386 which preluded the King's Peace (Xen. *Hell.* 5. 1. 31), and from that year until Philip of Macedon began the invasion of Asia in 336, the complete subjection of the Greeks of Asia was never seriously challenged. On three occasions one or other of the leading states of Greece, Sparta, Athens, and Thebes, gave military support to satraps in revolt, but with no thought of liberating the Asiatic Greeks.[1] Panhellenists like Agesilaus of Sparta or Jason of Pherae might talk of liberation, but they did nothing and could do nothing.[2] For all practical purposes the King's Peace had settled the matter. This chapter is concerned with the King's progress over twenty-five years towards that successful conclusion.

There were, broadly, three phases. In the first Tissaphernes, the satrap in Sardis, was the chief agent of Royal policy; he secured in a treaty of alliance Sparta's formal recognition of the King's right to Asia and with his help and encouragement Sparta began to rid Asiatic cities of Athenian control. In the second phase Cyrus, the younger son of Darius II, formed a close working relationship with Lysander, who was dedicated to the cause of destroying the Athenian Empire. Able to rely on the support of Cyrus, Lysander succeeded in his aim, thus ridding the King's land of Athens. Sparta made no attempt to take over and Asia was for the while the King's. In the third phase Sparta sought to recover what she had abandoned but was brought to acknowledge that she could not protect the Greeks of Asia.

To understand Persian policy in the western part of the Empire, one must realize that the satraps were not free to do whatever they chose. Policy was made in Susa and when the Greeks want a change it is to Susa that they go, the most striking case being the embassy of Pelopidas in 367 BC and the counter embassies of other states (Xen. *Hell.* 7. 1. 33–8). When a satrap considered that a change of policy was desirable, he went in person to argue the case. In 392 when Tiribazus had failed to get the Greeks to agree to the terms he had agreed with

Antalcidas, he 'thought it was risky to side with the Spartans without the King's consent' and 'went up' to see him (Xen. *Hell.* 4. 8. 16). He was unsuccessful and the King sent down Strouthas to replace him and to implement a policy hostile to Sparta (ibid. 4. 8. 17). The King kept control. Important decisions had to be referred to him. When Dercylidas in 397 proposed to the two satraps Tissaphernes and Pharnabazus that there could be peace if the King would allow the Greek cities of Asia to be autonomous, the satraps required the King's consent to any deal (ibid. 3. 2. 20), for a deal would have meant a change of policy.[3] Likewise when Agesilaus appeared on the scene in 396 and made the same proposal, again Tissaphernes referred it to the King, receiving apparently the same reply (ibid. 3. 4. 5–6).[4] When the following year Tithraustes was sent down to replace Tissaphernes, he brought a new policy with him and was able to negotiate with Agesilaus without further ado (ibid. 3. 4. 25), for he knew what he could do. It was a centralized system indeed. When Diodorus drawing on Ephorus commented on the slow progress of Persian preparations in 373 BC to invade Egypt, he made this illuminating generalization (15. 41. 5)[5]—'as a general rule the commanders of the Persians are not fully in control but refer all matters to the King and have to await the response on every single issue'. What was true of commanders of Persian armies was no doubt true of satraps, perhaps especially those who held the most responsible posts. A probable instance is the making of the Treaty of Alliance between Sparta and Persia in 412/411. The text was finally agreed and accepted by both sides at a meeting at Caunus in Caria but the formalities were concluded 'on the plain of the Maeander' (Thuc. 8. 58). Certainly the text would have been referred to Sparta for approval, but probably also to Susa; the crucial definition of the sphere of the Royal authority was notably different from the one common to the first two drafts and probably required reference to Susa. What made such ready reference possible was the imperial postal system; and exchange between Sardis and Susa could be completed within two or three weeks.[6] Of course, the King might not always reply immediately but he was in a position to keep control. If a satrap did not give satisfaction, he could be removed as was Tissaphernes, the saviour of the King in the battle of Cunaxa, by Ariaeus, the King's opponent in that battle (Xen. *Hell.* 3. 4. 25). Tissaphernes came to disaster on account of a military failure.[7] Failure to carry out Royal policy is not heard of. Tiribazus was accused of favouring Sparta (Diod. 15. 9–11) but the evidence was not decisive. Xenophon said he gave money to Antalcidas, but 'secretly'

(*Hell.* 4. 8. 16). If he did do anything of which he knew the King would disapprove, he had to be very secretive indeed. Each satrap was served by Royal secretaries (Hdt. 3. 128. 3) on whose loyalty the King could count.[8]

These considerations are especially relevant to the conduct of Tissaphernes. He seemed to the Spartans duplicitous (Thuc. 8. 99), in which Pharnabazus may have concurred (Xen. *Hell.* 4. 1. 32), but that does not mean that the King was dissatisfied with what he was doing. So it is time to turn to the period when Tissaphernes was in charge of the war against Athens, that is, between the ending of the Peace of Callias and the coming of Cyrus.

Tissaphernes and the Greeks

Unhappily one must commence by complaining about Thucydides. In book 8, on which one must heavily rely, he shakes confidence in his knowledge and understanding of Persia. First he treats as separate treaties two documents that must have been drafts agreed upon by the negotiating parties but rejected either in Susa or in Sparta. Thus in the first (ch. 18) the definition of where the King held sway must have been rejected by the King on the grounds of its ambiguity. 'Whatever territory and cities the King holds or the King's fathers held' might be questioned on the ground that Darius' father, Artaxerxes I, had ceded control of the Greek cities of Asia, and his grandfather, Xerxes, had lost control of a large part of the Asian coast after 479. In this second draft (ch. 37), where this point had been addressed, the definition could be objected to in Sparta, as indeed that of the first draft could have been, on the grounds that Persian Kings had earlier held, albeit shortly, Greek cities in Greece (cf. ch. 43. 3). The point was therefore put beyond cavil in the third draft (ch. 58) that became, with the approval of Susa and Sparta, the final text of the Treaty of Alliance—'the territory of the King, such as is in Asia, is to belong to the King'. This was all an intelligible development. What strongly suggests that the first two of Thucydides' 'treaties' were merely drafts is the absence from them of a full prescript with date and the normal details which we find set out in the third (ch. 58. 1 and 2).[9] What confirms this view is that such prompt rewriting of treaties is quite unheard of in the Greek world. There could be dissatisfaction with a treaty and agitation for its abandonment, but in no case known to us did this lead to the rewriting of a treaty, especially when the text could be and plainly was approved by home governments. Thucydides has, one regrets to have to say, blundered.

A second point concerns the Persian undertaking to pay the wages of Spartan forces. When Tissaphernes first sent a call to Sparta to take the war to Ionia, he 'was promising he would provide pay' (8. 5. 5), and since at Miletus 'he provided a month's pay as he promised in Sparta' (29. 1), it is clear that these promises had not been put into any sort of formal agreement. Nothing was said of this in the first two drafts, and in the formal treaty there is no more than a clause to the effect that Tissaphernes 'should provide pay for the ships currently present *in accordance with what had been agreed*' (8. 58. 4). The reference must be to the original agreement at Sparta. Yet the matter of pay was important, and Thucydides must be found deficient in omitting it. Of course, it is evident that book 8 is uneven and incomplete and perhaps blame is out of place. However, it does show that Thucydides is a less reliable guide where the Persians are concerned.

One would certainly like to know more about what was thought in Sparta of these different versions. When the Peloponnesian War began, the Spartans looked to Persia for help and various appeals were made, but in 425 the King complained in the letter which he sent with Artaphernes and which the Athenians captured (Thuc. 4. 50) that, although many ambassadors had come to him, there had been a lack of consistency and clarity. One can only surmise that Sparta was divided in its attitude to Persia. They had begun the war proclaiming that they were liberating Hellas (Thuc. 2. 8. 4), but they recognized that they needed Persian help. The price of Persian help, however, was that they recognize the King's right to the whole of Asia including the Greek cities which were to be liberated from Athens. Hence the lack of consistency and clarity.[10]

In 413 BC Athens was down but not out. Sparta had to maintain the pressure from Decelea but she had actively to support Athens' allies in revolt. For this ships were needed and though a naval force could be assembled (cf. Thuc. 8. 3. 2) money was needed to pay for it and, even so, additional ships were much to be desired. Persian help, both financial and naval, had to be procured.

There was later a plain dichotomy between, on the one hand, those like Lysander who accepted that recognition of the King's right to control the Greek cities of Asia was the price that had to be paid, and on the other, those like Callicratidas who spurned Persian aid (Xen. *Hell.* 1. 6.

1–11). That was in the time of Cyrus and will be treated in due course. Was there such a division when the Treaty of Alliance was being made? The first approach from Tissaphernes was made in winter 413/412 (Thuc. 8. 5) but the Treaty of Alliance was not finally settled until late in the following winter (cf. 8. 58. 1 and 61. 1). Why did it take so long? Not until the final version was the King's right to Asia baldly stated, and it may be suggested that that bitter pill had required a good time to swallow. Even then explicit mention of 'the cities' was avoided. The eleven Spartiates sent out in part to treat with Tissaphernes included Lichas (8. 39). He was the one who later, when the treaty had been signed, sealed, and delivered, as it were, expressed the view that the Greeks of Asia should put up with subjection to Persia for the duration of the war (8. 84. 5). That is, alliance with Persia was for Lichas but a short-term ploy to secure the ending of the Athenian Empire.

Earlier, Lichas had taken the lead in finding the definition of the King's authority unsatisfactory (8. 43. 3). Now Therimenes, as Chalcideus before him, would have been incredibly stupid not to think of the interpretation that Lichas put on it, and likewise the authorities at Sparta, who had accepted the clause in the first place. Tissaphernes left the meeting with the eleven commissioners angrily (8. 43. 4). He could hardly have been hoping to bluff the various negotiators on the Spartan side into accepting a clause that would allow the Persians back into Boeotia. Certainly Thucydides does not read like that. The truth must rather have been that Tissaphernes was disgusted by Spartan havering and indecision. They were seeking, under the aegis of Lichas, a redefinition of the King's authority despite having twice accepted a statement about 'territory and cities'. One may surmise that the real crux for Lichas and his kind was the mention of 'cities'.

At bottom, Sparta was at best ambivalent with regard to Persia. After the exchange with Tissaphernes, who went off in a rage, the Spartan fleet and the eleven commissioners sailed for Rhodes 'thinking they would be able without expanding the alliance (ἀπὸ τῆς ὑπαρχούσης ξυμμαχίας) to maintain the fleet and not beg Tissaphernes for money' (8. 43. 4–44. 1). That was how the less realistic Spartans would ideally have liked to fight the war. It could not be done, as Lichas had to accept (8. 84. 5) and as Spartans generally after the battle of Arginusae accepted. Sparta needed Persia.

Did Persia need Sparta? At one point Thucydides has Alcibiades advising Tissaphernes on how he should deal with Sparta (8. 46). Tissaphernes, he said, should not be too zealous in bringing the war to an end, or be willing to bring the Phoenician fleet, or provide pay for further Greeks and so hand over the control to them of both land and sea; he should leave both parties to have a share of rule in the Greek world, and make it possible for the King to lead against those who were a trouble to him their opponents in Greece; otherwise, if rule over land and sea became concentrated on the one side, Tissaphernes would be at a loss for people he could support in destroying those who held the power, if he did not himself wish to rise up at great expense and danger and finish the contest; the more economical course was at a small fraction of the expense, and at the same time in safety to himself, to wear down the Greeks in struggle against themselves. Alcibiades went on to argue that the Athenians were more suitable for partnership with the Persians in rule; they were interested only in sea empire, whereas the Spartans sought to liberate all the Greeks. So, he said, Tissaphernes should play them off against each other and when he had wrested as much as possible from the Athenians, he should then get rid of the Peloponnesians from his territory. Thucydides adds his own comment. 'Tissaphernes was so minded on the whole, so far at any rate as one could guess from his actions' (8. 46. 5).

It is highly probable that it was Alcibiades himself who furnished Thucydides with this account of what was said, and Alcibiades was not necessarily to be believed. The presumption all through is that Tissaphernes was free to choose whatever policy he liked. He, it was said, was preparing Phoenician ships. That could hardly be the case. Phoenician ships would be 'prepared' in Phoenicia over which Tissaphernes had no control. Even when the ships came as far as Aspendus (8. 81. 3, 87. 1), they were perhaps still beyond his control. Indeed when Thucydides said that Tissaphernes was preparing to go to the Phoenician ships at Aspendus and ordered Lichas the Spartan to travel with him (87. 1), it sounds as if the purpose of the journey was rather to persuade the admiral of the fleet than to order him. It certainly was the case that Persian help for Sparta was less than generous and in effect enabled Athens to continue the war, but whether this was entirely due to Tissaphernes or a policy dictated from Susa is worth asking.

Thucydides clearly thought the policy was Tissaphernes' own. He could not have said (8. 46. 5) that 'Tissaphernes was so minded on the whole ($\tau\grave{o}$ $\pi\lambda\acute{e}ov$)' if Thucydides had suspected that he had had the order from Susa. However, since he made his assertion on conjecture based on Tissaphernes' actions, he clearly did not have solid information about Persian policy.

It is conceivable that the reason why Persia did not exploit Athens' preoccupation in the early years of the Peloponnesian War was that Artaxerxes saw it was to Persia's advantage to leave the two leading states to fight it out. It was an obvious enough strategy. But whether the policy originated in Susa or in Sardis, it is likely that it was not clearly formulated until Sparta had been induced to carry the war to the East Aegean or indeed before the revolt of major cities on the mainland of Asia, like Miletus, presented Persia with the problems which would arise if Spartan hegemony replaced Athenian Empire.

The two satraps of the satrapies bordering the Aegean in 412 BC were Tissaphernes and Pharnabazus and to a large extent they appeared to act independently. When Tissaphernes was supporting the Chians who were seeking to secure Spartan help if they revolted from Athens and was himself proposing alliance between Sparta and Persia, an embassy arrived from Pharnabazus requesting Spartan help in causing revolt in the Hellespontine area and trying independently to make alliance with Sparta for the King (Thuc. 8. 5. 4–6. 1). In the following year when Tissaphernes had made the Peloponnesian navy very discontented at his failure to provide either ships or adequate pay, Pharnabazus invited them to transfer themselves to his area (8. 99) as if the two satraps were equal and independent agents. Over a decade later when Pharnabazus had a meeting with the Spartan king, Agesilaus, he could not only boast of his financial support for Sparta during the Peloponnesian War but could also speak of Tissaphernes' duplicity (Xen. *Hell.* 4. 1. 32). Pharnabazus seems to have got on well with Greeks, Tissaphernes badly,[11] and it would certainly seem that the policy pursued by the latter was rejected by the former. One has the impression that Pharnabazus felt free to go his own sweet way. If policy was prescribed by the King, it must have been only in very broad terms.

Thucydides, however, described Tissaphernes as 'general in charge of the seaward peoples' ($\sigma\tau\rho\alpha\tau\eta\gamma\grave{o}\varsigma\ \tau\hat{\omega}\nu\ \kappa\acute{\alpha}\tau\omega$). The precise meaning of this term has been much debated[12] but it is clear that in some sense Tissaphernes was the senior man. He was the King's agent in fixing the terms of alliance with Sparta and all that Pharnabazus had to do with it was to attend the formal ceremony on the plain of the Maeander (8. 58. 1). The important question therefore is how free was Tissaphernes to act? Did the King know about and approve of his dilatory tactics? Or was Tissaphernes quietly subverting the Royal purposes?

It is 'the Phoenician ships', constantly promised and constantly expected and never arriving,[13] that point to an answer. As already remarked, fleets were 'prepared' in Phoenicia, which was not Tissaphernes' 'province', and the naval station at Aspendus was perhaps not within his territory.[14] It would seem therefore that the fleet of one hundred and forty-seven ships that came to Aspendus came by order of the King and whatever their mission was they were not to be prevented by a word from Tissaphernes. Now in the first two draft treaties the clause pertaining to the war against the Athenians (8. 18. 2 and 37. 4) makes no mention of Persian naval forces fighting along with the Peloponnesians, and the only question at issue between the Greeks and Tissaphernes concerns pay (8. 29 and 45). But by the time the final draft was hammered out it is presumed that 'the ships of the King will come' (8. 58. 6). So the decision to prepare a fleet must have been taken in Susa in the winter of 412/411. Such a decision would not have been taken lightly. Fleets were costly and a fleet of one hundred and forty-seven ships was large. It would have made such a difference to the balance of naval power in the coming summer that the King must have been intending out-and-out destruction of Athenian imperial power in the eastern Aegean. Such a force was not to be lightly dismissed by a word from Tissaphernes. The recall of the fleet from Aspendus must have been dictated from Susa.

An explanation of the retirement of the fleet has been found in a curious passage in Diodorus' narrative of events of later summer 411 (13. 46. 6).[15] It has been taken to show that there was revolt in Egypt in that year and to suggest that Tissaphernes was therefore obliged to return the ships to base. It reads as follows: 'Pharnabazus' (though evidently Diodorus meant Tissaphernes, another instance of his well-attested tendency to reverse names) 'wishing to defend himself to the Spartans over their complaints, was carrying on the struggle against the Athenians with more vigour, and at the same time with regard to the three hundred ships sent off to Phoenicia he told them that his reason for doing this was that he was informed that the King of the Arabs and the King of the Egyptians were plotting against Phoenicia.' Whatever this curious phrase (ἐπιβουλεύειν τοῖς περὶ Φοινίκην πράγμασιν) referred to, it was not declaring that Egypt was in revolt, and as far as is known Egypt did not have a king in 411. Odd allusions to unrest and petty disturbances that are found in various Egyptian documents of the period hardly prove that Egypt was in revolt.[16] Indeed, if the reason why the one hundred and forty-seven ships went back to Phoenicia was that Tissaphernes had been informed that there was more important work for these ships in Phoenicia, it is hard to conceive that Pharnabazus would shortly afterwards have been promising, as Thucydides asserts (8. 99), 'to bring the ships'. Whatever is behind this curious bit of Diodorus, it should not be used to account for the Persians not giving naval help to the Peloponnesians.

Why then did the Phoenician ships return to Phoenicia? One can only guess, but it is a reasonable guess, that there was a major change of policy on the part of the King. He had intended to see in the summer of 411 BC an end to Athenian imperial power. Then came the reversal. He decided to follow the policy which Alcibiades was to claim the credit for proposing but which Tissaphernes did not need Alcibiades to suggest. Whether it was Tissaphernes who proposed it to Susa or not, the order came from the King, to the fleet over which Tissaphernes had no control. No doubt his commanders would resort to fine words of the sort that Alcibiades would claim he had heard from Tissaphernes (8. 81. 3), but from 411 to the end of the war the King declined to intervene, despite the pleas of his son Cyrus to whom we must presently turn. Tissaphernes was left to explain the change of policy as best he could. The garbled story found in Diodorus (13. 46) was perhaps the explanation he gave.

Cyrus, the Greeks, and the Struggle for the Throne

Thucydides' narrative broke off, almost in mid-sentence, in late summer 411 BC and since Athenian activity was largely from then on concerned with the restoration of Athenian power in the Hellespontine area, for some years comparatively little is heard of Tissaphernes, but he did remain in Sardis as satrap and, for all we know to the contrary, still 'general of the seaward people' ($\sigma\tau\rho\alpha\tau\eta\gamma\dot{o}\varsigma$ $\tau\hat{\omega}\nu$ $\kappa\acute{\alpha}\tau\omega$ 8. 5. 4). Then came the change. In 407 BC Cyrus the Younger, the King's second son and the brother of the future Artaxerxes II, came 'down' as 'Commander of those who muster at Castolus' to conduct with the Spartans the war against Athens (Xen. *Hell.* 1. 4. 3). Tissaphernes retired, presumably to his estate in Caria (ibid. 3. 4. 12).

Tissaphernes lost his post and his extensive powers. He was not, however, a total outcast. When the following year the Athenians made an approach to Cyrus, they did so through Tissaphernes and Tissaphernes took their embassy before Cyrus (Xen. *Hell.* 1. 5. 8). In the Athenians' eyes at any rate he was not a wholly spent force, nor presumably in his own, for otherwise he would not have gone to support the embassy. What sort of change was there with the coming of Cyrus?

It has been argued that, when the Spartan envoys who returned with Cyrus from their meeting with the King declared that they had secured all they wanted from the King, they were confident that from then on all would be different from what it had been under Tissaphernes, and it has been claimed that they had sought and obtained a new treaty of alliance, the so-termed Treaty of Boiotios superseding that of 412/411; as a result 'the whole Persian policy changes at this point'.[17] This treaty is, to my mind, a chimera. If the result of Spartan negotiations at Susa was a new treaty, it must have involved, as the treaty it replaced involved, Sparta's allies (cf. Thuc. 8. 58) and could not have been kept secret. But Cyrus did try to keep secret the news of an important change by stopping the Athenian embassy which encountered him from returning to Athens with the news. There was to be change. Spartan complaints about Persian conduct under Tissaphernes were to be redressed. The Athenians would be unprepared for their bitter lesson. There was not a new treaty, but there was promised a new rigour in doing what had been promised.

Cyrus certainly did all he could to secure victory for Sparta. He provided the money necessary for the maintenance of the Peloponnesian fleet (cf. Thuc. 2. 65. 12). He had said to Lysander, when he first arrived in Sardis, that if funds provided by the King ran out he would use his own money (Xen. *Hell.* 1. 5. 3) and clearly he was as good as his word (ibid. 2. 1. 14, 2. 3. 8). Of equal importance was his encouragement of the Spartans to persist. The battle of Arginusae in 406 BC was a fearsome disaster for the Peloponnesian fleet. The nauarch Callicratidas began the battle with one hundred and twenty ships, of which he lost more than sixty-nine (ibid. 1. 6. 25, 26, and 34). Without the support of Cyrus Sparta might have given up the struggle. When Cyrus was called to the bedside of his ailing father, he gave Lysander 'the surplus monies' from his satrapy for the Peloponnesian fleet. Where Tissaphernes had been tight-fisted, Cyrus was open-handed indeed.[18]

But how far was Cyrus' generosity Royal policy? At his first meeting with Lysander, he had to declare that he could not go beyond the King's orders which fixed the rate of pay for Lysander's fleet at a half-drachma a day, but he was readily persuaded of the case for paying more and paid it out of his own pocket (Xen. *Hell.* 1. 5. 5–7). It looks as if the King had not changed his attitude. Cyrus brought down with him in 407 five hundred talents (ibid. 1. 5. 3), which would maintain a hundred ships for ten months, but it would seem that that was all the King was prepared to give. Two years later Cyrus told Lysander that 'the money from the King had been spent' despite there being a great deal of money available (ibid. 2. 1. 11). But the real proof of the King's lack of enthusiasm for the final defeat of Athens is provided by his failure to send again the naval force which he had withdrawn in 411. Xenophon does not say explicitly that Cyrus was seeking naval help. He merely has Cyrus tell Lysander 'not to fight a sea-battle unless he has a far greater number of ships' (ibid. 2. 1. 14). Plutarch (*Life of Lysander* 9. 2) is explicit. When Cyrus went up to his father, he asked Lysander 'not to fight a sea-battle with the Athenians before he came back and he said he would come back with a large naval force from Phoenicia and Cilicia'. Why had it not come earlier?

For the defeat of Athens an overwhelming naval force must have seemed essential. No one could have foreseen that incompetence on the part of the Athenian generals would lead to the total destruction of Athenian naval power at the battle of Aegospotami in 405 BC; Athens had one hundred and ninety ships in the Hellespont (Xen. *Hell.* 2. 1. 20); at the end of the day no more than ten of them remained. That was Lysander's good fortune. But Cyrus would have had to plan the assemblage of a joint fleet comparable to that which won the battle of Cnidus in 394 BC, and the Persian part of such a fleet would be provided only if the King approved. He never did. Despite fulsome words it never came.

Cyrus may have been sent by Darius to take command as a practical solution to the difficulties that had arisen between Tissaphernes and Pharnabazus. The two satraps had proved somewhat incompatible. Pharnabazus seems to have found Greeks congenial. He had two who had been exiled staying at his court and whom he used on diplomatic business (Thuc. 8. 6). When he had his meeting in 395/394 with Agesilaus, who awaited him lying on the grass, he disdained Persian ceremony and lay down on the grass likewise (Xen. *Hell.* 4. 1. 30). Tissaphernes kept, as it were, to his high horse. Thucydides did not bother to name his envoy to Sparta in 413/412 (8. 5). Later he used a bilingual Carian (8. 85. 2). Pharnabazus, to judge by his conversation with Agesilaus, spoke Greek freely. Tissaphernes may have understood Greek but he kept his distance with an interpreter, on one occasion none other than Alcibiades (Thuc. 8. 56), and it is no surprise that he was thought a double-dealer (Xen. *Hell.* 4. 1. 32). The Spartans in 411 finally had had enough of him and went north to Pharnabazus (Thuc. 8. 99).

The rivalry between the two, which continued to flourish in the 390s, was readily exploited during the Ionian War and a practical solution was to send the King's son to be in overall command.

Thus Cyrus could play a useful part. Unperceived perhaps by the King but not by Cyrus' mother, Parysatis, the command could play a more than useful part in the plans of Cyrus. In 407 BC Cyrus was only 16 years old.[19] His ambitions were large. He showed his true colours when in the course of 406/405 he had two sons of the King's sister put to death for not showing him due respect by keeping their hands enveloped in their long sleeves, as would be required only in the presence of the King (Xen. *Hell.* 2. 1. 8), Royal pretensions indeed on Cyrus' part. This was not long before he was summoned to his father's sickbed, but the man who was in Xenophon's obituary notice pronounced 'most kingly, most worthy to rule' (*Anab.* 1. 9. 1), came down bent on securing himself the means of claiming the throne if it was not accorded him through the 'specious argument' advanced by his mother that unlike his elder brother Artaxerxes he had been born after his father became King.[20] He needed military experience and got it by war against the Mysians and the Pisidians (Xen. *Anab.* 1. 9. 14, 1. 11). Above all he saw that if he had an adequate body of Greek hoplites his chances of success, if it came to fighting, would be immeasurably increased.

To get the necessary mercenaries, Cyrus needed to secure, as far as he could do so, the victory of Sparta. From the outset he and Lysander got on extremely well. Cyrus was readily persuaded to increase the rate of pay for the fleet, and was not to be deflected by Tissaphernes arguing for his policy of ambivalence (Xen. *Hell.* 1. 5. 2–9). Later, on his return to the command of the fleet, Lysander applied to Cyrus for money and despite having already given amply Cyrus gave (ibid. 2. 1. 11). All this might seem to show only that Cyrus was intent on being what he declared that his father had bidden him be, namely, 'most zealous for the war' (ibid. 1. 5. 2–3). So why should he be suspected of having a secret agenda? Why should he be thought of as preparing his forces for a possible future struggle for power?

It is Cyrus' treatment of Lysander's successor as nauarch, Callicratidas, which shows that Cyrus' motives were not above suspicion. What reason did he have for disdaining Callicratidas (Xen. *Hell.* 1. 6. 6–7)? Cyrus had told Lysander that his father had charged him strenuously to carry on the war against Athens (ibid. 1. 5. 3). Why should he have done so during one Spartan nauarchy but not during another? Clearly

Callicratidas did belong to those at Sparta who were uncomfortable with Persian help in the liberation of Hellas, but that would hardly be a reason for declining to support Sparta, especially considering that Callicratidas did not express his disgust until he had been disdainfully treated. Cyrus plainly got on with Lysander uncommonly well (ibid. 1. 5. 6; cf. *Oec.* 4. 20–5) but he spurned Callicratidas before he met him. One therefore cannot but suspect that Callicratidas' disgust with collaboration with Persia, a disgust shared by a sizeable faction at Sparta, made Cyrus realize that there was little to be expected from such people if his mother's argument about the succession (Plut. *Art.* 2. 3–4) did not prevail and he had to claim the throne by arms.

In the summer of 405 Cyrus was summoned to his father's sickbed and went in high hopes of being named successor (Plut. *Art.* 2. 3). Before his mother Parysatis succeeded in her scheming to have Cyrus given preference over Artaxerxes, Darius died and Tissaphernes, whom Cyrus had taken with him 'as a friend', promptly denounced Cyrus as plotting against his brother (Xen. *Anab.* 1. 1. 2). Cyrus was arrested and only saved from execution by his mother's pleas. 'When he went away having been endangered and dishonoured, he planned never again to be in his brother's power but, if possible, to become King in his stead.' This account by Xenophon suggests that it was not until Cyrus got away from Babylon and back to his satrapy that he began to plan revolt,[21] and obviously it was only then that he began to assemble his army under the pretext of attacking the Pisidians (Xen. *Anab.* 1. 1. 11, 2. 1, 9. 14). But that the idea had been forming in his mind before this is strongly suggested by Tissaphernes accusing him of treasonable designs while he was still in Babylon. His aspirations to Royal status may well have gone back to the period of his arrival in Ionia, and his attitude to Sparta and the conduct of the Peloponnesian War perhaps derived from this. He wanted Sparta to win outright, under the leadership of the sort of Spartans he could count on. If King Darius had been similarly minded about the war, it would not have been necessary for Cyrus to go and request a large fleet from Phoenicia and Cilicia (Plut. *Lys.* 9. 2).

There are imponderables. One cannot know when the health of Darius II prompted thoughts of the succession in the minds of Cyrus and, more importantly, Parysatis, his mother. Her devotion to Cyrus was certainly strong. She had the man who cut off Cyrus' head after his death on the battlefield of Cunaxa himself murdered (Plut. *Art.* 17). Her vengeance was bitter and unrelenting (cf. Ctes. F16 §59). Because

Tissaphernes had in 404 denounced Cyrus to Artaxerxes, she secured his execution in 395 though he had done nothing to deserve it (Diod. 14. 80. 6–8, and Polyaenus 7. 16). Her part in kindling Cyrus' ambition may be presumed to have been important. She was certainly considered responsible (Plut. *Art.* 6. 6).[22]

Whether Cyrus would have had more success with his brother, the new King Artaxerxes II, than he had had with his father King Darius in his request for ships, one cannot tell.[23] By the time Cyrus got back to Sardis, Lysander had seized his opportunity and destroyed the Athenian navy. It was time to be on with preparations for revolt and the long march up-country.

It would have been better from Cyrus' point of view if Lysander had had to wait for a Persian fleet to finish off Athens, but Cyrus had done sufficient to get from Sparta what he needed. 'He sent envoys to the Spartans to remind them of his services during the war against the Athenians and to call on them to give him military support (ἑαυτῷ συμμαχεῖν), and the Spartans, thinking the war would be to their advantage, decided to help Cyrus, and promptly sent out envoys to their own admiral, Samios by name, to do whatever Cyrus ordered' (Diod. 14. 19. 4). In reality Sparta had no option. Cyrus had shown himself a man of energy and determination and if help were refused he could be expected to turn against such ingratitude. Nor did Cyrus seem to be asking all that much. In the beginning the aim he professed was to campaign against rebellious Cilicians (Diod. 14. 19. 3) and though he may at a very early moment on the march have told Clearchus what his real aim was (ibid. 14. 19. 9), it is wholly unlikely that his envoys to the Spartans were empowered to say as much or were even privy to his plans. So the Spartans had to accede to Cyrus' request.

The Spartan contingent of seven hundred hoplites under Chirisophus was far from the largest, but the fact that it had been promised must have been an encouragement to the other forces being assembled in Sardis.[24] The Greek leaders had no doubt been assiduously courted by Cyrus and probably bought. Xenophon was pressed by his friend, Proxenus, to join the party; Cyrus, he told him, would be worth more to him than his own country (Xen. *Anab.* 3. 1. 5). Aristippus, one of the medizing Aleuad family of Larisa in Thessaly, was one of his 'friends' (ξένος), who successfully appealed to him for money and two thousand soldiers and got twice as much money and twice as many soldiers (ibid. 1. 1. 10), and who sent his boyfriend Meno with a thousand hoplites and five hundred peltasts when the time was ripe (ibid. 1. 2. 6). Cyrus was able to call on, almost call up, a wide circle of friends. A notable instance was the Spartiate, Clearchus, who was to play the leading part on the march to Cunaxa. He had gone as an exile to Cyrus, found great favour and been given the means to assemble a large body of mercenaries. He was certainly one of Cyrus' cronies (ibid. 1. 1. 9 and 2. 9), and in due season arrived at Sardis with one thousand hoplites, eight hundred Thracian peltasts, and two hundred Cretan archers. Cyrus must have thought he had spent his money wisely, and, above all, must have congratulated himself on doing what he had done towards the total defeat of Athens. The market was flooded with unemployed soldiers. Revolt and the struggle for the throne could begin.

The Complete Recovery of Ionia

The revolt of Cyrus was a purely domestic affair but its failure had very serious consequences for the Greeks. Cyrus, who got on so well with Greeks, might have contrived a happy autonomy for the Greek cities of Asia. After all, the years of peace with Athens had been satisfactory enough. A similar settlement might have been attempted if Lysander and other friends had held sway. The death of Cyrus and the loathing felt by Artaxerxes for the Spartans who had been the accomplices of his brother[25] created a quite new situation for the Greeks of Asia. In place of the lenient Cyrus, they now had to deal with Tissaphernes, who, having rendered conspicuous service to the King, 'was sent down as satrap of the places he previously ruled and also of those of Cyrus' (Xen. *Hell.* 3. 1. 3). Trouble for the Greeks was to be expected (Diod. 14. 35. 2–6). The Greeks of Asia appealed to Sparta to protect them, and in the spring of 399 BC Thibron arrived with a force, substantial enough, when the remnants of Cyrus' Ten Thousand were included, to present Tissaphernes with something of a problem. Thibron, however, accomplished very little and when the allies complained that he had let his army plunder Sparta's friends (Xen. *Hell.* 3. 1. 8) and he was replaced by Dercylidas, the shadow boxing continued. He promptly made a deal with Tissaphernes and went off to the satrapy of Pharnabazus, where after a lightning eight-day dance through Aeolis he made a deal with Pharnabazus (ibid. 3. 1. 8–2. 1) which was extended the following year (ibid. 3. 2. 9). When in the course of summer 397 he moved back south to the satrapy of Tissaphernes he found himself confronted by the combined forces of Tissaphernes and Pharnabazus. No battle ensued. Instead, there was a new truce, the terms of a full agreement being referred to Sparta and to the King (ibid. 3. 2. 13–20). All in all, in three whole years remarkably little happened.

In winter 397/396 BC all seemed to change. A Syracusan who had been in Phoenicia on a merchant ship, and had seen a Phoenician fleet in various stages of being assembled, allegedly to be, when complete, three hundred triremes strong, got on to the first ship leaving for Greece and took this exciting news to Sparta. 'Where they are bound for,' he added, 'I have no idea.' The Spartans in alarm called a congress of the Peloponnesian League and shortly King Agesilaus set off for Asia in command of eight thousand hoplites to which he would be able to add the army of Dercylidas (ibid. 3. 4. 1–4). A decisive struggle of East and West was to be expected.

In the Ionian War, the King's seriousness about the Greeks of Asia could have been judged, no matter what satraps might say, by his failure to send adequate naval forces to confront the Greek power of the Aegean. When in 397/396 word came that he could be shortly expected in Aegean waters, it seemed time for Sparta to be strenuous. But one cannot help suspecting it was all a mistake.

Egypt, about which the King was ever most solicitous, had been in revolt since before 401 BC,[26] presumably part of the usual accession troubles of a new king. Perhaps the large force under the command of Abrocomas, satrap of Syria when Cyrus began his revolt (Xen. *Anab.* 1. 4. 5), had been intended for invasion of Egypt,[27] but the whole plan had to be postponed after the confusions that the revolt had caused. By 397 it may have seemed safe to proceed with it again and the fleet of which the Syracusan brought word to Sparta was perhaps being prepared not for decisive intervention in Ionia but for the reconquest of Egypt. He had no idea where this fleet was bound for. Sparta jumped to perhaps the wrong conclusion and the whole charade of Agesilaus' Panhellenist flourish in Asia was prompted by a mistake.

This is, it must be emphasized, no more than a guess, but it has the merit of explaining why the King left the reconquest of Egypt so long unattended to. Isocrates (4. 140), and no one else, mentioned an invasion by Abrocomas, Tithraustes, and Pharnabazus which came to disaster. Some have set this invasion immediately after the King's Peace, but in that period Persia was preoccupied with the war against Evagoras of Cyprus. It seems more probable that the attempted invasion belongs in the period after Pharnabazus returned from his triumphant voyage with Conon to Greece in 393 BC (Xen. *Hell.* 4. 8. 1 and

2) when Tiribazus had replaced Tithraustes in Sardis, thus setting him free for service elsewhere, and before the revolt of Evagoras in 390 BC had begun to look serious.[28] On this hypothesis the victory in the battle of Cnidus in August 394 by which Spartan naval power was utterly destroyed made it possible for Pharnabazus, admiral of the Persian fleet, to take his victorious navy to support an invasion. Artaxerxes, in short, took on the all-important task of resolving the Egyptian problem as soon as he could, and he would have begun it earlier if Sparta had not misapprehended his naval preparations.

If the Greeks were deceived, so too in a sense was Artaxerxes. Agamemnon setting out for Troy had sacrificed at Aulis in Boeotia. Agesilaus in 396 sought to do the same, a way of proclaiming the significance of his assault on Asia (Xen. *Hell.* 3. 4. 4). This was not to be the petty campaigning of a Thibron or a Dercylidas. Agesilaus was thinking, and talking, big. In 395 (ibid. 3. 4. 20) he proclaimed that he was 'leading by the shortest way against the strongest points of the land', whatever he meant by that, and in 394 (ibid. 4. 1. 40) he was thought 'to be preparing to journey as far up-country as he could'.[29] Indeed in his encomium of Agesilaus, Xenophon spoke of him 'being minded and expecting to destroy the empire that formerly campaigned against Greece' (*Ages.* 1. 36).[30] All this Panhellenist claptrap was congenial to Xenophon. Other Greeks were more hard-headed. The Oxyrhynchus Historian (25. 4 Chambers) said that Agesilaus was planning in 394 to go against Cappadocia, and Isocrates in the *Panegyricus* (144) asserted that he conquered 'nearly all the land within the Halys' but at no point did Isocrates say anything about Agesilaus intending to topple the King from his throne. Still, Cappadocia was well along the Royal Road (cf. Hdt. 5. 49. 6). If Agesilaus and the Spartans were to succeed in detaching from the Empire the seaward satrapies in the way in which he sought to interest Pharnabazus in 394 (Xen. *Hell.* 4. 1. 34–7), the situation would be serious.

The performance of Agesilaus was comparatively feeble. In over two years campaigning, apart from pillaging the satrapy of Pharnabazus, he did very little indeed. When in 395, having proclaimed his intention to attack 'the strongest points of the land', he had ravaged the paradise of Tissaphernes at Sardis and then, having entrapped in an ambush the satrapal forces following him, had, it seemed, a clear road to the 'upper satrapies' (Diod. 14. 80), he crossed over the mountains to the valley of the river Maeander but he was dissuaded by unfavourable auspices from going on. This might seem typically Greek and admirably pious, if it were not that the Oxyrhynchus Historian (17. 4) shows that he tried only on the day he reached the river. He was perhaps too easily persuaded. Despite the grandiose words he was not much different from Dercylidas. His first act on arrival in Asia in 396 had been to make a truce with Tissaphernes while the King was consulted about the terms on which the Greek cities of Asia could be autonomous (Xen. *Hell.* 3. 4. 5). So much for the Grand Design.

What Agesilaus' expedition to Asia did achieve was that the fleet being got ready in Phoenicia was sent under the command of Pharnabazus to join Conon's fleet (Diod. 14. 83. 4–7). The ensuing battle of Cnidus finished Spartan naval power. With the outbreak of the Corinthian War Agesilaus and his army were recalled and the way was open for the King to have undisputed control of the whole of Asia, the King's Peace.

What Alcibiades is alleged by Thucydides (8. 45) to have advised Tissaphernes, had been proved sound, namely, that if the Athenians were thrown out of Asia the Spartans having liberated the Greeks of mainland Greece would not leave the Greeks of Asia to the mercy of the King. Under Cyrus, for whatever reason, the policy of Tissaphernes was abandoned, and by 399 the Spartans were in Asia professing to protect the Asiatic Greeks against Persian interference (Xen. *Hell.* 3. 1. 3 and 4). This was a novel situation for the King. Under the Athenian Empire, even after the ending of the Peace of Callias, Athenian forces did not ravage the satrapies, but after Thibron's force appeared in 399 BC the territories controlled by Tissaphernes and Pharnabazus were constantly under attack. Indeed in winter 395/394 the latter, in his meeting with Agesilaus, is found complaining 'I am put in such a position by you that I don't even have a dinner in my own land except for what I, like wild beasts, scavenge from what you leave' (ibid. 4. 1. 33).

In general, Artaxerxes seems to have judged that the satrapies had adequate forces to deal with Spartan attacks. Only when Agesilaus arrived with substantially larger forces than Thibron had had[31] and uttering grandiose threats did the King send down extra forces for Tissaphernes (ibid. 3. 4. 6 and 11). Clearly what he wanted above all was a peace treaty. Xenophon would have it thought that Tissaphernes declined battle in summer 397 out of fear of the Ten Thousand and thinking that all Greeks were like them, and so entered into peace negotiations with Dercylidas (ibid. 3. 2. 18–20). Actually the combined forces of Tissaphernes and Pharnabazus probably well outnumbered the Spartan army (cf. Diod. 14. 39. 5) and some of the Greeks were taking advantage of the tall corn on the Maeandrian plain to desert (ibid. 3. 2. 17). It is more probable that Tissaphernes had instructions to do the deal, the terms of which were that the Greek cities should be autonomous provided the Greek army left the country and the Spartans' harmosts left the cities. This agreement was to be referred to Sparta and to the King. Nothing came of it, because of the alarms and excursions that sent Agesilaus to Asia. But a similar agreement was proposed in 396 as soon as Agesilaus came on the scene (ibid. 3. 4. 5). Tissaphernes declared that if a truce was made during which the matter would be referred to the King he thought that Agesilaus could achieve what he wanted and could sail home. This agreement seems to have miscarried. The King had stiffened his terms as was shown by the declaration made by Tithraustes who was sent down in 395 to execute Tissaphernes and take over his command (ibid. 3. 4. 25–7). 'The King thinks it fit that you should sail home, and that the cities in Asia should be autonomous provided that they pay him the tribute that they used to pay.' This was too much for Agesilaus to decide without referring it to Sparta and the response of the Spartan authorities (ibid. 3. 4. 27) was in effect that the war should go on. So negotiations came to an end.

Xenophon would have it thought that the Corinthian War, which forced Sparta to recall Agesilaus and his army, was caused by Persian bribery (*Hell.* 3. 5. 1–2), a view imperiously rejected by the Oxyrhyn-chus Historian (10. 2); resentment against the Spartans and indeed hatred were long-standing. Isocrates in his letter *To Archidamus* of 356 BC (§§11–14) put his finger on it. Maintaining control over the politics of the cities of mainland Greece and seeking to liberate the cities of Asia from Persian control were inconsistent and too much for Sparta to manage. It was inevitable that Agesilaus and his army should be obliged to abandon the Asiatic Greeks. The naval victory of the Persian fleet in the battle of Cnidus of August 394 set the seal on it all. There would now be no question of negotiations between Sparta and Persia. The King would arrange things entirely to his own satisfaction.

In 392/391 the Spartans sought to make peace with the King on terms that amounted to total renunciation of the terms that they had sought over the previous decade. Antalcidas was sent to Tiribazus in Sardis to say that Sparta wanted peace with the King, 'the sort of peace the King desired'. They abandoned all claim to the Greek cities of Asia and they professed themselves content that 'all the islands and the rest of the cities of Greece should be autonomous' (Xen. *Hell.* 4. 8. 14). This was, as far as we can discern, very much the same as the King's Peace. For that Xenophon gives only the Royal Rescript in accordance with which the Peace itself was drawn up (5. 1. 31) and the terms have to be presumed and conjectured. However, it is clear from the Rescript that if either side in the Corinthian War did not accept the Peace the King would join forces with those who were willing and make war by every possible means. The only Greeks who hesitated in 387/386 were the Thebans and they were quickly brought into line (ibid. 5. 1. 32–3). In 392/391 things were different.

In Andocides' third oration, *On the Peace* of 392/391, he sought to persuade the Athenians to accept the peace, the terms of which he had shared in negotiating at Sparta. As Philochorus (F 149b) shows, the Athenians were not persuaded and the war went on. Yet instead of joining with the Spartans and supporting the war by every means, the King is shortly found sending down as replacement in Sardis for Tiribazus, who had been covertly leagued with the Spartans, Strouthas, who favoured the Athenians and was hostile to the Spartans. This is a paradox and calls for explanation.

Plutarch (*Art.* 22) declared that Artaxerxes always loathed the Spartans and he quoted Dinon of Colophon, whose life overlapped Artaxerxes' reign, to the effect that Artaxerxes thought the Spartans 'the most shameless of mankind'. Whether this was based on their support for Cyrus or on their seeking to liberate the Greeks of Asia in the 390s despite having accepted during the Ionian War that the whole of Asia belonged to the King, is unclear, but certainly Tiribazus did not dare openly to support the Spartans until he had persuaded the King to approve of such a change of policy (Xen. *Hell.* 4. 8. 16). Tiribazus failed in 392/391 and it was not until Antalcidas went up in person in 387 to see the King that the Persians agreed to act in concert with Sparta (ibid. 5. 1. 25). Perhaps the King and Antalcidas really did hit it off, as Plutarch (loc. cit.) would have it believed. Perhaps Strouthas was sent down in 392 because Antalcidas had not yet gone up.

However, states do not normally allow such personal considerations to affect judgement of their interest, and once the Persians had secured from Sparta the all-important concession offered in 392/391 there was no good reason to miss the opportunity. It may therefore be suggested that the real difficulty lay in the Panhellenist policy of Agesilaus.[32] When in 394 he was recalled with his army to the defence of Sparta, he assembled his Asiatic allies to announce his return home but added, 'If things go well in Greece, be assured that I will not forget you but I will be back again to do what you require' (ibid. 4. 2. 3). No doubt word of this reached Susa. If peace came in Greece, the King could expect the Spartans to forget their oaths and treaty obligations yet again and return to the war which they had perforce abandoned.

Sparta was not monolithic. In these years there was a division between the hard-headed sense of an Antalcidas and the high-minded championship of the liberty of the Asiatic Greeks led previously by Lysander, latterly by Agesilaus.[33] Variation of policy ensued. Agesilaus returned from Asia, fighting the battle of Coronea *en route*, in 394. He does not reappear in Xenophon's narrative until 391 (*Hell.* 4. 4. 19). In the interval came Antalcidas' embassy to Tiribazus in Sardis (ibid. 4. 8. 12–15), which must have been the outcome of a serious debate in Sparta about the new situation created by the battle of Cnidus and the triumphant voyage of Conon back to Athens (ibid. 4. 8. 1–10); if Athenian naval power was rising again, Sparta would again need Persian alliance. Only the policy represented by Antalcidas made sense.

Tiribazus too saw that Persia must side with Sparta and went to persuade the King of it (Xen. *Hell.* 4. 8. 16). Perhaps the King simply distrusted Sparta too much for a sudden conversion, but to appoint Strouthas who would positively side with resurgent Athens was going a great deal further than was sensible. It may therefore be suggested that the King's feeling of resentment for Sparta received a sharp reminder just after the collapse of the Peace being negotiated in Sparta, in the resurgence of Agesilaus. In early 391 Agesilaus is to the fore again and he collaborated with his step-brother Teleutias in an attack on Corinth (ibid. 4. 4. 19). Teleutias is indeed the index. In the run-up to the King's Peace of 387/386 he is reported by Xenophon making a speech to the fleet at Aegina in which he echoes the words of Callicratidas a decade and a half earlier (ibid. 5. 1. 17). 'For what could be more pleasing than to pay court to no man for the sake of money, be he Greek or be he Barbarian, but to be in a position to provide for ourselves, and from the source most creditable'-- by which he means by raiding the enemy and he proceeds to organize a raid on the Piraeus. This speech was made at the very time that Antalcidas had gone up to see the King (ibid. 5. 1. 25) and seek his aid in defeating the Athenians. Teleutias was in fact preaching Panhellenism. In 392/391 he is found in command of the Spartan naval forces in the Corinthian Gulf (ibid. 4. 8. 11), and this command coupled with the re-emergence of Agesilaus suggests that those who had refused to countenance the deal proposed by Tithraustes in 395 (ibid. 3. 4. 25–9) were again in the ascendant. News of that may have been what hardened the King against the suasions of Tiribazus.[34]

Athens, having rejected the peace proposed in Sparta in 392, should have been utterly crushed, but through Spartan folly was left free to get on with the re-establishment of her imperial power. She had two options. Either she could quietly and slowly rebuild without provoking Persia, which was the prudent method advised by Conon who by 391 knew a very great deal about how to work with Persia, or she could throw caution to the winds and go all out for the re-establishment of the Empire. The Athenians chose the latter course. In the course of 391, it would seem, ships were built and ready for use when Thrasybulus was sent out partly to support Athens' friends in Rhodes but with a general mission to rebuild Athens' alliances. Thrasybulus did not restrict himself to the islands and the European side of the Hellespont. How widely he intervened in Asia itself is unclear but to judge by his intervention in Halicarnassus which happens to be mentioned in a speech of Lysias and, above all, by his landing at Aspendus, very much a Persian base, where he sought to raise money, he clearly had no hesitation in provoking Persia. Overall his intentions were blatantly imperialistic. He revived financial institutions of the fifth-century Empire and the Great King was faced with the return of Athenian power in his territories. He had good reason to regret his having rejected the advice of Tiribazus.[35]

Sparta's offer in 392 of unqualified acceptance of the King's right to all of Asia having been rebuffed, Thibron was sent to Asia with a substantial force which together with troops assembled in Asia confronted Strouthas (Diod. 14. 99. 2). Thibron was killed and his army put to flight (Xen. *Hell.* 4. 8. 17–19), but with trouble looming in Cyprus[36] the King had reason now to accept Sparta's offer, especially considering the increase of Athenian naval power. When in 387 Antalcidas went to the King in Susa, the terms of peace were agreed, and he returned to the Aegean with the offer of peace or the threat of war. The King's Peace was the result (ibid. 5. 1. 25–31).

Time had shown that Sparta lacked the power at the same time to dominate Greece, and to liberate and guard the Greek cities of Asia, let alone attack Persia more widely. She tried in the 390s with serious consequences within Greece. Good sense nearly prevailed in 392 but was ruined by the starry-eyed ideology of Agesilaus and his ilk. Athens, in turn, having been restored by Persian naval victory in 394 to hopes of resurgence, ruined her chances by putting her fortunes in the hands of Thrasybulus. The King's Peace of 386 settled the business. Save for a brief intervention by Athens in the 350s for which she paid dear, the King's Peace kept the Greeks out of Asia until the king of Macedon took charge of Greece.

NOTES

1. For Athens, Diod. 16. 22 and *FGH* 105 F4, for Thebes, Diod. 16. 34. Sparta did no more than send Agesilaus on an embassy, to do what harm he could (Xen. *Ages.* 2. 26, 27, cf. Nepos, *Tim.* 1. 3).

2. For Agesilaus after the King's Peace, v.i. p. 218. For Jason, Isoc. 5. 119–20 (λόγῳ μόνον χρησάμενος) and Xen. *Hell.* 6. 1. 12 (for a sample of his talk).

3. Cf. Lewis 1977: 58, S. Hornblower in *CAH* vi² 1994: 58–9, Briant 1996: 356–7.

4. Xenophon omitted to record the result of this reference to the King, presumably because the alarms and excursions caused by the rumour of winter 397/396 (Xen. *Hell.* 3. 4. 1) took over. Xenophon claimed (*Hell.* 3. 4. 6) that Tissaphernes cheated, but since the terms under discussion were essentially the same as those under discussion in the abortive proposals of Dercylidas (ibid. 3. 2. 20) Xenophon was perhaps letting his prejudices affect his judgement.

5. Of course, there is no way of knowing how Diodorus' source, Ephorus, came to make such a judgement. He may have been generalizing from the western satrapies, but relations with Greece and with Egypt formed a large part of the Royal concerns.

6. Cf. Lewis 1977: 57 and n. 51.

7. Xenophon (*Hell.* 3. 4. 25) puts the severe treatment of Tissaphernes down to his failure to deal with Agesilaus. That he was not allowed to remain as satrap was perhaps due to his military failures, but his execution was an extra to please the terrible, vengeful mother of Cyrus, Parysatis (Diod. 14. 80. 6; cf. Plut. *Art.* 14. 10, 17. 1–3 and 9, 18. 6).

8. Cf. Lewis 1977: 14, 25 n. 143, 95 n. 57.

9. Cf. Andrewes 1981 ad Thuc. 8. 58, Lévy 1983, and especially de Sanctis 1951: 84–96.

10. V.s. p. 143.

11. V.i. p. 157.

12. Cf. Andrewes 1981: 13–16.

13. Thuc. 8. 46. 1, 59, 78, 81. 3, 99, 108. 1, 109. 1; Diod. 13. 37. 5 and 46. 6 (in each of which passages Diodorus in typical fashion named Pharnabazus instead of Tissaphernes).

14. Aspendus in Pamphylia on the river Eurymedon was a Persian naval base

in the 460s as the story of Cimon's double victory on sea and on land shows. Pamphylia was not part of Cyrus' large command (Xen. *Anab.* 1. 9. 7), and in 401 it seems to have been joined with Cilicia, to judge by the fact that the guard accompanying the wife of Syennesis on her visit to Cyrus was composed of 'Cilicians and Aspendians' (ibid. 1. 2. 12). It seems unlikely that Tissaphernes' command in 411 embraced a larger territory than Cyrus'. It is true that Aspendus was included in the Athenian Tribute Assessment of 425 (assuming that lines 156–7 of column II are rightly supplemented) and it might be thought that the city's status varied from time to time and that 401 is not relevant to 411 but, as has already been discussed (v.s. p. 143), that Assessment was a pretty wild affair and there is no reason to suppose that a single drachma ever came in from many of the places assessed. Phaselis was the eastward limit of Athenian power, and Pamphylia was perhaps always linked administratively to Cilicia. There would have been no need for Tissaphernes physically to go there if the ships and the base had been under his command.

15. Lewis 1958.
16. Cf. Briant 1988: 143.
17. Lewis 1977: 124–5. The supposed Treaty of Boiotios was accepted by S. Hornblower in *CAH* VI² 65. Cf. Briant 1996: 617 and 1006, where the arguments of Tuplin 1987*a* opposing the thesis are preferred. The only point not dealt with by Tuplin is Lewis's claim (p. 124) that 'there is evidence that there was a treaty and we have a clause from it'. Lewis was basing his case on Xen. *Hell.* 1. 5. 5. See Appendix 8.
18. Andocides (3. 29) spoke of the Persians contributing 5,000 talents for the war, a claim repeated, possibly echoed, by Isocrates in the 350s (8. 97). Lewis 1977: 131 n. 138 was rightly sceptical. It is more likely Andocides was inflating the figure of 500 which was the number of talents Cyrus said he had brought down with him (Xen. *Hell.* 1. 5. 3). If he was being truthful, his handing over to Lysander at their first meeting 10,000 darics (Diod. 13. 70. 3, Plut. *Lys.* 4. 6), which were not much more than 30 talents, must have seemed decidedly stingy. Persian grandees, to judge by the fulsome words of the tight-fisted Tissaphernes (Thuc. 8. 81. 3), were perhaps somewhat given to grandiose utterances, and to talk about 'driving the Athenians from the sea' (Plut. *Lys.* 4. 1) or 'instructions from my father to provide the Spartans with whatever they want' (Diod. 13. 70. 3). This latter utterance was made by Cyrus at his very first encounter with Lysander, the more colourful version of which is found in Xenophon (*Hell.* 1. 5. 3), and is not a reliable index of Royal policy. 500 talents, if Cyrus did actually bring as much, was not, as Lewis remarked (loc. cit.), all that ample and the King produced no more (Xen. *Hell.* 2. 1. 11). It was Cyrus not the King who displayed real zeal for the war (cf. ibid. 2. 3. 8).
19. Cf. Lewis 1977: 134.

20. Plut. *Art.* 2. 4. As Plutarch noted, the argument had been deployed in favour of Xerxes (Hdt. 7. 3. 2–4).

21. Ctesias' phrase in F 16 §57 (μελεται ἐπανάστασιν) does not imply that in Ctesias' mind Cyrus had not before his arrest in Babylon had any thought of an uprising if he did not succeed his father. The story in Xen. *Hell.* 2. 1. 8 concerning the execution of two high-ranking Persians before he went up to his father's sickbed, if it is true, had shown how Cyrus was minded. (Ctesias was probably present at the sickbed of Darius and his placing the death in Babylon is to be accepted. However, it may be noted that according to Xenophon (Hell. 2. 1. 13) he took ill in Media during a campaign against the Cadusians who lived on the west coast of the Caspian, while according to Plutarch (*Artax.* 3) Cyrus was denounced at Pasargadae. All three stories may be true, but, if they are, Cyrus must have been absent from his command longer than is commonly supposed and the time for preparing for revolt correspondingly less. He had perhaps begun to formulate plans in his mind before he went up to his father.)

22. The precise date of Darius' death is uncertain. Cf. Lewis 1977: 120 n. 81 and 135 n. 154.

23. By 401 BC Cyrus had twenty-five ships of his own (Xen. *Anab.* 1. 4. 2, 1. 2. 21), but whence and how he obtained them is unknown.

24. Cf. Xen. *Anab.* 1. 2. 3, and 9. The hoplites with Chirisophus were presumably Neodamodeis. Cf. the force sent out with Agesilaus in 396 (Xen. *Hell.* 3. 4. 2). But Neodamodeis were well trained and fought side by side with Spartiates.

25. Plut. *Art.* 22. 1.

26. Kienitz 1953: 76–7. For the situation in Egypt in 401 BC, Briant 1996: 638. The revolt had already broken out, as Xenophon shows (*Anab.* 2. 1. 14, 2. 5. 13). For the Egyptians in the King's army at Cunaxa (*Anab.* 1. 8. 9, and 2. 1. 6), Briant 1996: 1012. According to Dandamaev 1989: 243, 'after Darius I the Persian Kings were basically uninterested in the internal affairs of Egypt'. That *may* be true but it is clear that there was never any thought of forgetting about that satrapy, though a great deal of effort and money could have been more usefully directed elsewhere if Egypt had been allowed to detach itself as at some stage the satrapy of India had done. (Dandamaev, ibid. 273, opines that 'the loss of Egypt was a heavy blow to the Persians, because it deprived them of the main granary of the Empire'. One wonders whither *in* the Empire he supposes that Egyptian corn was exported.)

27. Cf. Dandamaev 1989: 273.

28. Kienitz 1953: 85 assigns this campaign to 385–3 with surprising confidence considering that the only evidence is the statement of Isocrates (4. 140), according to whom it ended in failure. He has been followed generally (cf. Lloyd in *CAH* vi² 347) but any dating of the campaign between the

King's Peace and 380 BC, the date of Isocrates' *Panegyricus*, raises a serious difficulty, namely, its relation to the King's war against Evagoras of Cyprus. Conceivably the King might have tried to deal with the Egyptian rebellion straight after the King's Peace and before he dealt with Evagoras or even during the Cyprian War, but that war is comparatively fully recorded by Diodorus (15. 2–4 and 8–9) and a Persian failure in Egypt should surely have affected the course of events. It appears not to have done so, and Theopompus' twelfth book the epitome of which is to be found in Photius (*FGH* 115 F103) covered the King's Peace and the war against Evagoras but there is no word of an unsuccessful attempt to deal with Egypt.

It seems therefore preferable to put this mysterious campaign in 392 and the immediately following year, and if this is perchance correct, it would be consistent with the King being on as soon as possible with a campaign aborted by Sparta's heady intervention in Asia in 397/396.

29. If Agesilaus had it in mind in 395 BC to follow the route taken by Cyrus six years earlier, 'the strongest points of the land' would, after Sardis, have included Colossae and then the fastness of Celaenae (Xen. *Anab.* 1. 2. 6–9), which would have been held by a garrison. These places were part of Cyrus' command but Agesilaus would have had considerable difficulty in taking them. Indeed Agesilaus was probably lucky to encounter unfavourable omens on the day he arrived at the Maeander and since he did not persist in trying his luck, he was able to forget about Celaenae in 395 (*Hell. Oxy.* 15. 4 Chambers). For 394 he seems to have planned another route, to judge by his reaction to the defection of Spithridates and the Paphlagonians (Xen. *Hell.* 4. 1. 28). Again, he was probably lucky to be recalled to the war in Greece. This enabled him to continue his big talk.

30. How grand was the Grand Design? Plutarch (*Ages.* 15. 1) speaks of Agesilaus having decided to make the King fight for his life and for the riches of Ecbatana and Susa. Whence Plutarch derived this can only be guessed, but no doubt there was plenty of high-flown talk about what might have been if he had not been recalled to Greece. Xenophon (*Ages.* 1. 36) contributes his share and declares in the *Hellenica* (4. 1. 41) that Agesilaus was preparing in 394 to march up-country as far as he could. The Oxyrhynchus Historian perhaps reflects a more sober view (25. 4 Chambers). Cf. Seager 1977: 183–4.

31. Thibron took to Asia 1,000 Neodamodeis from Sparta and 4,000 hoplites from the Peloponnesian allies, Agesilaus 2,000 Neodamodeis and 6,000 Peloponnesians (Xen. *Hell.* 3. 1. 4 and 4. 2). Xenophon did not record what happened to Thibron's army, but it is to be presumed that Agesilaus took them over. Diodorus (14. 79. 2) gives a total for Agesilaus' army in 396 BC of 10,000 foot and 400 horse. When Agesilaus returned to Greece in 394, he left 4,000 to guard the Asiatic cities (Xen. *Hell.* 4. 2. 5). Considering that

he could call on the military resources of the Greek cities of Asia (cf. ibid. 3. 2. 17, 4. 2. 5), Agesilaus had, in Greek terms, a large army.

32. Cawkwell 1976*a*: 66–71. A different view of Agesilaus' attitude to Persia is provided by Cartledge 1987: 192–6.

33. Accame 1951: 117–18 ('Le prime manovrate dal filopersiano Antalcida pongono la Grecia alle dipendenze del Gran Re, le seconde manovrate da Agesilao hanno un concetto panellenico e vogliono costituire la Grecia al di fuori del Gran Re e contro di lui'). This view is based on Plutarch (*Ages.* 23). Cf. Cawkwell 1976*a*: 68–9. De Ste Croix 1972: 161–2 takes a different view ('It would be futile to try to make Agesilaus into a "Panhellenist", nor is there any good cause for suspecting that he and Antalcidas were not pursuing substantially the same policy, at least between 392 and 383'), and is impressed only with Agesilaus' joke about 'Medes laconising', in which Cartledge 1987: 195 concurs. Both happily dismiss what else Plutarch says about the two men and take a serious view only of the joke. An index of Agesilaus' views, however, is provided by the criticism of Antalcidas implied by that undeniable Panhellenist, his stepbrother Teleutias (Xen. *Hell.* 5. 1. 13–17, where he echoes Callicratidas' criticism of Lysander in 1. 6. 7).

34. One wishes one could be more precise about the chronology of the Athenian year 392/391, under which Philochorus (F149) recorded abortive peace negotiations over 'the peace in the time of Antalcidas'. The general outline is clear enough; cf. Cawkwell 1976*b*: 271–2. But greater precision eludes us. It would appear that Teleutias was nauarch in 392 (cf. Beloch 1916: 279), an office the commencement date of which in the 390s is uncertain (cf. Sealey 1976), and it is not impossible that his capture of the Corinthian ships and docks in early 391 (Xen. *Hell.* 4. 4. 19) was not long after his assumption of office. However, although Xenophon's account of the Congress of Sardis (ibid. 4. 8. 12–15) follows his account (in 4. 8. 11) of Teleutias taking command of the fleet in the gulf of Corinth, it is likely that the Spartan protest to Sardis about Conon's actions (4. 8. 12) was made before some of the events of §11. So Teleutias' career does not provide a *terminus post quem* for the Peace negotiations. Similarly, the precise moment of Artaxerxes' rejection of Tiribazus' advice and of his appointment of the phil-Athenian Strouthas cannot be determined. That appointment prompted the Spartans to send to Asia Thibron, who proceeded to pillage and plunder the King's territory (4. 8. 17), the business of summertime, but that is all there is to go on.

Plutarch (*Ages.* 21. 1) says Agesilaus, 'being of very great influence in the city, contrived to have his stepbrother Teleutias put in charge of the fleet'. He is speaking of their combined attack on Corinth in 391. If this is true (and there seems no good reason to deny it), Teleutias was not necessarily appointed nauarch in the autumn of 392, the evidence as to the date of commencement of office being very varied (cf. Busolt–Swoboda 1926: 716 n. 1). So it is possible that the peace negotiations did not peter out until not long before Agesilaus and his stepbrother attacked Corinth in the early summer of 391 (a date suggested by the ravaging in Xen. *Hell.* 4. 4. 19). But precise dating in 392/1 is barely possible.

35. Cf. Cawkwell 1976*b*: 270–1, 275–7.

36. The chronology of the King's efforts to bring Evagoras to heel has excited much debate. Cf. Tuplin 1983: 178–82 and Stylianou 1998: 143–54. Evagoras appears to have been openly insubordinate from the date of Teleutias' capture of Athenian ships on their way to help Evagoras' 'who was at war with the King' (Xen. *Hell.* 4. 8. 24), an event variously assigned to 391, 390, and 389 (cf. Tuplin 1983: 182 n. 76). According to Diodorus (14. 98. 3), Hecatomnos 'the dynast of Caria' was put in charge of the Persian force that was to deal with Evagoras, and according to Theopompus (F103 §4) Autophradates, 'satrap of Lydia' (for which post cf. Chaumont 1990: 599–603), was to command the land forces and Hecatomnus the sea. It is clear from the order of matters recorded in Theopompus' twelfth book that these appointments belonged to the period before the King's Peace. Although Diodorus (14. 98. 4) speaks of Hecatomnos crossing to Cyprus, the preparations would in the Persian manner have taken a good time and probably the war had barely got going by the date of the King's Peace. Diodorus (15. 9. 2) says that the Cyprian War lasted for 'about ten years' that most of the time was 'occupied with preparations', and that warfare was continued for only the final two years. Isocrates in the *Panegyric* of 380 BC speaks of the King having already wasted six years in war, the 'six years' being presumably the period since the King's Peace.

9

From the King's Peace to the End of the Social War

THE King's Peace of 387/386, whatever its precise terms, ended the long dispute over the status of the Greek cities of Asia.[1] Not until the king of Macedon began to plan conquest with the Greeks of the mainland as his allies was Persian domination of any part of Asia challenged, save once. That was in 355 BC when the Athenian general Chares, needing to find money to pay his army and his fleet, campaigned in support of a rebel satrap. He was initially successful but the King's response was abrupt and decisive. He sent an embassy to Athens to require immediate withdrawal and to threaten massive naval support for Athens' allies in revolt and the complete defeat of Athens (Diod. 16. 22). Athens promptly complied. She not only ordered Chares to leave Asia; she made peace with her allies and ended the Social War. Asia was secure.

It is the other demand of the Royal Rescript leading to the Peace that has excited debate, namely, 'to allow to be autonomous all the other Greek cities, both large and small, except for Lemnos, Imbros, and Scyros, which are to belong to the Athenians as they did in old times' (Xen. *Hell.* 5. 1. 31). This exception met the objections made by the Athenians in 392 BC to the terms proposed by Tiribazus and similarly modified at the Congress in Sparta (Xen. *Hell.* 4. 8. 14, Andoc. 3. 12). It underlined the main point, that naval empire would no longer be possible. But how much did the King care about the affairs of the cities of Greece, how much did he do about it? Did he have any real influence on the history of mainland Greece?

Writing in 380 BC in the shadow of the King's Peace, Isocrates, burning with indignation over the abandonment of the Greeks of Asia, would have it thought that Greece was virtually subject to the King (4. 120–1). 'As things are, it is he [sc. the King] who disposes of the affairs of the Hellenes and orders what each city must do and all but sets up governors (ἐπίσταθμοι) in the cities. What else is lacking? Did he not decide the war and does he not direct the peace? Is he not now placed in charge of things? Do we not take ship to him as if to a master, to denounce each other? Do we not name him "the Great King" as if we had become his prisoners of war? Do we not in our wars against each other place our hopes of salvation in him, the man who would gladly destroy both Athens and Sparta?' These extravagant words seem to have been more relevant to the ending of the Corinthian War and the making of the Peace than to what was happening in the late 380s. We know of no appeals to the King or denunciations of other states in that period. Yet the events of the early 360s when both Sparta and then Thebes and the Greeks generally sought the King's support (Xen. *Hell.* 7. 1. 33), aptly exemplify the state of affairs Isocrates was denouncing, and his view of the King's Peace merits serious consideration. It cannot, however, be denied that in the three decades between the King's Peace and the ending of the Social War on no occasion did Persia give any great help to any Greek state and it has been possible for an account of the working of the Peace[2] to conclude thus. 'Its influence had never been more than intermittent and superficial. First the Spartans, then the Athenians, and finally the Thebans presented themselves as *prostatai* of the peace in order to achieve certain limited political goals. But no city ever allowed the existence of the peace to dictate its aims, and no city tried to make the peace work as a peace. If the terms of the peace were congruent with a state's objectives, then the peace was momentarily exploited; if they were not it was ignored. It might affect the manner in which an action was justified or the form in which a policy was expressed, but policies and actions were still determined, as always, by advantage and the facts of military power.' Is this view correct? Did the King have no real influence on Greek affairs?

In addressing this question, one is faced with the serious difficulty posed by our main source for this period, the *Hellenica* of Xenophon. He is manifestly unfair in his playing down of the Persian part for the first two decades. The problem is how far to compensate. For as long as Sparta was able to control Greece his account rigorously excludes even the formal role of the Persians. By merest chance of epigraphic survival we learn that 'the King' (i.e. his representative) was joined with 'the Athenians and the Spartans and the rest of the Greeks' in swearing to the King's Peace (*GHI* 118).[3] Not the faintest hint of this is to be found in Xenophon's account (5. 1. 32). All that could be asserted thereon would be that there had been a Royal Rescript. It is even more striking that the renewal of the Peace in 375 is presented as a purely Greek affair (6. 2. 1). 'The Athenians, seeing that the Thebans were increasing their power through the Athenians' efforts and were not contributing to the cost of the naval force, while they themselves were having a hard time of it with levies for the war, with piratical raids from Aegina, and with the defence of their territory, desired to desist from the war. Sending ambassadors to Sparta they made peace.' The evidence (Philoch. F151, Diod. 15. 38) is plain enough to show that in fact the new Peace was similar in form to the Peace of 387/386 and involved an embassy from the King. So too with the Peace of 372/371 just before the battle of Leuctra. It seems likely that it too involved a Royal demand for a renewal of peace.[4] These silences are outrageous. One might pretend that the Persian part did not really matter, but it happened and at least merited notice.

After 371, however, Xenophon became ever more explicit about the shameful trafficking of the Thebans with the Mede. The mission of Philiscus in 368 Xenophon did indeed record (7. 1. 27); it showed that at that date Persia was still recognizing the Spartan right to Messenia. When, however, the Thebans began to get the King's favour, Xenophon does not hold back. The full extent of their baseness is spelled out (7. 1. 33–8), and Pelopidas' mission to Artaxerxes in 367 BC is shown up as despicable medizing. It emerges that there was a Spartan envoy already at the Persian court and that that was what moved the Thebans to organize embassies to counter his claims, but that is not how Xenophon puts it. 'The Thebans, constantly scheming to take over the leadership of Hellas, thought that if they sent to the King of the Persians they could get some base advantage with him ($\pi\lambda\epsilon o\nu\epsilon\kappa\tau\hat{\eta}\sigma\alpha\iota$—a nasty word). So having already called on their allies with the excuse that Euthycles the Spartan was with the King, Pelopidas went up with the others friendly to Thebes.' When they got there, Pelopidas got a considerable base advantage with the Persian, for he could 'say that the Thebans were the only Greeks to fight on the King's side at Plataea and that they never afterwards campaigned against the King and that the Spartans made war on them because they had not been willing to go with Agesilaus against him . . .'. In the ears of Greeks this was shameful talk indeed. One wonders what Antalcidas had said in his various meetings with the King, Xenophon having omitted to say. Indeed all he said about the crucial embassy of 387 was that 'Antalcidas came down to the coast with Tiribazus, having secured that the King should join Sparta in the war unless the Athenians and their allies accepted the peace which the King was dictating' (5. 1. 25). Of other missions to Sparta, not a word. At the Congress at Thebes, however, that followed Pelopidas' mission (7. 1. 39), 'the Persian who brought the Rescript displayed the King's seal and read the terms', a remarkable contrast with the account Xenophon gave of the making of the King's Peace. All in all, if we had had to make do with the evidence Xenophon provides, we would have been led to think that between 386 and the battle of Leuctra in 371 the King had no part at all in the affairs of Greece.[5]

Xenophon's bias is manifest and any argument based on his silences is instantly to be suspected. But, it may be asked, was he all that misleading about the realities of Greek politics? Granted that he omits the formalities, is he not to be trusted in his detailed accounts of various incidents? But there too one is very uneasy. The Mantineans, for instance, attacked by Sparta in 385, are not represented by Xenophon as appealing to their rights under the King's Peace (5. 2. 1–2), nor are the Spartans represented as seeking to split up the city into the four 'villages' (κῶμαι) of former times under an interpretation of the King's Peace which had required 'the independence of cities both great and small' (5. 1. 31) and which had been used to break up the Boeotian state (5. 1. 32). But there certainly was more to it than Xenophon lets on. In the Ephoran version 'the Mantineans sent ambassadors to Athens asking for help, but the Athenians chose not to transgress the general peace (τὰς κοινὰς συνθήκας)' (Diod. 15. 5. 5), and in Polybius (4. 27. 5) the Spartans, in moving the Mantineans and 'settling them in several cities', denied they were in the wrong in doing so.[6] The King's Peace would appear to have been at issue despite Xenophon's ignoring it. Instead, he suggests that the Spartans were free to act because the Thirty Years Treaty made between Sparta and Mantinea after the battle of 418/417 BC (Thuc. 5. 81. 1) had expired this year (5. 2. 2), 'this year' being in fact 385,[7] a comment both provoking and to be suspected of concealment.

Elsewhere one can only wonder. Did the Acanthians for instance in 382 BC, when they came before the Spartan assembly, not make some appeal to the King's Peace. They were presumably party to it as were the Olynthians.[8] It is hard to believe that the King's Peace remained unmentioned. There is not a word of it in Xenophon (5. 2. 11–20). So too over the intervention in Phlius (5. 2. 8–10 and 3. 10–13), and the occupation of the Cadmea (5. 2. 25–36), Xenophon maintains a thundering silence. There is only one passage in the whole of Xenophon's account of the period from the King's Peace to the battle of Leuctra where fear of the King's displeasure surfaces and that is in the speech of Callistratus at the peace conference of 372/371 (6. 3. 12), but he raises the idea only promptly to dismiss it. For the rest the Persians had in Xenophon's view no influence on either Spartan policy or Greek reactions to it.

That is how Xenophon has told the story, but was it so in fact? It is here maintained that Xenophon seriously misrepresented the period. The truth began to emerge as Thebes became the King's preferred agent (v.i. p. 186) but the real index of the influence of Persia between the King's Peace and the Social War is the way Athens reacted to the threat of Persian interference in the succeeding decade. The last Common Peace in which Persia was involved was in 366/365. In 362/361 the Greeks rebuffed an approach by the satraps leagued in the Satraps' Revolt and refused to join in war against the King (*GHI* 145). Indeed it was declared, if he did try to interfere in Greece, the Greeks united in the Common Peace would defend themselves 'in a manner worthy both of the peace that has recently been made and of former deeds', by which presumably they were alluding to the Greek resistance in the Persian Wars. These brave words, suggestive of how the King had behaved towards the Greeks previously, were uttered while the King was distracted by the Satraps' Revolt which must have been thought by some to be leading to the independence of the westernmost satrapies.[9] That revolt did not last. Within a few years the new King, Artaxerxes Ochus, had restored order and required the seaward satraps to disband their mercenary armies.[10] They complied and Persia resumed, or was thought to resume, its threatening posture. This was made abundantly plain in the immediate sequel. Some of the disbanded mercenaries went to the Athenian general Chares. Taking them into service, he went to the aid of the rebel Artabazus and won a victory over a Royal army which Chares described in a dispatch to Athens as 'sister to Marathon' (Schol. Dem. 4. 19). The glory was short-lived. The King demanded the recall of Chares. The story was put about (Diod. 16. 22. 2) that the King promised Athens' enemies that he would join in the war with three hundred ships and share in the utter defeat of Athens. Not only did Chares get out of Asia. The Social War was brought to an ignominious conclusion. Athens feared Royal intervention.

If the Xenophontic view that the King was of no real importance in the previous three decades were correct, the reaction of the Athenians in 355 would be hard to explain. They might have deemed it prudent to avoid further entanglement in the internal affairs of the Persian Empire, but why would they have accepted the independence of those members of the Second Athenian Confederacy who had been in revolt? The explanation would seem to be that experience had cowed them.

This fear persisted. In 354/353 BC rumour reached Athens that the King was preparing to campaign against the Greeks.[11] Probably enough the expedition was directed to the recovery of the long rebel satrapy of Egypt, but the Athenian reaction was to seek to summon a general congress of Greeks (Dem. 14. 12). In seeking to dissuade the Athenians from such action, Demosthenes speaks of the King as being thought 'to plot against the Greeks' and he begins his argument by affecting to be of the same mind as his audience by declaring 'I consider the King is the common enemy of all the Greeks' (§§ 3 and 7). Nothing, as far as we know, came of the proposed congress. Perhaps fuller intelligence assured them that the expedition was not intended for Greece. But the whole affair shows that Persia was much feared.

Again, in 351/350 in arguing for Athenian help for the Rhodian democrats, Demosthenes felt constrained to argue against the fear that if Athens intervened in Rhodes, she might provoke the King to hostile action, and concluded that the danger from the King was not to Rhodes but to Athens and all the Greeks (Dem. 15. 11–13). Such a fear was behind the stock argument of rhetoric (cf. Aristotle, *Rhet.* 1393^{a}32–^{b}4), that the King must not be allowed to reconquer Egypt for if he did succeed he would promptly attack Greece. The Athenians were emboldened in 344/343 to make a haughty response to an appeal from the King (Philoch. F157). By then they could look to Philip of Macedon, but in general it may be asserted that fear of Persia was a constant force in Athenian political life from the early 350s. Demosthenes in his *Fourth Philippic* of 341 railed against the sort of person 'who fears the man in Susa and Ecbatana and says he is ill-disposed towards the city' but who takes a different view of Philip (§34). Indeed it was this fear that Philip was able to exploit.

But why did the Greeks so fear? Nothing of great significance had happened since the mid-360s. In the late 350s the King had responded to a Theban appeal for financial aid in the Sacred War with a subvention of three hundred talents (Diod. 16. 40. 2), hardly enough to make the rest of Greece tremble. It is true that the strenuous support of Cyrus had seen Sparta through in the Peloponnesian War, that in the Corinthian Persian ships had in 394 BC deprived Sparta of control of the sea and in 387 helped to force Athens again to her knees. Persian money had also played its part in the 390s. But all this was in response to Greek intervention in Asia and in no sense constituted a threat to Greece. It was also long past by the 350s. Why then were the Greeks so prone to fear in the 350s and the 340s? The answer that suggests itself is that Persian influence in the affairs of Greece for two decades after the King's Peace had been all too effective, let Xenophon disregard and suppress it utterly as long as Sparta was the chief instrument of Persian policy.

Once the King had transferred his favour to Thebes and declared his support for the independence of Messenia from Sparta (Xen. *Hell.* 7. 1. 36), the relationship between him and the chief instrument of Persian policy becomes plainer. The mission to the King in 367 BC of representatives of the Greek states (ibid. 7. 1. 33–8) led him to redefine his policy. A Rescript, to which an Athenian succeeded in having a codicil added (7. 1. 36), was the outcome. The Thebans summoned the Greeks to Thebes to hear it. The Persian, who brought the Rescript, displayed the Royal seal on the document and read out the contents. Thereupon the Thebans called on those who wished their friendship, to swear to the King and to themselves their acceptance of the terms.[12] When the envoys refused to swear without reference to their home states, the Thebans began the process of sending their own envoys to each state separately and ordering each to swear compliance with the Royal terms, thinking that each city on its own would hesitate to incur the enmity of both the Thebans and the King. The Corinthians, the first state approached, jibbed, saying that they had no need of oaths sworn along with others to the King (πρὸς βασιλέα κοινῶν ὅρκων). All this is on Xenophon's account (*Hell.* 7. 1. 39–40) astonishing when compared with his previous brevity and silence. It is clear that for this Royal peace the Thebans were to be the King's agents, and those who did not comply would face the hostility of both the King and his agents. The Thebans were to be προστάται, to borrow the term used earlier by Xenophon (5. 1. 36) to denote the role of the Spartans in 'establishing independence for the cities'.

It has been flatly asserted[13] that when Xenophon declared that the Spartans became προστάται, that word denoted simply that Sparta was in a position to throw her weight about and not that she was accorded any formal function of securing that the clauses of the King's Peace were observed. The one thing that can be firmly asserted is that the King's Peace did not merely repeat the clauses of the Royal Rescript read out by Tiribazus at Sardis in 387/386 (Xen. *Hell.* 5. 1. 30). Beyond that it is a matter for conjecture and there can be little to say to those who consider the silence of Xenophon conclusive.

However, it makes some difference to understanding of the relations of Greece and Persia in this period how one envisages Spartan action under the King's Peace. Did the King regard with complete indifference what happened in Greece and leave Sparta free to do whatever she chose? Or did the Peace create a system that left the maintenance of autonomy in Greece to the Spartans as the προστάται and called for the intervention of the King only when things looked like getting out of hand?

In renewals of the King's Peace it would seem that there was a sanctions clause providing for action against transgressors.[14] In 372/371 the clause permitted but did not require all those entering the Peace to join in helping wronged parties (Xen. *Hell.* 6. 3. 18) and in the Peace made after the battle of Leuctra (ibid. 6. 5. 2) action against a transgressor was made obligatory on all participants. In the confusion following on that Spartan disaster nothing was said about how joint action was to be managed; Athens had in 370/369 marched out without delay to the salvation of Sparta without deciding the matter, and discussions had to be held in the following spring about command (ibid. 7. 1. 1–14). There is no reason to suppose that such vagueness was not exceptional. In the Peace of 375 hegemony was shared,[15] Sparta on land, Athens on sea. The Peace made it explicit, as one would expect. These Peaces were both peace and alliance, as the Thebans sought to establish in the negotiations of 367 and 366 (ibid. 7. 4. 10; cf. 1. 39) and as it would appear was the case in the peace made after Leuctra (ibid. 6. 5. 2).[16] Of course the King's Peace of 387/386 *may* have been quite different and when Xenophon said the Spartans were προστάται, he *may* not have meant it other than in a loose sense. It *may* be that the King thought that the Greeks could be left entirely to themselves and to the bully-boy methods of Sparta, that chaos would suit his purposes best, and that there was no formal system to secure autonomy.

The King's purposes as displayed by the Royal Rescript of 387 (Xen. *Hell.* 5. 1. 31) were twofold. First, he sought to secure undisputed control over all of Asia. Secondly, he wanted a settled order within Greece that would occasion him the least trouble, and since trouble had come for him from naval power, essentially Athenian naval power, he would be best served by enforcing a system that required states to be autonomous. But autonomy would not flourish left to itself. Those who did not accept such a condition would have to be coerced by joint action, and provision for joint action would be referred to as συμμαχία. The Peace of Thebes in 366 (Xen. *Hell.* 7. 4. 6–10) illustrates this. In 367 at Thebes the Thebans (ibid. 7. 1. 39–40) had sought to institute a King's Peace with themselves the leading power, that is, peace and alliance (εἰρήνη καὶ συμμαχία). The attempt miscarried but was renewed in 366. It was only partially successful. The Corinthian envoys went to Thebes 'for the peace' but when the Thebans called on them to swear to not just peace but to peace and alliance, the Corinthians refused declaring that 'the alliance would not be peace but an exchange of one war for another'. The Peace of Thebes was made, but it was not like either preceding peaces or the peace made in 362 after the battle of Mantinea which contained sanctions clauses. That the King's Peace of 387/386 contained such a clause must remain a matter for conjecture, Xenophon having chosen not to go beyond giving the Royal Rescript, but it seems not unreasonable to suppose that the Peace established some sort of system and did not depend simply on the might of Sparta.[17]

Whatever the truth of that, clearly the King was, in Isocrates' phrase (4. 175), 'guardian of the Peace', ready to intervene when called on, and that was what happened in 376/375. At the battle of Naxos in September 376, the Spartan navy under the command of Pollis was heavily defeated. Of the 65 Spartan ships confronting the 83 Athenian, half were sunk or captured, and a large number of prisoners taken (Xen. *Hell.* 5. 4. 61, Diod. 15. 34. 5). It was a crushing defeat and gave Athens control of the seas. It was for Sparta and for Persia the very state of affairs that called for the King to intervene. It is therefore no surprise that in the middle of 375 the King called on the Greeks to join in a Common Peace 'similar to the Peace of Antalcidas' (Philoch. F151, Diod. 15. 38. 1). How exactly it came about, whether after the naval disaster of September 376 Sparta sent an envoy to either Susa or Sardis just as she appears to have done before the Peace of 372/371, Xenophon has taken pains to conceal but the main point is clear. When Persia's chosen power was not able to keep control, the King would and did intervene.

In 375 the Greeks came to heel, just as they did in 372/371. What must, however, be answered is why the renewal of peace of 375 did not last and had to be renewed four years later. On the face of it, it would hardly seem to suggest that the Greeks cared much about the King.

Xenophon's account of the period between the two peaces in the second chapter of the sixth book of the *Hellenica* is one of the least satisfactory parts of his history. He furnishes no explanation why Timotheus landed Zacynthian exiles on Zacynthus (§2) or why Sparta thought he was wrong to do so. He makes it seem that the large Peloponnesian fleet sent out under the command of the nauarch Mnasippus (§4) was Sparta's response to what Timotheus had done; yet he declares that

Mnasippus was sent to deal with Corcyra. At the least, there is serious chronological compression and confusion.[18] In addition, though in his introduction to the peace of 372/371 (6. 3. 1) he alludes to the Theban attack on Plataea, he does not recount it in his previous chapter where he reviews the breakdown of the peace of 375. Yet Thebes was the real impediment to peace.

The landing of exiles on Zacynthus occasioned no more than a diplomatic wrangle, which simply petered out. Certainly nothing came of it and for two full years there was peace between the leading powers of Greece. The first breach of the peace was in 373/372 when the Thebans expelled the Plataeans from Boeotia and razed their city to the ground, and although Mnasippus, the Spartan nauarch, con-ducted a siege of the city of Corcyra during the winter of 373/372, the large Athenian force commanded by Iphicrates and numbering finally 90 ships, apart from capturing 10 ships sent by Dionysius to help the Spartans on Corcyra, did practically nothing, though he was said to be preparing to ravage Spartan territory. It was, in short, a 'phoney' war.[19] In the course of the first half of 371 Sparta sent to Phocis King Cleombrotus and two-thirds of the Spartan army (*Hell.* 6. 4. 2), the force that was to come to disaster in the middle of the year at Leuctra, but was originally intended to protect the Phocians against Theban attack (ibid. 6. 3. 1).[20] There was, in short, no great war between Athens and Sparta that required settlement or outside help. Thebes was the problem.

Differing interpretations of events in Corcyra in 373 would inevit-ably have aroused suspicions and created tensions. In 375 Timotheus' defeat of a Spartan naval force at the battle of Alyzia (*Hell.* 5. 4. 65) had had the important effect on the peace of 375, which followed very shortly after, that Athens was in the peace accorded hegemony on the sea, and the presence of a large Athenian force in western waters in 372 in support of the faction that dominated the city of Corcyra was argu-ably no breach of the peace. It could have led to war, but did not do so. The real fester in Greek affairs was Theban expansionist ambition, not just within Boeotia but through central Greece generally. The attack on Plataea and on Thespiae and the threat to Phocis was a serious disruption of the peace and something had to be done about it. Sparta, in all probability, appealed to the King and a rescript duly arrived.[21] Peace was to be renewed and the expectation was that Thebes would see sense and accept, but there was an important modification. Those who chose to join in the punishment of aggressors were to be free to do so but no one was to be obliged (ibid. 6. 3. 18). Sensible men north of the Isthmus were afraid of the Thebans who would shortly become the leading military power of Greece and were already before Leuctra formidable. The peace was intended to rein in Thebes, and Thebes is the answer to the question why the peace of 375 did not last.

371 was a cataclysmic year. In the last month of the Attic year 372/371 the Greeks assembled in Sparta and swore to a renewal of the Peace.[22] Xenophon took care not to let the role of the King emerge. In his account of how the Athenians came to be involved in a new peace he gave their dissatisfaction with Theban policy in central Greece as the reason (*Hell.* 6. 3. 1), and rightly. But he omitted to ascribe a formal role to the King. The other evidence is, however, clear enough.[23] The King was indeed involved in this Peace. All the Greeks accepted it and at first the Thebans swore to it. By the morrow, however, they had changed their minds about having sworn and having been enrolled as 'Thebans' and they now demanded to be listed at 'Boeotians'. If Sparta had accepted this, it would have been tantamount to accepting that Boeotia was not a collection of autonomous city-states but was a united single state. A famous altercation between Agesilaus and Epaminondas ensued, at the end of which the Thebans withdrew and were declared not party to the Peace (ἔκσπονδοι).[24] The Athenians now expected the Thebans to be severely dealt with, and according to Xenophon the Theban representatives departed in complete despondency (*Hell.* 6. 3. 20), wishful thinking indeed.

Twenty days later[25] the military might of the Spartan army was brought low on the battlefield of Leuctra. The shock was felt throughout Greece. Athens in particular was by no means pleased and when summoned by the Thebans to join them in finishing Sparta off declined the opportunity (Xen. *Hell.* 6. 4. 19–20). In an attempt to take control of the confused situation the Athenians managed to effect some sort of reassertion of the King's Peace (ibid. 6. 5. 1–3). Whether this included the Spartans is uncertain but probable.[26] Certainly Thebes had no part and in the course of 370 the order long established by Sparta began to disintegrate. By winter 370/369 Thebes had not only answered the appeal of the Arcadians which the Athenians had rejected but had invaded Laconia, inviolate for centuries.[27]

It should have been clear to the King that the system established in the King's Peace and with modification reaffirmed in 375 and 371 was over. Sparta had passed from being the leading power of Greece to being just a contender for power within the Peloponnese. Support for Thebes was his only real option and in 367 when Pelopidas led the Theban embassy to Susa the King yielded to the Theban arguments and abandoned Sparta to its fate. A rescript was drafted requiring recognition of Messenian independence and the cessation of Athenian naval operations, a clause aimed presumably at Athenian efforts to recover her fifth-century colony of Amphipolis.[28]

The King's decision seems only logical. Why had it not been taken sooner? Indeed in 368 the King had sent Philiscus of Abydos with a summons to the Greeks to make a Common Peace (Diod. 15. 70. 2). Xenophon would have it that the initiative misfired because the Greeks did not consult the god (*Hell.* 7. 1. 27), but he adds that the Thebans would not agree to Messene being treated as not independent. Diodorus has it that Thebes insisted, as in 371, on Boeotia being regarded as one unified state. So the rescript brought by Philiscus must have been no different from previous rescripts. Why was the King so slow to face the fact that Sparta was, as leader of the Greeks, finished?

Thebes was able to curry favour the following year with arguments equally persuasive in 368. Pelopidas could say in 367 'that the Thebans were the only Greeks to have fought on the King's side at Plataea, that never afterwards did they campaign against the King, that the Spartans had gone to war with them for the very reason that the Thebans had refused to join Agesilaus in going against the King and had not allowed him to sacrifice to Artemis in Aulis where Agamemnon had sacrificed when he sailed out to Asia and captured Troy, and it greatly contributed to Pelopidas being honoured that the Thebans had been victorious in battle at Leuctra and had, plain to all, ravaged the Spartans' land' (Xen. *Hell.* 7. 1. 34–5). All this could have been said well before Pelopidas' embassy. Why had not the King dropped Sparta earlier?

The central problem for Persia was how to prevent a resurgence of Athenian naval power which could endanger the King's complete control of Asia. The King's Peace had prevented that and although Athenian defeats of Spartan naval forces at the battles of Naxos in 376 and Alyzia in 375 had given Athens the naval hegemony in joint actions in the enforcement of peace, that by no means gave her opportunity to set about restoring naval empire. Sparta and her Peloponnesian allies had naval potential which could, if necessary, be sustained with Persian help in confronting Athens, but Thebes was of no use in this respect. In 369 and 368 Artaxerxes may have simply decided to 'wait and see'. When in 367 the Spartans sent Euthycles to solicit the King's aid (Xen. *Hell.* 7. 1. 33), Pelopidas went to counter his influence and, probably without difficulty, won the King over.

Pelopidas persuaded the King to include in the Rescript the stipulation that the Athenians must 'haul up their ships'. The precise significance of this clause is debatable but at the least it must have meant, as already remarked, that the Athenians were to cease their efforts to recover Amphipolis.[29] When one of the Athenian ambassadors was heard to mumble protest, the King added a codicil 'And if the Athenians know of a fairer way than this, they were to go to the King and tell him' (*Hell.* 6. 1. 37). The Athenians returned home. The ambassador who had assented to the dealings of Pelopidas with the King, Timagoras, was put on trial and condemned to death. After that, it would seem, appeal was indeed made to the King and a new rescript came down recognizing Athens' right to Amphipolis, a challenging tergiversation (Dem. 19. 137).

Xenophon says nothing of this appeal and the amendment of the Rescript. He passes directly from the return of the Greek ambassadors and the execution of Timagoras by the Athenians to his account of the Congress at Thebes at which a Persian read the Royal Rescript (*Hell.* 7. 1. 39). That must, however, have been the amended Rescript. At the Congress Athens was presumably represented; the Thebans had called on 'all the cities' to send ambassadors and Athens had too much at stake to abstain. Yet Xenophon recorded no Athenian protest. So the Rescript read out at Thebes must have been the amended version.

How long the amending of the Rescript took can only be guessed, but it was perhaps no earlier than the spring of 366 when the Congress assembled in Thebes and whatever one makes of the exact chronology of that year it was a crowded and dramatic period.[30] The Congress of Thebes partly failed, as the Congress of Sardis in 392 had partly failed (Xen. *Hell.* 4. 8. 12–15). Just as on that earlier occasion Xenophon omitted to mention the ensuing Congress at Sparta, and if the third oration of Andocides had not chanced to survive we would have been gravely misinformed, so on this occasion Xenophon separates his account of the Congress of Thebes by two whole chapters on the petty affairs of Phlius and Sicyon from his account of the making of peace between Thebes and Corinth and other states. Hence scholarly confusion and disagreement, but what is plain is that although the Rescript announced at Susa contained the threat of Persian military compulsion which is to be presumed no less in the amended Rescript delivered at Thebes, the Corinthians and 'other cities' (Xen. *Hell.* 7. 1.

40) refused to conform. So, it will be asked, what now of Greek fears of Persia?

When at Susa the Royal Rescript was read out, the Athenian envoy who would not accept that collaboration with Thebes was inevitable, was heard to say 'By God, Athenians, it's time for you, it seems, to look for some other friend in place of the King' (ibid. 7. 1. 37). The only conceivable explanation of this remark is that the Athenian was threatening alliance with some dissident satrap, and one readily thinks of Ariobarzanes, satrap of the Dascylian satrapy, as a likely candidate. When in the middle of 366 Timotheus sailed out with orders to lend military aid to Ariobarzanes 'provided he did not breach the treaty with the King', and found that the satrap was 'in open revolt from the King' (Dem. 15. 9), the restriction placed on Timotheus showed that the intentions and the loyalty of Ariobarzanes were very questionable. In 367 there were suspicions and hopes of disloyalty, by 366 open revolt. Diodorus (15. 90–3) placed his whole account of the Satraps' Revolt under the year 362/361 and at that time 'the satraps' (*GHI* 145) appealed to the Greeks for alliance against the King. The appeal was made, as the inscription shows, shortly after the battle of Mantinea and the Common Peace which immediately followed it, but the Revolt went on right up to the accession of Artaxerxes Ochus in 359/358. So for nearly a decade from 366 the King had a great deal to preoccupy him. The Greeks in that period could make peace entirely without his participation and haughtily declare if he minded his own business they would be content to be at peace with him. 'If he keeps peace and does not set Greek against Greek ($\mu\dot{\eta}$ $\sigma\upsilon\nu\beta\acute{\alpha}\lambda\lambda\eta\iota$ $\tau o\dot{\upsilon}s$ $^{"}E\lambda\lambda\eta\nu\alpha s$), we will remain at peace with him' (ibid. ll. 9–12), a reply that showed how his earlier interventions were regarded and how his present troubles emboldened erstwhile submissive minds.

The evidence simply does not allow more precision about the diplomatic negotiations of 367 to 365,[31] but the general point is plain. While the King was dealing with the crisis of rebellious satraps along his Mediterranean seaboard, there was nothing he would or could do to control the Greeks. Athenian imperial ambitions burgeoned.

Athens had begun on the war to recover Amphipolis in 368.[32] The Thebans had seen that from the recovery of that rich and strategically important place the Athenians might go on to larger imperial designs and had persuaded the King in 367 to require cessation. The Athenians had in turn persuaded him to relax his ruling and recognize Athens' claim to the city (Dem. 19. 137). A congress of the Hellenes agreed to this and probably at the same time acknowledged Athens' claim to the Chersonese,[33] her other strategically important fifth-century colony. The Thebans may have assented in return for Athenian recognition of Boeotia as a unitary state[34] and the Hellenes generally may have seen no harm in recognizing claims unlikely to be realized. In 365, however, Athenian policy took a sinister turn. The Athenians had in 377 by the Decree of Aristotle renounced the detested instruments of fifth-century imperialism, cleruchies and other forms of land-holding in subject states, and as far as the members of the Second Athenian Confederacy were concerned they had kept their word. However, after the battle of Leuctra they had added no more states to the Confederacy and in 365 when Timotheus captured Samos the momentous decision was taken to install a cleruchy on the island. It was a shocking development, to judge by what Aristotle says of the debate in the *Rhetoric* (1384^{b}32); one of the speakers 'called on the Athenians to suppose that the Hellenes stood round in a circle, watching and all but about to hear whatever they decree'. Clearly it was a moment of great importance to the Hellenes. It was the first fruit of the King's preoccupation with setting his own house in order. Athens was free to return to her old imperialism.

Isocrates in the speech *On the Peace*, which he wrote in 355 at the conclusion of the Social War, attacked 'those who create the expectation that we will recover our holdings in the cities of the Empire and regain our former power' (§6). Elsewhere (§126) he spoke of Athens 'being abused for maltreating and extorting money from the Hellenes'. Xenophon in the *Revenues* of the same period was concerned to show that the city could prosper if it ceased to treat the allies unjustly. Clearly Athens had been treating Greek cities badly and although detailed evidence of the cause of the Social War is lacking, the policy that began in 365 must have proceeded apace. The only precisely recorded instance is the intervention of the general Chares in Corcyra (Diod. 15. 95. 3 under 361/360). He is said at that time to have been continually 'wronging the allies' and if the speech of Isocrates styled by Aristotle *On the Allies* (Συμμαχικός *Rhet.* 1418^{a}32) is rightly identified with *On the Peace*, Isocrates' whole attack on Athens' imperialist policy was specially directed against him. Demosthenes in his speech of 351, *On the liberty of the Rhodians*, took a more apologetic line. 'The Rhodians', he said (§15), 'resented you getting back what belonged to you', presumably a reference to the wars for Amphipolis and the Chersonese but perhaps a great deal more, namely, the whole range of overseas possessions renounced at the start of the Confederacy. Elsewhere (§3) he put the blame for stirring up the war on to the Carian dynast, Mausolus, but he also said that the rebel allies, the Chians, the Byzantians, and the Rhodians, accused the Athenians of plotting against them. The allusion, one suspects, was to the machinations of Chares, about which we are ill-informed. Without fear of Persia much could be attempted.[35]

From the end of the Peloponnesian War there were Athenians dreaming of the recovery of naval power. In the Corinthian War Conon wanted quietly to rebuild and avoid provoking Persia. Thrasybulus would not wait and his success reunited Sparta and Persia and the King's Peace was the result. This union worked effectively until the defeat of Sparta at Leuctra caused the greatest confusion. By 367 a new union of Thebes and Persia had begun to take shape. Then came the Satraps' Revolt which effectively took Persia out of Greek affairs for a decade, and Athenian imperialism flourished again with Chares playing a leading part. With the accession of the new King in 359/358 Persia began to recover itself. Artaxerxes Ochus, in 356 perhaps, ordered all the western satraps to dismiss their mercenaries. They all obeyed, save one, the satrap of Hellespontine Phrygia, Artabazus.[36] Chares answered his appeal for help, perhaps not appreciating the resolute mood of the new King. An embassy went from Susa to Athens to denounce Chares, and threatening rumours led to his recall and the ending of the Social War. Athens submitted. The Social War was ended and so were Athenian dreams of naval empire.

NOTES

1. The inclusion of Clazomenae, which is a mere seven hundred metres off the coast, in the King's domain in the King's Peace (Xen. *Hell.* 5. 1. 31) was natural. Cyprus, not obviously Asiatic geographically speaking, was to a large extent Asiatic culturally and was properly claimed by the King. Cf. Isocrates' ninth Oration, the encomium of Evagoras, where Evagoras is presented as the philhellene rising against the barbarism that had come from Phoenicia (§§ 20–1 and 47). The island had been dominated by Assyria, then Egypt until the Persians took over. In the negotiations between Athens and Tissaphernes recorded by Thucydides (8. 56. 4), Alcibiades on Tissaphernes' behalf 'made a claim for all Ionia and then the offshore islands . . .'. *Pace* Andrewes 1981 ad loc. this claim was probably for no more than what the King was to require in 387/386.

2. Seager 1974: 63.
3. Badian 1993: 41–2 reasserted the view 'that the King cannot be imagined as swearing an oath, on equal terms, to a Greek city' and protested against 'accepting an assertion in a solitary Athenian inscription' (namely, the Chios alliance *GHI* 118). Other sources, however, assert the same. Dionysius of Halicarnassus (*Lysias* 12) speaks of the Peace of 372/371 as the Peace which 'the Athenians and the Spartans and the King swore', a notice which it is generally believed derives from Philochorus. Xenophon too in the *Education of Cyrus* has Cyrus the Great 'giving oaths to the Hyrcanians' (5. 1. 22), and in his denunciation of the decline of good faith among the Persians speaks (8. 8. 2) of 'the King and his subordinates' swearing oaths. In the *Anabasis* (3. 2. 4) he speaks of the ἐπιορκία and ἀσέβεια of the King. Of course, the exchanges of oaths are with his subordinates (cf. *Hell.* 1. 3. 8 and 3. 4. 6) but the King was believed to be bound by them. Cf. Ctesias F15 §§ 50, 52, 53.
4. Cf. *Hell.* 6. 3. 19 (δέχεσθαι). V.i. n. 21.
5. Cf. Cawkwell 1981*a*: 69.
6. Plut. *Pel.* 4. 5–8 has Pelopidas and Epaminondas fighting beside the Spartans commanded by Agesipolis (cf. Xen. *Hell.* 5. 2. 3), clearly therefore the campaign of 385 BC. The Spartans 'being yet the friends and allies' received military aid (βοήθεια). One wonders what the alliance was. Perhaps it was under the sanctions clause of the King's Peace.
7. Cf. Beloch 1923: 230–1.
8. The 'Chalcidians', such being the title of the union formed in 432 BC by the states that revolted from Athens, naturally continued after the end of the Peloponnesian War and they joined the Grand Alliance of 395 BC opposed to Sparta (Diod. 14. 82. 3). In the 390s the Chalcidians made alliance with Amyntas, the King of Macedon (*GHI* 111). The name then disappears until the 370s when it is found on the left face of the stele containing the Decree of Aristotle (*GHI* 123, l. 101), if, that is, we reject the supplementation commonly made of the prescript of *GHI* 119, which would assign the decree to 384/383 when the name of the archon of 376/375 would fit equally well. When Xenophon has Cligenes of Acanthus address the Spartans and their allies about the situation in northern Greece in 382, he claims that Olynthus 'the largest city in Thrace' is absorbing neighbouring cities and creating a sympolity (*Hell.* 5. 2. 12–14). Clearly the Chalcidian union of the fifth century had ceased under the King's Peace but Olynthus, not content with the conditions of autonomy brought by the King's Peace, was expanding in the way the Peace had forbidden. After the Spartan campaign of the late 380s had reduced the Olynthians to subordination within the Peloponnesian League (Diod. 15. 31. 2, Xen. *Hell.* 5. 4. 54), the 'Chalcidians' did not reappear until they were registered as members of the Second Athenian Confederacy after the renewal of

the Peace in 375. (For the history of the Chalcidians, see Zahrnt 1971: 80–98.)

9. For accounts of the Satraps' Revolt, see S. Hornblower 1982: 170–82, and Briant 1996: 675–93, who clearly distinguished (p. 678) the two views, the one 'maximaliste' based mainly on Diodorus (15. 90–2), the other 'minimaliste' which is dismissive of Diodorus. A notable representative of this latter view is Weiskopf 1989 (on which see Moysey 1991). According to Weiskopf, 'what has been perceived traditionally as a major threat to Artaxerxes' control was in fact a series of local, but interrelated, troubles limited in duration to the 360s and in impact to western Anatolia' (p. 13). It is true that the evidence is very shadowy. The earliest evidence of revolt is Demosthenes 15. 9; Timotheus was sent out to assist Ariobarzanes provided he did not infringe the peace with the King, but on arrival he found that Ariobarzanes was 'openly in revolt from the King', and so he began his intervention in Samos, datable to 366 BC (v.i. p. 298). That Diodorus has set the whole account of the Satraps' Revolt in the single year, 362/361, is of no consequence; it is typical of his method, and should not be used to belittle him. He derives, presumably, from Ephorus, a contemporary of these events. When he speaks of 'joint action' by the rebels (90. 3), it is no surprise considering the combined appeal of 'the satraps' for Greek participation in war against the King of 362/361 (*GHI* 145). But what is really tell-tale of the extent and seriousness of the Revolt is the part played by Tachos of Egypt (92). That kingdom had been in revolt and had rebuffed repeated Persian efforts at reconquest for four decades. Its great strategic asset was the desert which invaders had to cross timing their invasion between the falling and the rising of the Nile. So why should Tachos have sallied forth to fight a Royal army advancing through the satrapy of Beyond the River? His strategy implies a much larger and wider 'joint action'.

10. Schol. Dem. 4. 19, a note treated with some scepticism by Briant 1996: 811–12, but perhaps unjustly. If Alexander could later require a general disbandment of mercenaries (Diod. 17. 106. 3), Artaxerxes Ochus could well have done the same. The one satrap who is recorded to have been in revolt after the accession of Ochus, Artabazus, revolted against him, it would seem, having returned to allegiance in the 360s (cf. Debord 1999: 393–6). The cause of his defection in 356 may have been family rivalry, to surmise from his being a grandson of Artaxerxes Mnemon. There is no evidence that he was supported by other satraps between 356 and 352, the year when he fled to Macedon (Diod. 16. 52. 3).

11. *Hypothesis* of Dem. 14, the date of which speech is given by Dionysius of Halicarnassus (*Letter to Ammaeus* 4).

12. One might wonder whether in Xen. *Hell.* 7. 1. 39 one should take the datives, βασιλεῖ καὶ ἑαυτοῖς, with ὀμνύναι or with φίλους, were it not that

in §40 the Corinthians say they have no need of oaths πρὸς βασιλέα.

13. Lewis 1977: 147 n. 80, reaffirmed by Seager in *CAH²* vi (1994), 118. I am unrepentant in my belief that there *may* have been a sanctions clause in the King's Peace under which Sparta acted legally against transgressors (cf. Cawkwell 1981*a*: 77–9), and, if so, Xenophon's word προστάται (*Hell.* 5. 1. 36) may refer to this. Of course, this must remain hypothesis, at least possible. The only hypothesis touching the King's Peace that is roundly to be rejected is that it is safe to stick with Xenophon.

14. Cf. Cawkwell 1981*a*.

15. Cf. Stylianou 1998 ad Diod. 15. 38. 4.

16. The word συμμαχικόν at *Hell.* 7. 1. 39 is to be noted. Of the peace of 362/361, made after the battle of Mantinea, Diodorus (15. 89. 1) uses the dual term κοινὴ εἰρήνη καὶ συμμαχία whereas of the peace of 366/5, where the Corinthians spurned the notion of συμμαχία (*Hell.* 7. 4. 10), Diodorus (15. 76. 3) speaks of εἰρήνη *tout simple*. The peace of 362/361 excites from Polybius (4. 33. 9) the description of the participants, σύμμαχοι, just as Demosthenes (16. 9) speaks of Athens being obliged to render military aid under that peace, terms which indicate alliance.

17. Unregenerate (cf. Cawkwell 1981*a*) I continue to maintain that there were no gates on the Piraeus at the moment that Sphodrias made his attempt (Xen. *Hell.* 5. 4. 20) because a clause of the King's Peace required it. Clark 1990: 64–5 following Sinclair 1978: 31–4 maintained that the Piraeus had no gates in early 378 simply because the Athenians had not bothered to put them on. The Piraeus was unwalled in 395 (Xen. *Hell.* 3. 5. 16) and despite suggestions that the walls of the Piraeus had never been completely restored there is no mention of walls as there is of gates. The curious thing is that the Athenians did not put on gates immediately after the raid of Sphodrias but only after his acquittal. According to Xenophon (*Hell.* 5. 4. 34), the consequences of that acquittal were threefold: gates on the Piraeus, construction of ships, and all-out military aid for the Boeotians. This threefold outcome seemed to me, and seems, to match the three-fold consequences reported by Diodorus (15. 29. 7), namely, declaration that the Peace had been broken and so war was to ensue, the build-up of military and naval power, and the admission of the Thebans to full membership of the Second Athenian Confederacy. Diodorus thus states formally what Xenophon states in his concrete manner. (One may compare Diodorus' formal foundation of the Grand Alliance of the Corinthian War at 14. 98 with Xenophon's allusive manner at 3. 5. 2, 4. 2. 10, 13 etc.— cf. Accame 1951: 53–63.) I do not renounce my hypothesis that the Peace had required Athens not to put gates on the Piraeus though of course it remains speculation.

    Nor do I confess manifest error over a clause about the building of ships, despite the strictures of Sinclair 1978 and Clark 1990: 57–60. Clark bases himself on the fact that in the navy list *IG* ${}_{\text{II}}{}^2$ 1604, which he may well be right in redating to 379–378, fourteen triremes are described as 'new' and so are almost certainly not left over from the Corinthian War. On the presumption that there was roughly the same proportion of 'new' to 'old' ships in the missing portion of the inscription as there was in the pre-served—a somewhat hazardous presumption in view of the fitful occur-rence of the term 'new' in the preserved text (e.g. thrice in lines 87–9)—he guesses there were between twenty-eight and thirty-three 'new' triremes. 'With 1604 now dated to 379/8' he declares (p. 57) 'it is no longer possible to suppose that Athens built these triremes in the first two years of the Peace.' I certainly never was supposing anything of the sort. If there was the sort of clause that I postulated, there must have been some provision for Athens to carry on the normal business of diplomatic contacts. In the Peace which concluded the Peloponnesian War, Sparta allowed Athens to have twelve ships (Xen. *Hell.* 2. 2. 20) and in the King's Peace there may have been more generous allowance. So the 'new' ships built after the events reported by Diodorus (15. 29. 7) following on the acquittal of Sphodrias in early 378 BC may well be some of those listed in *IG* ${}_{\text{II}}{}^2$ 1604. If Athens chose to provide 'new' ships for the routine business of state as the Peace probably allowed for, ships built in the second half of 379/378 in the flurry of shipbuilding implied by Diodorus would be recorded by the Naval Commissioners at the end of their year of office. (Perhaps the 'new' ship *Galateia* which was not allotted to trierarchs was completed very late in the year.) So I do not find Clark's arguments decisive against my hypothesis of a disarmament clause in the King's Peace, a clause the converse of what Alcibiades on behalf of Tissaphernes demanded of the Athenians in winter 412/411 (Thuc. 8. 56. 4).

18. Cf. Cawkwell 1963*a*.
19. The date of the Theban attack on Plataea, 373/372, is furnished by Pausa-nias (9. 1. 8). For the detailed chronology of that year, see Cawkwell 1963*a*: 84–8, which makes clear that there were two full years of peace after the renewal of the King's Peace in mid-375. This effectively persuaded the mercenary rowers, on whom Athens relied to complete the manning of their ships, that there would be no work for them in the immediate future. Timotheus in 373 had to go to the islands to complete the manning of his sixty triremes (Xen. *Hell.* 6. 2. 12). For Iphicrates' campaign of 372 and 371, ibid. 6. 2. 33–8.
20. Xenophon records the dispatch of Cleombrotus with two-thirds of the Spartan army to Phocis in 375 (*Hell.* 5. 1. 1) and speaks of him and his army in the prelude to Leuctra (6. 4. 2) as if he had been there continuously. It is inconceivable that so many Spartiates would have been absent from Sparta all that time. Either Xenophon has misplaced the dispatch or he has failed to record its return in 375 and its second dispatch in 371.

21. Dionysius of Halicarnassus, *Lysias* 12, deriving from Philochorus, shows that the King was involved and Xen. *Hell.* 6. 3. 18 speaks of 'the Spartans too' accepting the Peace; 6. 3. 12 has been variously interpreted but is consistent with the view that Antalcidas had waited to see how the rescript was received. There is sorry confusion in the accounts given by Diodorus of the peaces of 375 and 372/371 (15. 38, and 50. 4). Cf. Stylianou 1998: 321–6. The confusion arises from the account of 375. That of 372/371 straightforwardly asserts that that peace was made when the King sent an embassy calling on the Greeks to renew the Peace.
22. For the date, Plut. *Ages.* 28. 7.
23. V.s. n. 21.
24. Plut. *Ages.* 27. 7–28. 4.
25. V.s. n. 22.
26. The peace made after Leuctra, unlike that preceding, obliged all participants to join in military action against transgressors (Xen. *Hell.* 6. 5. 2). At §5 Agesilaus felt inhibited from intervening in Mantinea 'the peace having been made on the basis of autonomy'. At §10 the Spartans felt obliged to give military aid to the Tegeates κατὰ τοὺς ὅρκους, and went against the Mantineans 'on the grounds that they had attacked the Tegeates παρὰ τοὺς ὅρκους'. At §36 Xenophon, reporting the Spartan appeal for help, declares that 'the commonest argument was that Athens was obliged to help κατὰ τοὺς ὅρκους'. At §37 the Corinthians, who were part of the appeal to Athens, assert that they would be plainly in the wrong if they did not help the appellants. 'Will you not be acting in breach of the oaths? And oaths that you yourselves saw that all of us swore to all of you.' By 'all of us' the speaker cannot mean 'all of us Corinthians' because the peace had been sworn by 'the most senior magistrates in each city' (§3). So he must mean 'all the appealing cities', which included Sparta. For full discussion, see Sordi 1951.

Seager in *CAH* vi^2 p.186 commented on the peace after Leuctra thus: 'on paper the peace was a diplomatic triumph for Athens, and it is also of note as the first renewal of the Peace of Antalcidas in which Persia played no part. "The King's Peace" had become no more than a name . . .'. That is not the impression one derives from the negotiations of 367. The truth is rather that immediately after Leuctra there was a great hiatus; Sparta was in no position to take charge of anything and there was no time to seek Persian compliance nor would the King have anything to put in place of the Spartan dominance that had served him well for nearly two decades. The King, like all the Greeks, was nonplussed.

The oaths of this second peace of 371 obliged participants to abide by 'the decrees of the Athenians and the allies' (Xen. *Hell.* 6. 5. 2). It seems wholly unlikely that this referred to the Second Athenian Confederacy. The reference is rather to the sort of Hellenic decrees that recognized

Athenian claims to Amphipolis and the Chersonese or the Messenian claim to independence from Sparta. No such decree can be attached to 371. The first, that concerning Amphipolis, was probably passed at the assembly of spring 369 (ibid. 7. 1. 1). Cf. Cawkwell 1961: 80–1 following Accame 1941: 155–6, *pace* Buckler 1980: 252–4, who sides with Ryder 1965: 128–30. See Appendix 9.

27. For the appeal of the Arcadians, a decisive moment not noticed by Xenophon, Diod. 15. 62. 3 and Dem.16. 12. The main accounts of the invasion of Laconia are Xen. *Hell.* 6. 5. 22–32 and Diod. 15. 62. 4–67. 1.

28. From the (coloured) story in Aesch. 2. 26–9, it emerges that Iphicrates was sent out as general ἐπ' Ἀμφίπολιν, a command he held for 'more than three years', until he was replaced by Timotheus (Dem. 23. 149), named by Demosthenes general ἐπ' Ἀμφίπολιν καὶ Χερρόνησον. 'The war for Amphipolis', as Isocrates in 346 termed the war against Philip (5. 2), went on for twenty-two years until Athens had in the Peace of Philocrates to renounce her forlorn aspirations.

29. From Dem. 19. 137 it is clear that the outcome of the threatening protest of one of the two Athenian ambassadors in Susa in 367 (Xen. *Hell.* 7. 1. 37) was that the King accepted Athens' right to recover Amphipolis. If the King in 367 had meant no more than that the Athenians must leave Amphipolis, 'haul up the ships' would have been a curious way of expressing himself. Of course, if there had been a naval clause in the King's Peace of the sort I envisage (v.s. n. 17), the phrase could have meant a return to the original peace.

30. The King's answer to Leon's protest (Xen. *Hell.* 7. 1. 37) was to add a codicil to the Rescript he issued to the Greeks assembled at Susa. 'And if the Athenians are aware of any fairer arrangement, they should go to the King and tell him.' This seems to mean that an Athenian embassy would have to go in person to the King. Earlier Conon had gone to see the King by sea to Cilicia, then overland to Thapsacus, then by boat down the Euphrates to Babylon (Diod. 14. 81. 4), which would have taken much less time than if he had travelled by the Royal Road (Hdt. 5. 53). Whatever the truth behind the curious fragment of Damastes (*FGH* 5 F8) concerning an Athenian embassy going to Susa from Cilicia by river, which makes the claim that they reached Susa in forty days, a journey from Athens to Susa and back might have been made in four months. The summoning and assembling of the representatives of the Greek states in Thebes would also have taken time and since Athens was so important would probably not have begun before the King's important amendment to the Susa Rescript (Dem. 19. 137) had been received. All in all, the Congress of Thebes is likely to have taken place in 366.

31. See Appendix 9.

32. V.s. n. 28

33. See Appendix 9.

34. No source indicates when the unified state of Boeotia was accepted by the Greeks. It is to be presumed that the Thebans did not soften their intransigence over being recognized as 'Boeotians', which had asserted itself yet again at the time of Philiscus' mission to Greece in 368 (Diod. 15. 70. 2), and that when they joined in a Common Peace they only did so as Boeotians. In the peace after the battle of Mantinea, from which the Spartans alone were excluded (Diod. 15. 89. 2), their status as Boeotians must have been recognized and the question was never raised again until the federal unity was broken up by Alexander (Arr. *Anab.* 1. 9. 6). Somewhere between 368 and 362, 'Boeotia' had become respectable and it is likely to have been at the Peace Congress in Thebes in 366 where there was more than meets the eye in the pages of Xenophon.

35. Cf. Cawkwell 1981*b*: 52–5.

36. Artaxerxes Ochus acceded between late November 359 and April 358 (Parker and Dubberstein 1956: 19). The order to 'the satraps ἐπὶ θαλάσσης' (Schol. Dem. 4. 19) was issued only when he felt secure. Like all the Kings, Ochus, though no source provides an account of his opening months, would have had either accession troubles or fears of troubles and he may not have issued his disbandment order until 356. It is commonly assumed that Artabazus did not revolt until after the other satraps had complied with the order. This may be right, but since according to Diodorus (16. 22. 1) an army seventy thousand strong was assembled to deal with him which would have required quite some time to manage, the revolt of Artabazus probably began before the disbandment order was received.

10

The End of the Achaemenids

PANHELLENISTS delighted to sneer at Persia and Persians, especially at their military performance. Isocrates above all argued that whether Persia was strong or weak the Greeks should unite in attacking it but that in fact Persia would be easily overcome (cf. 4. 139–57). This was not, he conceded (4. 138, 5. 139), the opinion of all Greeks, but it was orthodox Panhellenism, as we can see in the *Anabasis* of Xenophon.[1] It is, however, in the postscript to *The Education of Cyrus* that it is most plainly displayed. Xenophon's experience of Persian warfare was limited to the battle of 401, the long march back, and minor operations along the Aegean seaboard. He made the most of it. For instance, his comments on the ineffectiveness of the scythe-bearing chariots (8. 8. 25) stemmed from what he had seen at Cunaxa (*Anab.* 1. 8. 20) although there was something to be said in their favour.[2] Again, he would assert that Persians were so poor in battle that they had to have Greek foot-soldiers in their armies (§26); they did indeed follow Cyrus' example and seek and use Greek mercenary infantry but the reason why they did Xenophon did not understand.[3] Likewise he declared that Persian good faith was much in decline (§3) largely because the officers of the Ten Thousand had been so faithlessly deceived—in truth a debatable matter.[4] Because the Ten Thousand had been ushered out of the pacified areas of the Tigris valley[5] and left to their fate amongst grisly Kurds and other breeds without the law, he could declare that Persia's enemies could move through the land more easily than their friends (§21). As to Persian neglect of physical fitness (§9), he probably had no more to go on than the sight of those white, soft Persian prisoners of war exposed for sale naked in Ephesus in 395 (Xen. *Hell.* 3. 4. 19). For their eating and drinking the whole day long (§9) he probably had no evidence at all, though he might have been expected to display more understanding of why in extremes of climate they used gloves and parasols (§17). The softness of the Persian use of carpets (§16) he could more properly spurn than could those of the Ten Thousand who took some home with them. The whole chapter is, in short, trivial denunciation, to be taken seriously only by Panhellenists, no support for theories of decline.

Despite what Xenophon has to say, the Persians were no push-over. There are those who tend to think that Alexander the Great could make no mistakes and that his victories over the enemies of Darius III followed as night follows day. They should be left to their hero-worship. Yet that great military genius allowed the King and his army to get between himself and his base in 333 and had to rush back the way he had come and fight in the battle of Issus for his survival. He did it with dash and won. Sober appraisal, however, makes one wonder whether Darius put Alexander in such a position by good luck or good management. There was perhaps more strategic talent in the Persian command than Alexander's adulators allow. At the battle of Gaugamela in 331, which was to decide the war, Darius prudently chose his ground. By letting Alexander come right into the heart of the Empire, Darius gave him the problems of supply on the long march and blocked the route to Babylon. If Alexander's army were defeated it could be the more easily destroyed.[6] The strategy was sound.

Alexander's tactical genius triumphed and the battle decided, as he had predicted it would (Arr. *Anab.* 3. 9. 6), who was to 'rule the whole of Asia'. But it was no walk-over. Quite apart from Indian and Persian cavalry passing through the Macedonian line where the formation broke (ibid. 3. 14. 4 and 5), an incident which has been variously interpreted, there was a moment when Parmenion, the commander of the left wing, sent a message to Alexander calling for his help (ibid. 3. 15. 1). There is much debate about Alexander's reaction. It is not even sure that the message reached him. But there is no question about it that there was a crucial moment when the battle might have gone either way. The battle was the end of Achaemenid Persia, but it was not a wholly ignominious end.

Theories of long-drawn moral decline may be left to moralists. But one is bound to wonder whether the Persian Empire could have checked the Macedonian advance more effectively, whether there were failures of policy. Artaxerxes II (Mnemon) seems, to judge by the long and widespread Satraps' Revolt, to have been a somewhat ineffective king, but his successor, Artaxerxes III (Ochus) was very different, 'unmatched for savagery and bloodthirstiness' as Plutarch (*Art.* 30. 9) declared. His blood-stained accession[7] had induced a more sober mood. When he ordered the disbandment of mercenary forces in the western satrapies, only one satrap failed to conform. The new king was known to mean business. Militarily he was successful. Others had constantly failed in their attempt to reconquer Egypt; he took command in person and succeeded, having first settled the troubles in Phoenicia. Perhaps if he had not been murdered military resistance might have been more effectively managed.[8] But one might wonder whether even without him policy could have been differently conducted in the west to deter the advance of Macedon.

Through the 350s and the early 340s the King could contemplate Greece and the Greeks with equanimity. The threat of Athenian intervention in support of the Greek cities of Asia was finished. The Royal ultimatum that ended the Social War (Diod. 16. 22) had also meant the end of the Second Athenian Confederacy as an instrument of Athenian naval power, and by 355 Athens was nearly bankrupt. Thebes, the leading military power of Greece, was embroiled in the Sacred War and exhausting herself in this senseless struggle. The Phocians having helped themselves to the treasures of Delphi, the Thebans needed money to maintain their military forces and in the late 350s had to appeal to the King for financial aid. He granted it to the tune of three hundred talents (Diod. 16. 40. 1) despite the legendary Royal niggardliness; it was better that Thebes should be able to pay her mercenaries herself than be forced to find employment for them abroad as she had recently felt obliged to do when she sent five thousand under Pammenes to aid the rebel Artabazus (Diod. 16. 34).[9] There was no danger of Greece uniting against Persia as had been attempted by Agesilaus in the 390s.

With the rise of Macedon things were quite otherwise. While Philip was concerned with the war against Athens over Amphipolis, which was in reality all part of his consolidation of power in Macedon itself, and with the settlement of the Sacred War, there was no reason for the King to be apprehensive. But in 346 an astonishing thing happened. Philip withdrew from Greece. He kept control of access, of course, by installing a garrison in the forts at Thermopylae (Dem. 9. 32, Philoch. F 56 b), but the withdrawal was startling. Athens had expected the worst. When news arrived that Philip was in Phocis, a decree was passed requiring that women and children and equipment be brought within the city, that forts be repaired and the Piraeus fortified.[10] Likewise in the Peloponnese, there had been hopes that Philip would intervene in support of the Messenians and to the destruction of Sparta, that many Greek states would join in, but also there had been fears that Philip would proceed to make himself master of Greece (Isoc. 5. 74–6).

Isocrates, writing on the eve of the Peace of Philocrates, tried to dismiss such ideas by saying that no descendant of Heracles would ever think of plotting against Greece (5. 76–8). But once Philip had withdrawn from Greece there was no more of such talk from Isocrates. In his letter of 345 (*Epistle* 2) the tone is quite different, impatience with Philip dealing with Illyrians and getting himself wounded but expectation that Philip 'will try to destroy the so-called Great King' (§11).

Philip had impressed a good number of the Greeks. The King would perhaps have hardly noticed him. Diodorus (16. 60. 4–5) speaking of Philip's settlement of the Sacred War and his withdrawal from Greece said that 'not only had he made for himself a reputation for piety and excellent generalship, but also he had made great preparations for the increased position that was going to come to him, for he desired to be appointed supreme general of Greece and to carry out the war against the Persians—which indeed happened'. It is customary to dismiss this statement as a judgement arising from hindsight. It is not sure from whom Diodorus drew this part of his narrative, the favourite candidate being Diyllus, the early-third-century historian. Whence Diyllus derived his information is quite unclear, though it is worth remarking that if the histories of Theopompus had any part that writer was with Philip in 342 and was well placed to decide why Philip had so surprisingly left Greece in 346. [11] Certainly someone had asked the right question and he did not need to wait until the League of Corinth had been established to find the answer. Indeed Isocrates' letter to Philip of 338 contains a suggestive passage (*Epistle* 3 §3): 'Many asked me whether I urged you to make the expedition against the barbarians or it was your idea and I concurred. I say I don't know for sure . . . but that I think you had had it in mind and that my speech fitted in with your desires.' It has been said[12] that this is just what Isocrates would have had the tact to say, that it proves nothing of what Philip had actually been thinking at the time that Isocrates wrote the speech *To Philip* in 346. That might be so if it were not that the 'many' who put the question to him clearly were thinking that Philip had had the idea by 346 whether on his own or at Isocrates' suggestion.

It remains credible enough that Philip had begun to look eastward by 346. He had, however, not to be too open about it and warn Persia of what was coming. At the same time it was prudent to do what he could to win over Greek opinion. Hegesippus in 342 derided the benefits which he said Philip had promised (Dem. 7. 33–5) and in 340 Demosthenes treated such promises likewise, but hints of benefits which would flow from sharing in a grand crusade against Persia may well have been conveyed in such general terms. Followers of Isocrates at any rate would have understood (5. 120, *Ep.* 3. 5).[13]

By 341 the secret was not to be contained. After the reconquest of Egypt, in 342 Artaxerxes set about dealing with rebellious elements along the Asiatic seaboard. He assigned the task to the man who along with Bagoas had distinguished himself in Egypt, Mentor of Rhodes, brother-in-law of Artabazus and so not unsuitable to exercise command on the fringes of the Empire.[14] In what capacity Mentor did so is uncertain but he proceeded to deal first with the dissident Hermias 'who had revolted from the King and taken control of many strong points and cities' (Diod.16. 52). Mentor captured Hermias by trickery and sent him up to the King, who had him interrogated under torture before putting him to death. Demosthenes, talking of him in the *Fourth Philippic* of 341, presumed that Hermias was apprised of Philip's plans and would be forced to confess all he knew. That, Callisthenes (*FGH* 124 F2) asserted, Hermias did not do, but the whole business implies that there were plans to be known, though it is not clear why Hermias should have been made privy to them.[15] The King, however, was clearly of the idea that something was afoot. In 340 he wrote to the seaward satraps (Diod. 16. 75. 1) instructing them to assist the Perinthians in defending their city against the Macedonian attack. To order intervention in Europe was a very serious move. Fear of invasion of Asia must, one can only presume, have been what prompted him.

There is before 340 very little known about the relations of Artaxerxes Ochus and the rising kingdom of Macedon. In the letter which, according to Arrian (*Anab.* 2. 14. 2), Darius sent to Alexander, he asserted that there had been 'friendship and alliance' between Philip and Artaxerxes, but when there was and even if there was, is quite unclear.[16] Likewise amongst the rumours which Demosthenes in the *First Philippic* of 351 counselled the Athenians against is the story that Philip 'has sent an embassy to the king' (§48), though whether there was anything in the rumour or it was pure imagination there is no knowing. We do know that Artabazus, rebel satrap of Hellespontine Phrygia, gave up his revolt and took refuge in Macedon (Diod. 16. 52. 3), and this may have occasioned diplomatic exchanges. But speculation is pointless. In 344 an embassy from Artaxerxes appealing for assistance in his Egyptian campaign (Diod. 16. 44) happened to coincide with an embassy from Philip (Philoch. F 157). The somewhat abrupt response of the Athenians to the King was perhaps occasioned by their confidence that they could count on Macedonian friendship.[17] This may have irritated the King but hardly amounted to trouble between the two powers. All in all, if there was increasing hostility, it cannot be discerned by us. But by 340 it was clear enough that there was likely to be a struggle.

Artaxerxes had by then put his house in order. First, and most importantly, he had dealt with the rebellion in Phoenicia, on which principally he relied for his naval power. It is unclear when precisely the rebellion began, but certainly by 346, the date of Isocrates' *Letter to Philip*, Cyprus, Phoenicia, and Cilicia were all in revolt (§102). By 344 the troubles were over and Artaxerxes was free to proceed with his campaign to recover Egypt, which the troubles in Phoenicia had obliged him to defer.[18]

A campaign to recover Egypt was not easily accomplished. Cambyses conquered it in the mid-520s. It revolted under Darius (Hdt. 7. 1. 3 and 7. 7). In the late 460s there was the major revolt led by Inaros which lasted six years and troubles continued for some time after (Thuc. 1. 104, 109–10, 112–13). In the last years of the century there was a revolt again (Xen. *Anab.* 2. 1. 14, 5. 13). The Persian response was prevented by the uprising of Cyrus,[19] and Egypt remained out of the King's control for sixty years. There were at least five attempts to recover it including two led by Artaxerxes Ochus[20] before he was finally successful in 343/342. Clearly it would have been sensible to abandon it. Repeated failure must have been considerable encouragement to those elsewhere contemplating revolt and, according to Diodorus (16. 40. 5), the Phoenicians and the kings of Cyprus were moved to revolt by the failure of the Royal Campaign of 351/350. But the Great King could not contemplate giving up the troublesome satrapy.

It is no surprise that Egypt was so difficult to recover. First of all, the approach march through the desert presented special difficulties, principally the water supply. The help of the Arabs had to be sought (cf. Hdt. 3. 4. 3 and 9. 1); indeed they were essential (ibid. 3. 88). Stores of fodder had to be built up (Diod. 16. 41. 5). Provisions had to be transported on camels and also by sea (cf. Diod. 20. 73. 3).[21] Weather could make it difficult for a fleet to play its part (cf. Diod. 20. 74). As an army approached the bounds of Egypt, it had to traverse the treacherous sands of the so-called Barathra, in which Ochus lost some of his army in 343/342 (Diod. 16. 46. 5). So much for the approach. The obvious, and practically the only way for an army coming from the north to enter Egypt was past Pelusium and along the Pelusiac arm of the Nile

Delta. Well-positioned land forces and the blocking of the river with warships could make progress slow and difficult, as Antigonus found in 306 (Diod. 20. 75 and 76). If an accompanying fleet were used to transport the army along to another arm of the Nile, things could go badly awry, again as happened in 306. Above all, there was the central problem in invading Egypt. The invasion had to be made as the Nile was falling and completed before it rose again.[22] In 373 Pharnabazus' attempt was literally a wash-out (Diod. 15. 43. 4). Invasion was, inevitably, late in the sailing season and Antigonus nearly lost his naval force (Diod. 20. 73. 3 and 74), but any delay endangered the success of the whole. All in all, the reconquest of Egypt was not easy, and it is no proof of military incompetence on the part of Ochus that he failed twice. In 343/342 he succeeded and while, to judge by Diodorus' account, he owed much to the Thebans and the Argives and their commanders, the credit for getting into Egypt and for doing so on schedule belonged to the King himself.

Artaxerxes Ochus was indeed an effective king, and according to Diodorus (16. 52. 2) when he assigned to Mentor of Rhodes the task of dealing with rebellious elements along the western seaboard of the Empire he 'appointed him satrap of the Asiatic coast and designated him supreme general in the war against those in revolt . . .'. If Diodorus were correct, it would have been unprecedented. In time past the satrap of one of the satrapies would have been put in control of all the military forces of the area. Cyrus as a royal prince was exceptional but there were frequent enough parallels to the position and power of Tissaphernes in the Ionian War (Thuc. 8. 5. 4)[23] to let us see that to appoint a Greek who was not already a satrap to supreme command of various Persian satraps and to be a satrap without a satrapy would have been monstrous in Persian eyes. One is bound to suspect that Diodorus' source, whoever that was, has quite absurdly exalted Mentor, just as later he was prematurely to accord similar powers to his brother Memnon. Whatever position and power Mentor had, his appointment was confined to dealing with Hermias and no more is heard of him. It is to be presumed that he died before the Macedonian advance troops landed in 336,[24] but it is to be noted that when Artaxerxes sent instructions about helping the Perinthians withstand the Macedonian attack, he wrote 'to the satraps on the sea' (Diod. 16. 75. 1) and Mentor is not mentioned. The only name mentioned by any author in connection with Persian help for Perinthus is that of Arsites, satrap of Hellespontine Phrygia (Paus. 1. 29. 10). That was in 340. So unless Mentor died very shortly after he had dealt with Hermias, the Diodoran account of his powers and position cannot stand and there is no reason to suppose that Artaxerxes Ochus had a new strategic vision of how to defend his empire.

He did not have to face the Macedonian onslaught. In 338 while Philip was engaged in the war with Athens, Artaxerxes was murdered by the trusty eunuch Bagoas.[25] Insofar as Philip was apprised of it, it must have been encouraging news. Accessions to the Great Kingship were commonly enough accompanied by internal disturbances and in this case there may well have been a further outbreak in Egypt. The evidence is hardly certain but the brief rule of Chababash, if it is rightly assigned to this period,[26] would have suggested to Philip that the order established in the western satrapies by Artaxerxes Ochus would prove brittle and that Persia would not be able to concentrate its forces on confronting a Macedonian invasion. Philip had every reason to be on with planning.

Early in 336[27] Philip dispatched Parmenion and Attalus to Asia, with a force ten thousand strong, if we may trust Polyaenus (5. 44. 4). Their orders were to liberate the Greek cities (Diod. 16. 91. 2). In the previous autumn the Greeks assembled at Corinth had declared Philip leader of the war against Persia. It is to be presumed that news of this reached the Persian court at no great interval. What did the King do about it?

The King was the newly acceded Arses, a very young man set up by Bagoas who, to secure his control over Arses, had the King's brothers killed. There must have been a great deal of confusion at court and it would not be surprising if the new League of Corinth's decision to attack Persia passed largely unattended. Arses lasted only two years before he too was murdered by Bagoas (Diod. 17. 5. 4). The new king, Darius III, had a reputation for valour (ibid. 17. 6. 1), but no doubt in the early months of his reign he was fully occupied with the customary cares of accession.

It is to be remarked that Persia had had previous experience of attempts to liberate the Greek cities of Asia, accompanied by grand trumpeting of larger designs. Agesilaus in the 390s commanded an army large enough to let him suppose he could do great things and pro-claim his intentions, but it all came to very little. The King sent down 'a large army' which combined with satrapal forces, carried on the war with Agesilaus, and in 336 the new king Darius was no doubt minded to cope with Parmenion and his ten thousand in much the same way. Nor was it certain that a greater invading force would follow. There had been plenty of big talk in the previous half-century of which nothing had come. Prudence would have told him to wait and see.²⁸ When Philip was murdered, the crisis seemed to have passed; the youth of his heir Alexander excited contempt (Diod. 17. 7. 1).

During the year 335 Alexander showed himself ever less and less contemptible and Darius set about preparing a large number of triremes and assembling a considerable army (Diod. 17. 7. 2). In the spring of 334 Alexander began his march eastwards (Arr. *Anab.* 1. 11. 3) and his army must have crossed from Sestos to Abydos in May. Parmenion was put in charge and the crossing was effected by the use of the 'one hundred and sixty triremes and many merchant ships' (ibid. 1. 11. 6). It was therefore well into the sailing season and if the triremes provided by the League of Corinth were there, why did the Persians not seek to prevent or disrupt? Were they so inert, so inept that they would not even attempt the obvious move?

The question would be the more acute if Diodorus' account of Memnon's grand strategy were to be accepted. According to Arrian (1. 20. 3), Memnon the Rhodian, brother of Mentor and brother-in-law of Artabazus, was, not long before the commencement of the siege of Halicarnassus, appointed to supreme command of 'lower' Asia and of the whole of the marine. He was clearly a man of bold strategic notions. In the council of the Persian commanders before the battle of Granicus he had proposed a scorched earth policy (Arr. *Anab.* 1. 12. 9) which was too much for the assembled generals, but showed the sort of radical measure which he was capable of conceiving. When Arrian recorded his death (2. 1. 3), he remarked that this above all damaged the King's cause at that time, and at the start of the same chapter he declared that Memnon in his supreme command proposed to turn back the war to Macedonia and Greece (2. 1. 1). Later Alexander before Tyre admitted the dangers of leaving the Persians free to operate by sea and he envisaged that if they regained control of the places on the sea, while he and his army advanced against Babylon and Darius, they with a larger force might transfer the war to Greece (2. 17. 2). Consistent with this picture, Diodorus declared that Memnon's successes in 333/332 caused great expectations within Greece (17. 29. 3), that the King expected that Memnon would 'transfer the whole war from Asia to Europe' (17. 30. 1), and that Alexander had had reported to him that Memnon was 'planning to campaign with three hundred triremes and a land army against Macedonia' (17. 31. 3). So there is no doubt that

Memnon did have this grand strategy. The question is when did he begin to advocate it.

Diodorus would have it that Memnon in the council of generals before the Granicus proposed not merely the scorched earth policy but also 'the transference of forces, both naval and land army, to Macedonia and the moving of the whole war to Europe' (17. 18. 2). Such a plan, however, was appropriate only when Memnon had been given overall command, and this only happened when Halicarnassus was about to be attacked. To secure the command Memnon dispatched his wife and children to Darius' court, to serve as guarantees for his good faith (Diod. 17. 23. 5–6). Not until he had taken over his full powers did he even begin to prepare the defence of Halicarnassus. His appointment was a measure of Darius' alarm and despondency and his grand strategy was conceived and advanced when there was practically no alternative. Diodorus was drawing on a source concerned to exalt Memnon and his brother Mentor. To the latter he ascribed position and power (16. 52. 2) to which he almost certainly did not attain,[29] to the former position and strategy, which were appropriate only to the desperate times following on the Granicus.

Generally speaking, the Persians were landlubbers. Insofar as they went in for naval forces, they tended to use them as the mobile wing of the army. The idea of preventing Alexander's crossing to Asia, so obvious to us, probably would not have occurred to them. But even if it had, there would have been a good reason why they would not have sought to do so. Darius ordered 'the construction of many triremes' after Alexander had begun to prove himself no mere stripling (Diod. 17. 7. 2). That must have been in the course of 335 and the new ships would simply not have been ready by May 334. Persian fleets always took a long time to assemble. The suggestive case is the fleet of which the Syracusan merchant in 397/396 brought news to Greece and which led to the dispatch of Agesilaus to Asia in summer 396. He said he 'had seen Phoenician triremes, some sailing into Phoenicia from elsewhere, some being provided with crews on the spot, and some still being constructed'. He added that 'he had also heard that they were to be three hundred in number' (Xen. *Hell.* 3. 4. 1). These were the ships that did not appear until August 394 when they joined with the ships of Conon to fight the battle of Cnidus. There were no doubt Phoenician ships always ready and these may have been used in 336, or whenever, for a quick dash to the Nile Delta to deal with the rebel Chababash, but the assembly of a fleet even to match the one hundred and sixty triremes on which Alexander chose to rely (Arr. *Anab*. 1. 11. 6) would have taken the usual time to manage. There is no need to ask where was the Persian fleet when the Macedonian army was crossing the Hellespont. Much of it was still in the shipyards.[30]

Arrian asserted (1. 18. 5) that there were four hundred Persian ships off Miletus in 334 and it might be supposed that, no matter how many were still under construction, surely enough of the fleet was ready early in the year to impede Alexander's crossing. The figure of four hundred is, however, highly suspect. Persian navies had for over a hundred years been reckoned in totals which other evidence by no means supports.[31] The famous instance is to be found in Thucydides' account of 411. He, with Thucydidean precision, declared (8. 87. 5) that one hundred and forty-seven ships came as far west as Aspendus. Diodorus spoke of three hundred, the number constantly given throughout the century. Perhaps the position with Phoenician and Cyprian ships was no different from that in Athens, where the total number of ships far exceeded the number of the battle-worthy. For instance the largest fleet put out by Athens during the Social War was no more than one hundred and twenty strong but the Navy list of 357/356 shows that there were in one condition or another two hundred and eighty-three.[32] Only new or fairly new ships were to be used in battle. Rumour might put the battle strength of the Persian fleet at three hundred, a figure confidently repeated before Greek ears, but the stark truth was perhaps that the battle-worthy ships numbered far fewer.[33] That would be why Alexander considered a fleet of one hundred and sixty would suffice. Of those only twenty were Athenian, and Athens could have been called on for far more. But he thought he knew how many Persian ships he could expect. In the event he found he had underestimated. By how much is unclear. Parmenion (Arr. *Anab*. 1. 18. 6) urged him to have a naval engagement. The Greek fleet would have been outnumbered, but unless the ever-cautious Parmenion was temporarily out of his senses one must doubt whether the Persian fleet was much greater than, say, two hundred ships strong.[34] There were presumably ships that could have sailed north to confront Alexander in May 334, but perhaps not enough ready to do battle against the Greeks. There is no problem therefore about the Persians not appearing in the Hellespont at the vital moment, nor could there have been any alternative strategy open to the Persians than to engage those interfering in Asia in the way that had been followed in the 390s.

Parmenion had been instructed 'to liberate the Greek cities' (Diod.

16. 91. 2). There was no reason for Darius to suppose that Alexander intended to conquer the whole of Asia,[35] and Darius may well have supposed that the satraps of the 'lower' satrapies could deal with the crisis just as Tissaphernes and Pharnabazus had done confronted by Dercylidas and then Agesilaus. In dealing with the latter, King Artaxerxes II had sent down an army (Xen. *Hell.* 3. 4. 6) and the satrapal armies that joined to face Alexander at the Granicus may well have been reinforced by forces sent down for the purpose. Indeed the number of generals Arrian lists (1. 12. 8) suggests it. How large the Persian army was is quite uncertain, Greek and Macedonian totals for Persian armies being quite unreliable. The two armies may have been roughly comparable in size.[36] When Memnon asserted (1. 12. 9) that the Macedonian army would be 'far superior' to the Persian, he was not necessarily thinking of numerical superiority, and there was no reason for the Persians to expect a crushing defeat.

It was a crushing defeat indeed, as the casualties attest (Arr. *Anab.* 1. 16). Eight of the Persian commanders died, about two thousand Persian cavalry also, and of the Greek mercenaries two thousand were taken prisoner, the rest perished. The Macedonian army showed itself in all its awesome power and effectiveness. One cannot, however, omit to remark on the poor tactics of the Persian command. To have the cavalry positioned along the top of a river bank to stop an enemy climbing up that bank seems ill-judged, for the horses' bellies would have been exposed dangerously. Also, by positioning the infantry well to the rear (Diod. 17. 19. 5) the generals made them almost irrelevant to the battle.[37] The Greek mercenaries fought well, but isolated from the cavalry they were slaughtered in large numbers.

The defeat meant that Darius had no hope of stopping Alexander in Asia Minor. Indeed the battle had deprived him of the men most suited to take command and the choice of the Rhodian Memnon was almost inevitable. He was made supreme commander[38] of not only all the seaboard satrapies of western Asia Minor but also the naval forces of the King. It was perhaps a desperate throw which certainly promised well. He gained control of Chios and much of the island of Lesbos and had Mytilene under siege when he died. With him died Darius' hope of a serious resurgence of Persian power in the West.[39]

How serious is, of course, hard to judge. If Memnon had carried the war into Macedonia itself and Greece, as Arrian (2. 1. 1) asserted that he intended, he would have had to face the forces of Antipater, which were not inconsiderable. According to Diodorus (17. 17. 5), there were twelve thousand foot and fifteen hundred horse. It is unlikely that Memnon would have been able to match this and an invasion of Macedonia could well have ended in disaster as great as the Athenian attack on Syracuse eighty years earlier. Assistance to rebellion within Greece itself might have had the desired effect, but that would have required the unity which Greeks found so hard to achieve. Memnon's nephew the young Pharnabazus, son of Artabazus, nominated by Memnon on his deathbed to take over command, had his minor successes, but altogether these were far less than Darius had perhaps hoped.[40] It was clear that Persia would have to fight for the Persian Empire by land.

Alexander had to be stopped as soon as possible. Darius could not be sure how far Alexander would come, but in case he was planning to do what Cyrus the Younger had attempted the sensible course was to prevent him reaching the Euphrates. So the conflict, if conflict there was to be, would have to be in the region of Cilicia where geography would impose restraints on Alexander's choice of routes; if he followed the route taken by Cyrus, he would come through the Belen pass into the plain where the Persians could deploy their cavalry and a decisive battle could be fought.

It was a life-and-death struggle for the Achaemenids. The battle of Granicus had sealed the fate of the satrapies of Asia Minor. On this battle would depend all to the west of the Euphrates. Darius, who had had experience of war against those seasoned warriors, the Cadusians, and been successful (Justin 10. 3. 3–5), resolved to take command himself. So down to the satrapy of Beyond the River he went to fight the battle of Issus.

All our accounts are based on Macedonian sources which had no evidence for Persian intentions. The numbers they give for the Persian army are ridiculous, and must be drastically reduced, but the crucial question about Darius' campaign of late summer 333 defies solution. Darius had taken up a position on the Amir Plain, suitable for his cavalry to do their worst,[41] but he chose to go north, and through the Bahçe Pass down to the narrow strip of land between mountains and the sea. Why did he do it? It was allegedly (Arr. *Anab.* 2. 6. 3) against the counsel of the Macedonian deserter Amyntas, who assured him that Alexander would come to him wherever he was to be found and that the King was in the best possible position where he then was for a battle. Whatever the truth of that, it remains puzzling that Darius made the move. Alexander had been delayed and Darius may have considered that it was unwise to try to keep his army together indefinitely. He may have had problems with supplies. It is also possible that Darius' army was not at all that large[42] and the confined battle ground he actually fought on was thought well suited to a defensive battle[43] whereby Alexander could be cut off from his base long enough for the Macedonians to have their own problems of supply; Aeschines (3. 164) indeed suggests as much. Above all, Darius may not have blundered into making Alexander turn his army round and retrace his steps. It is not inconceivable that it was a masterly strategic move. If the Macedonians had been checked, their position would have been difficult.

In the event the Macedonian army was just too good, despite fierce resistance by the Persians. According to Arrian (2. 11. 2), 'there was a fierce cavalry battle and the Persians did not give way until they realized that Darius had fled'. That sounds like cowardice, but it was probably not. For the Achaemenid cause it was essential that the holder of the throne did not get captured. Arrian's view of Darius' conduct is not shared by the so-called Vulgate. Diodorus (17. 34) presents a different picture.[44] Justin (10. 3. 6) speaks of his 'great valour'. Darius secured that he would fight another day.

That day came two years later. Alexander, by going to Egypt, gave Darius ample time to assemble forces from all over the east of his empire and the army of Gaugamela was a formidable array.[45] He chose his battleground in the area where Alexander was bound to come, and he prepared it. At Issus there had been no scythe-bearing chariots. At Gaugamela he would have the full two hundred and he saw to it that they would operate on levelled ground. His cavalry would be well suited. There was a convenient source of supplies at Arbela, whereas Alexander would have an increasing problem the further he advanced into unfriendly country and Mazaeus was assigned the task of slowing Alexander's progress. The strategy was sound.

Tactically, Alexander and the Macedonian army were too good for their foe. The Persians put their faith in their cavalry and in the disorder which their chariots were expected to cause. These chariots, posted in three different parts of the front, were spurned by Arrian's sources (cf. 3. 13. 5), having failed in their attempt to disrupt the Macedonian right wing, but they may have had some success elsewhere; perhaps they had a part in creating the gap for Indian and Persian cavalry to charge through, a mysterious episode in the account of Arrian (3. 14. 5).[46] In general the cavalry did well. On the Macedonian left there was 'a very stout cavalry battle' (3. 15. 4) and whatever happened after Parmenion sent his message calling for support (3. 15. 1) there was a period when the battle might have gone the other way. There were certainly significant casualties.[47]

It is notable that in both the great battles the Persians made little real use of their infantry, a striking contrast with the role of the Macedonian phalanx. Despite the virtues of the Greek hoplite mercenaries, the sarissa-bearing foot of Alexander's army were much their superiors, and Alexander used them in concert with other arms. By comparison the army of Darius was a congeries and all the training he had given it while it awaited the coming of Alexander could not make it a real match for the unified and battle-hardened force under the leadership of a tactical genius.

Afterwards Darius went east, perhaps not without desperate hopes, but shortly to his death. Whatever forces he might have gathered beyond the Caspian Gates, Alexander was now in control of the Persian Empire. Indeed, according to Plutarch (*Alex.* 34. 1), he was proclaimed 'King of Asia', and he showed that the war was over by sending a message to the Greeks declaring that 'all the tyrannies had been destroyed'. Shortly afterwards he discharged with full pay and a generous gratuity 'the Thessalian cavalry and the rest of the allies', sending them on their way down to the coast (Arr. *Anab.* 3. 19. 5). The war was over. The Persians had been punished for their acts of sacrilege. The promises made by Alexander's father in establishing the League of Corinth (Diod. 16. 89. 2) had now been realized. The Greeks could now rest content.

Many of them had wanted it so. In the awkward interval between the murder of Philip and the invasion of Asia it was to be feared by the Asiatic Greeks that the liberation they had been expecting might be postponed or even abandoned. So 'the Greeks dwelling in Asia' sent an envoy to Alexander to 'inflame and incite him to begin the war against the barbarians' (Plut. *Mor.* 1126 D). Certainly the reaction of the Greeks of the islands along the Asiatic coast to the restoration of Macedonian naval power (Arr. *Anab.* 3. 2) showed that the earlier successes of Memnon and Pharnabazus (ibid. 2. 1 and 2) had been far from popular. In mainland Greece opinion was divided. No doubt many shared the attitude of those Boeotian cavalrymen, who on their return to Greece set up an inscription proclaiming the view that they had been avenging the Greeks.[48] Isocrates' long years of preaching the Panhellenist view had not fallen on deaf ears. Indeed such attitudes had been greatly helpful to Philip seeking friends and allies. Demosthenes was not deceived. He correctly perceived Macedon to be a far greater danger to Greek liberty than the remote Persian power (10. 34). How many joined him in 341 in regarding Macedon as a greater menace than Persia is unclear, but by 331 and the revolt of Agis Greece was seething with discontent. It was too late. Macedonian domination had to be endured.

NOTES

1. Panhellenism in the *Anabasis* appears most plainly in Xenophon's speech aimed at encouraging the Greek mercenaries (3. 2. 23–7): Cawkwell 2004: 65–7.
2. Xenophon's criticism of the scythe-bearing chariots pertains to the quality of those who manned them and their training not to the usefulness of the chariots themselves. They were an enduring feature of grand Asiatic armies. We first meet them at Cunaxa in 401 BC (Xen. *Anab.* 1. 8. 20) where their effectiveness was barely tested by the Greeks; by declining to follow the order obliquely to advance to their left, the Greeks remained largely outside the action. In winter 395/394, however, one gets a glimpse of their usefulness, when Pharnabazus came on a sizeable part of Agesilaus' army foraging on flat ground. He put the two scythe-bearing chariots he had with him in front of the cavalry and charged the Greeks about seven hundred of whom had formed up to meet the attack. The chariots broke them and scattered them, and his cavalry then did great damage, killing about one hundred (Xen. *Hell.* 4. 1. 17–19). No major Persian land-battle is described after that until the invasion of Alexander. Scythed chariots do not figure in the accounts of Granicus and of Issus. In both battles the Persians adopted a defensive position along a river. Even if chariots were available, the terrain forbade their use, open space being necessary, and Darius in deciding his strategy in 331 was persuaded that his failure at Issus was principally due to his choice of terrain (Arr. *Anab.* 3. 8. 6). Darius had used a chariot for his getaway from Issus (ibid. 2. 11. 4), just as Xerxes had used a chariot in his invasion of Greece (Hdt. 7. 40. 4, 100. 1–2), but such provision was exceptional. At Gaugamela Darius deployed two hundred scythed chariots in front of his line (Arr. *Anab.* 3. 2. 6–7). According to Arrian (3. 13. 5–6), those opposite the right of the Macedonian army were easily dealt with. The part played by those opposite the left is unrecorded. They may have helped cause the break in the Macedonian line (ibid. 3. 14. 5), through which Indian and Persian cavalry passed. Chariots continued to be employed. Seleucus had one hundred and twenty at Ipsus in 301 BC (Diod. 20. 113. 4) and they are heard of as late as the battle of

Magnesia in 189 BC, when Antiochus' hopes of them were disappointed. Why did Hellenistic generals, like the Achaemenids, persist with them? Bar-Kochva 1976: 83 speaks of 'repeated failures' with an arm that was 'recognised as useless', which would make of these generals pretty stupid fellows. They were not that.

According to Xenophon in *The Education of Cyrus* (6. 1. 27–30), these scythed chariots were an innovation of Cyrus the Great. Their chief limitation, obviously, was that only flat terrain suited them, such as Darius had had prepared in 331 (Arr. *Anab*. 3. 8. 7), but they were employed for over three and a half centuries because they were deemed in certain circumstances worth using. Why then did Xenophon speak so contemptuously of the quality of the men who manned them (*Education of Cyrus* 8. 8. 24–5)? One suspects he knew no more about it than that the Greeks at Cunaxa had not suffered from Artaxerxes' chariots and that the only chariots they encountered had been without drivers. That was not necessarily due to cowardice on the drivers' part.

3. The great usefulness of Greek hoplites was shown in the battle of Plataea of 479 BC. There the Persian infantry, according to Herodotus (9. 62. 3), were not inferior to the Greeks in fighting spirit and force, but they lacked hoplite equipment and technique and resource in battle. This disparity continued. In that vast land where moving large bodies of infantry was very cumbersome the Persians concentrated on cavalry. They had the superb infantry, the Immortals, but they relied principally on cavalry forces drawing on the large pool of Greek mercenaries to supplement their infantry as and when it suited. This was sensible, not a proof of martial decline.

4. Xenophon (*Anab*. 2. 5. 38) said that a message from Ariaeus asserted that Proxenus and Menon had denounced Clearchus to Tissaphernes as having plotted against him. Xenophon did not elucidate. He clearly hated Menon (2. 6. 21–9) but one might have expected that if he could he would have refuted the charge against Proxenus, under whose aegis he had joined Cyrus' army. Ctesias (F27) held that 'the plot' was concocted by Tissaphernes and Menon to which Proxenus was enlisted. So there was indeed a plot of some sort. Tissaphernes may have had no part in it but he may have taken it seriously, more deceived that deceiving. Cf. Cawkwell 1972: 24–6.

5. Tissaphernes made no effort to block the march of the Ten Thousand up the Tigris although he had ample forces with him to do so (*Anab*. 2. 4. 13). This emerges from the last two chapters of the third book of the *Anabasis*.

6. As Alexander was well aware (Arr. *Anab*. 3. 10. 4).

7. Plut. *Art*. 30, Justin 10. 3, Valerius Maximus 9. 2. 7

8. Cf. Olmstead 1948: 489.

9. As Beloch 1922: 251 n. 1 remarked, the five thousand sent with Pammenes

must have been mercenaries. The Boeotians put into the field at the battle of Neon thirteen thousand (Diod. 16. 30. 4) and a decade earlier had sent a force of seven thousand under Pelopidas to Thessaly (Diod. 15. 80. 2), but it is wholly unlikely that they would have sent five thousand citizens as far away as Asia.

10. Dem. 18. 36, 19. 86 and 125.

11. Cf. Sordi 1969: xxxi–xxxiii. For Theopompus at Philip's court, Speusippus, *Letter to King Philip* 12. Cf. M. Flower 1994: 19–20.

12. Errington 1981: 78.

13. The general consideration advanced by Griffith in Hammond and Griffith 1979 (p. 460) continues to seem to me sound, namely, that Philip being of large political ambition would have been more likely to set his sights on the wealth of Asia than on the poverty of Greece. This was derided by Errington 1981: 79 as of no help in reaching 'certainty', and he proceeded to dismiss with confidence and contumely all possible indications of Philip's intentions. 'The only whisper of plans against Persia even in the following years is from 341, if the *Fourth Philippic* is a genuine speech of Demosthenes from this year' (p. 79), a whisper, it seems, easily forgotten when he advances his own notice of when Philip began to think of attacking Persia. 'The concrete idea of planning such an expedition indeed emerged not very long before Chaeroneia' (p. 81)—one wonders why on his exacting criteria he does not opt for after the battle and just before the foundation of the League of Corinth. 'Certainty' is a luxury rarely available to students of Ancient History. Mostly we have to make do with a paucity of evidence. If Philip did have ideas as early as 346 of attacking Persia, it was certainly prudent not to proclaim them, and he could only hint at what benefits Greece could derive from joining him and suffer the derision of Demosthenes and the like. Despite Errington's scorn I remain of the view that Philip withdrew from Greece in 346 because by then he had formed the plan of attacking Persia, the view of Diodorus (16. 60. 4).

14. For Mentor and his brother Memnon, see Bosworth 1980 ad Arr. *Anab.* 1. 12. 9.

15. For Hermias, see S. Hornblower in *CAH* vi^2 94–5. How Hermias could have become privy to Philip's preparations, is a mystery. It has become fashionable to say that Philip must have been planning to establish a bridgehead in Asia for his invasion, but such talk seems inappropriate to this period. Parmenion and Attalus were able to land a force of five thousand in 336 (Diodorus 16. 91. 2) apparently without difficulty, and Assos the capital of Hermias' fiefdom would have been of no use geographically speaking. An explanation must be sought in the connections between those termed by Theopompus (*FGH* 115 F 250) 'Platonians' and the court of Philip, though the search must be inconclusive. Hermias, along with Corisius and Erastos, was recipient of the *Sixth Epistle* of Plato, having

attended Plato's school in Athens (the evidence concerning Hermias is conveniently collected by Düring 1957: 272–83). His noble death was to be reported to the friends and the 'companions' (an official title perhaps—cf. *GHI* 165—but perhaps the companions had all been ἑταῖροι in the sense of *discipuli*: cf. Xen. *Apol.* 23) as an example of philosophic endurance, recounted by Callisthenes (*FGH* 124 F2). Most noteworthy in his circle were Aristotle, who married his niece, and Xenocrates. 'Platonians' were not remote from politics as the case of Euphraeus (Athen. 506e) shows, as does the list in Plutarch, *Against Colotes* 32, whence it emerges both that Xenocrates was asked by Alexander to produce advice (ὑποθῆκαι) about kingship and that it was a pupil of Plato, Delius of Ephesus, who was dispatched by the Greeks of Asia to beg Alexander to be on with the campaign of liberation. Speusippus, Plato's successor as head of the Academy, wrote to Philip on behalf of a friend visiting Macedon and went on (odiously) to ingratiate himself with Philip and to denounce his rivals. There certainly were 'Platonian' contacts with the Macedonian court and they may well have known what Philip planned and have communicated it to Hermias.

16. Cf. Bosworth 1980 ad loc., Hammond and Griffith 1979: 485–6, Briant 1996: 708.

17. Harris 1989 argued that Didymus' comment (col. 8. 11) that the Athenian response to the Persian request in 344/343 for alliance was in more contemptuous terms than was necessary was due not to the accounts of Androtion and Anaximenes to both of whom he refers, and of Philochorus, whom he cites, but to his own carelessness. 'The Athenians', Harris says (p. 40), 'gave the Great King exactly what he was looking for, a pledge to remain friendly, which was equivalent to an assurance that they would not support the Egyptian rebels.' On Diodorus' account (16. 44. 1–2) Artaxerxes was 'asking the largest Greek cities to join the Persians in the campaign against the Egyptians'. The Thebans and the Argives gave him what he was asking for, but the Athenians and the Spartans 'refused to despatch an allied force'. The Athenian reply was 'contumacious' in telling the King to keep away from Greek cities.

18. For the operations in Phoenicia, Diod. 16. 41–5. Cf. Kienitz 1953: 101–4, S. Hornblower in *CAH* VI² 90–3, Briant 1996: 701–6. The date of commencement of the Phoenician revolt is uncertain. Artaxerxes' abortive expedition to Egypt, to which Demosthenes referred in his speech *On the Liberty of the Rhodians* in 350/349 in terms which show that the expedition was already faltering (§§ 11, 12), encouraged the Phoenicians to revolt (Diod. 16. 40. 5). So if one thinks of trouble in Phoenicia beginning in 450/449, one is probably not far wrong. The King appealed to Greece for military aid in the conquest of Egypt early in the Attic year 344/343 (Philoch. F 157) and the campaign seems to have begun in the latter half of 343. The siege of Sidon was still continuing after the King appealed to the Greek cities

(Diod. 16. 45. 4 and 46. 4) and the city must have fallen in late 344 or early 343. For all this, Cawkwell 1963*b*: 121–3 and 136–8.

19. The large army of Abrocomas (Xen. *Anab.* 1. 4. 3 and 5) must have been intended for dealing with the Egyptian revolt. Cf. Briant 1996: 638.

20. Apart from the expedition of Abrocomas, Tithraustes, and Pharnabazus (Isoc. 4. 140), that of Pharnabazus (Diod. 15. 41–3), and the triumphant campaign of 343/342, there was the unsuccessful campaign of Artaxerxes Ochus of 351/350 (Diod. 16. 40. 3–5, Dem. 15. 11–12, Isoc. 5. 101) to which one may relate the rumour of Persian preparations which excited Demosthenes' speech *On the Symmories* (*Hypothesis* Dem. 14), and finally a shadowy campaign, led by Ochus but in the last years of his father Artaxerxes Mnemon (Trogus, *Prologue* 10; Syncellus 486. 20; cf. Briant 1996: 684). Considering the distractions of the Spartan interventions in Asia in the 390s, the Cyprian War of the 380s, and the revolts of the 360s, one can assert that the recovery of Egypt was the main obsession of the last seven decades of the Achaemenid Empire.

21. Theopompus (*FGH* 115 F 263) gives a vivid picture of what was in the King's train, presumably in 343, reflecting perhaps Greek notions of Persian luxury rather than sober report. Any experienced soldier knows that the more baggage an army has the slower the progress. Similarly one may question Hdt. 7. 190 and 9. 80–3.

22. For the dates of the Nile inundation, Hdt. 2. 19 and Lloyd 1976 ad loc. ('The Nile began to rise at Cairo *c.* 20th June and then started to fall rapidly at the end of September, though absolute low water was not reached until June', p. 96).

23. Cf. Hdt. 5. 25. 1, 7. 135. 1, Xen. *Hell.* 3. 2. 13, Diod. 14. 85. 4.

24. Cf. Kahrstedt, *PW* xv 965.

25. Diod. 17. 5–6, Darius III acceding about the time of Philip's murder, and Arses, who succeeded, having reigned for two years. So Ochus was murdered in 338 (*pace* the Oxyrhynchus Chronicle—*FGH* 255—which set the murder in 341–340).

26. The evidence for dating King Chababash is fully discussed in Kienitz 1953: 185–9, where he concludes that he was leader of a rebellion in the period between the murder of Artaxerxes Ochus and winter 336/335. Lloyd in *CAH* vi² 344–5 reviews the evidence but holds that Kienitz's case is 'not strong'. However, even if Kienitz's dating is correct, it is hard to believe that the revolt of Chababash was a very serious affair. After the successful invasion of 343/342, Ochus had had the walls of the most important cities taken down (Diod. 16. 51. 2) and Chababash may have been no more than Amyrtaeus in the late 450s, described by Thucydides (1. 112. 3) as 'the king in the marshes', or than Psammetichus, 'the king of the Egyptians' in Plutarch's phrase (*Per.* 37. 4), who sent a gift of corn to Athens in 445/444 (Philoch. F 119). At both times Egypt was

under Persian rule. So although a naval force may have gone down from Phoenicia to the Delta to give support to the satrap, Pherendates, one should not suppose that historical record has utterly omitted a major campaign to suppress a revolt in Egypt that might explain Persian failure to prevent Macedonian invasion in 336 and 334.

27. Justin 9. 5. 8. says it was 'at the beginning of spring'.

28. The biggest talker of all was Jason of Pherae (Xen. *Hell.* 8. 1. 10–12), who according to Isocrates (5. 119) was famed for words not deeds. Isocrates had by 336 been talking big for nearly half a century. According to Speusippus (*Letter to Philip* 13), he had tried to persuade Agesilaus to take on leading a Hellenic campaign against Persia, then he turned, presumably after the defeat at Leuctra had ruled out a Spartan, to Dionysius of Syracuse, then to Alexander of Pherae before fixing on Philip. The Great King had many inducements to 'wait and see'. Agesilaus had in Asia a large force. He took two thousand Neodamodeis from Sparta and six thousand from the Peloponnesian allies (Xen. *Hell.* 3. 4. 2) and gathered four thousand from the Asiatic cities (Diod 14. 79. 2). He proclaimed in 395 that he would lead his army against the centres of power (Xen. *Hell.* 3. 4. 20). He prepared 'to march up-country as far as he could' in 394, and when he was recalled he promised he would return to do what had been intended (ibid. 4. 1. 41, 2. 3). But it all came to nothing. Experience suggested that Parmenion's force was not necessarily something to get greatly excited about.

29. V.s. p. 204.

30. Anson 1989: 47–8 argued that the Persians did not use their fleet because they lacked suitable bases in the Hellespont.

31. See Appendix 4.

32. *IG* II² 1611 of 357/356 line 9, and 1613 of 353/352 line 302. For the Athenian fleet in the Social War, Diod. 16. 21. 1.

33. Cf. Arr. *Anab.* 2. 13. 4.

34. Brunt 1976 in the course of his discussion of 'Naval Operations 334–332' remarked (p. 453) that Arrian's figure of 400 for the Persian fleet off Miletus 'may be an over-estimate'. In view of Parmenion's urging Alexander to have a naval engagement (*Anab.* 1. 18. 6) it seems highly probably that 400 was indeed an over-estimate. Certainly it was for Arrian's Macedonian source merely an estimate and many of the ships may have been supply-ships. According to Diodorus (17. 29. 1), Memnon 'manned 300 ships', but the operations of his successors suggest far fewer in service. Arrian at 2. 2. 2 has them send 10 ships to the Cyclades and take 100 to Tenedos, and at 2. 13. 4 they send 'some of the ships' to Cos and Halicarnassus and 'set off with the hundred best sailers for Siphnos'. Of course these details may be misleadingly incomplete, but it does not sound as if there are anything like 300 ships with Memnon.

35. Darius is unlikely to have had any precise idea of what Alexander was

like, though the son could be presumed to intend no less than the father. According to Fredericksmeyer 1982, esp. 90–1, Philip had not only intended to overthrow the Great King and rule the whole of Asia, but also made clear his intention by his evident satisfaction with a response of the Delphic Oracle and the public performances by the actor Neoptolemos of poems anticipating the defeat and ruin of the Great King. This sort of talk was not new to Persian ears, and Philip was more hard-headed than to be taken in by it. A safer guide is to be found in the attitude of Parmenion, Philip's 'only general' (Plut. *Mor.* 177 C), to the offer by Darius to cede all the land west of the Euphrates (Arr. *Anab.* 2. 25. 1–3). Parmenion counselled Alexander to accept. Alexander rebuffed him, saying he would not be content with less than the whole.

36. Diodorus (17. 19. 5) said the Persian, as opposed to the Greek mercenary, infantry was one hundred thousand strong, an improbably large figure. Arrian (1. 14. 4) spoke only of the mercenaries. As Bosworth remarked (1980 ad 1. 12. 9), 'it is hardly likely that the infantry was solely represented by Greek mercenaries'. The satraps generally had some oriental infantry. Xenophon (*Anab.* 1. 8. 5), describing Cyrus' battle army at Cunaxa, spoke of τοῦ βαρβαρικοῦ ἱππεῖς and τὸ ἄλλο βαρβαρικόν, just as the army of the two satraps, Tissaphernes and Pharnabazus, encountered by Dercylidas in 397 was said to contain 'the Persian army, the Greek troops each satrap had, and the really large cavalry force' (*Hell.* 3. 2. 5). Neither the Greek nor the Macedonian writers were seriously interested in accurately describing oriental armies. When Diodorus (16. 22. 1) said that the satraps confronting Artabazus in 355 had forces seventy thousand in number, one should add 'more or less', or rather, 'a great many more or a great many less'.

37. There is comparable disposition of Persian forces opposing the Ten Thousand's crossing of the Centrites (Xen. *Anab.* 4. 3. 3–5).

38. Arrian refers to Memnon being already appointed by Darius 'commander of "lower" Asia and of the whole naval force' by the time Alexander was advancing on Halicarnassus (*Anab.* 1. 20. 3). Cf. Diod. 17. 23. 4. One can only guess when Darius made the appointment, but it must have been shortly after the news of the battle of Granicus reached him.

39. Arrian (*Anab.* 2. 1. 3) considered that the loss of Memnon was most damaging to the King's cause at that time.

40. According to Diodorus (17. 29. 3), the rumour of Memnon's coming had set Greece astir and he had made contact with 'many of the Greeks'. With his death all the hopes the King had placed in his plan to 'transfer the war from Asia to Greece' collapsed. For the youthful Pharnabazus, see Berve 1926: ii no. 766.

41. According to Arrian (*Anab.* 2. 6. 1), Darius had chosen open plain near the city of Sochi, the site of which is uncertain but the general area is clear enough (cf. Bosworth 1980: 201 and see map opp. p. 198).

42. See Appendix 3.
43. Where the natural barriers of the riverbank failed him, Darius covered his position by a palisade (Arr. *Anab.* 2. 10. 1). He clearly intended not to cross the river.
44. Cf. Curtius Rufus 3. 11. 7–12.
45. As to the numerical strength of Darius' army, there is little to be said beyond remarking that the Persian front somewhat overlapped the Macedonian. Cf. Brunt 1976: 509–11. What is striking is the rich parade of cavalry from the eastern parts of the empire—Sacans, Bactrians, Sogdians, Parthians. Of course, it cannot be said that there were certainly no such units at Issus, for the recovery of the Persian order of battle for Gaugamela (Arr. *Anab.* 3. 11. 3) provided the historians with the detailed information hitherto lacking. However, Darius had ample time to summon all that he needed. He chose a battleground on which he would be able to make the best use of his two hundred scythed chariots (ibid. 3. 8. 7). His army could be supplied from Arbela, sixty or so miles distant (ibid. 3. 8. 7 and 15. 5). The role of Mazaeus is variously described (Cf. Bosworth 1980 ad 3. 7. 1), but whatever delays he could cause Alexander would be to Darius' advantage. On all these considerations, cf. Briant 1996: 854.
46. V.s. n. 2 for chariots. Arrian says (3. 11. 6) 'the elephants were posted ahead of Darius' royal squadron, with fifty chariots'. They make, however, no appearance in the accounts of the battle, though according to Arrian (3. 15. 4) Parmenion 'captured the camp of barbarians together with the baggage train, the elephants and the camels'. Perhaps the Persian order of battle had been prepared in great expectation but the elephants were a bit late in arriving. Had they been there in the battle, the effect on the Macedonian cavalry might have been very considerable, the horses being quite untrained to face them.
47. Cf. Bosworth 1980 ad 3. 15. 4 and 6.
48. The dedication by the city of Thespiai is preserved in the *Anthology* iv. 334.

Appendix 1

Persian and Greek Naval Warfare: The *diekplous*

THE beginning of wisdom[1] is provided by Thucydides' account of the battle of Sybota in 433 (1. 49). Having recounted the dispositions of the opposed navies, he went on: 'When the signal was given on each side, they engaged and began the naval battle. Both sides had a large number of hoplites on the decks, and a large number of archers and javelin-throwers, for they were still equipped rather crudely in the old-fashioned way. The sea-battle was fierce, though not remarkable for naval skill, being more like a land-battle. For when they attacked each other, they did not easily get away by reason of the number and the mass of the ships, and they somewhat more relied for the victory on the hoplites on the deck; they stood and fought while the ships lay still. There were no *diekploi*, but they fought the sea-battle relying more on determination and strength than on expertise.' This is a very remarkable statement.

It would seem

1. that the old-fashioned method of fighting a sea-battle was to go alongside the enemy and leave the decision to the marines fighting hand to hand, the result being that the successful party captured the ship of the enemy;
2. that as late as 433 BC two major naval powers, Corinth and Corcyra and their allies were still practising this old-fashioned method rather than the modern method to be displayed by the Athenians in 429 (Thuc. 2. 89), the small Athenian squadron at Sybota having held back from the main battle and so abstained from 'ramming' (Thuc. 1. 49. 7),
3. that the old-fashioned method called for a large number of marines on the decks, on whom the victory depended and not on naval manoeuvring, principally the *diekplous*.

But did Thucydides know what he was talking about? There were *diekploi* in the battle of Lade in 494 BC (Hdt. 6. 12. 1, 15. 2). At Salamis there was a good deal of ramming (Hdt. 8. 84, 87. 2 and 4, 90. 2, 92.

1 and 2). At Artemisium *diekplous* was to be expected (Hdt. 8. 9), and in Herodotus' account of the battle of Alalia in *c*.540 BC the Phocaean ships are said to have had their rams (*emboloi*) buckled (1. 166. 2).[2] But if ramming was widespread practice by the time of the Persian Wars, why did the Corinthian and Corcyran navies not choose to employ it in 433 BC? The development of naval warfare has in general been constantly in the direction of longer-range weapons—boarding to ramming, broadsides to longer range naval artillery, many guns to fewer longer-range sixteen pounders, carrier-based aircraft to land-based bombers, and on to intercontinental ballistic missiles. So some explanation is called for as to why the Greeks having seen the future in at Salamis reverted to older methods at Sybota.

The tactic of *diekplous* is nicely delineated in the *Suda* s.v. *diekploi* thus: 'ramming and splitting up the enemy's formation and again wheeling round and ramming once more'. Two passages in Polybius exemplify it well (1. 51. 9, 16. 4. 13–14), showing that it continued into the second century BC to be 'highly effective in naval warfare' and the way to avoid heavily armed marines fighting in close combat. Who began it?

It might be thought, on the strength of Herodotus' account of the Greeks training for the battle of Lade in 494 BC and of the battle itself (6. 12. 1 and 15), that it originated in Ionia,[3] but this was probably not the case. Certainly Dionysius of Phocaea knew about the *diekplous* and tried to train the Greek crews, who jibbed at the effort, and in the battle the Chians did carry out *diekploi*, but the commander of a squadron of only three ships (6. 8. 2) being given command of the whole Ionian fleet is very odd. One would expect either that the commander of the largest contingent would be put in charge of the whole or that command would rotate. The exceptional position of Dionysius might have been due to his persuading the Greeks to try his bright idea of *diekplous*. Equally it may have been the case that he had had previous experience of Phoenician tactics[4] and it was generally accepted that his knowledge was the Greeks' best hope. At Artemisium in 480 BC the Greeks clearly regarded the *diekplous* as the regular tactic of the Persian fleet. In the preliminary stage of that naval encounter Herodotus has the Greek fleet go against the barbarians, because they wanted to test the barbarians' 'method of fighting including the *diekplous*' (8. 9). Whether the method of countering this tactic ascribed by the historian Sosylus, to Heraclides of Mylasa (*FGH* 176 F1) belongs to 480 has been much and fruitlessly discussed,[5] but Sosylus who is alleged to have instructed Hannibal in Greek literature (Nepos, *Hannibal* 13. 3), was probably well enough informed about Carthaginian, that is, Phoenician, naval matters and when he spoke of the tactics of *diekplous* as Phoenician, he is worthy of attention. But what above all suggests that the Persian fleet were in 480 deemed to hold the trump-card is that after the battle of Artemisium, in which according to Herodotus (8. 16–18) the two sides were evenly matched but in which Greek losses of ships and men were great, with half the Athenian contingent damaged, the Greeks were simply reluctant to face the Persian fleet in open water (8. 70) where the *diekplous* could have been exploited, and the Persian fleet went in to the confined waters between Salamis and Attica in great confidence and with disastrous consequences.

It is remarkable that before Salamis we hear nothing of ramming. Both at Lade and at Artemisium it is the 'capture' of ships that is recorded. The Chians at Lade 'were doing the *diekplous* and engaging in battle until they *captured* many enemy and lost most of their own' (Hdt. 6. 15). They had to put on each ship forty picked men from the city as marines. Clearly the climax of the *diekplous* was for them the sort of standing battle between the two sets of heavily armed marines,[6] just the sort of naval warfare Thucydides described as 'old-fashioned' (1. 49. 1–3). It was the same sort of operation Herodotus envisaged in the case of the ten ships Xerxes sent to reconnoitre round Sciathus (7. 179–81); two of the three Greek ships on guard there were *captured*, their marines variously treated. In the operations off Artemisium the Persians are represented by Herodotus as expecting to *capture* Greek ships (8. 6. 1, 10. 1 and 3), and the Greeks are claimed to have *captured* thirty of the enemy ships in the first engagement (8. 11. 2). In the decisive engagement the Egyptians are said to have *captured* five Greek ships with all hands (8. 17). There were, it is true, a good number of damaged and wrecked ships (8. 16. 3 and 18), but that could have been the result of head-on collisions[7] rather than of beam-ends ramming.

At Salamis although the Persian navy captured Greek ships (8. 85. 2) and the Greeks would have liked, according to Herodotus, to capture Artemisia (8. 93. 1), the emphasis is on ramming, and ramming by Greek ships (cf. 8. 84, 87, 90, 92). So too in Aeschylus' picture of the battle the Greeks win by ramming (*Persae* 408–20); there is no mention of marines fighting marines in hand-to-hand combat.[8] On the face of it, it would seem that at Salamis there was an important development in tactics.

From an early date Greek ships had been provided with rams and presumably they were used. At Alalia (Hdt. 1. 166) the twenty surviving

Phocaean ships were, after their rams were damaged, 'useless', and although that is the only indication we are given of the nature of a naval battle in the mid-sixth century, it is likely enough that the Phocaean tactics in 540 BC were typical.[9] Why then do we not hear of ramming in 480 BC before the battle of Salamis?

One answer to this question is that although Herodotus did not mention the use of the ram at Artemisium it is to be presumed. Thus in Herodotus' statement (8. 11. 2) that the Greeks 'captured thirty ships', 'captured' is glossed 'i.e. towed away after ramming'.[10] But why did he not say as much when at Salamis he is so insistent on ramming but makes little mention of capturing? There is no reason to think that the accounts of the two battles were written at a great interval between them. In any case the purpose of ramming was to sink ships, not to capture them. When Artemisia rammed the Kalyndian ship, it sank and there were no survivors (8. 87. 4, 88. 3). Likewise when the Samothracian ship, as the story went, rammed an Athenian ship, it began to sink, and when the Samothracian ship was rammed by an Aeginetan, it too sank but not before the Samothracian javelineers had driven the marines from the Aeginetan and got hold of the Aeginetan (8. 90. 2); that is, the rammer, not the rammed was 'captured'. Ships that had been rammed were not in any case worth capturing, certainly not in the middle of the battle. Towing away ships that were awash would be hard and timetaking work. Insofar as ships were captured in 480, it may safely be affirmed that generally speaking they had not been damaged by ramming.[11] Indeed Herodotus' narrative makes plain that ships were in general disabled or destroyed (8. 86. 1, 90. 1), not captured. Salamis and Artemisium were 'clean different'.

It must, further, be noted that no mention is made by Herodotus in his account of Salamis of the manoeuvre of *diekplous*. The account is very scrappy and unsystematic and it may be that he just happened not to describe any incident of the battle in which a *diekplous* was involved. It may also be that the waters between the island of Salamis and the coast of Attica were too confined. There is, however, another possibility. According to Plutarch in his *Life of Themistocles* (14. 3), Themistocles did not attack the Persian fleet until the hour of the day which always brought fresh wind from the sea and a swell through the narrows; this did not affect the Greek ships which lay lower in the water but did mightily affect the Barbarians' ships which were much higher and which could be slewed round by the wind. In this way they could have been exposed to Greek attacks. This passage has been almost universally despised and rejected.[12] If Plutarch has here preserved, whether distorted or not, a genuine piece of information, it would certainly explain why there is no mention of *diekplous* amid all this ramming.

All in all, the battle of Salamis was a freak. The Greeks rammed and won, but when Cimon went out to confront the Persian fleet at Eurymedon a decade or so later, he adapted the Athenian ships to carry a large number of hoplites (Plut. *Cim.* 12. 2). The Persian fleet in 480, according to Herodotus, carried over thirty marines (7. 184. 2) armed with hoplite equipment (7. 100. 3), and this accords with his statement (6. 15. 1) that at Lade the Chians, trained by Dionysius of Phocaea to play the Persian fleet at their own game, had forty marines on each ship, equipped as hoplites (6. 12. 1). So at Eurymedon Cimon fought the battle not as Themistocles had fought at Salamis but in the Oriental fashion, and Greece in general as the battle of Sybota was to show remained wedded to the 'old-fashioned way'. Only the Athenians, so constantly active with their fleet, got ahead and achieved a dreaded mastery of the open seas. History temporarily went into reverse at the final battle in the Great Harbour at Syracuse in 413 BC, when they had to fight in confined space (Thuc. 7. 62 and 66. 2), a battle which like Salamis was a freak.

The only instance of *diekplous* known before the Peloponnesian War is that of the Chian ships at Lade, which, Herodotus declares, led to the capture of numerous ships of the enemy[13] and to the capture of the majority of their own and the disabling of a number of others (6. 15. 2–16. 1). Perhaps the Chians rammed some of the enemy but that was hardly a satisfactory way of *capturing* ships. Since they had had forty hoplite marines on each ship, the Chians must have been seeking the sort of battle that Sybota was, namely, 'trusting for the victory in the hoplites on the deck who stood and fought with the ships lying still' (Thuc. 1. 49. 3).

But how did the Persian fleet fight? Phoenician ships were of heavier construction than Greek triremes[14] and with their heavy complement of marines it is surprising that they could move faster than the Greeks. Yet they certainly did. Not only does Herodotus explicitly assert that Xerxes' ships moved faster (8. 10. 1), but his narrative recounts how of three Greek ships on guard off Sciathus two were quickly caught up and, after hand-to-hand fighting among the marines, captured, while the third, an Athenian trireme, headed north away from the combat to the mouth of the river Peneius and so its crew escaped by way of Thessaly (7. 178–82). The only explanation of why the heavier ships moved faster that presents itself is that at this stage of naval development the Oriental crews were better trained. Athenian naval superiority was to be won later, and only by long practice during the decades after the invasion of Xerxes.[15] In 480 many Athenians rowing must perforce have been very little used to rowing in a trireme, and since according to Herodotus (8. 42. 2) the Athenian ships were the fastest in the Greek fleet, the Greeks generally lacked experience and skill.

How then did the Persians use this advantage of speed? No doubt there would have been head-on collisions but to get alongside an enemy ship and give the marines scope for using their weapons the most satisfactory method must have been, at that date as later, to catch up from the stern, and then, while ships carried a large number of marines, get alongside and use grappling irons, long familiar in eastern waters, to hold the enemy fast.[16] In this way the Phoenicians could employ their tactic of *diekplous*, for which Dionysius of Phocaea had sought to train the Ionians (Hdt. 6. 12. 1) and which the Greek fleet at Artemisium had been eager to test (8. 9. 1). All that the tactic required was ample open water, which was precisely what Themistocles at Salamis insisted on the Greeks denying them (8. 60α).

None of the sea-battles between the Greeks and the Royal fleets between 480 and the making of the Peace of Callias is more than sketchily described, but there seems to have been an important change between the battle of Eurymedon in 469 and Cimon's last campaign in 450. In 469 Cimon sought, as has already been remarked, to play the Persian fleet at their own game, loading his ships with heavy-armed marines (Plut. *Cim.* 12. 2). In 450, according to Diodorus (12. 2), there was a battle in which the Greek triremes 'sank' many of the enemy's ships. This was perhaps the beginning of the supremacy of the Athenian navy based on the superiority of their skill and their tactics[17] as the early years of the Peloponnesian War would make plain.

Outside the pages of Thucydides the only moment in the pre-Hellenistic period where the tactic of *diekplous* is mentioned is in Xenophon's account of the battle of Arginusae (*Hell.* 1. 6. 31). There defence against it is made by the Athenian commanders and one might wonder whether it went out of use as the Greek world constructed ever bigger ships. However, Polybius' account of the sea-battle off Drepanum in 249 BC (1. 51. 9) speaks of it as a 'most effective' manoeuvre. Whether the Phoenician navy continued to employ it is quite unclear. Not only was there no detailed account of a battle involving the Phoenicians and Greeks after 450. Save for Cnidus in 394 there was no battle at all. The two nautical systems kept their distance from each other. Alexander declined to take on the Persian navy (Arr. *Anab.* 1. 20. 1). He thought that his Greek fleet would be no match for them. He may have feared their superiority in more than mere numbers.[18]

Indeed were it not for Thucydides' account of the operations in the Corinthian Gulf in 429 (2. 83–92) and of the battles in the Great Harbour of Syracuse in 413 (7. 39–41 and 7. 60–71) we would have a very feeble notion of naval warfare in classical Greece. Herodotus is no naval historian. His account of the battle of Salamis is ludicrously inadequate. Only the Phoenicians and the Greek subjects of the King play any part. The latter feature in the heroic exploits of the ruler of Herodotus' native city (8. 85) and in the account of an incident involving a Samothracian ship which turned out unlucky for some of the Phoenicians; they, allegedly, left the battle to complain to the King about his Greeks but he, seeing the Samothracians at that moment turning on a good show, ordered the decapitation of the complaining Phoenicians (8. 87–8, 90). On the Greek side only the Athenians and the Aeginetans appear to have fought. The Corinthian dead, whose epitaph we have (ML 24), died unrecorded by Herodotus, who reported Athenian slander (8. 94) but did not bother to discuss what the Corinthians actually did. All in all, a quite inadequate performance.

To sum up. One can speak only tentatively of the development of naval warfare before the Peloponnesian War. However, it is here proposed that the Phoenicians led the way. They could outrow Greek crews until after the battle of Salamis, even though their ships were heavier and carrying a large number of marines. They developed the manoeuvre of *diekplous* as an effective way of getting alongside an enemy ship and giving their marines the opportunity to board and capture. The Greeks endeavoured to imitate at the battle of Lade, 'capturing many ships and losing the majority of their own' (Hdt. 6. 15), but as late as 480 at the battle of Artemisium they were uncertain what to expect (8. 9). There may have been, to some degree, *diekploi* but no hint of it emerges in Herodotus. The Egyptians 'captured' five Greek ships, but the damage done to ships and the destruction may, for all we know, have been caused by ships colliding prow to prow, the manner in which in 334 BC Alexander ordered ten of his ships at Miletus to attack five ships of the Persian fleet (ἐμβάλλειν ἀντιπρώρους Arr. *Anab.* 1. 19. 10), the very manner in which the Corinthians attacked the Athenians near the entrance to the Gulf of Corinth in 413 (ἀντίπρωροι ἐμβαλλόμεναι Thuc. 7. 34. 5). Then came Salamis and abundance of ramming. But it was a freak battle. To confront the Persian fleet at Eurymedon Cimon took out ships laden with hoplites, decks adapted for making best use of them in the close-quarters fighting. By the beginning of the Peloponnesian War the Athenian fleet and no doubt the ships of the ship-contributing allies were highly trained and highly skilled, their main tactic being the *diekplous*, which demanded speed and skill for the ramming, while the rest of Greece was still following out-of-date practice (Thuc. 1. 49). In 429 Peloponnesian forces were plainly terrified of the Athenian *diekplous*, crowding together as a mere twenty Athenian ships circled around them like a stoat around a rabbit, and bent above all on avoiding open water where the Athenians could deploy their skills (Thuc. 2. 83–92, esp. 83. 5, 86. 5, 89. 8). That was the age of the fully developed *diekplous*, the Athenian speciality. In the confines of the Great Harbour of Syracuse it was back to head-on ramming (Thuc. 7. 36. 3–4, 40. 5). The Athenians sought to make the best of an old-fashioned job and sought to grip the enemy's ships with grapples and to rely on their marines to finish the business (Thuc. 7. 62. 3–4, 70. 3–5). But this reversion was temporary. At Arginusae in 406 BC the Athenian generals had to adapt their formation to prevent the Peloponnesians' sailing through (Xen. *Hell.* 1. 6. 31).

NOTES

1. However, Wallinga 1993: 172–3 presumes that at Sybota both Corinth and Corcyra *chose* to put to sea with their ships undermanned, which meant that neither could employ *diekplous* but committed themselves to seeking to decide the battle by close-quarters fighting between marines. He omits to explain how it came about that both sides fixed on the same tactic. The battle was not in confined waters where such tactics would be more effective (cf. Phormio's remarks in 429 BC—Thuc. 2. 89. 8), and a smaller force of fast ships dashing in to perform the *diekplous* against a fleet of undermanned sitting ducks would have been more to be expected from one side or the other at least. Wallinga argues that neither Corcyra nor Corinth had the manpower fully to man the large numbers of ships each possessed in 433, but that is equally true of Athens, the majority of whose rowers were mercenary (Thuc. 1. 121. 3, and 143. 1, *pace* S. Hornblower's scepticism). As Thucydides shows (1. 31. 1 and 35. 3), Corinth certainly assembled rowers from other places, evidence belittled by Wallinga on the grounds that at the battle of Sybota both Corinth and Corcyra fought

in 'the old-fashioned way' (1. 49. 1); why, he wonders, would they have chosen to fight in this way? The obvious explanation is that only Athens had 'modernized', that the rest were still trusting to the tactics Cimon expected to follow at Eurymedon thirty or so years previously.

Wallinga is persuaded that 'in the Athenian navy undermanning was habitual' (p. 174). His evidence is not impressive. Certainly Conon in 407 did concentrate his force of rowers from one hundred ships on to seventy (Xen. *Hell.* 1. 5. 20) but at that late date in the war when Athens, and the trierarchic class in particular, as the institution of the syntrierarchy shows (Lys. 32. 24 of 410 is the first recorded instance), was becoming even poorer, it was possible for Peloponnesian commanders to do what the Corinthians are alleged to have advocated just before the outbreak of war (Thuc. 1. 121. 3), namely, to lure oarsmen from Athenian ships for higher pay, as Xenophon (*Hell.* 1. 5. 4) notes. Likewise, the Sicilian Expedition was exceptional. No doubt the troop-carriers (Thuc. 6. 43) had a skeleton rowing force, for otherwise the five thousand one hundred hoplites could not have been accommodated in the forty ships, and once the hoplites had landed in Sicily, both the ships and their limited crews had to be employed, though Thucydides does not inform us how. Such mixed expeditions of fighting ships and troop-carriers may have been familiar enough. The Potidaea campaign of 432–429 BC, for instance, involved four thousand hoplites (Thuc. 2. 58. 3) and thirty (1. 59. 1) and, later, forty ships (2. 61. 1). But whatever use was made of sparsely manned troop-carriers after their primary purpose was fulfilled, it seems wholly improbable that if there was to be serious fighting at sea the 'fast-sailing' ships should be slowed by having some of their rowers taken away, especially considering the efforts that trierarchs made to excel in speed (cf. Thuc. 6. 31. 3). In any case, the Sicilian Expedition was exceptional. Major naval engagements were not to be expected. It would be unsafe to generalize from it.

Speed was all-important in the developed naval tactics of the Athenian navy, and no general would be so stupid as to take out ships undermanned if he could possibly help it, whether there were to be close-combat between marines or not. Of course, in any set of oared ships some would have 'sailed better' than others. Training made all the difference. It was not a matter of whether they were fully manned or not. (When Wallinga calls in a remark in Xenophon's *Oeconomicus* (8. 8) to support his case, he misunderstands. Xenophon, beginning with §3 of that chapter, was arguing that orderly arrangement was all important in armies as also in a ship loaded with men who do everything ἐν τάξει, which is the reason for their formidable, admirable speed.)

All in all, it was not by choice that both sides at Sybota fought in the 'old-fashioned manner'. They did not know any other.

2. Nowhere else do we hear of rams being 'buckled' (ἀπεστράφατο). The

Phocaean rams at Alalia must have been very ineptly applied. Perhaps the pentekonters which carried the Phocaeans west in 546 BC did not have bronze rams fitted (cf. Morrison and Williams 1968: 280). Indeed since Herodotus chose to term the Phoenician fleet mere 'boats' (πλοῖα), one wonders how fighting-fit they were. He said that the Phocaeans won a 'Cadmean victory' with forty ships destroyed and the remaining twenty rendered 'useless' and afterwards they gathered up the women and children and moved to Rhegium, which looks very much like a crushing defeat and not a triumph of Greeks over Phoenicians. Thuc. 1. 13. 6 speaks of a Phocaean victory but it is questionable whether he was referring to Alalia (see S. Hornblower 1991 ad loc.). Herodotus omits to say that the Phocaeans, having been not totally destroyed, counted that a triumph. The buckling of the Phocaean rams may have been in head-on collisions.

3. Speaking of the naval operations of 480, Hammond in *CAH* IV² 553–4 said, 'The chief difference between the Greek fleet . . . and the Persian fleet was in tactics. The Greeks had developed to a fine art the tactics suited to ramming, one of which was the *diekplous*, and they carried only a small number of marines.' Later he remarks 'The Phoenicians may well have invented that manoeuvre . . .'. There seems some confusion.

4. There were Ionians and Aeolians in the forces which Cambyses took against Egypt, including a Mytilenean trireme (Hdt. 3. 1. 1, 13. 1 and 14. 4 and 5, which proves the ship had a complement of two hundred).

5. Cf. Hignett 1963: 393–6.

6. I take the phrase καὶ τοὺς ἐπίβατας ὁπλίσειε at Hdt. 6. 12 to mean 'and use the marines as hoplites'.

7. V.i. p. 228.

8. At 8. 92 an Aeginetan ship rammed a ship of Sidon, which was taken rather than sunk. In what state the ship was after being rammed is unclear. Its being 'taken' may mean no more than that the Persians (and the valiant Greek captured off Sciathus) were taken on the Aeginetan ship and the disabled Sidonian left to flounder. There was hardly time in the middle of the battle to tow a hulk ashore. The problem of the Persian marines may have been abruptly disposed of.

9. V.s. n. 2.

10. The gloss is made in Morrison, Coates, and Rankov 2000: 54.

11. But v.s. n. 8.

12. Aeschylus' *Persae* 386 has battle commence at dawn which is not to be pressed literally (cf. Pelling 1997: 3–5). In Herodotus (8. 83) there is time for Themistocles to address an assemblage of marines. It is indeed credible that the Persian fleet should have moved under cover of darkness into a position to confront the Greek fleet, for to move by daylight into the bay in defile would have been dangerously to expose to attack their leading ships, but they had to wait for the Greeks to come forward. So it is

credible that the Greek commanders waited until the suitable moment to advance. It may be true that 'it is impossible to predict weather with any degree of certainty anywhere in the Aegean' (Frost 1980: 154) but if it did indeed happen to start blowing before the advance was made, Themistocles would naturally have been said to have waited for the wind. That he was commended for far-seeing cunning would be no surprise.

A more troubling question arises over what Plutarch says about the Greek ships, namely, that they were lighter and lay lower in the water. The evidence for the Phoenician ships is not very substantial but seems to justify the view of Basch 1969, esp. 160–2, that they stood higher out of the water. According to Thucydides (1. 14. 3), Greek ships were not fully decked at that stage, whereas Herodotus (8. 118) tells a story which implies the opposite about Phoenician ships, and which is consistent with what Plutarch says of them. The real difficulty lies in the remark Herodotus attributes to Themistocles (8. 60α), namely, that the Greek ships are heavier (βαρυτέρας). Does this not show that Plutarch did not know what he was talking about? Not necessarily so. The weight of the Greek ships was not relevant to Themistocles' argument. He should have been saying that they would be disadvantaged in open water by their comparative slowness. Indeed it looks as if Herodotus was making Themistocles talk as Herodotus had made the Persians think at Artemisium, that the Persian fleet would outnumber and 'outsail' the Greeks (8. 10. 1), and there is much to be said for Stein's suggestion of βραδυτέρας in place of βαρυτέρας. Perhaps then Herodotus' text should not in this matter have the last word. Plutarch's evidence cannot be so lightly dismissed. That Plutarch proceeds to name Ariamenes as the Persian admiral who was killed in the battle when Herodotus had named Ariabignes (8. 89, 7. 97) seems no great fault. Herodotus had named an Ariamenes in connection with the battle and in a somewhat mysterious sentence (8. 90. 4, for which cf. Macan 1908).

13. Herodotus' statements about enemy losses arouse scepticism. If the Chians did indeed 'take many ships' of the Persian fleet (6. 15. 2), what became of them? Likewise at Artemisium the Greeks 'took thirty ships' (8. 11. 2), but we hear nothing more about them nor about their crews. Did they all jump overboard except for the brother of the king of Salamis? At 8. 14. 2 the Greeks 'attacked Cilician ships' and destroyed them. In the final engagement (8. 16. 3) 'although many ships of the Greeks were destroyed, far more still of the barbarians were destroyed and far more men.' One wonders whether at least some of these glittering successes were achieved against supply ships, 'the Phoenician merchant men' (γαῦλοι), (cf. 8. 97. 1, 6. 17). Losses at Salamis were not recorded save for the statement that 'the majority of the ships were damaged' (8. 86; cf. 91), though after the battle the Greeks 'expected that the King would still use his surviving

ships for another sea-battle' (8. 96. 1) and in 8. 97 he is found preparing
for another sea-battle, as indeed at 108. 1 are the Greeks. One could wish
for a fuller account of the Ionians' success in 498 against 'the Phoenicians' (5. 109. 1), the force which had transported 'a large Persian army'
from Cilicia to Cyprus (5. 108. 1) and which after landing the army and
rounding the north-east cape of Cyprus, evidently making for Salamis (as
was the army) ran into the fleet sent by the Ionians (5. 109. 3) who got the
better of them (ὑπερεβάλοντο). How many were transports and how large
a force of Phoenicians was involved Herodotus did not say. One may be
pardoned for scepticism.

14. Cf. Basch 1969 (but see Morrison, Coates, and Rankov 2000: 45).
15. Presumably the Athenian ships of 480 BC were no differently constructed
     from those of other Greek states, but Herodotus declared that they 'moved
     faster' (8. 42. 2), a remark which may have been more true of his own day.
     Corinthian optimism in 432 about matching Athenian naval skill in the
     Peloponnesian War was firmly dismissed by Pericles who declared that
     Peloponnesian landlubbers would not find it easy to catch up the Athen-
     ians who had been practising uncontested ever since the Persian Wars
     (Thuc. 1. 121. 4 and 142. 5–7).
16. Head-on collisions were always possible, as in the battle of Chios of 201
     BC (Polyb. 16. 4. 11). For grappling irons, Casson 1971: 121 n. 87; Thucydi-
     des makes Nicias in 413 speak as if grappling irons were new (7. 62. 3) but
     their use was casually mentioned in 425 (4. 25. 4) and they could well have
     been in use much earlier.
17. Cf. Livy 37. 30. 2, who remarks: '*robore navium et virtute militum Romani
     longe Rhodios praestabant, Rhodiae naves agilitate et arte gubernatorum et scientia
     remigum.*'
18. *CAH* vi² 330.

Appendix 2

Histiaeus

THERE are endless uncertainties about Histiaeus. In the text it is argued that he may well have sent a message to Aristagoras warning him that it was time to revolt, because he knew that once the attack on mainland Greece had begun it would be too late. But why did Darius send him down to Sardis? And when he joined the Ionians, did he seek to help or hinder the Revolt?

Histiaeus was, or claimed to have been, privy to all Darius' plans (Hdt. 5. 106. 3). No doubt he had proved his worth in council, and the reasonable guess is that he secured his return to the West by suggesting that he would be equally valuable to Artaphernes, that he understood his countrymen in a way that Artaphernes could not. Certainly Darius could have had no expectation that Histiaeus would be able to return directly to Miletus, but he could have been led to hope that informal, secret contacts might help secure an early return of his native city to allegiance.[1]

As to what Histiaeus actually did in Sardis one can only state that Herodotus' account is doubly unsatisfactory. If Artaphernes really had suspected him of complicity in the Revolt (6. 2), he would have had him arrested and tried, not left him free to slip away by night. More importantly, it is wholly unlikely that Histiaeus would have had secret discussions with Persians 'about revolt' (6. 4). A satrap might revolt from the King, but subordinates, however critical of the King's brother in office, would have been so unlikely to heed a Greekling seeking to persuade them to 'follow the Lie' (the phrase frequent in the Behistun Inscription) that Histiaeus would surely not have tried. However, Artaphernes is said by Herodotus to have put many of the Persians to death, and report of such a purge may well have reached his informants. There is a possible solution. Zgusta 1956 pointed to the occurrence of Iranian names in Lydian vernacular inscriptions and in contexts which made it virtually certain that we are dealing with Lydians. Indeed, the adoption of Iranian names became widespread. We may be sure that the temple attendant in the temple of Artemis at Ephesus, Megabyzus, to whom Xenophon entrusted belongings in 394 (*Anab*. 5. 3. 6) was not a Persian; likewise, the Halicarnassian magistrate, Megabates son of Aphyasis, colleague of Phormio son of Panyassis (who may have been Herodotus' uncle) (ML 32), was not Persian. Iranian names occur throughout Caria: they 'may surely indicate "iranization" rather than, or in addition to, an actual Iranian presence'.[2] Such adoption of Iranian names may well have spread amongst the Lydians since the defeat of Croesus, and by 496 there may have been a number of prominent Lydians at Artaphernes' court,[3] whom Histiaeus had wooed with suggestions of renewed Lydian independence. If news of men so named being executed reached the Greeks on the coast, by the time it reached Herodotus these Lydians could have been thought of as Persians. If this hypothesis were correct, it both throws light on Aristagoras' attack on Sardis and illuminates Histiaeus' intentions. However, the evidence of Herodotus being what it is, such hypotheses must remain unverified, if irrefutable.

As to Histiaeus' purposes once he had joined the Ionians, there is ample room for conjecture. As remarked in the text, Herodotus' statement (6. 29) that Histiaeus at the moment of his capture 'expected that he would not be put to death by the King for his present offence' is poor evidence, mere guessing or slander, and if his severed head did indeed receive honourable burial (6. 30. 2), that proves nothing about what he had been trying to do. The King could forgive. The sins of Miltiades, which caused him to flee before the Phoenicians, were not visited on his captured son, Metiochus (6. 41). More strikingly, the man who in 401 saved the day at Cunaxa, Tissaphernes, was in 395 executed on the orders of King Artaxerxes II by Ariaeus, the very man who had led the Orientals in the rebel host of Cyrus the Younger (Polyaenus 7. 16, Diod. 14. 80. 8). Ariaeus must have been forgiven. Histiaeus could have been likewise. Neither the circumstances of his capture nor the honourable treatment of his remains argue anything about his purposes.

It would be no surprise if Histiaeus, frustrated of his hopes of taking charge of the Revolt, turned to privateering, which was precisely what Dionysius of Phocaea did (Hdt. 6. 17). But there is one element in the story which suggests that Histiaeus at Byzantium was seeking to help the rebel cause. He persuaded the Lesbians to let him have a naval force and so they manned eight triremes (Hdt. 6. 5. 2f.). This was before the battle of Lade, and the Phoenician fleet was to be expected. The Lesbians contributed seventy ships to the rebel forces and they must have realized that every ship would count. So they must have been persuaded of the usefulness of Histiaeus' plans, and furthermore the Lesbians who manned the eight ships must have continued to be confident that they were helping and not hindering the interests of their own island.[4] With the same Lesbians he went against Chios after hearing the outcome of the battle, and then with 'many Ionians and Aeolians' he campaigned against Thasos. That these operations were not mere opportunist marauding is shown by his hasty return to Lesbos on receiving news of the movement northwards of the Phoenician ships (Hdt. 6. 28). Clearly he meant to confront them or in some way prevent them from controlling the island, and the best sense one can make of all this is that he intervened in Chios because he feared the island was going to come to terms with the Persians, and that he attacked Thasos, which was rich (cf. Hdt. 6. 46), to get money to continue the struggle. Perhaps Histiaeus in a forlorn way was trying to maintain resistance when resistance could only be in vain, like his son-in-law Aristagoras a sort of hero of Greek liberty. But, of course, any such view is mere conjecture. Herodotus' informants hated and belittled Histiaeus and all we can do is wonder. In any case he had little effect on the history of the Revolt and the Persian recovery.

NOTES

1. Heinlein 1909 proposed that Histiaeus' aim was 'aus den griechischen Inseln ein von dem persischen Königs abhängiges Inselreich zu gründen'. Literal acceptance of Herodotus' statement (5. 106. 6, 6. 2) that Histiaeus promised Darius that he would make Sardinia (Σαρδώ) tributary to Persia is absurd; no doubt he may have beguiled Darius with his colourful talk and 'from Sardis to Sardinia' might have been a particularly beguiling line, but it need reflect his real intentions not one jot.
2. Cf. S. Hornblower 1982: 26, 140, 351, and 2002: 72. One may compare the name Psammetichus, the 6th-cent. tyrant of Corinth; he was no Egyptian!
3. At *Cyrop.* 8. 6. 10 Xenophon has Cyrus urge his satraps to have the young at their court for proper training (a system similar to the Macedonian 'Pages'). The older Lydians, if we may take Myrsos, son of Gyges (Hdt. 5. 121), as typical, saw where their advantage lay and served the new power. Young Lydians may have borne Persian names but nourished anti-Persian sentiments.
4. Hdt. 6. 26. 1 has him seizing 'the merchantmen of the Ionians' as they sailed out of the Pontus, a somewhat baffling detail. We know that Teos imported

corn in the early 5th cent. (ML 30). Other Ionian states may have done the same, and Histiaeus and his Lesbian ships may have been concerned to divert corn from cities which the Persians had already recovered. Herodotus' remark does not exclude the possibility that Histiaeus was diverting traffic on its way to mainland Greece.

Appendix 3

Persian Armies

T H E successes of Persian armies[1] are more striking than their failures. The attitude of modern Greek historians is inevitably affected by the failure of the great invasion of Greece in 480/479, coupled with the repeated unsuccessful attempts to recover Egypt. The latter, how-ever, are readily explicable. The approach to Egypt posed peculiarly difficult supply problems, as Antigonus discovered in 306 (Diod. 20. 73–6), and attack had to be timed to coincide with the falling of the Nile; any delay of the sort almost inevitable in the movement of large armies meant that that annual inundation prevented success. Then, too, the Delta was naturally on the side of the defenders.[2] So failures against Egypt argue little about the efficiency of Persian arms. As to the failure in Greece, the explanation offered by a speaker in Thucydides (6. 33. 5) is, as I have argued elsewhere,[3] the right one; quite apart from unspecified strategic errors on the part of the Persian High Command, there was a serious shortage of supplies ($\dot{a}\pi o\rho\dot{\iota}a\ \tau\hat{\omega}\nu\ \dot{\epsilon}\pi\iota\tau\eta\delta\epsilon\dot{\iota}\omega\nu$) which brought the great army to disaster, the common lot of large armies operating in foreign territory at the full stretch of communications. For in warfare success and failure depends in large measure on supply, and the Persian failure in 479 should remind us how brilliantly successful Persian armies so frequently were. One has only to think of the con-quest of what was to be the satrapy of India, of the conquest of Egypt, of the advance into Europe including the crossing of the Danube. These were very great feats of arms, and the Persians must rate as one of the greatest military powers of history.

To the Greeks Persian successes were due principally to their over-whelming superiority of numbers, just as Greek successes were ascribed to the valour of free men facing impossible odds.[4] Such a view was due in part to national pride, in part to a failure to comprehend the mean-ing of very large numbers. Herodotus did not pause to consider the practical implications of the movement of an army of 1,700,000 men against Greece (7. 60. 1),[5] just as the Macedonian historians did not blench at the idea of Darius moving an army of 600,000 through the

Amanus Gates to cut Alexander's line of communications (Arr. *Anab.* 2.
8. 8), or of Darius assembling 1,000,000 infantry for Gaugamela (ibid.
3. 8. 6). Such totals were not just to magnify the victors' achievements.
They were accepted because they were incomprehensible. Ctesias
(*FGH* 688) unblushingly had Semiramis collect an 'army of 1,700,000
infantry, 210,000 cavalry, and almost 10,600 scythed chariots' (F1 5.
4), elsewhere an army with 3,000,000 infantry (F1 17. 1), and put into
Sardanapalus' pyre ten million talents of gold and a hundred million
talents of silver (F1q). Such numbers Greeks could not take seriously
enough even to deride. In the same way Xenophon, who had been
at the battle of Cunaxa, gave the total of the King's army as 900,000
and remarked that Abrocomas with his 300,000 was late for the battle
(*Anab.* 1. 7. 11–13), Ephorus modestly fixing on 'not less than 400,000'
(Diod. 14. 22. 2), just as 300,000 recurs elsewhere (Diod. 11. 74. 1, 75. 1,
15. 2. 1). All these totals are absurd, and show only that large numbers
were beyond Greek comprehension. But they have a legacy, to wit,
that historians are tempted to think of Persian armies as exceptionally large and, if so, largely untrained. Thus the real nature of Persian
military power is obscured.

Every satrapy had and had to have its own forces both for the control
of the subject peoples and for defence against outside attack (Xen. *Oec.*
4. 5). Was there also, as has been claimed,[6] a Palatine army ever available for the King to use on his major expeditions? Isocrates spoke of
'the army which goes around with the King' (4. 145) but it is clear from
Xenophon's account in the *Cyropaedia* (7. 5. 66–70) that this was no other
than the ten thousand Immortals whom we meet under the command
of Hydarnes in 480 (Hdt. 7. 83) and of whom one thousand formed
an elite unit. Herodotus (7. 41) regarded these thousand, 'the best and
noblest of the Persians', carrying spears with golden pomegranates on
the butt, as a separate body, but it is clear they were part of the ten
thousand Immortals, as Heraclides (*FGH* 689 F1) makes plain, and as
the title of Chiliarchus shows; that important officer commanded the
Immortals.[7] The Thousand were all Persians. The Ten Thousand, to
judge by the sculptures of Persepolis and the coloured bricks of Susa,
comprised other Iranian peoples,[8] but they are the Royal Guards
found around the King in the centre of the battle-line at Gaugamela
(Arr. *Anab.* 3. 11. 5). In addition to this infantry, there was a unit of
1,000 elite Persian cavalry who are mentioned in Herodotus' account
of Xerxes' march from Sardis (7. 41), the King's 'Royal Squadron' as

Arrian (*Anab.* 3. 11. 6) terms them, the King's Own (οἱ συγγενεῖς ἱππεῖς) 'picked for their valour and loyalty, consisting of 1,000 in one squadron' as Diodorus describes them (17. 59. 2).[9] That was all there was for certain in 'the army that goes around with the King'. Herodotus spoke also of 10,000 Persian horse in the march from Sardis (7. 41. 2), but they may have been Persian cavalry assembled from the satrapies, like the 500 cavalry that Tissaphernes took with him when he went to inform the King of Cyrus' plans (Xen. *Anab.* 1. 2. 4). The alleged Palatine army was no more than the Royal Guards. As Darius said in his Behistun Inscription, 'The Persian and Median army which goes with me, this was a small force' (II §25). There is no reason to think there was ever anything more. If the King wanted to assemble a large army, he had specially to summon forces from the satrapies.

The satrapal armies were well displayed in the troubled times after the accession of Darius I. Each of the rebels was able to field an army large enough to confront what Darius sent against them. For instance, 'the Median army which was in the palace' (i.e. the palace of Media) 'became rebellious from me, and went over to that Phraortes' (DB II §24). These satrapal armies, which were of fixed strength, were annually reviewed and their military fitness was reported on (Xen. *Oec.* 4. 5–7). Training is to be presumed. In any case they were regularly employed on policing the satrapies and defending them against marauders. Thus when the King needed to assemble a large army, he had ample military forces to draw on, though of course the assembly took time. For instance, as the Ten Thousand made their way up the left bank of the Tigris, they were passed by a large force under King Artaxerxes' bastard brother on his way to help in the battle already fought (Xen. *Anab.* 2. 4. 25). The unusually long period allowed by Xerxes for preparation and assembly of forces for the invasion of Greece (Hdt. 7. 20) was perhaps principally for the construction of the fleet, but major expeditions seem regularly to have taken two years to prepare; witness the various assaults on Egypt.[10]

Since armies were so assembled from remote satrapies, one is tempted to suppose that a Royal army was a mere congeries of all sorts and conditions of soldiers, so diverse in kind and equipment as to make proper tactical use impossible. A major influence in this is the so-called Army List of Herodotus (7. 61–86), which groups 43 different peoples in 29 units of infantry with names of commanders under 6 generals, and states that 14 of these 43 furnished cavalry, horse-drawn chariots, or camels; two cavalry commanders are named. The motley nature of this army is heightened by various descriptions of their armament. All the peoples named appear in Herodotus' satrapy list (3. 89–94) save the Hyrcanians (7. 62) and the Ligyes (7. 72), who may have been omitted there by accident, and the names of the commanders are, it would seem, respectably Iranian.[11] The ethnographical notes are dubitable, or even inaccurate, but if Herodotus had an army list, he may have added information derived from some other source or sources of information such as Hecataeus, the fragments of whom show that he probably treated of all the peoples described by Herodotus (cf. FF 205, 282, 288, 289, 292, 293, 294) and included notes of their dress (cf. FF 284, 287, 328, 358).[12] It would not be just to dismiss the list simply because such additions can be queried by reference to the sculptures of Persepolis, or because it seems to be refuted by Herodotus' narrative: I refer especially to his description of the manner in which the 8,000 Sagartian cavalry are said to have operated, with the use of the lasso, never heard of in the accounts of Plataea and of Thermopylae, where those who fought outside the wall would have been very vulnerable to such an attack. That is all perhaps misapplied Herodotean colour.[13] The list itself can be considered separately. Nonetheless it seems to be of no use for the characterization of Xerxes' army.

The names of the alleged commanders may be respectably Iranian but are they the commanders of 480/479? None of the subordinate commanders appear later in Herodotus' account of operations in Greece, save for Artabazus son of Pharnaces (7. 66) who seems to have been almost on a par with Mardonius in 479 (cf. 9. 4),[14] and Pharandates, son of Teaspis (7. 79), whose presence at Plataea is argued by the presence of his concubine (9. 76. 1). If the list really does relate to 480/479, the advancement of Artabazus would be surprising. He was commander of the Parthian and Chorasmian foot in Herodotus' list, and neither people is mentioned in connection with the operation at Thermopylae. More surprising is the promotion of Mardontes son of Bagaios to joint command of the fleet in 479 (8. 130. 2); he commanded infantry from the Island peoples of the Red Sea in Herodotus' list (7. 80), a curious change of role. These oddities may be tolerated perhaps, for promotion may not have been by merit in the field or by suitability of experience. The serious case is Artaÿktes, son of Cherasmis, who is listed (7. 78) as commander of the Macrones and Mossynoeci, two peoples living on the southern shore of the Black Sea (cf. Xen. *Anab.* 4. 8. 1, 5. 4. 2). Herodotus noted that he was regent of Sestos. Not only would it be very strange for a man to command troops with whom he had no immediate connection, but also it is clear from Herodotus' account of the end of Artaÿktes that he was not part of the expeditionary force in 480 (9. 116). Of course, Herodotus may have been mistaken in adding his note about the regency of Sestos and have identified two different bearers of the name, but it is equally possible that there is here a sign that whatever Herodotus was using it was not the Army List of 480.

The order of battle found in the Persian camp in 331 (Arr. *Anab.* 3. 11. 3)[15] is frequently appealed to as a possible parallel, but in the case of Herodotus' list there are difficulties. Two of the commanders lack patronymics, 'Artochmes married to Darius' daughter' (7. 73) and 'Tigranes, an Achaemenid' (7. 62). One would expect an official list to follow the same procedure in all cases. Furthermore if an official list gave the names of subordinate commanders of infantry units, presumably it would have done the same for the subordinate cavalry commanders. Herodotus cites no such names. Did he mean his readers to presume that the infantry commanders of the peoples providing cavalry commanded their cavalry as well? But that is not the way that armies are run or operate. There were, allegedly, separate cavalry commanders for the whole (7. 88). So the cavalry may be supposed to have been brigaded together and not with individual infantry units, and the lack of subordinate cavalry commanders' names is suspicious. Then, too, there are some surprising omissions. The Dahae, brigaded at Gaugamela with the Bactrians and the Arachosians (Arr. *Anab.* 3. 11. 3), do not appear in the pages of Herodotus (unless they are the Daoi mentioned (1. 125. 4) as a nomadic Persian people on a par with the Mardians, the Dropikoi, and the Sargartians, which the Dahae certainly enough were not).[16] They were important enough to be listed in Xerxes' Daiva inscription (X Ph 26). Did they play no part in 480 in the assembly of the nations? The Mardi were a Median people despite what Herodotus says, and their presence in 480 may be subsumed in his term Μῆδοι (7. 62), but one would expect to find mention of the Cadusians, who were prominent militarily not only later (cf. Xen. *Hell.* 2. 1. 13, Diod. 15. 8. 4, 17. 59. 5) but also before the rise of Cyrus the Great (Ctes. F5).[17] They may lurk behind Herodotus' Κάσπιοι (7. 67), but in a list that names so many less remarkable peoples their omission is striking. And what too of the Arachosians?[18] The 'land' was mentioned in the Behistun Inscription (D B iv §§47, 48), as secured by Darius after fighting. Did they have no part in 480? Herodotus' list is either too long or too short for 480. Finally, it is to be noted that in the battles of 480 and 479 we hear only of Iranian troops, save that having given the Persian order of battle for Plataea Herodotus added that 'Phrygians, Mysians, Thracians, Paeonians and the rest were present, mixed up' as well as Egyptians and Ethiopians who had previously served as marines (9. 32), which looks like an attempt to find a role for the countless voiceless hopeless throng.

But if the army list is not what it professes to be, what is it, or rather from what has it been constructed? Surely enough Herodotus had the names of the six generals of the infantry, and of the commander of the Immortals, and the names of the two cavalry commanders (7. 82, 83, 88). The latter are never mentioned again, but the former are named again when the army was divided into three corps[19] for the march westwards (7. 121) and an anecdote about one of them is recorded later (8. 26). But this list of commanders can be detached from the rest. As already noticed, Herodotus gave no names for the subordinate cavalry commanders and this prompts the speculation that the core of the so-called Army list is a list of 'lands' and 'governors'.[20] Varying numbers of 'lands' are recorded in the Old Persian inscriptions, at Behistun 23, in D Pe 26, in D Se 28, in the first Naqš-i-Rustam inscription 30. These variations reflect partly the growth of the empire, partly perhaps some flexibility in its organization. The list given by Herodotus in book 3 (89–94) numbers only 20, but it is notable that the only names of peoples in his 'Army List' not found in his satrapy list are the Hyrcanians and the Ligyes while all the peoples of his satrapy list appear in his 'Army List' save for the Hytenni, the Aparitae, the Pausicans, the Pantimathii, Dareitae, and Thamanaeans. These omissions seem of little consequence, save for the last, if it is right that they are the Greek version of the Arachosians, but the general coincidence of the satrapy list and the 'Army List' suggests that the second is in essence the same as the first with the addition of governors' names. That would, at any rate, make sense of one curious feature of the 'Army List', the seemingly over-subordinate role of the joint commander of the Marathon expedition, Artaphernes, son of Artaphernes; as satrap of an enlarged Sparda, his position would be as honourable as that of his father, Artaphernes son of Hystapes, the brother of Darius. The same name would also give an indication of the date of the list of satrapies, if such it is. The elder Artaphernes would appear to have been back at court when Darius died and the succession was debated (Justin 2. 10. 9), and his son may have succeeded him as satrap of Sparda at some time after 490. On the other hand Artaÿktes was not yet 'hyparch' of Sestos, an appointment, one might guess, of special importance once preparation for the crossing of the Hellespont was in hand. So the explanation of Herodotus' 'Army List' may be proffered, that it is a list of satrapies and satraps from early in Xerxes reign, to which Herodotus has added ethnographical notes culled from Hecataeus.[21]

However, whatever one makes of Herodotus' list, it seems preferable to leave it out of account in characterizing the army of Xerxes. Whoever else went on the great invasion of Greece, the army was essentially Iranian, and the impression one gets of a motley array[22] should be erased from the mind and not allowed to colour one's picture of the various great armies we hear of throughout Achaemenid history.

In presenting such a picture, the question of numbers is crucial. Did the Persians succeed by reason of overwhelming numbers, or were they only moderately superior in numbers but highly effective as a fighting force? The very large numbers furnished by Greek and Macedonian historians have been almost universally rejected, but others have been reluctant to reduce them further than they feel obliged and it is common to postulate a land army of 300,000 in 480, the figure that is to be found in Ctesias and other fourth-century historians. It is the burden of the present discussion that Persian armies were never anything like as large as this and that the drastically lower estimates of Delbrück[23] are much nearer the truth.

In general, the great invading armies of antiquity were not, it would seem to modern eyes, large. Hannibal set out from Spain, according to Polybius (3. 35), with 50,000 foot and about 9,000 horse; by the time he reached Italy they were down to 20,000 foot and 6,000 horse (3. 56) and with these for sixteen years he remained undefeated. For the great attack on Antiochus III in 189 the Romans had an army of about 30,000 and were confronted by 70,000 of all sorts of troops from all parts of the Seleucid realm, including the most eastern peoples. Alexander began his invasion of Asia with something like 43,000 foot and 6,100 horse and confronted the might of Asia at Gaugamela with about 40,000 foot and 7,000 horse (Arr. *Anab.* 3. 12. 5).[24]

Nor, to judge by the history of the Successors, was the might of Asia ever assembled in such numbers as to produce totals of great magnitude.[25] The largest army of which we are informed by Diodorus, drawing on Hieronymus, was that of Antigonus in his invasion of Egypt in 306, 80,000 infantry and 8,000 horse (20. 73. 2).

Were then the Achaemenid armies numerically so very different?

It might be supposed that a fairer estimate of their size might be made by considering the *total* number of combatants in the battles of the Hellenistic age. At Ipsus in 301, for which unfortunately the text of Diodorus fails us, 134,000 infantry and 20,500 cavalry, on Plutarch's account (*Demetrius* 28. 6), took part, while at Raphia in 217 there were more than 140,000 men in all on the field of battle, to follow Polybius (5. 79), though some have argued for a total 25,000 less.[26] If two conflicting powers of Asia could put together such totals, perhaps, it might be argued, the Achaemenids could easily have mustered as many, and perhaps more, on their own side.

But there are universally compelling reasons why armies should be no bigger than the military task requires. First, there is the problem of keeping armies supplied with food and water, and with all the reserves of equipment to replace losses and damage. The Greek historians made little of this aspect of warfare[27] and presume on their readers' understanding. For Persian armies we are even more in the dark. Herodotus remarked (7. 187. 2) on the huge amount of grain the Persians must have had to transport to feed the numbers he credited them with, but beyond that he gave little attention to how the Grand Army of 480 was supplied and how the immense problems that its provisioning posed were overcome. He noted the establishment of dumps of food along the route as far as Macedonia (7. 25). He paid no attention to how provision was made for the march southwards or for the maintenance of the army once it was in Greece. He noted the presence of female bakers (7. 187. 1). The transport of grain-mills, for example, or the actual organization of the commissariat or the manifold supply services for the repair of wagons and weapons he took for granted. Fortunately, Xenophon had served in a Persian army, and when he wrote his account of the campaign of Cyrus the Great against the Lydians he could draw on this experience. The *Cyropaedia* (6. 2. 25–3. 4) helps us to understand just how much had to be carried on a campaign, and the vast diversity of the necessary supplies helps to fill out the picture provided by a colourful fragment of Theopompus (263) concerning the invasion of Egypt in 343. However, it must be remembered that the invasions of Egypt and of Greece were, as far as supplies were concerned, comparatively easy, for those armies could be in some degree supplied by sea (cf. Diod. 16. 40. 6, Hdt. 7. 25. 2). For operations in the most eastern parts of the Empire the Persians' problems were as great as those of the army of Alexander, so admirably illuminated by D. W. Engels, *Alexander the Great and the Logistics of the Macedonian Army*. Indeed they were probably greater, for there is no sign of the Persians making self-denying ordinances of the sort that Alexander made (Curtius Rufus 6. 6. 15). All in all, even for an army no larger than the Macedonian, the logistic problems were immense, and this consideration alone helps to explain why armies were no bigger than they were in the well-attested period of the Successors.[28]

At all points, one fact is clear. Let an army carry as much as it possibly could on beasts of burden, and plainly that is how much of the food and probably water was carried in the invasion of Greece, wagons, and wagons in great numbers, were deemed indispensable. They surface at only one moment in the narrative of Herodotus, when he mentions that the Greeks found wagons in the Persian camp containing sacks of gold and silver cauldrons (9. 80. 2),[29] but Xenophon knew what he was talking about in his frequent allusion in the *Cyropaedia* to wagons, not just to carry articles of Oriental luxury, but 'many objects of all kinds' (7. 4. 12). All this is not merely to generalize from the special arrangements made by Cyrus the Younger for the provisioning of the Ten Thousand (*Anab.* 1. 10. 18); there were other wagons (1. 5. 7, 7. 20). Alexander's army had its wagons; although on his march to Bactria he severely reduced their number (Curtius Rufus 6. 6. 15; cf. 6. 11. 3), there were wagons on the march through the Gedrosian desert (Arr. *Anab.* 6. 25. 2). That was an army in which special attention must have been paid to logistics; the Persians were no doubt no less amply provided with transport.

This necessary element in the supply system leads to the other major determinant of the size of Persian armies, namely, the problem of controlling and using an army the column of which on the march inevitably extended many miles. No matter how many abreast troops could be marched in open territory, the wagons had to move for the most part on roads and where there were defiles the troops are hardly to be thought of as marching more than three abreast, and the transport for each unit had to move close behind the unit (cf. Xen. *Anab.* 1. 7. 20, *Cyrop.* 4. 2. 2).[30] Similarly with the burden-carrying animals. Thus an army of 60,000 could on the march be spread out over a great many miles. At three abreast and with suitable intervals to avoid the concertina effect, familiar to anyone who has been part of a long column, such an army could be extended for 30 miles. Since opposing forces exploit their geographical advantages to the full, the bigger the army the more cumbrous its movement and the less manoeuvrable its fighting troops. Thus there were powerful disincentives to fielding armies of immense size, and it may be postulated that no matter how large the resources in manpower of a state, the requirements of supply and manoeuvrability imposed their own restraints and that is why the armies of the Successors were no larger than they were. What is true of them is surely true of the Persians too.

The exact numbers of Persian armies are denied us, but speculation is possible. One indication is provided by the vital part played constantly by mercenary soldiers, on which the Persians relied. Clearchus, on whose Ten Thousand Cyrus the Younger had rested his main hope of victory (cf. *Anab* 1. 8. 13), said to Tissaphernes, 'As to the Egyptians, with whom I am well aware you are especially enraged, I do not see what allied force you could use to punish them the more effectively than the one that is with me' (*Anab.* 2. 5. 13) and for the various invasions of the fourth century Greek mercenaries were always sought and used. In the invasion of the 370s Iphicrates led a mere 20,000 according to Diodorus (15. 41. 1), according to Nepos (*Iph.* 2) 12,000. In 343 there were 10,000 Greeks in all in the invading army (Diod. 16. 44. 4). If there were as Diodorus asserted 200,000 or 300,000 in the Persian army on each occasion (15. 41. 3, 16. 40. 6), why were these small mercenary forces so important? In an army the size of those we meet in the period of the Successors they could play the central part that the Macedonian phalanx was to play, but their importance must have diminished the larger the army became. Alternatively, if they were the decisive factor there was no advantage to be gained in putting with them gigantic numbers of other troops. However, it must be conceded that such an argument will be of little force with those who believe that one Greek hoplite was worth twenty of an Oriental rabble.

Consideration of four great battles which are more than sketchily attested is more helpful, namely, Plataea, Cunaxa, Issus, and Gaugamela, which will be treated in reverse order. For Gaugamela Alexander's forces were numbered about 40,000 foot and 7,000 horse (Arr. *Anab.* 3. 12. 5), figures consistent with other information about his army and thus acceptable, but 'the whole army of Darius was said to number about 40,000 horse, 1,000,000 foot . . .' (ibid. 3. 8. 6).[31] These vast throngs of infantry, however, do not play any part in the battle or its aftermath[32] and may readily be forgotten. The only indication of how many were in the Persian army is to be found in the fact that whereas Darius was in the centre of his line, Alexander who was roughly opposite him was with the Companion cavalry which was stationed to the right (with the right-flank defence units outside it) (Arr. *Anab.* 3.

11. 5 and 8. 13. 1). Thus the Persian line must have been nearly twice as long as the Macedonian. There is no knowing how deep the Persian formations were, but unless they were very much deeper it is unlikely that the army of Darius was over 100,000 in all. As to the assertion in Arrian (*Anab.* 3. 8. 6) which derives perhaps from Ptolemy, that Darius had 40,000 cavalry, one should be sceptical. For the battle of the Granicus, Arrian gave 20,000 as the number of the cavalry (1. 14. 4) but Diodorus (17. 19. 4) asserted that they were 'more than 10,000' and one suspects that in the absence of precise evidence of numbers there was some wild guess-work on Ptolemy's part, and that his figure for Darius' cavalry at Gaugamela is no more worthy of respect than his figure for the infantry. The figures we get from Hieronymus for the period of the Successors urge moderation. In 323 Peithon obtained 8,000 horse from the eastern satrapies (Diod. 18. 7. 3), and in 317 Eumenes assembled from the same area 4,600 horse (Diod. 19. 14), the individual totals being revealingly low, 400 from Persis, 700 from Carmania, 610 from Arachosia, 400 from Paropamisadae, 1000 from Areia and Zranka, and from India 500. At Gabiene in 316 of the 9,000 horse in Antigonus' army, 2,000 were Medes (Diod. 19. 39. 2, 40. 1). Similarly at a later date, namely at Magnesia in 189, the analysis of Antiochus the Great's army (Livy 37. 40) suggests that the cavalry potential of Asia was nothing like as great as Arrian's figure for Gaugamela would suggest. There is, therefore, no case for supposing that Darius' army was huge because his cavalry were so numerous that, on analogy with other armies, his infantry must have been huge. The truth is rather that in defence of his throne in the heart of his kingdom Darius did not have an army enormously greater than Alexander's.

For Issus, according to Arrian (*Anab.* 2. 8. 8), 'the whole army of Darius was said to be about 600,000 fighting men', and similar ample totals occur elsewhere.[33] Callisthenes had 30,000 cavalry and 30,000 Greek mercenaries (F 35); his figures for the other parts of Darius' army have not survived. Polybius (12. 17–18) censured him for his failure to realize that even the cavalry and the mercenaries alone could not be deployed on a battlefield fourteen stades wide. These criticisms may be 'superficial and petty' as Beloch described them,[34] but they show plainly that the numbers are absurdly exaggerated. Darius' army was probably numerically superior to Alexander's, but there is some reason to think it was not vastly so. The exact site of Sochi where Darius encamped to await Alexander (Arr. *Anab.* 2. 6. 1) is uncertain but its general location is clear enough; it was two days' march from the Syrian Gates and presumably lay on the main route from the Belen Pass to Thapsacus on the Euphrates, the route taken by Cyrus the Younger in 401 (Xen. *Anab.* 1. 4. 4, 6, 9, 11). To reach Issus by the Bahçe Pass and the Amanus Gates required a march of nearly 100 miles. Unfortunately an exact timetable cannot be drawn up. According to Arrian (*Anab.* 2. 6. 1, 2), as soon as Alexander in Mallus learned that Darius was in Sochi, he set out in haste and in two days he had reached Myriandrus, but one does not know how up to date his intelligence was. Darius may have been on the move northwards for some time. But even if he took six days,[35] the distance covered means that his army was by no means large. He had to keep with him a supply train sufficient to maintain his army for more than a few days, for he did not know that the battle would be fought so soon after reaching the Cicilian plain. So even with an army of 60,000 movement was bound to be slow.[36] With a huge army it is inconceivable that such a distance would have been covered in the available time. Even to debouch from the Amanus Gates would have taken an army of 60,000 the best part of a day. Darius' surprise march argues against his army being very large.

For Cunaxa, again the King's army must not have been much greater than Cyrus' army. Cyrus, like Artaxerxes, stationed himself in the centre of his army (Diod. 14. 22. 6, Xen. *Anab.* 1. 8. 13; cf. Arr. *Anab.* 2. 8. 11 and 3. 11. 5) and when Artaxerxes' army was near enough to show that the Greeks would miss the King if they advanced directly on a line parallel to the river, Cyrus called on them to march obliquely at the King's centre (Xen. *Anab.* 1. 8. 12). Such a manoeuvre was conceivable only if the King was not far to the left of the Greeks. Again there is no knowing how deep the formations of his army were drawn up. Xenophon's assertion (*Anab.* 1. 8. 9) that each people (ἔθνος) marched in a solid rectangle (ἐν πλαισίῳ πλήρει) is no more helpful than his other statements about the Royal army. Even if the average depth was twenty, the total strength was probably not much more than 50,000, if as great. If the contingents of Abrocomas and the King's bastard brother had arrived in time (ibid. 1. 7. 12, 2. 4. 25), the total might have risen to 80,000 but there is no case for positing a much higher figure. After all, Cyrus knew what he had to expect. He had an army of which 13,000 Greeks formed half the battle-line, and which contained a mere 2,600 cavalry (ibid. 1. 8. 5, cf. Diod. 14. 22. 5–7). If he could expect that the King would muster a comparatively huge army, he would not have set out in the first place. The whole story supports the view that Royal armies were not greater than their Hellenistic successors.[37]

Yet when the invasion of Greece is in question, an army of a different order of magnitude is envisaged. Herodotus' fantastic totals have been rejected, but a reluctance to reduce them further than need be seems to have been generally prevalent. The arguments of Maurice[38] have been influential; pointing to Herodotus' statements about the army drinking rivers dry (7. 43. 1, 58. 3, 108. 2), he posited that the total cannot have exceeded 210,000 for otherwise multitudes would have died of thirst, which is no doubt reasonable. But he and others took these statements of Herodotus as literally true[39] and used them as proof of the size of the army, which is far from sensible, for they belong with such comic stories of the immensity of the invading force as the enclosure for counting by the myriad (7. 60. 2). Maurice's great service was to draw attention to the logistic problems of moving large armies; the criterion he proposed has been seriously misleading. The other powerful influence has been Herodotus' 'Army List'; to accommodate under six generals 29 subordinate units with a separate unit of 10,000 Immortals large totals have been excogitated. As argued above, that list should be left out of consideration. The serious question must be faced. Was the Royal army of 480 utterly different in size from later Achaemenid armies?

Consideration of the battle of Plataea is the only means of answering this question. Herodotus had under Mardonius' command 300,000 troops (9. 32. 2; cf. 8. 100. 5 and 113. 3), but such a total has no more to recommend it than other Greek estimates of Persian armies. There are three real indications. First, Herodotus states that the Persians constructed a fortified camp at Scolus which was ten stades square (9. 15), that is, just over a square mile in area, and no army with its transport much more than half the size of Herodotus' 300,000 could have been accommodated in such a space, but there was no point in constructing it if it could not provide protection for the whole army. Secondly, to take Herodotus' account of the movements of Mardonius' army at their face value (9. 13. 2–15. 1), the army seems to be small enough to move quickly and compactly.[40] Thirdly, when Herodotus recounted the battle order of the two sides (9. 28–31), he put the Persian left opposite the Spartans and Tegeans on the Greek right, and the Boeotians and other medizing Greeks opposite the Athenians on the Greek left. On neither flank was there an overlap. Now, although he says there were about 60,000 light armed, his Greek line was composed of 38,700 hoplites. His figures for the various Greek contingents are in some cases suspect,[41] and the total number of hoplites may in fact have been considerably less, but even as they are given, they imply a Persian army of not much greater strength than the Greek. It might be supposed that Mardonius' army was in much greater depth, but although Herodotus says the Persian contingent opposite the Spartans was much more numerous being in a greater number of ranks and, even so, covering the Tegeates as well, he does not say as much of other contingents or of the whole Persian array. So Herodotus' order of battle suggests that Mardonius' army was not much greater than the Greek hoplite array. (It is to be noted that Thucydides puts into the mouth of Hermocrates a remarkable statement which should have given historians furiously to think (6. 33. 5 f.) to the effect that the Persian army in the invasion of Greece did not have numerical superiority. For Thucydides only hoplites seriously counted and in writing Hermocrates' speech he was probably thinking only of hoplites.)[42]

These arguments are hardly compulsive but they do support the view that the Persian army that fought at Plataea was not vastly greater than other later Achaemenid armies. But, it is countered, that army was merely the remnant of Xerxes' great host. Did not Thucydides, so contemptuous of pretty stories ($\tau\grave{o}\ \mu\upsilon\theta\hat{\omega}\delta\epsilon\varsigma$), accept that Xerxes retired after Salamis with the greater part of his army (1. 73. 5)? So perhaps the invading army of 480 was indeed enormous? However, as has long ago been pointed out,[43] if he had an escort under Artabazus which returned to Mardonius (Hdt. 8. 126. 1, 129. 3), he did not have a large part of the army with him and despite Thucydides' acceptance of the story it is hardly to be accepted. Mardonius was left in command of a force deemed sufficient to deal with the united Greeks in battle. What more demanding task had there been in 480? The crucial military problem in that year was how to penetrate Thermopylae, but that was not a task in which enormous numbers of land troops would have helped. Xerxes' plan was to outflank the Greek resistance by using his navy. In the event, chance having depleted his navy, he outflanked the Greeks by a surprise march through the mountains, but at no time could he have imagined that huge numbers would do other than impede his progress. As Beloch[44] wrote over eighty years ago 'it is indeed clear that Xerxes would not have led to Greece hundreds of thousands for which he had no use and which would only have needlessly increased his difficulties of supply, great as they already were'. The great army of 480 was not numerically so different from the armies of the next century and a half.

Armies of the magnitude here envisaged sound small in modern ears, but to the ancients they were large indeed. So what, it will be asked, do such considerations matter? But they do indeed matter. In an army of 50,000 to 70,000, such bodies of crack troops as the 10,000 Immortals assume much greater importance. They were outstanding both for valour and discipline, not just in Xerxes' mind (Hdt. 7. 103. 5) but also in Herodotus' (7. 83. 2), and it is no surprise that they were the unit chosen for the difficult night march to take Leonidas from the rear (7. 215), no mean feat. But they were not alone. The Medes and Cissians were also in their way crack troops, and with the Persians formed a solid well-trained nucleus; they failed against the defenders of Thermopylae (7. 210), only for reasons of geography. The Greek victory at Plataea was won not against ill-disciplined hordes, but against the excellent Iranian troops to whom the Kings had owed their successes in many campaigns.

Plataea was decisive in Persian military development, for it established the superiority of the Greek hoplite, of the spear over the bow, of Greek protective armour over the comparatively ill-protected Persian. The Persians were, according to Herodotus (9. 62), 'not inferior in courage or in physical strength' and indeed the Persian infantry was adjudged by the Greeks the best of the infantry in Mardonius' army (9. 71), but their equipment and methods were no match for the Spartans (9. 62, 63), and for the next century and a half the Achaemenids looked to Greek mercenaries to form the core of their infantry wherever Greeks had to be faced. But their methods of warfare did not remain unchanged. Some attempt was made in the course of the fourth century to produce an Iranian counter to Greek infantry. Evidence about the body of hoplites 'the so-called Cardaces' whom Darius placed on either side of the Greek mercenaries at Issus (Arr. *Anab.* 2. 8. 6) is slight.[45] They are not specifically mentioned in the order of battle at Gaugamela, and must be presumed to be included in the Persian mixed cavalry and infantry (ibid. 3. 8. 3), but as early as the Satraps' Revolt they are to be found in the army sent against the rebel Datames (Nepos, *Datames* 8. 2). But the most striking development is in the role of the cavalry. Herodotus' account of Plataea is far from satisfactory. He claimed that the cavalry was stationed 'separately' (9. 32. 2) but gave no indication where. In the battle the Scythian cavalry were adjudged the best on the Persian side (9. 71. 1) and it is not unlikely that they were part of the cavalry that attacked the Spartans (9. 60) and that the Bactrians, Indians and Scyths to the right of the Medes (9. 31) were principally cavalry. So perhaps the array at Plataea was not so different from that of Cyrus the Younger at Cunaxa, cavalry on the wings and in the centre. By the time of the Macedonian invasion, however, the role of the cavalry was different, fighting in the front of the infantry. Another development was the use of scythe-bearing chariots, which are generally derided because in the two battles when they appear in our evidence, at Cunaxa (Xen. *Anab.* 1. 8. 19–20) and Gaugamela (Arr. *Anab.* 3. 13, Diod. 17. 53), their effect is belittled, perhaps unjustly; Seleucus had 120 of them at Ipsus (Diod. 20. 113. 4, Plut. *Demetrius* 28. 6) and continued to use them (Plut. ibid. 48. 2); indeed they were still in vogue as late as the reign of Antiochus the Great (Polyb. 5. 53. 10, Livy 37. 41). They were perhaps of more use in disrupting the enemy than the accounts of Cunaxa and Gaugamela lead us to suppose.[46] In any case there were tactical innovations and developments, and Persian armies were not motley arrays. The Greeks and Alexander did not win because victory was easy.

NOTES

1. For compact statements about Persian armies, see Meyer 1944: 63–73 and Ehtécham 1946: 62–76.
2. The first difficulty Cambyses, like subsequent invaders, faced in penetrating Egypt was traversing the desert approaches (Hdt. 3. 4. 3, 5. 3) which he solved by requiring Arabs to deliver supplies of water, allegedly in camel skins (Hdt. 3. 9). Then his army had to cross the swampy area, called 'the Barathra' (Diod. 1. 30. 4). Special arrangements had to be made for supplies (cf. Diod. 16. 40. 6 and 20. 73. 3). Crossing a desert was always demanding (cf. Xen. *Anab.* 1. 10. 18 and *Cyrop.* 6. 2. 25–38), but in the invasion of Egypt timing was all important. It was necessary to go in as the Nile was falling and complete the campaign before it rose. V.s. pp. 203–4. Egypt was peculiarly difficult militarily to deal with, and both Alexander the Great and the Emperor Augustus took pains to secure that it did not fall into dangerous hands.
3. V.s. pp. 113–15.
4. Cf. Hdt. 7. 228; Lysias 2. 41; Isoc. 4. 71; Plato, *Menex.* 240d.
5. Cf. Young 1980.
6. Wade-Gery 1958: 215. Cf. discussion by Young in *CAH* iv[2] (1988) 91–2. Evidence for the Royal escort in Briant 1996: 197.
7. For the 1,000 elite, cf. Marquart 1896: 225, and for the military role of

the Chiliarch, Junge 1940: 32–5. Herodotus (8. 113) asserted that all the Immortals, save Hydarnes, stayed in Greece with Mardonius, but presumably the Thousand went with Xerxes.

8. Cf. Junge 1940: 35 n. 2 and Olmstead 1948: 238.

9. Cf. Hdt. 8. 113. 2 τὴν ἵππον τὴν χιλίην.

10. Cf. Diod. 15. 41. 5. In Hdt. 5. 31. 4 Artaphernes has to get Royal approval for the attack on Naxos. There was an invasion of Egypt in 351, and the rumour that prompted Demosthenes' speech *On the Symmories* of 354/353, was presumably caused by preparations for it. The plainest case is provided by the rumour of Persian preparations in winter 397/396 (Xen. *Hell.* 3. 4. 1) which came to fruition in the battle of Cnidus of August 394. The lengthy period of preparation for the invasion of Greece in 480 envisaged by Herodotus (7. 20) may not have been fully four years, but even if it was not, it is plain that Herodotus thought that Persia took a long time to prepare for a campaign (cf. 7. 1. 2).

11. Cf. D. M. Lewis in Burn 1984: 600–2.

12. Cf. Armayor 1978*b*.

13. Herodotus at 7. 64 confuses the Saka tigrakauda (for whom see Hdt. 3. 92. 1 and Herzfeld 1968: 327–8) and the Saka haumavarga. Cf. Asheri 1990: 317–18.

14. Artabazus, while subordinate to Mardonius (9. 42. 1), had a substantial force under his command (9. 66. 2), seemingly of Medes (9. 77. 2), and was clearly a very senior person (cf. 9. 66. 1). If, as Herodotus' list would have it (7. 66), he commanded the Parthians and the Chorasmians in 480, his rise in a matter of months would have been indeed remarkable.

15. Not everyone has accepted Arrian's claim at its face value (cf. Bosworth: 1980 297–8).

16. For the Dahae, *PW* iv. 2 1945 and Herzfeld 1968: 321–2, and for the Daoi *PW* iv. 2 2133.

17. Cf. Xen. *Cyrop.* 5. 2. 25 and 3. 24.

18. The Arachosians appear at Hdt. 3. 93. 2 as Thamanaioi (cf. Herzfeld 1968: 332–4).

19. It has generally been presumed that the six generals were each in command of a corps, but the pairing of generals for the march is curious, each of the first three being joined with one of the second three. Were there three corps each with a senior and a junior commander? Hence the three divisions of cavalry? Presumably Masistius (9. 20) replaced the disabled Pharnuces (7. 88); cf. Munro, *CAH* iv (1st edn., 1926), 272 n. 2. Perhaps the relationship of Artabazus to Mardonius in 479 BC, definitely subordinate (9. 42) but forward with counsel (9. 41 and 66. 1), is another case of dual command.

20. In view of the argument of Cameron 1973, it seems best to avoid the terms 'satrapies' and 'satraps'.

21. Cf. Armayor 1978*b*: esp. 8.
22. Cf. Briant 1996: 208–9.
23. Delbrück 1975 in chapter 1, 'Army strengths: Introductory Material', pointed to the wild exaggerations of numbers in other armies. He then posed a series of realistic criteria which demand much lower totals for the Persians. Cf. Young 1980, where similar good sense prevails.
24. For Antiochus' army and the Romans in 189 BC, Appian, *Syriaca* 31–2 and Livy 37. 39–40. For Alexander's army, Brunt 1976: lxix–lxxi.
25. Launey 1987 (8–10) tabulates the evidence.
26. See Walbank ad Polyb. 5. 65. 1–10. Appian, *Proem.* 10 speaks in a general way of very large forces in Ptolemaic Egypt, but Polybius, our chief authority, gives the actual figures for the battle of Raphia (for which see Will 1982: 37–9).
27. Discussed by Anderson 1970: ch. 3.
28. For the supply of Alexander's army, see Engels 1978: 22–4 and 24 n. 39, 123–30, 144–5, which provide sobering matter for thought. Cf. Young 1980: 222–37.
29. But see 7. 41. 1 for transport in the march from Sardis.
30. If the soldiers' weapons were carried on wagons (as in Xen. *Anab.* 1. 7. 20), each unit's wagons would have had to be close at hand, not miles away at the end of the column. Presumably the covered wagons in which the senior officers' 'lady-friends' travelled (Hdt. 7. 83. 2, 9. 76. 1) stayed close; cf. Xerxes' own covered wagon (7. 41. 1).
31. According to Curtius Rufus (4. 12. 13), there were 45,000 horse and 200,000 infantry.
32. Cf. Marsden 1964: 32–7. His argument is here adopted.
33. See Bosworth 1980: 209.
34. Beloch 1923: 355.
35. Alexander must have inquired closely into the source and date of the intelligence, and it is unlikely that it was more than three or four days out of date.
36. Cf. Engels 1978: 153 for a table of rates of march.
37. This paragraph repeats the argument of Cawkwell 1972: 37–8.
38. Maurice 1930: 210–35. Cf. n. 23 supra.
39. Cf. Burn 1984: 328 'There is every reason to think that he derived these details from a genuine account of the march.' Are we to envisage the whole army advancing on a river at the same moment to drink?
40. Both these points were made by Delbrück 1975.
41. Cf. Beloch 1916: 74–7, not accepted by Hignett 1963: 437.
42. Burn 1984: 330 quotes this passage of Thucydides.
43. Busolt 1895: 712 n. 4.
44. Beloch 1916: 71.
45. For other evidence see Bosworth 1980: 203.
46. See Ch. 10, n. 2.

Appendix 4

The Persian Navy

'ALL the kings of the entire world from the Upper to the Lower Sea—
all the kings of the West land living in tents, brought their heavy tributes
and kissed my feet in Babylon.'[1] Thus Cyrus on the Cyrus Cylinder,
and it is commonly presumed that this involved the submission of the
kings of Phoenicia, which Herodotus regarded as a voluntary act (3.
19. 3).[2] But, having obtained this formal submission, the Persians had
no direct interest in Phoenicia and Phoenician naval forces until Cambyses came down on his way to Egypt and organized a naval force for
the invasion. That is why Herodotus made an eminent Persian say that
Cambyses 'gained Egypt and the sea' (3. 34. 4).

That naval force was composed largely of Phoenicians, but included
Cyprians, Samians, and one Mytilenean trireme at least (Hdt. 3. 19. 3,
44. 2, 13. 2 and cf. 14. 4 and 5), and it seems likely that it was assembled
from all the naval powers of the Mediterranean seaboard. After Egypt
had been conquered, the naval forces of that kingdom were available
to the King, which had been considerable enough in the first half of
the sixth century to engage the Tyrians in battle (Hdt. 2. 161. 2) and,
according to Diodorus (1. 68. 2), to defeat them (Diodorus speaks of
'Phoenicians and Cyprians'). Cambyses had indeed 'gained the sea'.
Did he organize a navy? There certainly were 'navies'. The Ionians at
the start of the Ionian Revolt had sufficient ships to transport the Persian forces to Naxos and to sail to Cyprus and oppose the Phoenician
ships which had transported the army to Cyprus, and these ships could
be described as being at the disposal of Artaphernes (Hdt. 5. 30. 5, 32,
108. 2, 112. 1). But was there a Persian navy, with all the organization
that such a term implies?[3]

Regardless of what the King required, cities had to have ships.
There was, as far as we know, no regular Persian navy patrolling the
seas, and piracy was constantly to be expected. It was necessary too to
provide for the common business of transporting envoys. Even Athens
in 404 was left with the right to maintain a small number of ships, presumably to provide for such matters. So the King had no need to fear

that if ever he wanted to assemble a fleet there would be no competent builders of warships or competent crews. His purposes might have been adequately served by leaving the subject maritime peoples to their own devices. When a major naval effort was required, the necessary forces could have been ordered, without the expense and trouble of maintaining a regular Persian navy.

The one exception was perhaps Phoenicia. Herodotus remarked (3. 19. 3) of Cambyses' 'fleet' in Egypt that 'the whole naval force depended on the Phoenicians' and the same could have been said generally of Persian naval expeditions. It is not necessarily significant that the party of Persian grandees who accompanied Democedes on the voyage of reconnaissance early in Darius I's reign could requisition and get manned immediately two triremes and a supply ship in Sidon (Hdt. 3. 136. 1); that could have been done on the orders of the King, no matter whether the Phoenician ships were part of the Persian navy or not.[4] But some Royal supervision, if only by the satrap, was necessary if the Phoenician ships were to be maintained in the numbers and the state of preparedness to form the nucleus of any naval armament the King ordered. After all, the Phoenician kings within the *pax Persica* had no longer to fear for their security. Their main danger, navally speaking, had been removed with the incorporation of Egypt within the Empire, and since navies are costly to maintain, why should the Phoenician kings have continued to bother? Yet there were Phoenician ships sufficient in number to transport a Persian army, asserted by Herodotus (5. 108) to have been 'large', to Cyprus in the unforeseen emergency caused by the Cyprians joining in the Ionian Revolt. So perhaps the Kings did directly concern themselves with the maintenance of the Phoenician fleet. For the rest, there seems no reason why the King should not have left naval states to their own devices and called on them to produce ships only when he needed them. He may, as Diodorus (11. 3. 7) asserted of the Greek ships in the invasion of Greece, have paid for the construction of the ships, but that in no way implies any regular naval organization. Apart from ensuring that the irreducible minimum of ships was maintained in Phoenicia, the King may well have been content to leave the naval states alone and to call on them only when he was preparing for a major partly naval expedition.[5]

That in part explains why, whenever a naval expedition was required, a considerable period of time was needed for its preparation. When, for instance, report reached Sparta in 397/396 that a royal fleet of three hundred ships was being assembled in Phoenicia, 'some having already sailed in from elsewhere, some having been manned on the spot and some being still in course of being fitted out', and Agesilaus was sent to Asia to meet the threat, it was not until August 394 that a substantial Persian fleet could confront the Spartans (Xen. *Hell.* 3. 4. 1).[6] Of course in all ancient naval warfare it was the new ships that were the most valuable in conflict and that is principally why the number of Athenian ships that actually fought were far smaller than the numbers recorded on the Navy lists.[7] But Athens could get out a fleet of one hundred and twenty at no very great interval of time, and she must have constantly been in a state of naval preparedness which Persia never matched. In that sense at least, apart from the Phoenician fleet, Persia lacked a regular navy and presumably a regular naval organization.

Consistently with this, Persian ideas of naval strategy remained always those of a land power that regarded ships as the mobile wing of land forces rather than as a means of dominating the seas. Herodotus pictured a debate of naval strategy before Xerxes in which the Spartan king, Demaratus, advocated the use of a substantial portion of the fleet in assaulting cities of the Peloponnese (7. 234–7). It is unlikely to be historical, partly because it is doubtful whether Herodotus had any information about the inner councils of the King,[8] partly because it presupposes a highly improbable number of ships on the Persian side, but nevertheless the argument put into the mouth of Achaemenes, the commander of the Egyptian contingent (7. 97), in opposition to Demaratus, is generally suitable for Persian naval operations. He advocates keeping fleet and army together. 'The whole naval force will assist the land army, and the land army will assist the navy as they move together' (7. 236. 2). That was typical not only of the various invasions of Egypt, where the navy had the all-important role of helping to keep the land army supplied, as well as assisting it by landing troops in the rear of enemy defensive positions (as had no doubt been planned for Thermopylae), but also of most of the Persian naval expeditions. For instance, the fleet that fought at Lade in 494 did not appear until a large land army was moving against Miletus (Hdt. 6. 6) and in 480 when suitable forward naval bases were available in the Cyclades (Hdt. 6. 96, 8. 46. 3 f.), the fleet moved in close contact with the land army and there seems to have been no thought of engaging the Greek navy before the advance to Thermopylae had ever begun, just as when the fleet withdrew to Asia in 479, the Phoenician ships, which were ever what Alexander is said to have termed in 333/332 'the most numerous and strongest part of the fleet' (Arr. *Anab.* 2. 17. 3), were dismissed (Hdt. 9.

96. 1) and no attempt was made to check the progress of the Greek navy into eastern waters.[9] It is the lack of real naval strategy which explains why there were on two occasions in the Pentekontaetia land and sea battles at virtually the same moment (Thuc. 1. 100. 1, 112. 4). Only when Greeks took command, was Persian naval power used in an essentially naval way, viz. under Conon in the 390s, and Memnon in the late 330s. For the rest, the Persians remained, navally speaking, unadventurous and inert. Is it likely that an empire so blind to the real uses of sea-power established and maintained a formal naval organization?

A sign of there being no Persian naval organization is given by the difference between the Phoenician ships and those furnished by the Asiatic Greek states. If the Persians had organized their navy as opposed to merely calling on the subject states to furnish ships, it seems likely that they would have seen to it that all their triremes were of similar construction. The Phoenician triremes were the best sailers in the fleet of 480 (cf. Hdt. 7. 44 and 96) but that was probably due to superior oarsmanship. They certainly could outrow the best triremes of the opposing Greek fleet, as Herodotus asserted in his account of Artemisium (8. 10) and as was demonstrated by the incident of the ten Persian ships overtaking the Greek ships stationed off Sciathus (the one that escaped did so only by fleeing northwards as the others unsuccessfully sought the sanctuary of Artemisium) (Hdt. 7. 179–82). After all, 480 was early days for the development of the Greek rowing skills which would manifest themselves in the course of the Pentekontaetea. But quite apart from the arguments of L. Basch[10] about the construction of Phoenician triremes, it is clear enough from the Greek evidence that Greek triremes were different. Plutarch (*Them.* 14. 3) asserted that they were of lighter draught and lower hull (ἁλιτενεῖς καὶ ταπεινοτέρας) and Thucydides (1. 14. 3) said that the ships that fought in 480 'did not yet have decks throughout their whole length'. This latter is the really tell-tale item. For it is clear that the Phoenician ships carried a larger number of marines than would have been possible for the narrow outrigged Greek ships. The proof of this is that when Cimon went out on the Eurymedon campaign, he made, according to Plutarch (*Cim.* 12. 2), an important modification to the design of triremes, in order to play the Phoenicians more effectively at their own game of what Thucydides (1. 49) was to term 'the old-fashioned style' of 'a land-battle' at sea; for whereas Themistocles' ships had been designed for 'speed and being easily turned (περιαγωγή)', Cimon had his made 'broader and with a gangway for the decks' so that 'with a large number of hoplites they could fight more effectively when they bore down upon the enemy'. This not only makes clear what Thucydides (1. 14. 3) was alluding to in his remark about decks, but also shows that Basch's picture of broader, taller Phoenician triremes is correct. In the 480s Greek and Phoenician triremes were quite different.[11] But were the East Greek triremes 'Phoenician' or 'Greek'? In view of Herodotus' account of Dionysius of Phocaea's training of the fleet that fought and lost at Lade, it would seem that they were 'Greek'. He made the marines hoplites (τοὺς ἐπιβάτας ὁπλίσειε 6. 12. 1) and packed them on to the ships forty strong (6. 15. 1). Herodotus does not discuss how he was able to do this. Presumably in Thucydides' phrase he made 'decks throughout their whole length.' What does seem likely is that he was innovating. The East Greek triremes were not accustomed to such methods and so although they had been available to the Persians for two and a half decades before the Ionian Revolt, they do not seem to have been standardized, and this argues somewhat against a centralized organization of a Persian navy.

Of course, it might be argued that the naval potential of the East Greeks hardly mattered to the Persians and that their being different is not so significant as the uniformity of the ships from the Levant. One cannot avoid taking sides in the controversy between Basch and Lloyd,[12] innocent bystander though one inevitably is. Lloyd contends that the triremes built by the Pharaoh Necho (Hdt. 2. 159. 1) were Greek-inspired and Greek-designed and indeed he denies that the Phoenician ships were any different. Both points are here, wisely or unwisely, rejected. The Phoenician influence throughout the Levant was so strong that the powers of the Levant imitated Phoenician models and methods, and, as Basch maintains, the three-banked Phoenician ships were essentially different from the Greek. What Cyprian ships were like is quite unattested, but in an island where Phoenician influence was so strong[13] one would expect their ships to be Phoenician in type. Similarly nothing is known of Cilician ships, but again they may be presumed to have been Phoenician.[14] This presumed uniformity, however, in no way argues the existence of Persian organization. Phoenician methods had long dominated the Levant.

All in all, it seems preferable to suppose that the King took what he needed on the fairly rare occasions that a large naval force was required. The subject peoples had to do what they were told. To postulate a regularly organized and maintained navy seems neither necessary nor sensible.

The size of the 'navy' is a more serious problem. For the understanding of the wars of Greece and Persia, it is necessary to form some idea of how large the naval forces available to the Kings were before one can consider how effectively the Kings used their power.

There is a curious contrast between the massive numbers of ships furnished by Herodotus for the wars down to 479 and the numbers encountered in a wide variety of sources from 478 to 331. All through the Diodoran narrative for this latter period the figure of 300 ships recurs again and again, and without much argument. Delbrück[15] postulated that the Persian ships that fought at Artemisium in 480 numbered between 200 and 300, and that the Grand Fleet of 480 was no greater than the fleets assembled in the fourth century. Such I *believe* to have been the case.

The Diodoran figure of 300 is not merely from Ephorus. That source would account for the total of the Persian fleet against Egypt in the 450s (11. 75. 2, 77. 1), for the fleet proposed but never fully assembled in the Ionian War (13. 37. 4; cf. Thuc. 8. 87. 3), for the figures for the Cyprian War in the 380s (15. 2. 1) and the invasion of Egypt in the 370s (15. 41. 3). But 300 is the figure Diodorus no longer drawing on Ephorus gives for the fleet of Memnon in 333/332 (17. 29. 2) as for the fleet of Artaxerxes in the 340s (16. 40. 6), just as it is the figure given by Ctesias for the invasion of Egypt by Megabyzus in the 450s after the failure of Achaemenides with a force of 80 ships (F14 §§ 36, 37). It is also the figure of rumour. The news that sent Agesilaus to Asia in 396 was that the King was assembling a fleet of 300 (Xen. *Hell.* 3. 4. 1), and the Social War came to an abrupt end in 355 when 'word was put about that the King had promised Athens' enemies that he would join them in fighting the Athenians with 300 ships' (Diod. 16. 22. 2).

The naval reaction to the Macedonian invasion is of special interest. Darius certainly had serious reason to fear. In 336 a substantial Macedonian army was landed in Asia charged with the liberation of the Greek cities (Diod. 16. 91. 2) and the King ordered the 'preparation of many triremes' (Diod. 17. 7. 2). This resulted in Memnon having a fleet of 300 ships (Diod. 17. 29. 2). It is true that Arrian gave the total for the Persian fleet off Miletus in 334 as 400 ships (*Anab.* 1. 18. 5). He *may* be correct. It was a time of great danger and a supreme effort was called for. The totals of individual contingents, however, are more consistent with the smaller total of triremes. When the ships of Aradus, Byblos, and Sidon went over to Alexander, they numbered 80, and the Cyprians who followed suit numbered 120 (Arr. *Anab.* 2. 20). Diodorus (17. 14.

1) put the strength of the Tyrian fleet that prepared to fight Alexander at 80. The Cyprians and the Phoenicians were the real danger in the Persian fleet (Arr. *Anab.* 1. 18. 7), though other small contingents are heard of, namely, 3 Cilician triremes, 10 Lycian, and a single trireme from Iasos (Arr. *Anab.* 2. 20. 2, 1. 19. 11). It looks as if, at this moment of supreme crisis for the Persian Empire, the King assembled a fleet of 300. Even if Arrian's figure of 400 is right and 334 an exception, the point is clear. In the fourth century Persian fleets were regularly no more than 300.

Was it different in the fifth century? It has already been remarked that large Persian naval armaments only happened when the King gave special orders for their assembly, for cooperation with a large land army. When the land army was disbanded, the fleet was dismissed. That is presumably why Pausanias could sail to Cyprus in 478 with 20 ships from the Peloponnese, 30 from Athens and 'a number ($\pi\lambda\hat{\eta}\theta$os) from the other allies' (Thuc. 1. 94. 1), hardly more than 100 ships in all one would suppose. He cannot have expected a major fleet to confront him and in the event there was, it would appear, no opposition at all. Similarly Pericles could sail into eastern waters with a mere 50 ships, Ephialtes with 30 (Plut. *Cim.* 13. 4), and when during the Samian Revolt report came that 'Phoenician ships' were on their way, Pericles did not abandon the siege and set out with his full fleet of 115 ships to meet them, but took only 60 (Thuc. 1. 116); there had been no time for the assembly of a major Persian fleet and Pericles had to fear only the regular Phoenician nucleus, which cannot have been all that great. But it is the size of the major Athenian navies in the Pentekontaetea that is tell-tale. The largest navy to sail east was the force that took part in the Eurymedon campaign, 250 ships if we may trust Ephorus (F191 l. 66, cf. Diod. 11. 60. 5). For the rest, 200 is the figure twice recorded (Thuc. 1. 104. 2, 112. 2). Of course, as time went on, the Athenians, and the Greeks, gained confidence. Lysander in 396 thought that the Spartans would have the better of it with their navy (Xen. *Hell.* 3. 4. 1 f.). The Persians were expected with 300 ships, and, although precision is impossible, it is inconceivable that anything like that number would be available to the Spartan command. Lysander must have been confident that Greek naval skill would be superior to a numerically vastly superior Persian navy. So too Alexander in 334 was content with a mere 160 ships to cover his move to Asia (Arr. *Anab.* 1. 11. 6). It is true that when the full Persian naval force confronted him at Miletus, he realized that 'his navy would be no match in battle for the Persian' (ibid. 1. 20. 1), and he may have underestimated the number of ships the Persians could assemble by 334, but, equally possibly, he was content with 160 for the opening phase of his invasion of Asia because he had confidence in Greek naval superiority. Such might be said for both of Cimon's campaigns after Eurymedon, but for Eurymedon itself the case was different. It ended in a crushing defeat for the Persians (for reasons discussed elsewhere), but in prospect Cimon had every reason to regard it as a great crisis of naval power. That he went with 250 ships suggests that he had no expectation of overwhelmingly large numbers of ships to confront. The figure furnished by Ephorus (F 191) was in fact 340. Even if it is correct, there is no knowing how many of them were fighting ships. Thucydides (1. 100) spoke of the capture of 'triremes of the Phoenicians' and the destruction of them all to the number of 200. One has the impression that that was the total of the fighting ships. One may be misled. But in general it may be affirmed that the Persian navies of the fifth century were never much in excess of 300.

What then of the earlier period? Herodotus' total of 1,207 triremes (7. 89. 1) and 3,000 lesser craft (7. 97) is not worthy of discussion, but the figure of 600 which he gives for the Scythian Expedition (4. 87. 1), the battle of Lade (6. 9. 1), and the expedition to Marathon (6. 95. 2) has attained some sort of respectability.[16] It is to be noted that the first was said to have been composed entirely of Asiatic Greeks (4. 89. 1), the second came from the Levant, and the third likewise, for the whole force was assembled in 490 in Cilicia (6. 95. 1). The figure for the Scythian Expedition seems absurd. For what purpose would Darius have needed such a large number of triremes? There was no naval force to confront him. (According to Ctesias (F13 §20), a satrap of Cappadocia had made an earlier Scythian expedition with 30 pentekonters.) The bridging of the Bosporus would appear to be a matter separate from, and ordered at the same moment as, the provision of ships for the fleet (4. 83. 1), and when the fleet was instructed to sail to the Danube, Herodotus gave no hint that it was much diminished by boats left at the Bosporus (4. 89). As to the bridging of the Danube, some triremes may have been used, but one would suppose that it was principally a role for pentekonters (cf. 7. 36. 1). Why take ships rowed by large crews to use when ships with small crews would do equally well? The figure of 600 triremes at the Danube can hardly be taken seriously. Similarly with the expedition to Marathon. Minimal naval resistance was to be expected, and there would appear never to have been any question of it. Of course, the horse-transports were included in the total of 600 (6. 95. 2) and presumably troop-carrying ships, though Herodotus at no point mentions such a category, but the force that went to Marathon must have included a large number of supply ships, a matter of which evidence is scarce. Thucydides recorded that the 134 triremes and two pentekonters that went to Sicily in 415 were accompanied by 120 so-called ὁλκάδες and 100 merchantmen (πλοῖα) perforce, and many others of both types voluntarily (6. 43, 44). When Democedes' party set off in two triremes, they were accompanied by a so-called γαῦλος, the distinctively Phoenician merchantman (Hdt. 3. 136), but that was not war and no doubt whatever supplies were needed were bought whenever a city was visited. When Artaxerxes III invaded Egypt in 343, he had, according to Diodorus (16. 40. 6), 300 triremes and 500 supply ships, but the march through the desert may have required an exceptionally large number of the latter. Thus the proportion of supply ships in 490 cannot be determined, but if Herodotus was correctly informed that 600 ships went to Marathon, the vast bulk of them may not have been fighting ships and Herodotus have erred only in describing the whole armada as 'triremes'. So too with the 600 ships which he says appeared before Miletus in 494 (6. 9). Many of them may not have been fighting ships.[17] By such means Herodotus' figure of 600 may be made respectable but in view of his abandoned totals for 480 one suspects that he was far from accurately informed about Persian numbers. The figure of 600 so widely favoured for 480 is hardly rendered more respectable by its occurrence earlier in Herodotus' narrative.

It seems reasonable to suppose that Xerxes took to Greece what he deemed to be sufficient to accomplish his military objectives. He may have made generous allowance but since every fighting ship surplus to what he judged necessary created extra supply problems, he had a strong incentive to keep the numbers of the fleet down. What naval resistance had he to expect? When he began to make preparation for the invasion of Greece in 484 (Hdt. 7. 20. 1), the potential naval resistance of Greece could not have been rated highly. In 480 the Greek fleet depended for its success largely on the 200 Athenian ships, which had been begun in 483/482 (Ar. *Ath. Pol.* 22. 7, Dion. Hal. *AR* 8, 83. 1),[18] but earlier in the decade the Athenian fleet had numbered a mere 70 ships (Hdt. 6. 89, 132), largely pentekonters not triremes (Thuc. 1. 14. 3). Herodotus would have it that the 200 were built merely for the war against Aegina (7. 1. 144); it was this war that 'forced the Athenians to take to the sea'. Thucydides removed this belittling of Themistocles' foresight by saying that the ships were built 'at a time when the Barbarian was expected' (1. 14. 3). Clearly when Xerxes gave his orders he had no expectation that the Greek fleet would total anything like 300 (and Themistocles' proposal was framed in response to news of preparations). Delbrück[19] used this to argue for an upper limit of 300, claiming that 'at the Persian court one certainly had no idea what exceptional efforts the small state had made at the last moment'. Tarn[20] found it 'incredible' that Xerxes should have been ignorant of Themistocles' shipbuilding. Perhaps he was right to do so. Modern ideas of the speed of communications in the Persian Empire[21] encourage one to suppose that the King was promptly informed of developments in the Aegean. But the extent of Athens' sudden affluence may have been slow to show itself plainly and the intelligence may have been too late to affect Xerxes' plans. In any case it would seem unlikely that it could affect them. Every Persian major naval expedition took time to prepare, and the four years Xerxes allowed for preparation must have been judged necessary primarily for the construction of ships. News received in, say, early 482 would have been too late to affect the building programme.

There is also another consideration. Xerxes put his trust, navally speaking, in the superiority of Phoenician seamanship. He was pleased, but probably not surprised, when the Sidonians outrowed the rest of the fleet in the race at the Hellespont (Hdt. 7. 44). No matter how many ships the Greeks prepared, he doubtless was assured that their seamanship would be no match for the Phoenician; as Pericles was later to assert (Thuc. 1. 142. 6) 'naval skill is not easily acquired' (and Pericles went on to speak as if Athenian skill was developed after the Persian Wars). Why then should Xerxes have feared that the navy ordered in 484 would be inadequate?

Herodotus concluded his account of the destruction of the 200 ships that he had circumnavigating Euboea (8. 7, 13) with the surprising remark that 'everything was being done by the god to secure that the Persian navy was made equal with the Greek and not be much more numerous'. Herodotus' gods are not mocked. What they would, that they secured. This was before the operations off Artemisium, for which he furnished the precise numbers of the Greek navy, 324 triremes and 2 pentekonters (8. 1, 14). That must have been therefore roughly the total of the Persian fighting ships Herodotus envisaged. But although his narrative provides a means of reducing his grand total, the attempted circumnavigation of Euboea must be dismissed as fabrication; the 250 nautical miles to be covered would have taken too long to be worth attempting when, if Xerxes had intended to destroy the whole Greek fleet, his purpose would have been more effectively achieved by his dispositions for battle.[22] Herodotus' other means of reconciling the enormous numbers he had given for the Persian fleet with what he had implied about Persian naval strength in the battle of Artemisium is the storm on the Magnesian coast; he would have it that no less than 400 ships on the most conservative estimate were lost (7. 190), and by ships he evidently means fighting ships, for in the following chapter he adds that corn transports and other merchantmen were destroyed beyond number. All this may have put Herodotus' historical conscience to rest, but it should arouse our scepticism. Greek triremes were not the place to have a good night's sleep, and a fleet would land to secure it (cf. Xen. *Hell.* 6. 2. 29). It is unlikely that a Phoenician trireme was any better. So the triremes would all have been drawn up on beaches, as Herodotus indicates some were (7. 188. 3). No doubt the supply ships were anchored off-shore and the losses would have been of these. But even here one is sceptical about the scale of the losses. It is not improbable that the whole fleet did not move as one, for merchantmen would not have sailed at the same rate. Supposing that the triremes reached the Sepiad strand in a day from Therme, as Herodotus asserts (7. 183. 3),[23] one could certainly not suppose the same for supply ships, and unless the latter had set out earlier, they would not have reached the same place. To judge by the story of the capture of the fifteen ships of Sandoces (7. 194), movement from the Sepiad strand was staggered. Why should it be different from Therme? So one cannot help wondering just how great the losses due to the storm were, but whatever they were, they must have been principally, if not entirely, of supply ships.

As to the losses in the operations at Artemisium, one is sceptical here too. It is curious that all fifteen of Sandoces' ships should have been captured so easily (7. 194 f.). They appear to have made no sort of fight of it and, despite the presence of the tyrant of Alabanda on one and of a high-born Paphian on another, one wonders whether they were fighting ships. Perhaps they were. In two engagements in the afternoons of the two days before the decisive battle (cf. 8. 15), Herodotus has the Greeks capture thirty ships (8. 11. 2) and destroy 'Cilician ships' (8. 14. 2). One would be grateful to have been told how this happened and what became of those captured ships. Likewise in the real battle on the day of the assault on Thermopylae (8. 15. 1) 'though many ships of the Greeks were being destroyed, far more still of the ships of the barbarians' suffered the same fate (8. 16. 3). Since he goes on to say that 'half of the Athenian ships were damaged' (8. 18), i.e. a matter of ninety ships, the Persian losses were seen to be great indeed. The Egyptians captured five Greek ships, and since they did best presumably few others were captured. No Persian losses are detailed. So the credulous can get rid of as many as they please.

There is one challenging point about the number of Persian ships. Aeschylus says (*Persae* 341 ff.) that 207 were 'arrogant in their speed' (ὑπέρκομποι τάχει), and the figure of 207 seems to have influenced Herodotus in fixing his total of 1,207 (7. 89. 1). Whence came this precise number? The notion of 'fast ships' is familiar. Thucydides said that of the 100 Athenian ships that went to Sicily '60 were fast, the rest were troop-carriers' (6. 4. 3) and Demosthenes in his *First Philippic* said that the force he wants sent out to carry on war constantly will need an escort of 'ten fast triremes, for since Philip has a navy we will need fast triremes to ensure that the force sails in safety' (§22). Clearly they mean by 'fast triremes' fighting ships. Is it possible that this is really what Aeschylus means, that the fighting ships of Xerxes' navy were 207 in number?[24] After all, when one saw an ancient fleet on the move, one would hardly be able to distinguish those that moved faster and count them. However, a different explanation is also possible, that by the ships 'arrogant in their speed' Aeschylus referred to ships of Phoenician construction, presuming that Basch's distinction between Greek and Phoenician triremes is correct. They must have been easily counted. If Herodotus were indeed correct in his figure of 300 for the Phoenician contingent, the 207 might be supposed to be all that remained of them by the time of the battle of Salamis. But in view of the number of Phoenician ships which we meet during the invasion of Alexander this does not seem satisfactory. Then, if ever, the Persians needed the most that Phoenicia could produce. Yet what Alexander termed 'the most numerous and strongest part of the Persian navy, that of the Phoenicians' (Arr. *Anab.* 2. 17. 3) totalled a mere 160 (Arr. *Anab.* 2. 20. 1, 80 from Sidon and Aradus; and Diod. 17. 41. 1, 80 at Tyre). It is true that in the Phoenician Revolt of the 340s Sidon, by especial efforts, itself produced 100 triremes and quinqueremes (Diod. 16. 44. 6), but it is unlikely that in 480 a single city would have been called on to produce such an enormous number of rowers. So 200 seems too large for the Phoenician contingent, let alone 300. But if Basch is right in his view that the Egyptian ships were built on the Phoenician model, and if it is right to suppose that the Phoenician style prevailed in Cyprus and indeed throughout the Levant, 207 would be the number not of

Phoenician ships but of Phoenician-style ships at the battle of Salamis. It is notable that in his account of the battle Herodotus says nothing of Cyprian or Cilician ships and confines himself to the Ionians and the Phoenicians, as is not surprising if the basic distinction was between the two types of trireme. So the figure of 207 may represent the strength of Levantine ships and since the number of Greek-style ships is indeterminable, we reach an impasse.[25]

There is finally no proof possible that Delbrück's conservative estimate is right. But when one considers the regular size of Persian navies after 478 and notes the readiness of Cimon to sail into eastern waters in 469 with a fleet of perhaps 250 ships[26] while yet there was no reason to think that Greek skill could match Phoenician in combat on the open sea, and furthermore when one considers that Xerxes had no reason to plan or fear to face a large Greek fleet in 480, one should, I hold, incline to Delbrück's conservative view. At the least, those who hold to a total of 600 need to explain what was so different about the naval situation in 480 and the immediately succeeding years from the rest of Persian history. Of course the naval resources of the Greek islands were not available to the King after 479 BC[27] and for a large part of the fourth century Egypt was in revolt, but only if the King was concerned always to mobilize every ship he could, might those defections be used to argue that the Royal fleets of the century and a half after the invasion of Greece had to be smaller.[28] The figure of 300, however, appears so constantly and in such varied circumstances that it would seem that 300 was what different Kings regarded as suitable. After all, fleets like armies need to be kept supplied. A fleet larger than what was needed would have been a hindrance. A fleet of 300 sufficed at all times, 480 BC included I suspect. For proper understanding of Persian power one must emancipate oneself from the Navy List as well as the Army List of Herodotus.[29]

NOTES

1. Translation of Pritchard 1969: 316.
2. Cf. Mallowan 1972: 9.
3. Under consideration here are the views of Wallinga 1987 and 1993 ('The traditional view of Persian sea-power must be abandoned. The Persian naval arm consisted of Persian ships manned at the oars by subjects: its

creation made Cambyses conqueror of the Sea (Hdt. 3. 34. 4)', p. 122).

4. One may note the prominence of Sidonian commanders. Cf. Hdt. 8. 67, where the Sidonian king is seated in council beside the King and above the king of Tyre; also Diod. 14. 79. 8 where the Sidonian 'dynast' has command of the eighty ships from Phoenicia. He was not, of course, an admiral in 480 (cf. Hauben 1970), but it seems likely that at that period Sidon was the naval headquarters of Phoenicia. By the second half of the 4th cent. Tripolis, that artificially created capital where the three leading Phoenician cities, Aradus, Sidon, and Tyre, formed the three discrete parts, where common council was held, and where ships were docked (cf. Diod. 16. 41. 1, Strabo 16. 2. 15 754C, Arr. *Anab.* 2. 13. 2 and 3), was clearly naval headquarters. The precise source of the intelligence urgently brought to Greece by a Syracusan concerning the assemblage of a Persian fleet in 397/396 (Xen. *Hell.* 3. 4. 1) is unclear; he claimed to have observed some Phoenician triremes 'sailing in from other places, others being manned on the spot, and some still being fitted out'. It could have been Tripolis or it could have been Sidon. But in 480, to judge by the order of seating in the King's naval council (Hdt. 8. 67), Sidon was considered the senior Phoenician state and presumably before the foundation of Tripolis it was the King's naval headquarters.

5. The passage on which Wallinga heavily relies is a statement in Diodorus (11. 3. 7) concerning the review of the fleet of 480 conducted by Xerxes at Doriscus; of the three hundred and twenty Greek ships alleged to be present Diodorus asserts that the Greeks themselves provided the crews but the King supplied the ships. That could have been true when a special effort to assemble a large force was being made, perhaps every ten or so years, but there is no sign of a large standing navy. Rather the contrary in fact. In 478 Pausanias set out for eastern waters with fifty plus ships (Thuc. 1. 94), just as later we hear of Pericles with fifty ships and Ephialtes with a mere thirty sailing beyond the Chelidonian Isles 'without being confronted by any naval force of the Barbarians' (Plut. *Cim.* 13. 4). That might have been mere luck but that such small forces could be sent out argues that there was no great standing navy to be feared. Of course, if the King had had an Ionian division in this putative standing navy, by 478 he had lost it, but there were, in addition to Phoenicians, both Cyprians and Cilicians which he could have used (Thuc. 1. 112. 4). So why did they not confront Pericles and Ephialtes and Pausanias? The inevitable response is that the Persians did not have a standing navy apart from the Phoenicians.

6. The Syracusan who hastened to Sparta with news of Persian naval preparations said he did not know where this fleet was to be sent (Xen. *Hell.* 3. 4. 1) and it is possible that it was intended for an Egyptian campaign and was diverted to Ionian waters because the Persians got wind of the dispatch

of Agesilaus. But no matter whither it was intended it still took a remarkably long time to get there, for the battle of Cnidus was not fought until August 394. Preparations always were drawn out; cf. Hdt. 5. 32 for the Naxian expedition, 6. 48. 2 for the campaign of 490, 7. 1. 2 for the Great Invasion of Greece, Diod. 11. 71. 6 for the invasion of Egypt in 460, etc. The assembly of even a purely Phoenician force could be represented by Tissaphernes as a thing not to be quickly accomplished (Thuc. 8. 87. 3, 5). When Pharnabazus persuaded Artaxerxes II to prepare a naval force and put Conon in command of it, he took money and sent instructions to the kings in Cyprus to get ready one hundred triremes, but Conon had to make do with forty ships (Diod. 14. 39). When Artaxerxes was persuaded to act against Evagoras, he sent out orders to satraps to build ships (Diod. 14. 98. 3) and the Persian preparations took 'a long time' (ibid. 15. 2. 1). Since preparations could take several years (cf. Diod. 15. 41. 2 and 5), what would have been the point of having an imperial fleet and an imperial naval organization? And since the useful life of a trireme was not short, where would the ships have been kept in fallow times? It was much better for subject kings and rulers to manage their own naval resources and respond when called on, as seems to be implied by Diodorus' account of the response to the revolt of Evagoras (14. 98). Wallinga 1993: 133 argues that three hundred of the Greek ships at the battle of Lade (Hdt. 6. 8) 'were in fact Persian ships which the Ionians appropriated at the beginning of the revolt—200 are expressly described as such by Herodotus (5. 30. 5)—and that the Ionian cities built 53 in addition to that number during the revolt.' How many ships there were in the various Greek cities at the beginning of the revolt is beyond conjecture, but since the Greek cities had almost six years to build ships to face the inevitable Persian response to the revolt the totals given by Herodotus seem perfectly credible without recourse to the hypothesis of a large reserve of Persian ships.

7. In the Social War of 357 to 355 BC Athens sent out two fleets of sixty ships (Diod. 16. 21. 1) to deal with the rebels at a time when she had 283 triremes in all (*IG* ii² 1611, ll. 3–9), just as in the Lamian War of 323/322 170 ships fought in the battle of Amorgos (Diod. 18. 15. 8) at a time when she had in all 365 ships (cf. Ashton 1977: 1–10, treating of *IG* ii² 1631, ll.167–74). Many of the triremes must simply have been kept in the docks out of reluctance to destroy them (cf. Gabrielsen 1994: 127–9). In the Navy List for 357/356 (*IG* ii² 1611) ships are placed in different categories, 'the firsts', 'the seconds', 'the thirds', 'the specials'. It is hard to imagine what these categories comprise other than ships of different ages, and the 'thirds' were probably not used. For the life of triremes, cf. Clark 1993: 163–74 and Gabrielsen 1994: 129–31.

8. Demaratus is an unlikely source. He had, for whatever motive, given advance notice of the invasion (Hdt. 7. 239) as something the Persians

would have wished to stop him doing, and he would not have been declaring afterwards that he had urged on the King a more effective strategy. Artemisia also is unlikely, for she does not figure in Herodotus' account of the debate.

9. For joint operations, cf. Hdt. 6. 43. 1 and 44. 1 (Mardonius in 492), Thuc. 1. 100. 1 and 112. 4 (virtually simultaneous land and sea battles), Ctesias F14 §36 and Diod. 11. 71. 6 and 77. 1 (Egyptian expedition of early 450s), Diod. 15. 41. 3 and 42 (Egyptian expedition of the 370s), Diod. 16. 40. 6, 48. 3 (subjection of Egypt in 343). For the special conditions of the approach to Egypt, cf. Diod. 20. 73–6 (Antigonus' abortive attack of 306).

10. Cf. Wallinga 1993: 59–62; Morrison, Coates, and Rankov 2000: 45.

11. Herodotus' highly unsatisfactory account of the battle of Salamis is almost entirely concerned with actions fought against Greek ships in Xerxes' fleet. The sort of ship on which Xerxes travelled on his way home (Hdt. 8. 118), was similar to that from which, in Plutarch's account (*Them.* 14. 3), Ariamenes 'shot arrows and fired javelins as from a wall'. The only difficulty is presented by Hdt. 8. 60α, where Themistocles is made to say that the Greek ships were 'heavier' (βαρυτέρας). No manuscript shows any variant; there is no hint of βραδυτέρας as conjectured by Stein. The explanation offered by Macan (1908 ad loc.) was that 'heavier' might be taken to mean 'less easy to manage' (χεῖρον πλέουσας) and be referred to the crews and seamanship rather than to the actual ships. Morrison and Williams 1968: 134 explain Themistocles' words as a reference to the Greek ships not being 'dried out' as the Persians' had been at Doriscus (Hdt. 7. 59. 3), but the Greeks must have had sufficient notion of where the Persian array was, to have dried out their own ships, at least in relays. Perhaps Stein's conjecture was right and Themistocles was urging avoidance of battle on open sea because the Phoenician ships, although bigger (Plut. *Them.* 14. 3), were better handled and moved, when they had space to work up speed, faster.

12. Basch 1969, Lloyd 1972, 1975*b*, and 1980, and Basch 1980.

13. Cf. Gjerstad 1979.

14. Although Thucydides (1. 112. 4) mentioned Cilician ships in the fleet that was defeated off Cyprus in 450, the only later mention is in connection with the fleet that fought at Cnidus in 394 (Diod. 14. 79. 8) where in addition to 80 triremes from Phoenicia there were 10 from Cilicia. Of course, Thucydides may have used the term 'Phoenician' as shorthand for the various Levantine contingents (cf. 1. 100 and Tarn 1908: 205 n. 15), just as Herodotus speaks simply of 'Phoenician' ships at Salamis and omits mention of Cyprians and Cilicians (8. 85). Cf. ML 24. But one cannot help wondering whether the role normally assigned to the Cilician cities was to provide transports. To the Levantine fleet that went over to Alexander in 332, while Cyprus contributed 120 ships, Mallus and Soloi contributed

between them a mere 3 (Arr. *Anab.* 2. 20. 2), no other contingents being mentioned. So by the later 4th cent. the potential of Cilicia in fighting ships was not great. Minor piratical craft are heard of in large numbers later (Appian, *Mith.* 96), but in general Cilicia was never a naval power of any consequence. The 'Cilician ships' attacked and destroyed at Artemisium in 480 (Hdt. 8. 14. 2) seem to have been on their own and it is unlikely that a mere part of the fighting fleet would have been so used. Perhaps they were supply ships on their way in the late afternoon to the land-forces before Thermopylae.

15. Delbrück 1975: 99–100.
16. Hammond 1959: 229 and 1973: 268–70 accepts Herodotus' totals, which would entail enormous supply problems (cf. Young 1980: 223–4) and indeed manpower problems. Wallinga 1993: 171–85 sidesteps these by arguing that the Persian fleet was undermanned as indeed was, he holds, regularly the case in Greek fleets of the 5th cent. and that a trireme could move with a hundred rowers, all of which seems a very improbable device to salvage Herodotus' credit; one would have expected the Persians to have fewer but faster ships in preference to a huge surplus of underpowered; if they were providing for surplus to requirements, one would have thought it was extra rowers not extra ships that were needed, for illness, disease, and casualties might, as ever, affect the fighting efficiency of the navy. (Cf. Appendix 1, n. 1 for further discussion of this theory.) Green 1970: 61–2 reduces Herodotus' figure by postulating that although Herodotus had been accurately informed he had failed to subtract the large number of ships used in the bridging of the Hellespont. Burn 1984: 330–2 argues similarly. Beloch 1916: 67–70 explained Herodotus' total as being tailored to fit supposed totals in the Trojan War and postulated an actual total of not more than 500 at the beginning of the campaign. Tarn 1908 accepted the figure of 600, having argued for five divisions of 120 ships. Hignett 1963: 345–50 settled for 600. Only Delbrück contended that the Greeks outnumbered the Persians at Salamis.
17. Any naval force supporting ground troops or siege operations and so not free to roam needed supply ships. For instance the Hellenic fleet of 160 ships that Alexander had with him for the crossing to Asia and down the Asiatic coast as far as Halicarnassus (Arr. *Anab.* 1. 11. 6, 20. 1) was accompanied by 'many merchantmen'. When Mausolus was said to have had 100 ships at the siege of Sestos (Xen. *Ages.* 2. 26), many may have been supply ships; when Idrieus in the 340s was called on to act against the Cyprians, he sent forty triremes and that could well have been the best he could manage. If 200 ships did indeed go against Naxos in 499 (Hdt. 5. 31. 4) many of them were presumably transports of one kind or another.
18. Cf. Cadoux 1948: 118.
19. Delbrück 1975: 99–100.

20. Tarn 1908: 203.
21. Cf. Lewis 1977: 57.
22. Beloch 1916: 88–90, followed by Hignett 1963: 386–92, found Herodotus' account incredible. It should, in fairness, be added that Hammond in *CAH* iv² 553 accepted the whole story without a tremor. Cf. Lazenby 1993: 129.
23. An assertion concerning which cf. Tarn 1908: 210–16.
24. V.s. n. 14.
25. Herodotus' figures for Greek naval strengths are not necessarily reliable. Although he had declared (8. 18. 1) that half the Athenian ships at Artemisium had been damaged and although there had hardly been time or opportunity for repairs, he gave exactly the same total at Salamis (8. 1. 1, 14. 1, 44. 1). Also he made the full Greek strength at Salamis 378 triremes and 7 pentekonters (8. 48), whereas Aeschylus who took part in the battle made it 310 (*Persae* 339–40). So the 353 ships at the battle of Lade in 494 BC (6. 8) may be misleadingly large. But even if he was correct about that, there is no reason to take that as a guide to the numbers of 'the Ionians' (8. 85. 1) in the Grand Fleet of 480 BC. For one thing, the 80 Milesian ships (6. 8. 1) must have been a thing of the past (6. 20), but quite apart from that the large numbers of Chian and Lesbian ships assembled in the supreme crisis of the Ionian Revolt may not have been required by the King in 480; in the Samian Revolt of 441/440 BC there were only 55 in all from Chios and Lesbos combined (Thuc. 1. 116. 2 and 117. 2) with similar low totals in Athenian service in 430 BC and on the Sicilian Expedition (ibid. 6. 31. 2 and 43). Similarly, one notes that the Samian contribution to the Egyptian campaign of Cambyses, at a time when Samian naval power was at its height, was only forty triremes (Hdt. 3. 44. 2). There is no way of knowing what Xerxes required for the invasion of 480.

    It is also to be noted that 'the Ionians' of Hdt. 8. 85. 1 may reflect the Persian usage of using the word for Greeks in general and in 480 the Ionian division of the fleet included Samothracians (8. 90. 2) and perhaps the Dorians commanded by Artemisia (7. 99). Probably 'the Ionians' at the battle of Salamis were quite different from the Ionians at Lade, and certainly their numbers are quite beyond conjecture.
26. The manuscripts of Plut. *Cim*. 12. 2 vary between 200 and 300. Diodorus 11. 60. 3 gives 200 Athenian plus 100 allied ships. Ephorus (*FGH* 70 F 191 frg. 9, 10) gave 250 against 340 barbarian ships (for which latter figure cf. F 192).
27. According to Isocrates 4. 135, most of the fleet used by Tiribazus in the war against Cyprus in the 380s came from Ionia. Xen. *Ages*. 2. 26 has a naval force of 200 ships operating under Mausolus in the 350s.
28. *Pace* Morrison, Coates, and Rankov 2000: 44 n. 17.
29. The Navy List (7. 89–96) seems to emanate from the same stable as the

Army List. The accoutrements and weapons of each people are again given, this time even more irrelevantly. Cf. 91 where the dress and weapons of the Cilicians are reported, none of much importance for life at sea! As to the numbers of ships provided, one might compare the statement in Justin (9. 5. 6) where the total military potential of the League of Corinth was far greater than any Greek army on the field of battle.

Appendix 5

Thermopylae and 'the way into' Greece

ACCORDING to Herodotus (8. 31), Xerxes, having destroyed Greek opposition at Thermopylae, moved into Phocis by invading Doris from Trachinian territory and by that route invading Phocis. This has always been a puzzle, and indeed remains so. Why take so great pains and incur such losses at the Gates, when he could, perfectly easily it would seem, get into central Greece by another route? Various answers have been given which there is little point reviewing, but some notice must be given of a new and revolutionary answer to the puzzle.

The theory is most fully developed in Szemler, Cherf, and Kraft's *Thermopylae. Myth and Reality in 480 BC* (Chicago, 1996). They argue that Xerxes entered Greece by what they term 'the Isthmus Corridor', a broad highway across high places in existence and indeed in use from much earlier times, that in 480 BC there was no road through the Gates which an army with all its baggage train and wheeled vehicles could use to enter Greece, that at that time the Gates were a dead end and only of interest to Xerxes because the Greeks had chosen them as their command post whence contact could be maintained with the navy at Artemisium. What has prompted this, at first hearing bizarre, theory is a series of geological explorations along the coastline as it was in 480 BC, which they claim show that there could have been no road along which historians have constantly envisaged the Persian army advancing or at any rate being able to advance had such a route been chosen.

There is an inconsistency in this theory. They point to the speech Arrian set in the mouth of Alexander at Opis (*Anab.* 7. 9. 4), where Alexander asserted of his father Philip that 'after he had humbled the Phocian people he made the access to Greece broad and easy instead of narrow and difficult', and they refer to various allusions in inscriptions to works at Thermopylae (*SIG*³ 220, 243 D 42–5, 250 D 43–5). So regardless of geological soundings, there must have been something there for Philip to widen and make easier, and this early route may well have been useful enough for Persian purposes in 480 BC.

The real answer, however, to this new theory is that made by

Pritchett, most notably in vol. v of his *Studies in Ancient Greek Topography* (1985) where he reviewed the post-Herodotean testimonia on the use of the Thermopylae Pass (pp. 191–3). What he said in *Studies* vi (1989) would no doubt command general assent: 'I find it hard to believe that the sinking of seven cores in the Malian Gulf proves that the record of the crucial military importance of Thermopylae attested in Herodotus, Thucydides, Xenophon, Demosthenes, Hyperides, Diodorus and Polybius is false.' It is not just what men said about the Pass but what they did. There is no point in going over all this evidence, but it may be useful to focus on the period between the Battle of the Crocus Field in 352 BC and the occupation of Phocis by Philip in 346. In 352 when news of the result of the battle reached Athens, the Athenians, to stop Philip coming into Greece, 'occupied the pass (*angustias*) of Thermopylae in a policy similar to that of the previous occupation when the Persians were coming' (Justin 8. 2. 8). In Diodorus' version of that event (16. 38. 1 and 2), Philip 'was advancing to the Gates to make war against the Phocians; the Athenians checked him from going through the pass' (παρόδους, the word Diodorus in his account of the Persian Invasion had used of Thermopylae, e.g. at 11. 4. 1 and 5. 2) 'and Philip retired to Macedon'. Similarly, when Demosthenes referred to this Athenian expedition (19. 84, 18. 32), it was simply 'to the Gates'. There was no thought on the part of the Athenians or of Philip of this 'Isthmus Corridor'. Were they all stupid ignoramuses?

Similarly, with the tragic events of 346 BC when Philip 'occupied the pass of Thermopylae' (Justin 8. 4. 12). The Athenians failed 'to bolt' the Gates and Philip got 'inside' them (Dem. 18. 32, Aesch. 2. 130, 3. 80). The Gates were thought to be on the way in. No alternative appears to have occurred to either the victor or the vanquished. All thoughts were on Thermopylae.

Are we then to suppose that those who wrote the history of those years and those who made speeches and sought to shape public policy were all living in Cloud-cuckoo-land? For most historians at any rate, the 'facts' of geological inquiry do not destroy the record of what men thought and did. There must be something wrong with these 'facts', though only a geologist will be able to discern it, an uneasy conclusion.

Why then did Xerxes turn back after ridding himself of Greek opposition at the Gates and enter central Greece by way of Doris? His precise route may be debated (cf. Pritchett 1982: 211–33, and Szemler, Cherf, and Kraft 1996: 79–95) but it was, according to Herodotus 8.

31, somewhere west of Thermopylae. So why had he apparently disregarded it previously?

Answers can only be conjectured. If Xerxes was aware before the battle of the route he took after it, he may have concentrated his efforts on Thermopylae because, although he thought that frontal assault was unlikely to succeed, he was counting on naval victory to enable him to attack the Greeks at the Gates from their rear as well as on their front. Such a naval assault was unnecessary once the outflanking march by the path Anopaia became a possibility. He could have had, after all, little idea what forces and what conditions a march over the mountains would produce. Herodotus said that the forces available to Leonidas included the Opuntian Locrians 'in full force' and a thousand Phocians (7. 203. 1), the latter being the force set by Leonidas to 'defend their own land' (7. 217. 2). But were these thousand Phocians the most that Phocis could put in the field? There seems to be a distinction between the 'full force' of the Locrians and the thousand Phocians. Before ever the Phocians laid hands on the treasures of Delphi and were thereby able to raise the large mercenary forces, they seem to have been a considerable power. For instance, Cleombrotus in 457 BC took a force of 1,500 Spartan hoplites and 10,000 of their allies to deal with the Phocians (Thuc. 1. 107. 2), and at the start of the Corinthian War Ismenias led nearly 6,000 against them and at the end of a long hard battle nearly 1,000 Phocians lay dead (Diod. 14. 82. 7–9). So it is highly likely that in 480 the Phocians could field a good many more than the thousand Herodotus talks about. Where were they then? It seems all too probable they were ready to help defend Doris and that the Dorians 'were taking the side of the Mede' (Hdt. 8. 31) only after the Greek failure at Thermopylae. All in all, it is no surprise that Xerxes concentrated on the Gates.

What is surprising, if Szemler, Cherf, and Kraft are right about there being a high highroad, this Isthmus Corridor, well known from ancient times, is that in 339 BC the Athenians were dumbfounded when Philip occupied Elateia (Dem. 18. 168–79). The Thebans too seem to have thought that by occupying Nicaea (Philoch. 56b) they were secure. Both of them must have been counting on the Phocians to keep the Macedonian army out. So if there was this Isthmus Corridor, it was defensible.

Appendix 6

The Themistocles Decree

AMAZING and shocking though it may seem to many, there is no mention in Chapter 5 of the decree discovered at Troizen and first reported in 1960. This, the so-called Themistocles Decree, has been endlessly discussed and there is no consensus about whether it is, or is based on, an authentic decree of 481 or 480 BC, or is a fourth-century fabrication. Lazenby 1993: 102–4 has treated of it, to my mind, admirably, and here I confine myself to stating the main reasons I have for disregarding it.

If the decree were authentic, Herodotus would be in several respects seriously discredited but it will hardly suffice to seek to discredit the decree merely by showing where it conflicts with Herodotus. However, there are three general considerations for confidence in Herodotus and grave dissatisfaction with the decree.

1. The whole procedure of a decree ordering strategy is inconceivable.
In the decree the Athenian people are shown making an important strategic decision without reference to the existence or the operation of the Hellenic League. Once word reached Greece that the Persians were coming, it must have been obvious that no one state on its own could keep them out and there was no point in Athens seeking to go it alone. The League was formed probably in later 481, and Herodotus represents the members at an early date seeking to secure as wide participation as possible, and embassies were sent to Sicily (7. 153), Corcyra (7. 168. 1), and Crete (7. 169. 1), as well as to Argos (7. 148), and the representatives of the member states (πρόβουλοι 7. 172. 1) were established at the Isthmus in time to receive a Thessalian appeal when Xerxes was about to cross to Europe (7. 172. 1). It would have been essential that there should be, in Greek terms, a *hegemon*, and Sparta was the chosen power and the Spartan Eurybiades the general commander of the Greek navy (8. 2). So an *Athenian* decree taking the decision to send out ships to Artemisium is, historically speaking, unthinkable. (If, however, it were argued, as has been attempted, that the Athenians passed their

decree in 481 before the Hellenic League was operating, half the Athenian navy would have been expected to be out in northern Euboea long before there was any possibility of operations and needing to be kept supplied in a way that simply did not happen at that stage of Greek naval developments—a wholly absurd theory.)

2. The implied strategy of the decree is wholly improbable.

Regardless of what Herodotus says, it must have been clear to the states' representatives meeting at the Isthmus that there was only one strategy for united Greek resistance seriously to be considered and that was to try and stop the Persians getting through the Gates. That was, in prospect, a naval problem. Geography meant, as they must have thought, that the Persian army could be kept out provided that the Persian navy could be prevented landing a force immediately to the east of the Gates. To have the best chance of securing this, the Greeks, considering the expected superiority of the Persian navy, would have had to put all the Greek naval power possible in position to confront the enemy. Artemisium would not be a mere holding position. Navally speaking, it would be their desperate last chance. But in the decree, the Athenians are pictured sending only half their naval strength to Artemisium, to my mind a very improbable picture indeed.

Of course, even on Herodotus' account the Athenian navy was divided. Fifty-three of the one hundred and eighty Athenian ships at Artemisium did not arrive until the second day's fighting (8. 14. 1), and he offers no explanation of their last-minute arrival. If they had been kept back in case a Persian force was sent around Euboea, they abandoned that idea well before word of the disastrous effects of the storm, which Herodotus believed destroyed a circumnavigating force, could possibly have reached them. A more likely explanation is perhaps that not all the ships could be manned and equipped in time to set out together.

Again, on Herodotus' account other Greek states contributed more ships to the Greek fleet at Salamis than at Artemisium (8. 1 compared with 8. 42–8). Save for the Aeginetans, these other Greek contingents added up to very few, and in any case Herodotus' figures for Salamis are very suspect, his total being markedly different from that of Aeschylus, who took part in the battle. As to the Aeginetans, 'there is something amiss with the numbering of the Aeginetan fleets' (Macan 1908 ad Hdt. 8. 46. 1). According to Herodotus (8. 46. 1), 'the best sailing ships' of the Aeginetans numbered thirty. Despite his assertion that there were only eighteen at Artemisium (8. 1), there may have been a larger number, for Herodotus' total is greater than the sum of the contingents. The precise situation is unclear. What is clear is that there is no colour to be derived from Herodotus for the idea of a large Greek reserve force. Once Artemisium had been decided on for the navy, the strongest fleet possible had to be sent there. The idea which is implied by the Decree that Artemisium would be a holding operation with the real conflict to be fought well to the south could be conceived only in hindsight. In 480 before the battle it was unthinkable.

3. A decision to evacuate Attica before the fleet went out to Artemisium is to be thought on balance unlikely.

According to Herodotus, the proclamation to Athenians to save their families by what means they could was made after the fleet returned from Artemisium (8. 41. 1), but he also has the Persian fleet arrive in Phalerum (8. 66. 1) within nine days of the battle (cf. Lazenby 1993: 111–12). How long the Athenian ships took to return home is unclear but on Herodotus' timetable there could have been six or seven days at the most for the evacuation to be effected. Hence the allure of the version of the 'Themistocles' Decree, which has the Athenians deciding by formal decree to evacuate Attica at the same time as the fleet was ordered out to Artemisium.

However, long before the Themistocles Decree had been heard of, scholars had been criticizing and rejecting the Herodotean timetable (cf. Hignett 1963: 195), and, considering the distance to be travelled, the terrain, and the possibility of hostility, one is inevitably inclined to lengthen the time for the march and so to adjust the time for the fleet's arrival at Phalerum, which would not have been safe before the army had removed all posssible opposition to the landing. So there must have been more time for the evacuation than Herodotus allows.

In any case, there is a very strong reason for not putting the evacuation where the Decree puts it. When the Athenian fleet returned from Artemisium, they expected, according to Herodotus (8. 40. 2), to find the Peloponnesians out in full force in Boeotia in a position to resist the Barbarian. Consistently with this, he had earlier (7. 206) stated that when the Spartans sent out the force under Leonidas, they intended to go out themselves in full force shortly, and in 479 he has the Athenians (9. 7β) tell the Spartans that they had agreed to go to Boeotia and oppose the Persians but had stood by and watched them invading Attica. Thucydides too has the Athenians, in speaking of their role in the salvation of Greece, say that they took to the sea and were not enraged because the Spartans had not previously gone to their aid (1. 74. 2). Of course,

Thucydides may have been simply following Herodotus, but it seems wholly credible that the High Command at the Isthmus should have considered what was to be done if the Greek fleet failed against the Persian and the defence of the Gates had failed. Peloponnesian states may well have privately decided to write off all of Greece north of the Isthmus, but there must have been a plan to convince the Megarians, the Athenians, and the Boeotians that they would not be left defenceless. Similarly, Athenian leaders may have privately formed the plan of evacuation well in advance, but they could hardly have declared as much by a formal decree if they were not to be seen to be writing off all the other Greeks between them and the advancing Persians. The only reasonable strategy, therefore, must have been to confront the foe, if he broke through the Gates, in Boeotia, a desperate last chance, Plataea a year early. Herodotus' last-minute proclamation makes better sense than the 'Themistocles' Decree.

For these three reasons the inscription must be regarded as bogus.

Appendix 7

The Peace of Callias

THE debate goes on and on and, for many, tedium holds sway. I have set out my reasons for holding (strongly) that there was a Peace made in 449 BC in *Phoenix*, 51 (1997), 115–30, and there is no point in expounding them here. Briefly they were:

1. the absence of operations between 449 and 412, especially after 431;
2. the improbability of the Peace being invented to show up the shameful King's Peace, considering that the first mention of the Peace is made by the very man who could least be expected to be duped or willing to be duped, namely, Isocrates;
3. Ionia was unwalled in 427 BC (Thuc. 3. 33. 2), which at the least shows that there was no physical obstacle in the way of the Persians resuming control but which is best understood as a positive requirement of the Peace.

Nor is it necessary to redevelop the argument I advanced against the hypothesis of Badian 1993: 1–72 that there were two Peaces of Callias, one where Diodorus' account (12. 4) placed the Peace, in 449 BC, and the other in the 460s after the battle of the Eurymedon. Unless Thucydides is wildly misleading, Athens cannot be supposed to have made peace with Persia until after the Spartans dismissed the Athenian army from Ithome and in a general diplomatic revolution Athens, the King's arch enemy, made alliance with the King's arch friend, Argos, and gave up the alliance that had been made with Sparta against the Persian (Thuc. 1. 102. 4). Until Thucydides' account is despised and rejected, there is no need for further discussion.

What should be confronted is the argument of Meister 1982: 6–22 that apart from Diodorus' formal statement, which he dismisses as a confusion (28–31), the evidence for a peace is all to be related to the 460s (and since there clearly was not peace between Athens and Persia in the late 460s and indeed later, the only explanation of all this evidence, he argues, is that the Peace of Callias was a later and much

embroidered invention). It is true that Athenian naval campaigns in
the eastern Mediterranean are very similar and would have been easily
confused by Diodorus if they had not been differentiated by the names
of the Persian commanders, at the Eurymedon Tithraustes on sea and
Pherendates on land (Diod. 11. 60. 5 and 61. 3), but in 449 BC Artabazus and Megabyzus (Diod. 12. 3. 2). The evidence for a Peace after
Cimon's last campaign in 450/449 is not to be so lightly dismissed as
Meister supposed. As to the rest of the evidence, despite his conviction
that it is all concerned with a supposed peace with Persia in the 460s,
the evidence of Callisthenes as presented by Plutarch (*Cim.* 13. 4) is
crucial. As Bosworth 1990 has shown, Callisthenes did not, it would
seem, deny that there was a peace treaty. He simply did not mention
it. He argued, perhaps in the introduction to his *Acts of Alexander*, that
what conditioned the relations of Athens and Persia was the defeat of
Eurymedon which constrained the King's actions. For such a view
the actual Peace of 449 BC merely formalized legally what had been
established in fact almost two decades earlier. This perhaps is what
the writer in the *Suda* had in mind (s.v. Καλλίας). The Greek is curious—τοὺς ἐπὶ Κίμωνος τῶν σπονδῶν ἐβεβαίωσεν ὅρους. If it had said
τῶν ἐπὶ Κίμωνος σπονδῶν, that would have meant assuredly that the
writer thought that there was a peace made in the time of Cimon which
Callias later confirmed, that is, the Badian hypothesis. As it stands, the
writer may have meant that Callias confirmed in his treaty the bounds
established in Cimon's time, that is, the effect of Eurymedon was to
exclude the Persians from west of the Chelidonian Isles and this exclu-
sion was later enshrined in the Peace of Callias. In any case one can
hardly be impressed by such a lexicographical entry and, as far as the
other passages assembled by Meister are concerned, one may assert
that none of them demands a date for the Peace of Callias immediately
after the battle of the Eurymedon. The Peace is to be left where Diodorus placed it, and it was the first peace between Athens and Persia.

So much by way of orthodox response to new heresies. What is
intended in this appendix is to consider the terms of the Peace. In Diodorus (12. 4. 5) they are set out concisely, but a moment's thought raises
questions that call for answers. If the Greek cities of Asia were all to be
autonomous, how were 'the Greek cities' indisputably defined? If the
satraps were not to go within three days of the sea, what, for instance, of
the satrap at Dascylium which was much less than three days from the
sea? And what of the places in his satrapy like Atramyttium (modern
Edremit) which Pharnaces (Thuc. 5. 1) accorded to the Delians? Were

such places now to be beyond the reach of Persian authority? And did Diodorus delineate the full scope of the Peace? In treaties excessive concision can lead only to disputes, and it is best to spell out fully what is intended. There must have been more to the Peace than Diodorus set down.

We have the text of only one treaty between Persia and a Greek state and that is the treaty negotiated by Sparta in winter 412/411 (Thuc. 8. 58) together with the two preliminary drafts (chs. 18 and 37). (What is commonly referred to as the King's Peace (Xen. *Hell.* 5. 1. 31) is the text of a Royal Rescript, not of a treaty.[1]) One can see the Spartan and the Persian negotiators seeking a form of words acceptable to both parties, the first two versions defining the area of Royal authority, both clearly uncongenial to the Spartans, the third a firm assertion of the King's right to 'Asia'—'the King's territory such as is in Asia is to belong to the King'. In the case of the Peace of Callias an acceptable form of words would have been less easy to find. 'The Greek cities' alone would not have done. There were too many cities disputably Greek or barbarian, like for instance Aspendus, for which an Argive origin might be claimed (cf. Strabo 14. 4. 2 667C).[2] Nor could 'the Greek cities' be defined by an area. There were too many non-Greeks living mixed up with Greeks. For instance, as the remainder of the Ten Thousand came southwards in 400–399 BC, they found in the valley of the river Caïcus a mix-up of barbarian and Greek, and this had probably been the situation during the period of the Peace of Callias.[3] How then were 'the Greek cities' of the Peace defined? The answer would have had to be clear and, to judge by the manner of the Spartan–Persian treaty of 412, one would expect it to have been concise. It may therefore be suggested that alliance with Athens was the criterion—τὰς κατὰ τὴν Ἀσίαν Ἑλληνίδας πόλεις ὅσαι τῶν Ἀθηναίων σύμμαχοι ὦσιν, or the like.[4] After all, 'Asia' was the King's as Herodotus (9. 116. 3; cf. 1. 4. 4) writing in the heyday of the Peace of Callias asserted. 'The Persians think that all of Asia belongs to themselves and to the reigning King (τοῦ αἰεὶ βασιλεύοντος).' So the Peace probably began with an assertion of Royal sovereignty over the whole of Asia (cf. Thuc. 8. 58. 2), with the autonomy of Athens' allies added, provided they kept their side of the bargain.

Time would show 'autonomy' to be a somewhat nebulous concept, though in the 440s it was thought to mean something clear enough for Sparta to consider that an autonomy clause in the Thirty Years Peace of 446 BC would be a real check on Athenian imperialist designs.[5]

No doubt Athens viewed the guarantee by the King of autonomy for Athens' allies in the Peace of Callias similarly, and the idea endured as the terms of the truce offered in 395 BC by Tithraustes show (Xen. *Hell.* 3. 4. 25). In addition there was the assurance that, if Athens kept faith, there would be no military interference. But precisely what this involved is problematic.

Diodorus (12. 4. 5) spoke as if the restriction concerned only satraps, but Isocrates twice (7. 80, 12. 59) spoke as if there was a ban on Persian armies crossing the river Halys on the way 'down'. What Herodotus said of that river (which is the modern Kizil Irmak) is roughly correct, that it 'cuts off pretty well all the lower parts of Asia' (1. 72. 3), and he constantly speaks of it as a dividing line (1. 6. 1, 1. 28, 1. 103. 2, 1. 130. 1) as indeed did Thucydides in referring to the realm of Croesus (1. 16), but it is also clear that it was for Herodotus a point on a road, the Gates through which it was inevitable that those crossing the river had to pass (5. 52. 2). If it was named in the Peace of Callias as Isocrates suggests it was, did the clause assert that no army would go from east of the river Halys towards the sea (καταβαίνειν)?

Wade-Gery's notion of a Palatine Army[6] has been discredited (cf. pp. 238–9) and when large armies were to be assembled special efforts had to be made, but certainly Royal armies did often enough come west of the Halys. Is it to be supposed that the King accepted in 449 BC that he would not be able to exercise the full Royal power over 'the peoples living within the river Halys' (Hdt. 1. 28)? He could deny himself the Greek cities, but time would show what could in the middle of the fifth century have easily been foreseen, namely, that revolt by satraps was a serious possibility. In fact, in the early part of his reign Artaxerxes, as Ctesias (F14) shows, had been confronted with revolts in Bactria, then Egypt, then Syria—the last requiring two successive 'Persian armies'—and he must have been very conscious of the dangers of revolt in the periphery of the Empire. It is, therefore, inherently unlikely that the King would have accepted a restriction which could so seriously threaten the cohesion of his realm.

How then, it may be asked, could the river Halys have been mentioned in the Peace? 'Provinces', 'countries' in the Persian Empire (*dahyava* in Old Persian) were groups of 'peoples' (ἔθνεα in Herodotus, constantly). There was no Halys line. 'Across the Halys' perhaps designated an area, just as 'Across the river' (*Ebir-nari*) designated the area which later formed the Roman province of Syria.[7] Croesus' kingdom comprised the peoples living to the west of the Halys (Hdt. 1. 6, Thuc.

1. 16), and to define the area within which the Peace of Callias would apply mention of the river Halys would have been convenient. Just as Herodotus (5. 102. 1) could speak of 'the Persians who hold satrapies (νομοί) within the river Halys', so the area within which satraps could not go down to the sea could be so defined. If Isocrates thought, as he might seem to have thought, that the treaty prevented the Persians crossing the Halys with an army, probably he misunderstood.[8] In any case it is the clause governing satraps that challenges.

'The satraps of the Persians are not to go further down to the sea than a distance of three days journey from the sea' (Diod. 12. 4. 5). One of them, viz. the satrap of the Dascyleian satrapy, had his satrapal seat within three days of the sea. Quite apart from that there were places near to the sea which were not Greek. The cluster of towns in the Caïcus valley has already been mentioned. They are Pergamum, Parthenion, Apollonia, Halisarna, Teuthrania (Xen. *Anab.* 7. 8. 8–17); none of them are to be found in the Tribute Lists; all were plainly enough held by the Persians in 401 BC and it is reasonable to suppose that that had been their condition throughout the fifth century. Did the Peace of Callias put them out of the reach of Persian power? In 422 BC Pharnaces gave Atramyttion to the Delians removed from Delos to live in (Thuc. 5. 1). Despite its position on the coast Atramyttion never appears on the Athenian Tribute Lists. It appears to have been a Lydian foundation[9] and perhaps remained largely non-Greek, under the control of the Oriental power, and that control was evidently sure enough for the satrap at Dascylium to be able to impose a rabble of Delians on the city. Again it is to be noted that Magnesia on the Maeander, not far from the sea, did not feature on the Athenian Tribute Lists and had in the sixth century been the headquarters of the satrap Oroetes (Hdt. 3. 122 and 125). One suspects that it continued in the fifth century to be dominated by Persia. Artaxerxes had 'given' it to Themistocles and in winter 412/411 the Spartan commander went there to have discussions with Tissaphernes (Thuc. 1. 138. 5 and 8. 50. 3). But if Magnesia did remain Persian controlled between 449 and 412, how was Persian power exercised? Nor is the question posed in just one or two special cases. As A. H. M. Jones remarked,[10] 'the quota and assessment lists of the Delian League show that the Greek cities hitherto mentioned [i.e. in his account of Greek colonies in Asia Minor] by no means occupied the entire coastline. Interspersed between them were scores of other communities, some Greek and some barbarian . . .'. The Greek communities may have been covered by the Peace of Callias, but what of the rest? In 334 BC Alexander let Priene be free, but there were also 'those who were not Prienians and who lived in villages' and Alexander required these people to pay the tribute to him (*GHI* 185). Their subjection to the King may not have been new, but have derived from the system established in the 540s. The area along the coast of Asia three days from the sea was by no means entirely the territory of Greek cities.[11] The Lelegian cities later synoecized into Halicarnassus are a case in point, as were the Pedaseis established on Milesian territory in 494 BC (Hdt. 6. 20).[12] To whose control were they subjected in the Peace? Were they quietly forgotten about and their tribute simply not collected?

It seems very unlikely that such places were left to do what they liked. For one thing, Persians like Asidates (Xen. *Anab.* 7. 8. 9) would surely have needed protection against Mysian brigands. Law and order could not have been kept if the satrap was without the means of enforcement, and when the Peace was made the King could have foreseen it. So how was the clause set out guaranteeing the Greek cities safety from Persian military action without making normal government of the non-Greek areas impossible?

Isocrates perhaps provides a clue. In each of the passages in which he alludes to the restrictions under the Peace on Royal military and naval freedom (7. 80, 12. 59), he speaks of *armies*, and it may be suggested that the clause in question placed a ban on the *assembling* of armies. Each satrap had his own guards (Xen. *Oec.* 4. 6). An army was assembled at the place where the assembly (σύλλογος) was called (ibid.). The normal place of assembly for Sparda and the Dascyleian satrapy was Thymbrara on the Plain of Castolus (Xen. *Cyrop.* 6. 2. 12, *Anab.* 1. 1. 2, 1. 9. 7, *Hell.* 1. 4. 3), as it probably was in 499 BC, when, with Sardis under attack, 'the Persians who have satrapies within the river Halys' assembled to go to the aid of the Lydians (Hdt. 5. 102. 1), but perhaps not always so. There were, as there had to be, for normal administration and for policing the King's territory within three days' march of the sea, detachments of troops. What was forbidden was the *assembling* of an army and its advance into 'no army's land'. But whatever is thought of this suggestion, it is not to be thought that in 449 BC the King undertook to leave the non-Greek parts of the coastal strip to crime and brigandage and complete *laissez-faire*.

Concerning the geographical limits of Persian naval activity there is a minor difficulty. Diodorus, in his formal statement of the terms (12. 4. 5), gave Phaselis as the southern limit.[13] Elsewhere (Dem. 19. 273, Plut.

Cim. 13. 4) the Chelidonian Isles are named. In late sources (Aristodemos and *Suda*) both are given. One can see why Phaselis might be named when one considers what a useful navigating mark Mount Olympus just behind it might have been for ships coming along the coast from Aspendus, clearly an important naval base, just as the Chelidonian Isles would have been for ships cutting across the Pamphylian Sea. What is odd is that Phaselis regularly paid tribute to Athens. Being to the east of the Chelidonians, it could be expected to be wholly controlled by Persia. The city depended on its trade with Greece and it was in her interest to continue to pay; but why did Persia allow the anomaly? The right explanation is probably that the city was part of Lycia[14] and that the Lycians were one of the 'peoples' in the area Within the Halys, but the Chelidonian Isles had to be used as a nautical limit.

The real difficulty in the naval clause is raised by the demand made of the Athenians in 412/411 by Alcibiades on behalf of Tissaphernes (Thuc. 8. 56. 4). 'He asked them to allow the King to build ships and sail along by his own territory as, and with as many ships as, he wishes.' It is hard to accept that the King accepted a restriction on his construction of ships. Recent events had made him aware that Egypt could only be kept subject if there was naval support for the army. Nor would Athens have any means of monitoring. In the King's Peace there would be, I believe, a ban on Athens rebuilding her navy,[15] but she could not have done so without prompt detection and Spartan reprisal. The two Peaces are therefore in this respect quite dissimilar, and a limitation on shipbuilding seems very unlikely. On the other hand, Alcibiades' demand seems to presuppose that there was a limitation despite the determination of commentators to deny it. Andrewes commented on ναῦς . . . ποιεῖσθαι καὶ παραπλεῖν τὴν ἑαυτοῦ γῆν 'the verbs must be taken closely together and understood as ναῦς ποιησάμενον παραπλεῖν . . . the King's right to build ships elsewhere is not in question'. But why say 'having made ships, sail along'? He could not have sailed along without ships, nor presumably did it mean that Royal dignity required *new* ships. Either Alcibiades was being surprisingly silly or there really was some restriction at which we can only guess. One had better leave it at that.[16]

NOTES

1. Cf. Cawkwell 1981*a*: 71.
2. Presumably Thrasybulus went to Aspendus in 391 BC because he regarded it as a Greek city (Xen. *Hell.* 4. 8. 30).
3. Cedreae in Caria of which the inhabitants were said to be μιξοβάρβαροι (Xen. *Hell.* 2. 1. 15) was perhaps not untypical. Cedreae regularly paid tribute to Athens, after as before the Peace.
4. If the deal proposed by Dercylidas and Tissaphernes (Xen. *Hell.* 3. 2. 20) had been made into a treaty, a similar formula covering 'the Spartans and their allies' (cf. Thuc. 8. 58) would have sufficed. Likewise the deals of Agesilaus (Xen. *Hell.* 3. 4. 5 and 25).
5. Cf. Badian 1993: 137–42.
6. Wade-Gery 1958: 215–16.
7. Leuze 1935: 28, Frye 1984: 113. The letter of Darius to Gadatas (ML 12) speaks of 'Across the Euphrates' as the area from which Gadatas had transferred plants to his own satrapy.
8. Isocrates may have meant that within the area designated as 'Within the river Halys' an army could not go down to the sea, i.e. had to keep away from the coast at least three days' march. It is unfortunate that the date of the Revolt of Pissouthnes (Ctes. F 15 §53) is uncertain, but if it is correct that it was Athens' alliance with his son Amorges that broke and terminated the Peace, it would seem that Darius sent an army from outside the area designated as 'Within the Halys' during the period of the Peace.
9. Cf. Strabo 13. 1. 65 613C. Cf. Jones 1937: 34.
10. Jones 1937: 28–9.
11. Jones 1937: 33.
12. For the Lelegians, S. Hornblower 1982: 9–13 and 89–90. For the Pedaseis, Hdt. 1. 175, Strabo 13. 1. 58–9 611C. Cf. Ruge, *PW* XIX. 1 26.
13. As do Isocrates (4. 118, 7. 80, 12. 59) and Lycurgus (*In Leocr.* 73). The various designations are collected in Wade-Gery 1958: 213.
14. *Suda* s.v. Κίμων says Phaselis was Pamphylian, but Strabo (14. 3. 9 666C) treats of it as part of Lycia (cf. 14. 4. 1 667C).
15. Cf. Cawkwell 1973: 51–5, an argument turning on the comparison of Xen. *Hell.* 5. 4. 34 and Diod. 15. 28–9. But see Stylianou's Commentary on Diod. 15. 29. 7.
16. Some have assumed that the restriction on a Royal fleet sailing along the coast of Asia Minor must have been due to the Peace of Callias, but of course Alcibiades could have been seeking an assurance that the Athenians would not attack a Royal fleet, fear not treaty up till then having kept the Persians away. But the demand for the Athenians to let the King build ships is challenging. What was stopping him? And why should Alcibiades

have so spoken? Cawkwell 1997: 121 rashly presumed that there is here an allusion to the Peace, but some will prefer to suppose that Thucydides had Alcibiades stating the obvious.

Appendix 8

The Alleged Treaty of Boiotios

W H E N the young Cyrus in spring 407 BC, accompanied by the Spartan embassy led by Boiotios, came down to assume his large command, the Spartans declared that 'they had got from the King everything they needed' (Xen. *Hell.* 1. 4. 2, 3). Lewis 1977: 124–5 proposed that Boiotios had made a new treaty of alliance between Sparta and Persia. Although no terms of this postulated treaty survive, Lewis claimed to have found an echo of it in Cyrus' reply to Lysander on the subject of naval pay. Lysander had asked for a full drachma per man per day and Cyrus said that he could not exceed the King's instructions, that 'the agreement (τὰς συνθήκας) . . . is to give thirty minas a month per ship [i.e. a rate of half a drachma per man per day] for as many ships as the Spartans choose to maintain' (Xen. *Hell.* 1. 5. 5). Since there is no such clause in the treaty of winter 412/411 BC (Thuc. 8. 58), it must, according to Lewis, have been in the postulated treaty of Boiotios. Andrewes in *CAH* v² (p. 489) and his commentary on Thuc. 8. 58. 5 accepts the theory.

In the first draft of summer 412 BC (Thuc. 8. 18) nothing was said about the King paying the wages of forces sent out by Sparta and the Peloponnesians. In the second, of the following winter, a clause was included which required the King to pay the cost of any *army* which the King called for (8. 37. 4), but there was no mention of naval matters. In the final version a clause appears requiring 'Tissaphernes to provide pay for the ships currently present (νῦν παρούσαις) in accordance with the terms that have been agreed (κατὰ τὰ ξυγκείμενα) until the King's ships come' (8. 58. 5). When and what was this agreement? Earlier that winter Tissaphernes 'had paid a month's pay, just as he undertook in Sparta, at the rate of an Attic drachma per man for all the ships, but he was willing from then on to pay at the rate of half a drachma while he sought the King's approval; he said that if the King gave the order he would pay at the rate of a full drachma' (8. 29. 1). Andrewes (1981 ad loc.) supposed that between that time and the final treaty the King had made a ruling, to which τὰ ξυγκείμενα refers.

A ruling by the King was hardly to be termed 'an agreement', and, unless one postulates diplomatic negotiations of which Thucydides makes no mention whatsoever, one can only suppose that 'the terms that had been agreed' were those which had been promised in the name of Tissaphernes by his envoy to Sparta at the time of the first appeal (8. 5. 5) and presumably accepted by Sparta, terms indeed that Tissaphernes cited to justify his conduct over pay (ὥσπερ ὑπέστη ἐν τῇ Λακεδαίμονι, 8. 29. 1). The συνθῆκαι to which Cyrus referred in his answer to Lysander in 407 (Xen. *Hell.* 1. 5. 5) were, it is here proposed, none other than the original agreement made in Sparta in the name of Tissaphernes.

When both Pharnabazus and Tissaphernes separately sent envoys to Sparta in winter 413/412 BC to try to get the Spartans to ally with the King (Thuc. 8. 5. 5, and 8. 6), they were no doubt acting with the King's consent. It must have been realized at Susa that, if a fleet was to be quickly equipped and manned, money would be required and that the King would in all likelihood have to pay. So it is probable enough that the satraps knew the rate of pay which the King would pay. If the satraps undertook to pay more, they would have to pay it themselves. Hence the figure of a half drachma on which Tissaphernes had to insist, until the King could be persuaded otherwise (Thuc. 8. 29. 1). Tissaphernes' envoy had, on the satrap's behalf, undertaken to pay at the rate of a full drachma for every ship Sparta sent out, but when it became a burdensome obligation he reverted to the Royal rate, which continued to apply in Cyrus' time (Xen. *Hell.* 1. 5. 5), though Cyrus, like Tissaphernes, chose in the first month to subsidize it out of his own pocket. Because all this had been arranged at Sparta before any Peloponnesian ships set out for eastern waters, the draft treaties left the topic out of consideration, save that in the final version Tissaphernes was to pay κατὰ τὰ ξυγκείμενα, i.e. the terms agreed in Sparta.

The Spartans had felt very discontented with the way Tissaphernes was behaving, principally over pay (cf. Thuc. 8. 78 and 85. 3). Hence the embassy of Boiotios, which returned professing themselves completely satisfied, the King having removed the satrap who had been accused of causing so much trouble. No new treaty of alliance was needed, and none made.

Appendix 9

366 BC

CHAPTER 76 of Diodorus book 15 gives under the year 366/365 a series of notices which apparently come from his chronographic source. First come the Athenian archon and the Roman military tribunes, at that period taking the place of the consuls. Then comes the seizure of Oropus, followed by the synoecism of Cos. At the end there is a note about various literary figures of the period. All this is typical of Diodoran citations of his chronographic source. Embedded between Cos and the literary note is the following:

At the same time as these events the King of the Persians persuaded the Hellenes to end the wars and arrange with each other a Common Peace. And so the so-called Spartan–Boeotian War was ended which had gone on for more than five years, starting with the Leuctra campaign.

The notice in general is typically chronographic, and the last sentence settles the question. The whole chapter is composed of chronographic citations.[1]

The note speaks merely of 'common peace', unlike the account of the Peace made in 362 directly after the battle of Mantinea where Diodorus speaks of 'peace and alliance' (15. 89. 1). Since this latter notice seems not to derive from the chronographic source, no direct comparison of phrase would be apt, but, at least, the absence of 'alliance' in the earlier notice is consistent with Xenophon's account of the Peace made between Thebes and Corinth, Phlius and other unnamed states (*Hell.* 7. 4. 10). When the Corinthians arrived in Thebes for *the* peace, the Thebans 'were requiring them to swear to alliance as well', but the Corinthians replied that 'alliance would not be peace but a change of war' but that 'they were there, if the Thebans so willed, to make the just peace'. Thus far, at any rate, concord between Xenophon and Diodorus.

In the ninth chapter it has been argued that after the Congress at Susa where Pelopidas persuaded the King to put a stop to Athenian naval ambitions, presumably in particular Athens' efforts to regain control of Amphipolis, there was further diplomatic exchange between Athens and the King and he was induced to retract this Royal demand. The King 'sent down' a Rescript declaring, in Demosthenes' phrase (19. 137), that Amphipolis was again to belong to Athens when on the earlier occasion he had declared that city to be his friend and ally. This process of getting the King to change his ruling would have taken time and may well have extended into 366. In any case the Thebans summoned to Thebes representatives from *all the cities* to hear the Royal Rescript (*Hell.* 7. 1. 39), and the Congress could not have been quickly assembled. Furthermore, the Rescript which the Persian envoy read out was surely the amended Rescript which Athens had sought. Since all the cities were summoned and Athens had a special interest which would have made her representation compellingly desirable, and yet the Athenians appear to have made no public protest, it must have been a Rescript which did not discontent them, that is, the second Rescript. So, allowing for the diplomatic exchanges and for the assembling of the Congress and not forgetting that the seas were not reliably navigable until April,[2] one must suppose that the Congress was no earlier than the spring of 366.

This means that the Congress of Thebes may have preceded the making of the peace by no great interval, though precise dating is not possible. Diodorus' chronographic source may have confused or misunderstood his information, as presumably many suppose, but at least his statement about the peace ending the Spartan–Boeotian War which has lasted 'more than five years' (15. 76. 3) may be accepted. He said it began with the Leuctra campaign, and the date of the battle was the fifth of Hecatombaeon, 371/370 (Plut. *Ages.* 28. 7). Whether one counts by Attic archon years, or by twelve-month periods, 'more than five years' takes one into 366/365. But how far? Xenophon records the third Syracusan expedition in support of Sparta as happening 'at pretty much this time' (*Hell.* 7. 4. 12), and this suggests that the peace was made before the end of the sailing season.

'Involved and uncertain'[3] the chronology of the 360s certainly is and no more is claimed here than that the Congress of Thebes and the making of peace were not necessarily separated by a large lapse of time. Xenophon chose for whatever reason to insert the affairs of Phlius and Sicyon between them and to round off his account of the Congress with the sentence: 'And this attempt of Pelopidas and the Thebans to gain the dominating power was in this way put an end to'

(7. 1. 40). Inevitably one thinks of the similar sentence that rounded off his account of the peace Congress at Sardis in 392: 'in this way this peace came to nothing and each envoy went home' (4. 8. 15). This is a monstrously misleading sentence, as Andocides' speech *On the Peace* makes abundantly clear. Is Xenophon's concluding remark concerning the Congress of Thebes similarly to be regarded?

In his *Third Philippic* of 341 Demosthenes (§16) spoke of 'Chersonese, which the King and all the Hellenes decided (ἐγνώκασιν) belongs to you Athenians.' When was this decision made? Elsewhere (19. 253) he spoke of 'Amphipolis which the King and all the Hellenes decided (ἔγνωσαν) belongs to you.' We are less in the dark about Amphipolis. Opinion is divided as to when exactly all the Greeks first decided that Athens' claim to the city was just, but it was certainly before 368 when Iphicrates began his efforts for over three years to recover the city.[4] As Accame pointed out,[5] when Hegesippus said (Dem. 7. 29) that 'the Hellenes and the King of the Persians decreed and agreed' that the place belonged to the Athenians, it may be that the decree and the agreement were not made on one and the same occasion; the Hellenes may well have passed the decree when the King was not represented and the Royal assent may have been granted considerably later. So it is possible that the decree about Amphipolis was one of the sort of decrees which the participants in the Peace after Leuctra swore to observe (Xen. *Hell.* 6. 5. 2). Whatever the truth of that, it seems that the King, to Pelopidas' satisfaction, pronounced in his Rescript of 367 against the Athenian claim to Amphipolis and that in answer to Athenian protest and threat he changed his mind and sent down a Rescript acknowledging the Athenian claim. This new Rescript must have been the one which the Persian brought and read out at Thebes (ibid. 7. 1. 39). Xenophon, as is now only to be expected, said nothing of the content of the Rescript or the full proceedings at Thebes but the Greeks at that meeting may well have taken their decision about Chersonese as well as their crucial decision about the independence of Messene. Nor is any other occasion easily to be imagined.[6] If the decision does belong to 366, it is no surprise to find Timotheus, who replaced Iphicrates in 365, on the successful conclusion of the siege of Samos turning his attention to the Chersonese and using his fleet and army for this purpose, though of course as soon as the Hellenic decision had been made the Chersonese could well have been added to Iphicrates' cares. Timotheus was made general ἐπ' Ἀμφίπολιν καὶ Χερρόνησον (Dem. 23. 149) but Iphicrates in the later period of his command may have been the same, having initially been merely στρατηγὸς ἐπ᾽ Ἀμφίπολιν (Aesch. 2. 27).

Now for the *Archidamus* of Isocrates. The dramatic scene and date of the speech is a meeting of the Spartan assembly at a time when certain Peloponnesian states had indicated that they could not continue the war against Thebes whether Sparta went along with them or not (cf. §91) and so have asked Sparta to release them from their obligation as members of the Peloponnesian league to have the same friends and enemies as Sparta. Sparta is urged by the son of the aged Agesilaus to fight on and never to assent to the loss of Messene. It matches the situation described by Xenophon in *Hell.* 7. 4. 6–11. There the Corinthians sent envoys to Thebes to ask whether they would get peace if they came. When the Thebans replied in the affirmative, the Corinthians asked to be allowed to go to their allies seeing that they intended to join with those who wished in making the peace and to let those who preferred to continue war do so. The Thebans consented and the Corinthians went to Sparta and asked to be allowed to make peace. The Spartans assented, saying that they themselves would not accept the loss of Messene. The Corinthians then went to Thebes to the peace. It is clear that both Xenophon and Isocrates are dealing with the closing moments of the Peloponnesian League.

In Xenophon's account, the Corinthians seem to know what peace would entail. Of course a clause recognizing the independence of Messene was, in view of the dealings of Pelopidas with the King the previous year, only to be expected, but it is noteworthy that Xenophon thrice speaks of the Corinthians making *the* peace.[7] In Isocrates (§27) Archidamus is represented speaking as follows: τῷ μὲν βαρβάρῳ τὴν Ἀσίαν ὡς πατρῴαν οὖσαν ἀποδιδόασιν . . . ἡμᾶς δὲ Μεσσήνην ἀποστεροῦσιν. The present tenses strongly suggest that he is referring to clauses of the proposed peace. The Corinthians were not proposing to make just a peace. They were proposing to enter *the* peace, the terms of which they knew full well. But why should a clause about the King's right to Asia touch the Corinthians, or for that matter the Phliasians, whom Xenophon mentions, or the Epidaurians, whom Isocrates (§91) mentions but Xenophon does not, or the Argives whose participation Xenophon happens to mention later by way of showing up their perfidy (7. 4. 11)? Such a clause was the standard demand of the King from 412 onwards, but what was it doing in a peace between Thebes and sundry Peloponnesian states? The answer which is to my mind probable is that the peace the Corinthians were offered is the Peace on offer at the Congress of Thebes, the peace envisaged in the Royal Rescript but to which the Corinthians originally refused to swear, a King's Peace of which Diodorus' chronographic source spoke.

Xenophon, living in Corinth, described the events of 366 from a Corinthian point of view, but even that was done sparingly. He declared that the Corinthians refused to swear oaths to the Theban envoys saying that they in no way needed 'oaths sworn in common to the King' (πρὸς βασιλέα κοινῶν ὅρκων 7. 1. 40). He did not explain the Corinthian refusal. When at Susa the King had asked Pelopidas what he wanted the Rescript to contain, Pelopidas had proposed, in addition to the independence of Messene and the cessation of Athenian naval activity, a sanctions clause to the effect that, if the Spartans and the Athenians did not comply, there should be a military campaign against them and any city that refused to join the campaign would be proceeded against first (7. 1. 36). The King had agreed and put such a clause in the Rescript. Presumably it was included in the Rescript delivered at Thebes. Such a sanctions clause was particularly hard on members of the Peloponnesian League. To go against Sparta would have been both a contravention of their oaths to Sparta and inviting the vengeance of the gods. So it is readily understandable why the Corinthians declined to swear. Some adjustment on the part of the hegemonic power was necessary, and release from obligations for Sparta's allies would have to be sought. The spur to seeking that release was provided by the Athenian Arcadian alliance (7. 4. 2) and the appeal to Sparta of the remaining members of the Peloponnesian League ensued (7. 4. 7–9).

To the Congress of Thebes the Thebans, according to Xenophon (7. 1. 39), summoned envoys 'from all the cities'. The envoys declared that they had come to hear the Rescript, not to swear oaths; if the Thebans wanted oaths, they bade them send envoys to the cities. Xenophon then records only the Corinthian refusal, but, he adds, 'other cities' reacted likewise (§40). How many cities, let alone which, he does not say. He omits to say how or why the Argives swore to the same terms (7. 4. 11). There was more to it than he lets on.

Xenophon is not, one supposes, dishonest. He may forget and he may misremember, but he does not tell outright lies. However, it is not to be doubted that he was 'economical with the truth'. It never ceases to amaze that he can recount the history of the 370s and the 360s without mentioning the name of Pelopidas more than once and then as ambassador (7. 1. 33), not as soldier leading the Sacred Band. More relevantly here and more amazingly, he says not a word about the

Congress in Sparta that followed the Congress in Sardis in 392. So one is emboldened to dissent from the general opinion that Diodorus' 'very vague report cannot stand against the detail given by Xenophon'.[8] He is here, it is maintained, misleadingly incomplete. The peace of the Rescript read out at Thebes was after delay generally accepted albeit shorn of its sanctions clause. As Diodorus said, it was peace *tout simple*, unlike the peace and alliance sworn to after the battle of Mantinea.

But, it must be asked, why did the Thebans give in to the demand that the sanctions clause which Pelopidas had called for at Susa be dropped from the peace that was finally sworn? It is the contention of this book that in the course of 366 satrapal discontent passed from a smouldering state to the blazing Satraps' Revolt, during which Greece was free of Persian influence.[9] Thebes could and had to go on alone.

NOTES

(In this appendix I have the temerity to persist with the view I espoused in 1961 practically *contra mundum*—cf. Stylianou 1998: 485–9, who defends my view and lists its main critics.)

1. For Diodorus' Chronographic Source, see Stylianou 1998: 25–49, esp. 31 and 43–5. For the scope of such literature, *FGH* 244 T2 and for a (restricted) sample, *FGH* 255.
2. Cf. Casson 1971: 270–2.
3. The phrase of Stylianou 1998: 446.
4. Iphicrates began on his period as 'general against Amphipolis' in 368, shortly after the death of Alexander II of Macedon (Aesch. 2. 27–9), and was replaced 'over three years' later (Dem. 23. 149) by Timotheus who was made 'general against Amphipolis and the Chersonese' at the conclusion of his siege of Samos (Isoc. 15. 112) in late 365.
5. Accame 1941: 155.
6. Accame 1941: 155 and 165 presumed that the decree concerning the Chersonese was passed at the same time as that concerning Amphipolis, but unless the manner in which orators alluded to the matter misleads us (as is admittedly perfectly possible) the only occasion for the King, by means of a Rescript, and for all the Hellenes to take a decision would have been at a Common Peace. So, to make clear my position, I propose that the decree of the Hellenes about Amphipolis was passed either at the peace of 371/370 or, as Accame 165–6 opined, at the conference of spring 369, but this decree did not receive Royal assent until the Congress of Thebes in

366, and that the decision of the Hellenes concerning the Chersonese was
taken in 366 at the same time as Royal assent was given to both Athenian
claims. It is notable that the only evidence about Iphicrates' operations in
the 360s shows no concern with the Chersonese, which only came on the
agenda when Timotheus took charge of operations in the north Aegean.
Buckler 1980: 252–3 disputed the view advanced in Cawkwell 1961: 82
that Athens would not have been slow to act against Amphipolis and the
Chersonese once each claim had been recognized by the Hellenes. Operations in the north began in 368, seemingly at that date concerned only with
Amphipolis. Iphicrates had only a small naval force, 'more to keep an eye
on things than to besiege the city' (Aesch. 2. 28)—not surprisingly, for such
a siege which had been considered too much for Athens in the heyday of
her naval power would have required a large force. Iphicrates probably
took the view of the Emperor Tiberius, *plura consilio quam vi*. Timotheus
in 365 took his army and navy first against the Chersonese and promptly
captured Sestos and Crithote (Isoc. 15. 112). Each general acted without
delay when the decision of the Hellenes allowed him.

7. Of the Royal peace before Leuctra, Xenophon says (*Hell.* 6. 3. 18) 'the
   Spartans voted δέχεσθαι τὴν εἰρήνην'.

8. Quoting Salmon 1984: 380. Similarly, Ryder 1965: 137.

9. It would greatly help if one could determine whether Timotheus was sent
   out to Asia after the peace was sworn. He was sent out to help Ariobarzanes,
   but the decree contained the proviso 'provided he does not break up the
   peace with the King' (Dem. 15. 9). When he got to Asia, he found, Demosthenes continued, that Ariobarzanes was openly in revolt from the King
   and so he turned aside to besiege and capture Samos. The siege lasted for
   ten months (Isoc. 15. 111), and since Diodorus (18. 18. 7) declared that the
   Samians he caused to be exiled returned at the end of the Lamian War after
   forty-three years, Samos must have fallen in 365/364. This is hardly precise, but two minor bits of evidence suggest that the siege had begun by the
   autumn (Polyaenus 3. 10. 9, [Aristotle] *Econ.* 1350[b]54–7). So he must have
   begun the siege in, say, September and have gone out on his voyage after
   the Etesian winds of 366 had ceased. (Cf. Beloch 1923: 246.) The proviso of
   the decree that sent him out could have been added either before or after
   the Congress of Thebes or could have been merely a general reference
   to the King's Peace as an enduring presence just as it is referred to in the
   peace made after Leuctra in which the King did not take part (Xen. *Hell.* 6.
   5. 1–3). It may be added that Demosthenes' remark (15. 9) that 'Samos was
   kept under guard by Cyprothemis, whom Tigranes the King's hyparch
   had set up' is of uncertain value. The Greek name suggests that the guard
   was a band of mercenaries; 'hyparch' appears to be Demosthenes' word
   for 'satrap', a term which he never uses (cf. 23. 142), but no satrap called
   Tigranes is known in this area at this period and he must have been some

holder of subordinate office, in a world where it might have been said: *de minimis non curat rex*. All in all, the relation of Timotheus' dispatch and the swearing of the peace at Thebes cannot be determined.

LIST OF WORKS REFERRED TO
IN THE NOTES

ACCAME, S. (1941), *La lega ateniese del secolo IV a.c.* (Rome).

—— (1951), *Ricerche intorno alla guerra corinzia* (Naples).

AKURGAL, E. (1983), *Alt-Smyrna* (Ankara).

ANDERSON, J. K. (1970), *Military Theory and Practice in the Age of Xenophon* (Berkeley).

ANDREWES, A. (1981), *A Historical Commentary on Thucydides*, vol. v (Oxford).

ANSON, E. M. (1989), 'The Persian fleet in 334', *Classical Philology*, 84: 44–9.

ARMAYOR, O. K. (1978a), 'Did Herodotus ever go to the Black Sea?', *Harvard Studies in Classical Philology*, 82: 45–62.

—— (1978b), 'Herodotus' Catalogues of the Persian Empire in the light of the monuments and the Greek literary tradition', *Transactions of the American Philological Association*, 108: 1–9.

ASHERI, D. (1990), *Erodoto: Le storie: Libro III* (Milan).

—— (1997), *Erodoto: Le storie: Libro I*, 4th edn. (Milan).

ASHTON, N. G. (1977), 'The naumachia near Amorgos in 322 BC', *British School at Athens*, 72: 1–11.

AUSTIN, M. M. (1990), 'Greek tyrants and the Persians, 546–479 BC', *CQ* ns 40: 289–306.

BADIAN, E. (1993), *From Plataea to Potidaea: Studies in the History and Historiography of the Pentecontaetia* (Baltimore).

BALCER, J. M. (1972), 'The date of Herodotus IV.1, Darius' Scythian expedition', *Harvard Studies in Classical Philology*, 76: 99–132.

—— (1983), 'The Greeks and the Persians. The process of acculturation', *Historia*, 32: 257–67.

—— (1984), *Sparda by the Bitter Sea: Imperial Interaction in Western Anatolia* (Chico, Calif.).

BAR-KOCHVA, B. (1976), *The Seleucid Army: Organisation and Tactics in the Great Campaigns* (Cambridge).

BARNS, J. W. B. (1953), 'Cimon and the first Athenian expedition to Cyprus', *Historia*, 2: 163–76.

BASCH, L. (1969), 'Phoenician oared ships', *Mariners' Mirror*, 55: 139–62, 227–45.

—— (1980), 'M. le Professeur Lloyd et les trières: Quelques remarques', *JHS* 100: 198–9.

BELOCH, K. J. (1916), *Griechische Geschichte*, 2nd edn., vol. ii 2 (Berlin and Leipzig).

——(1922), *Griechische Geschichte*, 2nd edn., vol. iii 1 (Berlin and Leipzig).

——(1923), *Griechische Geschichte*, 2nd edn., vol. iii 2 (Berlin and Leipzig).

——(1927), *Griechische Geschichte*, 2nd edn., vol. ii 1. (Berlin and Leipzig).

BERVE, H. (1926), *Das Alexanderreich auf prosopographische Grundlage*, vol. ii: *Prosopographie* (Munich).

——(1967), *Die Tyrannis bei den Griechen* (Munich).

BICKERMAN, E. J. (1963), 'A propos d'un passage de Charon de Mytilène', *Parola del Passato*, 18: 241–55.

BIGWOOD, J. M. (1978), 'Ctesias' description of Babylon', *American Journal of Ancient History*, 3: 32–52.

BOFFO, L. (1983), *La conquista persiana delle città greche d'Asia Minore* (Memorie della Classe di Scienze Morali e Storiche dell'Accademia dei Lincei, 26/1; Rome).

BORZA, E. N. (1990), *In the Shadow of Olympus* (Princeton).

BOSWORTH, A. B. (1980), *A Historical Commentary on Arrian's History of Alexander*, vol. i (Books 1–3) (Oxford).

——(1988), *Conquest and Empire: The Reign of Alexander the Great*. Cambridge.

——(1990), 'Plutarch, Callisthenes, and the Peace of Callias', *JHS* 110: 1–13.

——(1995), *A Historical Commentary on Arrian's History of Alexander*, vol. ii (Books 4–5) (Oxford).

BOYCE, M. (1982), *A History of Zoroastrianism*, vol. ii (Leiden).

BREITENBACH, H. R. (1967), 'Xenophon', *RE* IX A 2, cols. 1569–1928.

BRIANT, P. (1985), 'Dons de terres et de villes: l'Asie Mineure dans le contexte achéménide', *Revue des Études Anciennes*, 87: 53–71

——(1988), 'Ethno-classe dominante et populations soumises dans l'empire achéménide: Le Cas d'Egypte', in A. Kuhrt and H. Sancisi-Weerdenburg (eds.), *Achaemenid History*, vol. iii (Leiden), 137–73.

——(1996), *Histoire de l'empire perse* (Paris: Fayard).

BRUNT, P. A. (1976), *Arrian: History of Alexander and Indica, I: Anabasis Alexandri Books I–IV* (London and Cambridge, Mass.: Loeb Classical Library).

BUCKLER, J. (1980), *The Theban Hegemony, 371–362 BC* (Cambridge, Mass).

BURN, A. R. (1984), *Persia and the Greeks: The Defence of the West, c. 546–478 BC*, 2nd edn. (London: Duckworth).

BURY, J. B. (1897), 'The European expedition of Darius', *Classical Review*, 11: 277–82.

BUSOLT, G. (1895), *Griechische Geschichte*, 2nd edn., vol. ii. (Gotha).

—— and SWOBODA, H. (1926), *Griechische Staatskunde*, vol. ii (Munich).

CADOUX, T. J. (1948), 'The Athenian archons from Kreon to Hypsichides', *JHS* 68: 70–123.

CALDER, W. M. (1925), 'The Royal Road in Herodotus', *Classical Review*, 39: 7–11.

CAMERON, G. G. (1943), 'Darius, Egypt, and the "lands beyond the sea" ', *Journal of Near Eastern Studies*, 2: 307–13.

CAMERON, G. G. (1973), 'The Persian satrapies and related matters', *Journal of Near Eastern Studies*, 22: 47–56.

CARGILL, J. (1977), 'The Nabonidus chronicle and the fall of Lydia: Consensus with feet of clay', *American Journal of Ancient History*, 2: 97–116.

CARTLEDGE, P. A. (1987), *Agesilaus* (London: Duckworth).

CASSON, L. (1971), *Ships and Seamanship in the Ancient World* (Princeton).

CASTRITIUS, H. (1972), 'Die Okkupation Thrakiens durch die Perser und der Sturz des athenischen Tyrannen Hippias', *Chiron*, 2: 1–15.

CAWKWELL, G. L. (1961), 'The Common Peace of 366–365 B.C.' *CQ*, NS 11: 80–6.

——(1963a), 'Notes on the Peace of 375/4', *Historia*, 12: 84–95.

——(1963b), 'Demosthenes' policy after the Peace of Philocrates', *CQ*, NS 13: 120–38, 200–13.

——(1970), 'The fall of Themistocles', in B. F. Harris (ed.), *Auckland Classical Essays Presented to E. M. Blaiklock* (Auckland, New Zealand: Auckland University Press), 39–58.

——(1972), 'Introduction' to *Xenophon: The Persian Expedition*, trans. by Rex Warner (Harmondsworth, England: Penguin Books), 9–48.

——(1973), 'The foundation of the Second Athenian Confederacy', *CQ*, NS 23: 47–60.

——(1976a), 'Agesilaus and Sparta', *CQ*, NS 26: 62–84.

——(1976b), 'The imperialism of Thrasybulus'. *CQ*, NS 26: 270–7.

——(1978), *Philip of Macedon* (London).

——(1979), 'Introduction' to *Xenophon: A History of my Times*, trans. by Rex Warner (Harmondsworth, England: Penguin Books), 7–46.

——(1981a), 'The King's Peace'. *CQ*, NS 31: 69–83.

——(1981b), 'Notes on the failure of the Second Athenian Confederacy', *JHS* 101: 40–55.

——(1997), 'The peace between Athens and Persia', *Phoenix*, 51: 115–30.

——(2004), 'When, how, and why did Xenophon write the *Anabasis*?', in R. Lane Fox (ed.), *The Long March: Xenophon and the Ten Thousand* (Yale University Press), 47–67.

CHAUMONT, M. L. (1990), 'Un nouveau gouverneur de Sardes', *Syria*, 67: 579–608.

CLARK, M. (1993), 'The Date of *IG* II² 1604', *British School at Athens*, 85: 47–67.

——(1993), 'The Economy of the Athenian Navy in the Fourth Century BC', Oxford D.Phil. thesis.

COOK, J. M. (1961), 'The problem of classical Ionia', *Proceedings of the Cambridge Philological Society*, NS 7: 9–18.

——(1983), *The Persian Empire* (London: Dent).

—— and NICHOLLS, R. V. (1998), *Old Smyrna Excavations: The Temples of Athena* (Supplementary Volume 30; London: British School at Athens).

CUMONT, F. (1933), 'L'iniziazione di Nerone da parte di Tiridate d'Armenia', *Rivista di filologia e d'istruzione classica*, NS 11: 145–54.

DANDAMAEV, M. A. (1989), *A Political History of the Achaemenid Empire* (Leiden).

—— and LUKONIN, V. G. (1989), *The Culture and the Social Institutions of Ancient Iran* (Cambridge).

DANOV, C. M. (1976), *Alt-Thrakien* (Berlin).

DAVIES, J. K. (1971), *Athenian Propertied Families 600–300 BC* (Oxford).

DEBORD, P. (1999), *L'Asie mineure au IVe siècle (412–323 a.C.)* (Talence: Ausonius).

DELBRÜCK, H. (1975), *History of the Art of War*, vol. i: *Antiquity*, (translation by W. J. Renfroe, Jr, of *Geschichte der Kriegskunst im Rahmen der politischen Geschichte*, 3rd edn., 1920) (Lincoln, Nebr.).

DELEBECQUE, E. (1957), *Essai sur la vie de Xénophon* (Paris: Klincksieck).

DE SANCTIS, G. (1932), 'Aristagora di Mileto', in *Problemi di storia antica* (Bari), 63–91.

——(1951), *Studi di storia della storiografia greca* (Florence).

DE STE CROIX, G. E. M. (1972), *The Origins of the Peloponnesian War* (London: Duckworth).

DEUBNER, L. (1956), *Attische Feste* (Berlin).

DREWS, R. (1973), *The Greek Accounts of Eastern History* (Cambridge, Mass.).

DÜRING, J. (1957), *Aristotle in the Ancient Biographical Tradition* (Göteborg).

DÜRRBACH, F. (1893), 'L'Apologie de Xénophon dans l'*Anabase*', *Revue des Études Grecques*, 6: 346–86.

EDDY, S. K. (1973), 'The cold war between Athens and Persia c. 448–412 BC', *Classical Philology*, 68: 241–58.

EHTÉCHAM, M. (1946), *L'Iran sous les Achéménides* (Fribourg).

ENGELS, D. W. (1978), *Alexander the Great and the Logistics of the Macedonian Army* (Berkeley).

ERRINGTON, R. M. (1981), 'Review discussion: Philip II', *American Journal of Ancient History*, 6: 69–88.

EVANS, J. A. S. (1969), 'Notes on Thermopylae and Artemisium', *Historia*, 18: 389–406.

FEHLING, D. (1989), *Herodotus and his 'Sources': Citation, Invention, and Narrative Art*, (Leeds: Cairns).

FLOWER, H. I. (1991), 'Herodotus and Delphic traditions about Croesus', in M. A. Flower and M. Toher (eds.), *Georgica: Greek Studies in Honour of George Cawkwell* (London: Bulletin of the Institute of Classical Studies, Supplement 58), 57–77.

FLOWER, M. A. (1994), *Theopompus of Chios* (Oxford).

—— and MARINCOLA, J. (2002), *Herodotus: Histories Book IX* (Cambridge).

FORNARA, C. W. (1971), *Herodotus: An Interpretative Essay* (Oxford).

—— and SAMONS, L. J., II (1991), *Athens from Cleisthenes to Pericles* (Berkeley).

FREDERICKSMEYER, E. A. (1982), 'On the final aims of Philip II', in W. L. Adams and E. N. Borza (eds.), *Philip II, Alexander the Great, and the Macedonian Heritage* (Washington: University Press of America), 85–98.

FROST, F. J. (1980), *Plutarch's Themistocles: A Historical Commentary* (Princeton).

FRYE, R. N. (1984), *The History of Ancient Iran* (Munich).

GABRIELSEN, V. (1994), *Financing the Athenian Fleet: Public Taxation and Social Relations* (Baltimore).

GARNSEY, P. (1988), *Famine and Food Supply in the Graeco-Roman World* (Cambridge).

GERA, D. L. (1993), *Xenophon's Cyropaedia* (Oxford).

GJERSTAD, E. (1979), 'The Phoenician colonisation and expansion in Cyprus', *Report of the Department of Antiquities, Cyprus*, 230–54.

GOMME, A. W. (1945), *A Historical Commentary on Thucydides*, vol. i (Oxford).

GRAF, D. F. (1985), 'Greek tyrants and Achaemenid politics', in J. W. Eadie and J. Ober (eds.), *The Craft of the Ancient Historian: Essays in Honor of Chester G. Starr* (Lanham, Md.: University Press of America), 79–123.

GREEN, P. (1970), *The Year of Salamis 480–479 BC* (London: Weidenfeld & Nicholson).

HALLOCK, R. T. (1969), *Persepolis Fortification Tablets* (Chicago).

HAMMOND, N. G. L. (1959), *A History of Greece to 322 BC* (Oxford).

—— (1973), *Studies in Greek History* (Oxford).

—— (1980), 'The extent of Persian occupation in Thrace', *Chiron*, 10: 53–61.

—— and GRIFFITH, G. T. (1979), *A History of Macedonia*, vol.ii (Oxford).

HANFMANN, G. M. A. (1983), *Sardis from Prehistoric to Roman Times* (Cambridge, Mass.).

HARMATTA, J. (1953), 'A recently discovered Old Persian inscription', *Acta Antiqua Hungarica*, 2: 1–14.

—— (1976), 'Darius' expedition against the Sāka Tigraxaudā'. *Acta Antiqua Hungarica*, 25: 15–24.

HARRIS, E. M. (1989), 'More Chalcenteric negligence', *Classical Philology*, 84: 36–44.

HARRISON, E. B. (1972), 'The south frieze of the Nike temple and the Marathon painting in the Painted Stoa', *American Journal of Archaeology*, 76: 353–78.

HAUBEN, H. (1970), 'The King of the Sidonians and the Persian imperial fleet', *Ancient Society*, 1: 1–8.

HEINLEIN, S. (1909), 'Histiaios von Milet', *Klio*, 9: 341–51.

HERZFELD, E. (1968), *The Persian Empire: Studies in Geography and Ethnography of the Ancient Near East* (Wiesbaden).

HIGNETT, C. (1963), *Xerxes' Invasion of Greece* (Oxford).

HIRSCH, S. W. (1985), *The Friendship of the Barbarians* (Hanover, NH).

HORNBLOWER, J. (1981), *Hieronymus of Cardia* (Oxford).

HORNBLOWER, S. (1982), *Mausolus* (Oxford).

—— (1987), *Thucydides* (London: Duckworth).

—— (1991), *A Commentary on Thucydides*, vol. i. (Oxford).

—— (1996), *A Commentary on Thucydides*, vol. ii. (Oxford).

—— (2002), *The Greek World 479–323 BC*, 3rd edn. (London: Routledge).

HUXLEY, G. L. (1966), *The Early Ionians* (London: Faber).

JACOBY, F. (1922), 'Ktesias', *PW* xi. 2, 2032–73.

JONES, A. H. M. (1937), *The Cities of the Eastern Roman Provinces* (Oxford).

JUNGE, P. J. (1940), 'Hazarapatis', *Klio*, 33: 13–38.

KENT, R. G. (1953), *Old Persian: Grammar, Texts, Lexicon*, 2nd edn. (New Haven: American Oriental Society).

KIENITZ, F. K. (1953), *Die politische Geschichte Ägyptens vom 7. bis zum 4. Jahrhundert vor der Zeitwende* (Berlin).

KLEINER, G. (1968), *Die Ruinen von Milet* (Berlin).

KRAAY, C. M. (1976), *Archaic and Classical Greek Coins* (London: Methuen).

KUHRT, A. (1988), 'Earth and Water', in A. Kuhrt and H. Sancisi-Weerdenburg (eds.), *Achaemenid History*, vol. iii (Leiden), 87–99.

—— (1997), review of R. Rollinger, *Herodots babylonischer Logos*, *Classical Review*, 47: 108–9.

LANDELS, J. G. (1980), *Engineering in the Ancient World* (London: Chatto & Windus).

LATEINER, D. (1976), 'Tissaphernes and the Phoenician fleet', *Transactions of the American Philological Association*, 106: 267–90.

LAUNEY, M. (1987), *Recherches sur les armées hellénistiques*, 2 vols. (Paris: De Boccard).

LAWRENCE, A. W. (1979), *Greek Aims in Fortification* (Oxford).

LAZENBY, J. F. (1993), *The Defence of Greece* (Warminster).

LEDGER, G. R. (1989), *Re-counting Plato* (Oxford).

LENDLE, O. (1995), *Kommentar zu Xenophons Anabasis: Bücher 1–7* (Darmstadt).

LEUZE, O. (1935), *Die Satrapieeinteilung in Syrien und Zweistromland von 530–320* (Halle).

LÉVY, E. (1983), 'Les trois traités entre Sparte et le Roi', *Bulletin de Correspondance Hellénique*, 107: 221–41.

LEWIS, D. M. (1958), 'The Phoenician fleet in 411', *Historia*, 7: 392–7.

—— (1977), *Sparta and Persia* (Leiden).

—— (1985), 'Persians in Herodotus', in M. H. Jameson (ed.), *The Greek Historians: Literature and History: Papers Presented to A. E. Raubitschek* (Saratoga, Calif.), 101–17.

LLOYD, A. B. (1972), 'Triremes and the Saïte navy', *Journal of Egyptian Archaeology*, 58: 268–79.

—— (1975a), *Herodotus Book II: Introduction* (Leiden).

—— (1975b), 'Were Necho's triremes Phoenician?'. *JHS*, 95: 45–61.

—— (1976), *Herodotus Book II: Commentary 1–98* (Leiden).

—— (1980), 'M. Basch on triremes: some observations', *JHS* 100: 195–8.

LORAUX, N. (1986), *The Invention of Athens: The Funeral Oration in the Classical City* (Cambridge, Mass.).

MACAN, R. W. (1895), *Herodotus: The Fourth, Fifth, and Sixth Books* (London: Macmillan).

——(1908), *Herodotus: The Seventh, Eighth, and Ninth Books* (London: Macmillan).

MACGINNIS, J. D. A. (1986), 'Herodotus' description of Babylon', *Bulletin of the Institute of Classical Studies*, 33: 67–86.

MAGIE, D. (1950), *Roman Rule in Asia Minor*, 2 vols. (Princeton).

MALLOWAN, M. E. L. (1966), *Nimrud and its Remains* (London: Collins).

——(1972), 'Cyrus the Great', *Iran*, 10: 1–17.

MARQUART, J. (1896), *Untersuchungen zur Geschichte von Eran* (Göttingen).

MARSDEN, E. W. (1964), *The Campaign of Gaugamela* (Liverpool).

MARTIN, T. R. (1985), *Sovereignty and Coinage in Classical Greece* (Princeton).

MARTIN, V. (1965), 'La Politique des Achéménides: L'Exploration, prélude à la conquête', *Museum Helveticum*, 22: 38–48.

MASARACCHIA, A. (1998), *Erodoto: Le storie: Libro IX*, 3rd edn. (Milan).

MAURICE, F. (1930), 'The size of the army of Xerxes in the invasion of Greece, 480 BC', *JHS*, 50: 210–35.

MAZZARINO, S. (1947), *Fra oriente e occidente* (Florence).

MEIGGS, R. (1972), *The Athenian Empire* (Oxford).

MEISTER, K. (1982), *Die Ungeschichtlichkeit des Kalliasfriedens und deren historische Folgen* (Palingenesia, XVIII; Wiesbaden).

MEYER, E. D. (1944), *Geschichte des Altertums* vol. iv/1, 4th edn. (Stuttgart).

MITCHELL, B. M. (1975), 'Herodotus and Samos', *JHS* 95: 75–91.

MOMIGLIANO, A. D. (1933), 'Dalla spedizione scitica di Filippo alla spedizione scitica di Dario', *Athenaeum*, NS 11: 336–59.

——(1975), *Alien Wisdom* (Cambridge).

MORRISON, J. S., and WILLIAMS, R. T. (1968), *Greek Oared Ships 900–322 BC* (Cambridge).

—— COATES, J. F., and RANKOV, N. B. (2000), *The Athenian Trireme* (Cambridge).

MOYSEY, R. A. (1991), 'Diodorus, the satraps and the decline of the Persian Empire', *Ancient History Bulletin*, 5: 111–20.

MURRAY, O. (1988), 'The Ionian Revolt', in *Cambridge Ancient History*, vol. iv (2nd edn.), 461–90.

NICHOLLS, R. V. (1958–9), 'Old Smyrna: The Iron Age fortifications and associated remains on the city perimeter', *British School at Athens*, 53–54: 35–137.

OLMSTEAD, A. T. (1948), *History of the Persian Empire* (Chicago).

ÖZYIĞIT, ÖMER (1994), 'The city walls of Phokaia', *Revue des Études Anciennes*, 96/1–2: 77–96.

PARKER, R. A., and DUBBERSTEIN, W. H. (1956), *Babylonian Chronology 626 BC–AD 75* (Providence, RI).

PEISSEL, M. (1984), *The Ants' Gold* (London: Harvill Press).

PELLING, C. B. R. (1997), 'Aeschylus' *Persae* and history', in C. Pelling (ed.), *Greek Tragedy and the Historian* (Oxford), 1–19.

POMEROY, S. B. (1994), *Xenophon, Oeconomicus: A Social and Historical Commentary* (Oxford).

POWELL, J. E. (1935), 'Notes on Herodotus II', *CQ* 29: 159–63.

PRITCHARD, J. B. (1969), *Ancient Near Eastern Texts*, 3rd edn. (Princeton).

PRITCHETT, W. K. (1982), *Studies in Ancient Greek Topography*, iv: *Passes* (University of California Classical Studies, 28; Berkeley).

——(1985), *Studies in Ancient Greek Topography*, vol. v (University of California Classical Studies, 31; Berkeley).

——(1989), *Studies in Ancient Greek Topography*, vol. vi (University of California Classical Studies, 33; Berkeley).

RHODES, P. J. (1981), *A Commentary on the Aristotelian Athenaion Politeia* (Oxford).

ROBERTSON, M. (1975), *A History of Greek Art*, 2 vols. (Cambridge).

ROBERTSON, N. (1976), 'The Thessalian expedition of 480 BC', *JHS* 96: 100–20.

ROLLINGER, R. (1993), *Herodots babylonischer Logos* (Innsbrucker Beiträge zur Kulturwissenschaft, 84; Innsbruck).

ROSTOVTZEFF, M. (1910), *Studien zur Geschichte des römischen Kolonates* (Leipzig).

——(1941), *Social and Economic History of the Hellenistic World*, vol. ii. (Oxford).

RUBINCAM, C. R. (1979), 'Qualification of numerals in Thucydides', *American Journal of Ancient History*, 4: 77–95.

RYDER, T. T. B. (1965), *Koine Eirene* (Oxford).

SALMON, J. B. (1984), *Wealthy Corinth* (Oxford).

SEAGER, R. J. (1974), 'The King's Peace and the balance of power in Greece 386–362 BC', *Athenaeum*, 52: 36–63.

——(1977), 'Agesilaus in Asia: Progapanda and objectives', *Liverpool Classical Monthly*, 2: 183–4.

SEALEY, B. R. (1976), 'Die spartanische Nauarchie', *Klio*, 58: 335–58.

SHIPLEY, D. G. J. (1987), *A History of Samos 800–188 BC* (Oxford).

SHRIMPTON, G. (1980), 'The Persian cavalry at Marathon', *Phoenix*, 34: 20–37.

SINCLAIR, R. K. (1978), 'The King's Peace and the employment of military and naval forces 387–378', *Chiron*, 8: 29–54.

SMITH, S. (1944), *Isaiah XL–LV*, being the British Academy Schweich Lectures, 1940 (Oxford).

SORDI, M. (1951), 'La pace di Atene 371/0', *Rivista di Filologia*, 79: 34–64.

——(1969), *Diodori Siculi Bibliothecae Liber Sextus Decimus* (Florence).

STARR, C. G. (1962), 'Why did the Greeks defeat the Persians?', *Parola del Passato*, 17: 321–9.

STEVENSON, R. B. (1985), 'Fourth-Century Greek Historical Writing about Persia in the Period between the Accession of Artaxerxes II Mnemon and that of Darius III (404–336 BC)', Oxford D.Phil. thesis.

STOCKTON, D. L. (1959), 'The Peace of Callias', *Historia*, 8: 61–79.

STYLIANOU, P. J. (1998), *A Historical Commentary on Diodorus Siculus Book 15* (Oxford).

SYME, R. (1988), 'The Cadusians in history and fiction', *JHS* 108: 137–50.

SZEMLER, G. J., CHERF, W. J., and KRAFT, J. C. (1996), *Thermopylae: Myth and Reality in 480 BC* (Chicago).

TARN, W. W. (1908), 'The fleet of Xerxes', *JHS* 28: 202–33.

TARN, W. W. (1951), *The Greeks in Bactria and India* (Cambridge).

TAYLOR, A. E. (1948), *Plato: The Man and his Work*, 5th edn. (London: Methuen).

THIRLWALL, C. (1845–52), *The History of Greece*, 8 vols. (London: Longman, Brown, Green & Longmans).

TOZZI, P. (1978), *La Rivolta Ionica* (Pisa).

TUPLIN, C. J. (1983), 'Lysias XIX, the Cypriot war and Thrasyboulos' naval expedition'. *Philologus*, 127: 170–86.

——(1987*a*), 'The treaty of Boiotios', in A. Kuhrt and H. Sancisi-Weerdenburg (eds.), *Achaemenid History*, vol. ii (Leiden), 133–53.

——(1987*b*), 'Xenophon and the garrisons of the Achaemenid Empire', *Archäologische Mitteilungen aus Iran*, 20: 167–246.

——(1993), *The Failings of Empire* (Historia Einzelschriften, 76; Stuttgart).

UNGER, E. (1915), 'Die Dariusstele am Tearos', *Archäologischer Anzeiger*, 1915: 3–17.

VANDERPOOL, E. (1966), 'A monument to the battle of Marathon', *Hesperia*, 35: 93–106.

VOLKMANN, H. (1954), 'Die Inschriften im Geschichtswerk des Herodot', in *Convivium (Festschrift K. Ziegler)* (Stuttgart), 41–65.

VON WILAMOWITZ-MOELLENDORF, U. (1937), *Kleine Schriften*, vol. v/1 (Berlin).

WADE-GERY, H. T. (1958), *Essays in Greek History* (Oxford).

WALBANK, F. W. (1957), *A Historical Commentary on Polybius*, vol. i (Oxford).

WALLINGA, H. T. (1984), 'The Ionian Revolt', *Mnemosyne*, 37: 401–37.

——(1987), 'The ancient Persian navy and its predecessors', in A. Kuhrt and H. Sancisi-Weerdenburg (eds.), *Achaemenid History*, vol. i (Leiden), 47–78.

——(1993), *Ships and Sea-Power before the Great Persian War: The Ancestry of the Ancient Trireme* (Mnemosyne Supplement, 121; Leiden).

WATERS, K. H. (1970), 'Herodotus and the Ionian Revolt', *Historia*, 19: 504–8.

WEISKOPF, M. (1989), *The so-called 'Great Satraps' Revolt' 366–360 BC* (Historia Einzelschriften, 63; Stuttgart).

WELLES, C. B. (1966), *Royal Correspondence in the Hellenistic Period* (Rome).

WEST, S. R. (1985), 'Herodotus' epigraphical interests', *CQ* 35: 278–305.

——(1991), 'Herodotus' portrait of Hecataeus', *JHS* 111: 144–60.

WESTLAKE, H. D. (1989), *Studies in Thucydides and Greek History* (Bristol).

WILL, E. (1979), *Histoire politique du monde hellénistique*, 2nd edn., vol. i (Nancy).

——(1982), *Histoire politique du monde hellénistique*, 2nd edn., vol. ii (Nancy).

WINTER, F. E. (1971), *Greek Fortifications* (London: Routledge & Kegan Paul).

WISEMAN, J. R. (1978), *The Land of the Ancient Corinthians* (Göteborg).

YOUNG, T. Cuyler, Jr (1980), '480–479 BC: A Persian perspective', *Iranica Antiqua*, 15: 213–39.

ZAHRNT, M. (1971), *Olynth und die Chalkidier* (Munich).

ZGUSTA, L. (1956), 'Iranian names in Lydian inscriptions', in F. Tauer, V. Kubíčková, I. Hrbek (eds.), *Charisteria Orientalia Rypka* (Prague).

INDEX

CPSIA information can be obtained
at www.ICGtesting.com
Printed in the USA
BVHW051640210722
642645BV00016B/149

9 780199 299836